An
Empire
of Touch

GENDER AND CULTURE

GENDER AND CULTURE

A Series of Columbia University Press

Nancy K. Miller and Victoria Rosner, Series Editors
Carolyn G. Heilbrun (1926–2003) and Nancy K. Miller, Founding Editors

For a list of titles, see pages 321–22.

An Empire of Touch

Women's Political Labor and the Fabrication of East Bengal

POULOMI SAHA

Columbia University Press
New York

Columbia University Press wishes to express its appreciation for assistance given by the American Comparative Literature Association's Helen Tartar First Book Subvention Prize and the UC Berkeley English Department in the publication of this book.

Columbia University Press
Publishers Since 1893
New York   Chichester, West Sussex
cup.columbia.edu

Library of Congress Cataloging-in-Publication Data
Names: Saha, Poulomi, author.
Title: An empire of touch : women's political labor and
the fabrication of East Bengal / Poulomi Saha.
Description: New York : Columbia University Press, [2019] |
Series: Gender and culture | Includes bibliographical references and index.
Identifiers: LCCN 2018042035| ISBN 9780231192088 (cloth : alk. paper) |
ISBN 9780231549646 (e-book)
Subjects: LCSH: Women in development—India—Bengal—History. |
Women—Political activity—India—Bengal—History. |
Women textile workers—India—Bengal—History. |
Nation-building—India—Bengal. |
Bengal (India)—Politics and government. |
Bengal (India)—History.
Classification: LCC HQ1240.5.I4 S24 2019 | DDC 305.420954/14—dc23
LC record available at https://lccn.loc.gov/2018042035

Columbia University Press books are printed on
permanent and durable acid-free paper.

Printed in the United States of America

Cover design: Noah Arlow
Cover image: © Victoria and Albert Museum, London

For Dorothy McCulloch and Aagami Mohiraaj

Dorian Gray wore those gauzes from Dacca
known as woven air, running water, evening
dew, that transparent cotton a dead art
now, dead for over a hundred years,
No one can imagine, my grandmother says,
what it was to wear, just to touch, that cloth.

—Agha Shahid Ali, "Reading Dorian Gray in Kashmir"
(1983 draft of "Dacca Gauzes")

Contents

Acknowledgments

A cknowledgment is such a thin word for the texture of generosity, care, and love to which I am beholden and because of which this book is possible. *An Empire of Touch* bears vividly the touch of so many people, as do I. Writing this book for the last seven years has taken me from Providence to New Delhi to Dhaka to Berkeley—with various detours in Carlisle, Calcutta, El Cerrito, and Barrington—in an at-times dizzying circuit, over and over. Miraculously, it has also found me home in all of those places. For the host of social relations and objects that have made that possible, I am deeply grateful.

My thanks to Wendy Lochner at Columbia University Press for her commitment to seeing this book through to the very end. Lowell Frye and Kat Jorge at CUP ushered this book through production; I thank also the CUP design team for the beautiful cover and Ben Kolstad for overseeing the copyediting. I am honored and grateful that Nancy K. Miller and Victoria Rosner chose it for their Gender and Culture series, which has included some of the books that have most shaped my thinking. Thanks to the anonymous readers who offered me such excellent and detailed feedback on the manuscript; this book is better for their insight. I thank the generous support of the Hellman Family Foundation. This book's final form is owed enormously to the research time and support that made it possible. The American Comparative Literature Association's Helen Tartar First Book Subvention Prize critically made possible the production of this manuscript. Research for this book was also supported by the Pembroke Center for Research and Teaching on Women at Brown University, the Foreign Language and Area Studies Fellowship, and the UC-Berkeley Humanities Research Fund. The Institute for International Studies sponsored the workshop for the manuscript at a critical juncture. It was so heartening to have this project recognized and supported by the Mount Holyoke College Alumnae Association's 1905 and Hannuum-Warner Fellowships as my time there as an undergraduate formed the base of my scholarly life. It was there that I was lucky enough long ago to start learning from Amy Martin how to read in ways that spectrally limn this book. Her friendship and love these many years are a great gift.

While a graduate student at the University of Pennsylvania, I had the good fortune to be a part of an intellectual community of faculty and students whose influence on my thinking I discover in new ways daily. I thank Ania Loomba, Suvir Kaul, and David Eng for their time, support, and generosity in advising the dissertation that set the stage for questions I was able to ask when I began this book. Also at Penn, I am grateful to Srilata Banerjee, Nancy Bentley, Jim English, Jed Esty, Amy Kaplan, David Kazanjian, Heather Love, Jo Park, Jean-Michel Rabaté, and Paul Saint-Amour. Although I never had the chance to take a class with him, Peter Stallybrass's remarkably humane and textured understanding of the social life of objects has been a guidepost. One of the deepest joys of Penn was the phalanx of fellow grad students with whom I got to think, commiserate, and celebrate: GerShun Avilez, Paige Contreras-Gould, Stephanie Elsky, James Fiumara, David Gardner, Isabel Geathers, Matt Goldmark, Chris Hunter, Jillian Ingold, Jen Jahner, Adrian Khactu, Jeehyun Lim, Sarah Mantilla, Will Nessly, Emily Ogden, Michelle Strizever, Mecca Sullivan, Thomas Ward, and Emily Weissbourd. Christen Mucher's been on this road with me since South Hadley and is still my favorite raised eyebrow in a room. My writing group produced a world of engagement and solidarity that made writing a dissertation live and communitarian work. Thank you, then especially, to Julia Bloch, Megan Cook, Sarah Dowling, Emily Hyde, Greta LaFleur, Melanie Micir, Jessica Rosenberg, and Emma Stapley.

The first glimmers of this project emerged at Brown University, during a year at the Pembroke Center. I thank in particular Cal Biruk, Michelle Cho, Denise Davis, Joe Fischel, Donna Goodnow, Hunter Hargraves, Martha and Artemis A. W. Joukowsky, Lynne Joyrich, Suzanne Stewart-Steinberg, Elizabeth Weed, and Debbie Weinstein. At Dickinson College, my gratitude to David Ball, Sarah Kersh, Patricia Moonsammy, Sarah Niebler, Ash Nichols, Sharon O'Brien, Susan Perabo, Siobhan Phillips, Jerry Philogene, Tom Reed, Claire Seiler, Jacob Sider Jost, Dean Neil Weissman, and particularly Kelly Winters-Fazio. I learned a great deal from my students—especially Alejandro Heredia—and colleagues during my time there. The friendships of Jenny Kelly, Marisol LeBron, Crystal Moten, and Martha Schoolman were the happiest surprise of Carlisle. I will meet them at any Chili's any time they want.

This book came to life at Berkeley. The support, remarkably rigorous and enthusiastic engagement, and sheer good cheer of colleagues have made this book thicker than I could have anticipated and the labor of its making far more fun, too. Elizabeth Abel, Janaki Bakhle, Dan Blanton, Mitch Breitweisser, Lawrence Cohen, Kathleen Donegan, Catherine Flynn, Joshua Gang, Mark Goble, Amanda Jo Goldstein, Kevis Goodman, Joshua Guzman, Dori Hale, Grace Lavery, Abdul JanMohammed, Bob Kaufman, Steven Lee, David Marno, Barbara Metcalf, Maura Nolan, Sam Otter, Genaro Padilla, Christine Philliou, Sonia Katyal, Kent Puckett, Leigh Raiford, Harsha Ram, Juana Maria Rodriguez, Scott Saul, Elena Schneider, Sue Schweik, Namwali Serpell, Katie Snyder, Hertha Sweet Wong, Elisa Tamarkin, Leti Volpp, and Bryan Wagner all read, grappled with, and hashed out thoughts and chapters in various forms, much to the benefit of this whole book. Steve Justice's generosity saved the day. I thank Malcolm Potts for taking the time to share with me his experiences in Bangladesh and for opening up new avenues of research that the archive might have foreclosed. Stephen Best, Nadia Ellis, and Steven Goldsmith's extensive feedback on the manuscript at my mid-career was a light that went off, illuminating the arc of the project and dark corners I had been too hesitant to venture into on my own. Individually and collectively, their engagement with the manuscript was essential to honing its final form. I especially thank Stephen Best for helping to me to get to Berkeley in the first place. Eric Falci, Lyn Heijinian, and Emily Thornbury prove that intellectual life is an endeavor best shared with laughter and forged over many a drink. Donna Jones has been a cheerful champion of my work since I arrived at Berkeley and instrumental to securing many a necessary resource. Colleen Lye has helped shepherd this project and me through varied uncertainties and enjoining a kind of rigor and precision that raised the stakes of the work—all with unstinting fortitude and determination. Judith Butler and Wendy Brown have believed in me, inexplicably, all along. Raka Ray is my model for an ethical, fun, committed feminist life in the academy. Sanchita Saxena and Puneeta Kala have made a sweet spot of respite and care in the center of campus. The sudden and delightful fact of Natalia Brizuela's friendship has brought so many things together and been the source of such fun. I am so glad to walk alongside Abhishek Kaicker, Damon Young, and Dora Zhang, leaving no man behind.

My research in Bangladesh owes everything to the generosity and patience of my interlocutors, friends, and family. When things appeared hopeless, people responded with ceaseless alacrity, opening their homes to me, sharing memories, digging through old material. The human archive was truly the pleasure of working on the latter chapters. Firdous Azim has been a bastion of encouragement and stalwart advocate of the continuing lived relevance of feminism and the postcolonial. Without hesitation, Rubana Huq made herself, her factories, and the writing of women who work there available to me; I am very grateful for her kindness. Maleka Khan's contribution can't simply be thanked: She opened up her personal archives and memory to me and, in so doing, opened up a whole world of thought. I have tried to follow her excellent example and do well enough by the Girl Guide oath. I hope that, despite his skepticism about my brand of "theory-speak," Binayak Sen will recognize here traces of the inspiration of his remarkably capacious and keen thinking that spans disciplines. Sukanta Sen's generosity and easygoing nature are beyond compare. He has been untiring with his help; without him the last two chapters would not exist. Kakoli Talukder and Soumik Sen were the most cheerful and enthusiastic companions. Thanks also go to Tamera Abed; Sharif Uddin Ahmed; Maleka Begum; Goutam Chakraborty; Faizul Latif Chowdhury, Director of the Bangladesh National Museum; Jharna Das of the Gandhi Foundation; Md. Elias Miah at the National Archives; Ruby Ghuznavi; Abdul Halim; Mufidul Huq, Director of Muktijuddho Jadhughaar; Anisul Huq; members of Naripokkho; Minister of Cultural Affairs Asaduzzaman Noor; Tariq Omar Ali; Pavel Partha; Ratna Kar; Abdur Rouf; Bibi Russell; Bulu and Seuty Sabur; Chandi Saha; Chandra Sekhar Saha; Sumona Sharmin; Cesar, Ronon, and Rai Talukder. During this writing, Shahidul Alam, photographer and founder of the Drik Gallery which has taken on the muslin project, was imprisoned in Bangladesh for speaking out against the current government; his commitment to art as politics is an inspiration.

Many thanks to the weavers at the *jamdani polli* of Sonargoan. I owe a special debt of gratitude to Aktara, Jayeka Akhter, Jesmine Akhter, Lima Akhtar, Afrozi Begum, Lajju Begum, and Rehana Yesmin, all workers at the Mohammadi Group factories, for sharing with me their writing—their words are what I returned to over and over and to which I write.

In New Delhi, Shahid Amin leapt to my assistance when all archival excavation seemed to fail. I thank Nishita Jha, Shuddhabrata Sengupta, and Aman Sethi for genuinely curious and insistently rigorous inquiries into "the book" and their willingness to adopt me into their world. Anjali and Rajesh Sethi's care and cheer are treasures. Early wanderings in the city that laid the foundation for this work are indebted to the formidable Primla Loomba. My time at Shantiniketan, made possible by Amartya Sen's hospitality, was a signal flare at a moment where the shape of a book was as uncertain as the course of my own life. For his kindness and affection, as well as transformative conversations while meandering through the local *gram*, I am deeply grateful. Many thanks to Dr. Tapati Mukherjee, Director of Rabindra Bhavan at Visva Bharati University;

Nilanjan Banerjee, Special Officer of Rabindra-Bhavan; Arabinda(da) Nandy at the Pratichi Trust; and Emma Rothschild.

This project has been made possible by moments of serendipitous generosity by many people but Jill Sabella in particular appeared as though conjured, and the gift of her archive stands as a reminder to me of the interconnectedness of thinking and being in the world. At various points, as the stakes of this book were coming into focus, the critical engagement by keen readers and inter-locuters made all the difference. I thank Sunil Agnani, Anjali Arondekar, Neilesh Bose, Joshua Branciforte, Indrani Chatterjee, Nusrat Chowdhury, Drew Daniel, Bina D'Costa, Daniel Elam, Kathleen Frederickson, Elaine Freedgood, Avishek Ganguly, Inderpal Grewal, Lauren Heintz, Naveeda Khan, Madhumita Lahiri, Deepti Mistri, Durba Mitra, Nasser Mufti, Chris Nealon, Michael Ralph, Pooja Rangan, Ellen Rooney, Parama Roy, Mrinalini Sinha, Harris Solomon, and Robert Young. Peter Betzer pointed out the extraordinary use of an object too often seen as ubiquitous; I thank him for this insight and for his, and Susie Betzer's, continuing sweetness. The insights of Sangeeta Ray and Mrinalini Chakravorty brought richness and depth, and their friendship happiness. For invitations to share this work and for rich feedback, thanks to the Princeton Arts Initiative and Paul Muldoon; the Jackson School of International Studies at the University of Washington and Sunila Kale, Christian Novetzke, Priti Ramaswamy, and Anand Yang; and the University of Virginia's Institute of the Humanities and Global Culture and Mrinalini Chakravorty, Sheila Crane, Debjani Ganguly, Geeta Patel, and Kath Weston; BRAC University in Dhaka and Firdous Azim, Samia Huq, Seuty Sabur, and Binayak Sen; IIT-Bombay and Amrita Banerjee, Paulomi Chakraborty, and Ratheesh Radhakrishnan; and the English Departments of the University of Albany, Johns Hopkins University, and Vanderbilt University.

Much of the research time for this book was spent in archives—my own fever unabated. This book would not have been possible without the resources of the Asiatic Society of Kolkata, Bangla Academy, the British Library, Butler Library at Columbia University, Bryony Davis and the Freud Museum London, Hough-ton Library at Harvard University, the Indian National Archives, the Liberation War Museum (Muktijuddho Jadughaar) in Dhaka, the National Archives of Ban-gladesh, the National Library of India, the Nehru Memorial Museum Library, Mary Brower and the Providence Athenaeum, Rabindra Bhavan at Visva Bharati University, and the West Bengal State Archives. Many thanks to the various librarians, archivists, and fellow burrowers who made those dusty days fly by. An early version of chapter 1 appeared as "Women on Fire: Sati, Consent, and the Revolutionary Subject" in *differences: A Journal of Feminist Cultural Studies* 24, no. 3 (2013). Initial thoughts from chapter 2 began to be worked out in an arti-cle entitled "Singing Bengal into a Nation: Tagore, Nationalism, and Colonial

Cosmopolitanism," in the *Journal of Modern Literature* 36, no. 2 (2013). For use of the images included, I thank: The Victoria and Albert Museum, London, for permission to use the cover image; the West Bengal State Archives, Kolkata for access to the photograph of Pritilata Waddedar from the Police Archives; the LIFE Picture Collection for permission to reproduce the Margaret Bourke-White image of M. K. Gandhi; the Freud Museum of London for permissions for the photograph of the ivory Vishnu statuette; Rabindra Bhavan, (Institute of Tagore Studies and Research) Archives, Visva-Bharati University in Santini-ketan, for providing the two images of Rabindranath Tagore and Sigmund Freud's meeting; and finally, beyond all formal thanks, the private collection of Jill Sabella, which granted permission to use the two images of women in the Rehabilitation Center in Dhaka and also donated the remainder to a forthcom-ing digital archive on the Bangladesh war for independence.

In February 2017, Leela Gandhi, David Theo Goldberg, and Ankhi Mukher-jee descended upon Berkeley to spend a day working through the manuscript, guiding it into clarity. I am grateful for their time, energy, and kindness, which radically improved the book. It should be said that all shortcomings that remain are my own. Leela Gandhi saw, with laser precision, the stakes of the book and was the best playmate in thought at this stage. David Theo Goldberg offered me relationality—as a theoretical concept for the book and as a modelled intel-lectual practice. Ankhi Mukherjee's excellent suggestion that the book move cognitively rather than phenomenologically was a reminder I have kept near at hand. Special thanks to Thiti Jamkajornkeiat for his careful reading and inci-sive thoughts, and to Colleen Lye, who was able to translate scales of interven-tion for me at a critical moment. Ramsey McGlazer's research support has been invaluable and his calm counsel and eagle eye for detail have been lifesavers. I am lucky to have had him through this. I thank Sherine Ebadi for the precision and alacrity of her last-minute assistance (twice over!) and Laila Riazi for her indispensable help in the final push. Cathy Hannebach's editorial assistance at an earlier stage of the manuscript was enormously helpful.

For being unsurpassable comrades and friends in this strange and wonder-ful life, my thanks to Sarah Besky, Cal Biruk, Kathleen Frederickson, Chris Boots Hansmann, Hunter Hargraves, Emily Hyde, Leon Hilton, Abigail Horne, Sumayya Kasamalli, Sonia Katyal, Jenny Kelly, Wendy Korwin, Christina Leon, Cristina Mora, Al Nading, Tianna Paschal, Anjuli Raza Kolb, Debarati Sanyal, Prerna Singh, Elizabeth Steeby, Aileen Teague, Karen Tongson, and Chris Zepeda-Millan. The hours of laughter and psychoanalytic commiseration with Michelle Cho, in-person closing down every restaurant in Providence and virtually on Skype, have kept me sane, brought great joy, and made my thinking ever clearer. Sarah Dowling has run many miles with me, as has Julia Bloch. I am very grateful for their company on the long road and the surety of their friendships and intellectual ferocity. Azeen Khan keeps me honest and her faith in the possibilities of the psyche remains my example. I owe Maxe Crandall and his toes many bathtubs full of rosé. It is as though I've known Abhishek Kaicker and Stacey Van Vleet forever. By becoming my family, they made Berkeley my home: I am very grateful.

Writing this book, and living this strange life, have taken me away from "civilian" friends and family more often than I might like. For their infinite patience with the unending process and sweetly feigned interest, thanks and love to Katherine Betzer, Molly Flanagan, Naomi Garber, Brooke Goldstein, Sean McCanty, Sandy McCulloch, Abir Muhuri, Pradip Muhuri, Prapti Muhuri, Shukla Muhuri, Anjali Talukder, Banani Sen, Debattama Sen, Taposh Talukder, Tapti Sen, and Uma Jaan Singh. Swami Atmajnanda has been my pocket Sanskritist; his enthusiasm, care, and faith buoy me. My father, Tulshi Saha, demonstrates his love through work and sacrifice. His willingness to do anything I needed has made the impossible possible; I hope I have made him proud. Despite her extensive worries, my mother, Parbati Saha, has been steadfast in her support of my aspirations and committed to my freedom. Her intellectual contributions to this project are vast and I would not be here without her.

Everyone should be so lucky as to have a ride or die like Greta LaFleur. She has been instigator, confidante, life partner, and bad-idea bear since 2005—there's no one I would rather be in this world with. Taco, you're the best. Freud may not have actually said that a fulfilled life consists of *lieben und arbeiten*, but Aarti Sethi shares with me every day the life-giving pleasures of working alongside love. For revealing such magic, for all the alchemies tiny and profound, and much more, she has my gratitude. For everything else, I just hope she knows. Marge at second base kept life an adventure. Becky huffed me into attachment. Steve found me just in time. And made it just right.

Three people's absence marks this book as much as their presence has my life. I would like very much to have been able to put this book into Swami Sarvagatananda's hands; I think he would have been delighted. The last time we spoke, Rosemary George signed off with "so much left to say"—so much of this book is me still talking to her. I hope each day to be a tribute to Nita Mahalanobish's gentleness and good humor. The world has less a little less light in it without each of them.

In all the ways that matter, this book begins with my grandmother, Dorothy McCulloch, who is my true north. She has always been the source of unconditional and unstinting love, relentlessly cheerful support, and great mischief and fun. And it ends with Aagami Mohiraaj, whose name brings with it the future and who is the wonder of my life. They are my very favorites and this book is for them.

An
Empire
of Touch

Cezanne Course 19th Julia
Critical I might Hist. Jeff
(problem) teach
formalist Theme Theory
theoret one 2-3 historical periods
Fall Film
1 sem   5
1 indep.   Introduction   45 21
                              46×2 34
                              47   35
                                   37
                                   40
                                   42
                                   43
                                   44

Introduction

I n 2013, Drik, a visual arts agency in Dhaka, Bangladesh, undertook the ambitious project of conjuring from centuries of extinction the storied cotton muslin for which the city was once famed. While Pliny notes the exportation of Bengal muslin as early as 77 CE in his *Naturalis Historia*, testifying to the long life of the commodity, it was in fact perfected for the Mughal court. That cloth, nearly pellucid in its fineness, became one of the most valued global objects as it circulated across Europe to fill trousseaus and garb an imperial elite in the eighteenth and nineteenth centuries. Nine yards of it folded into a matchbox were said to have been presented to Queen Victoria in honor of her wedding. Known as *bafta hawa*, or woven air, *Dhakai* (from Dhaka) muslins carried in their vaporous weave the name of a place that became synonymous with the artistry and magic of their manufacture. True muslin has not been manufactured for nearly two centuries—popular apocrypha of its disappearance contends that the British, unable in Manchester mills to approach its quality, amputated the thumbs of master weavers.[1] Today, it largely appears in museum displays, trapped behind glass so as to avoid contact with the bodies that it was made for but that now threaten its material integrity. It is preserved in private collections and as family inheritance, passed down between women and repurposed into new forms.

In attempting to retrieve muslin, to restore it to the Bangladeshi nation and a global economy, Drik encountered its paradoxical allure. Its value as a commodity derived from the enigma of its becoming, the irreconcilability of the technology of its manufacture and its actual object life. How could cotton spun by hand and woven on bamboo come to be finer than gossamer, so diaphanous as to almost disappear? And yet be so durable as to outlast the memory of its making by so many years? Hyperartisanal, muslin, though "handmade," disappeared the body of its manufacturer. Historical accounts of the fabric can only attribute its "almost incredible perfection" to the possibility that it may have been the "work of fairies or insects, rather than of men."[2] The touch of no mere human hand, it seemed, could produce cloth so numinous; as a result, the object has been shorn of the site and labor of its making. But Drik's hope of muslin's return fundamentally depended on the promise of that touch: that having been handmade, the fabric might be made again by hand.

Though the courtly weavers who are credited with producing the cloth were male—participants in a hereditary occupation in which the precise alchemy of muslin production was passed down from master weaver to son—the process by which muslin came into being was permeated by the touch of female hands from seed to cloth. *Dhakai* muslin is an object of a particularly feminine economy of labor and consumption. Only master weavers knew all aspects of the process, for fear that proprietary techniques would be stolen, but the muscle memory of its fabrication was distributed throughout a kin network. Women of those households engaged in intimate contact with the material life of cotton. From sowing cotton seed to handpicking bolls to spinning, pigmenting, and starching thread to embroidery, their labor was central to the production of a fabric that would travel across the imperial world as a conjugal commodity. John Forbes Watson, in his 1866 *Textile Manufactures and the Costumes of the People of India*, notes that the most fabled aspect of muslin—the fineness of its thread—came from the hands of women under the age of thirty (not in keeping with our contemporary notion of the aged spinster) who spun "early in the morning before the rising sun dissipates the dew on the grass."[3] Watson locates the essence of muslin's magical constitution in the touch of young women, in the glancing contact of their fingers twisting filaments barely endowed with enough moisture from the morning dew to be perceptible to the eye. Bound in the fibers of fabric that would be layered into bridal gowns and courtly vestments alike was the somatic trace of those young women; their bodies came to constitute the substance of the mythical cloth alongside cotton, starch, and dye. Particulate remains of touch adhere to fabric weave, carrying in the textile remnants of laboring forms to be pressed against, to exfoliate and accumulate from, the body of the wearer. In this way, we might say that a corporeal memory of muslin abides even now in the bodies of women by and for whom it was made, despite its disappearance from a commercial marketplace.

In the same year that Drik began its muslin project, in May 2013, just twenty kilometers away from its offices, the Rana Plaza commercial building in Savar collapsed, killing nearly 1,200 garment workers inside. The sixth major disaster at a Bangladeshi garment factory, Rana Plaza is to date the deadliest factory incident in history. As the death toll rose, bodies of young women, who comprise 85 percent of the ready-made garments labor force, were lined up along the corridors of a local high school to be identified. Images of the demolished building and of the casualties circulated through the international media, galvanizing consumer outrage in the United States and the United Kingdom in particular, where the majority of the clothing made in the factories was sold at Gap, H&M, Wal-Mart. Vibrant cloth—the concatenation of manufactured apparel and clothing on human remains—was laminated by concrete rubble, a final fusion of laborer to commodity. Common comparisons between Rana Plaza and the New York Triangle Shirtwaist Factory fire in 1911 collapsed time and histories of labor exploitation into a singular failure of liberal rights wherein Bangladesh became the uncanny echo of a prior moment of Western industrial development and progress. Bangladesh, it would seem, never fully shares in the modernity of global capital, even as it clothes it. Because the garments sector is credited with Bangladesh's recent economic growth and signals the potential for the country to wean itself off the international aid apparatus on which it has depended since its independence in 1971, the predominance of women's bodies at Rana Plaza (in the building wreckage and at its periphery as witness) embodied for a consumer public in the Global North the gendered cost of the cheap cotton knit apparel that rested as second skin on their own bodies, just as it rested on the dead bodies of workers in the building.

Like the historical *Dhakai* muslin, contemporary machine-woven cotton bears in its fiber the somatic sign of touch from its manufacture. Far tighter in its warp and weft structure than its handwoven kin, this cotton does not announce its proximity to the manufacturing body as did muslin or the handloomed cotton (*khadi*) popularized by Mohandas K. Gandhi during the Indian nationalist movement; those fabrics, by design, distance the textile through its touch—muslin too ethereal for human skin and *khadi* markedly rough—even as they vouchsafe the historical trace of the hand. Mill-cotton's technological feat is that it so closely resembles the skin it rests upon. (Cue Calvin Klein's coy acknowledgement that "Nothing gets between you and your Calvins.") "Ready-made," the garments that are now the referent of Dhaka in a contemporary global imagination are disembodied as their local predecessors had been. No human hand appears in the image of these machinic, ubiquitous textiles, once again shearing from cloth the labor and site of its making. But through the rupture of disaster in 2013, the manufacture of this cloth announced itself.

Beyond the coincidence of shared location and time, these fabric phenomena—these objects that do not appear to be of a shared aesthetic order—are bound in a common lineage of the non-normatively reproductive and insistently political life of women's labor in East Bengal (modern-day Bangladesh). From *Dhakai* muslin to *khadi* to ready-made knitwear, cotton fabric materializes an intimate history of touch that ranges both British and American empires. Placed alongside literary text, archival encounters, and other material objects, these textiles tell a new story of political imagination and commitment from the standpoint of East Bengal, a space both foundational to, and excluded from, familiar conceptions of postcolonial studies—and one in which women are central political actors and laboring subjects.

As metaphor, textiles have a rich, and markedly feminine, citational life from mythology to Deconstruction.[4] Derived, in English from the Latin *texere*, *textile* and *text* share the etymology "to weave"; this is the same branch that gives us *techne* in the derivational tree rooting itself in the Sanskrit *taksati*, meaning "shaper" or "fabricator."[5] Penelope weaving and unweaving the sign of her own widowhood; Arachne and Athena set against one another to render in fabric the stories of the gods; Freud's diminutive sense of women's invention of weaving and plaiting as prostheses of phallic lack; Jacques Derrida on feminine writing in the face of radical finitude, "You're dreaming of taking on a braid or a weave, a warp or a woof, but without being sure of the textile to come, if there is one, if any remains and without knowing if what remains to come will still deserve the name of text, especially of the textile in the figure of a textile."[6] Textile opens itself up into writing, into being rendered into writing, into making legible. But this book militates against the impulse to stabilize narrative by way of the metaphoric life of textiles. Rather, it returns to Marx and his concerns about what of the history of human labor is denuded in the commodification of the object: that "as soon as it emerges as a commodity, it changes into a thing which transcends sensuousness."[7] *An Empire of Touch* refuses object transcendence as a discursive practice, investing instead in a practice of immanent sensuousness not just what a body can do, or what a body can make, but the host of social relations and somatic practices that communicate by way of touch. Thus, over five chapters, this book develops a set of reading practices committed to materiality which read for the presence of human labor, for what is intimate and tactile. Despite abstractions and atrophies by which the manifest presence of labor would seem to be effaced from objects, an accumulative, tangible relationality persists within and beyond that of exchange. Historically, our conception of labor has been mediated by two abstractions. The first is of the touch of work itself, effaced in the object made commodity; the second is of the gendered body, personalized and domesticated. But what seems to disappear in fact has a material—indeed, textilic—life. I look to touch to bring to the surface the materiality and intimacy of labor. This is a form of reading predicated upon and transcending the critical diagnoses of absence and failure that have historically marked East Bengal and (post)colonial women both.

Beginning with the 1905 division of the British colonial state of Bengal into East and West—the fault line along which the region would again be split in 1947 and nationalized in 1971—this book traces the fissures of a colonial policy of gendered partition that long outlived the Raj. East and West Bengal's partition in 1905, I contend, is in fact the uncoupling of text from textile. From it, West Bengal inherits the humanistic legacy of literature and historiography; East Bengal inherits a world of objects, raw material, and embodied labor. In the wake of 1905, West Bengal and the Indian nation-state to which it eventually came to belong are set up to offer an intellectual genealogy of political becoming; East Bengal and its future Bangladesh state-form come to be the repository of touch. Contemporary industrial labor of female garment workers in Bangladesh bears the mark of that attempt to disaggregate the site of politics, figured as masculine and modern West Bengal, from the feminized and ancestral site of natural resources in East Bengal, even as the relationship between the two lobes of the region remains co-constitutive and intimate.

Bengal, in this way, comes to be historically and disciplinarily cleaved in two. Indeed, for all of the scholarly attention to Bengal in history and literary studies, East Bengal has been a curious lacuna, subsumed under the sign of a unified Bengal, romanticized as the spectacularly maternal source of raw material and poetic feeling that fed an urban political intelligentsia in West Bengal, or disavowed as a ghostly remnant of a prior India. Scholarship, too, has been divided between the qualitative work of postcolonial studies, which has long faced claims of Indocentrism, and the densely quantitative methodologies of development economics that have characterized studies of and interventions in Bangladesh. Since 1971, when it was declared (in a phrase apocryphally attributed to Henry Kissinger) "an international basket case," Bangladesh has received nearly $50 billion in foreign aid, of which nearly half has been in the form of loans. Its now-lauded progress toward middle-income country status has proved it an exemplar of a development state. In its case, growth and modernization have been driven not by state enterprise and domestic capital investment but by gender-targeted foreign aid and nongovernmental organizations. It is precisely these gender-targeted policies and programs that Amartya Sen has recently credited for the fact that Bangladesh now ranks higher in human development indices (what he terms markers of qualitative well-being) than India.[8] Women's reproductive health, literacy, life expectancy, and income—measures of their *empowerment* (to use the neoliberal buzzword with which we will hope to dispense by the end of this book)—are, in this way, vehicles of individual and national mobility. Since the Grameen Bank was awarded the Nobel Peace Prize in 2006 for its microloan programs aimed at rural Bangladeshi women, its model of collateral-free, high-interest, socially regulated loans has been exported to dozens of countries. Thus, Bangladesh's two major global exports of ready-made garments and gender-targeted microfinance are today intimately tied to its representative women.

Over the more than a century on which this book focuses, East Bengal persists within the ambit of two empires: the British colonialism by which it was originally bifurcated and the American empire of debt on which its statehood was erected. By taking as our focus this East Bengal, irreducible to either colonial forebear or contemporary state, the intellectual and ideological continuity between discourses that produce and sustain definitions of the postcolonial nation and its political possibilities comes into stark relief. We see the endeavor of postcolonial sovereignty and the claims of its stillbirth in a fresh light.

The bodies and labor of East Bengali women uphold global projects of intervention and quantifications of development on the one hand and symbolize reproductive national futurity on the other—passed on from one imperial form to another. To interrupt the insidiously depoliticized homology between women and nation which the familiar historical nationalist iconography of *Banga/Bharat Mata* (Mother Bengal/India) repeats, this book focuses on unruly feminine subjects: virgins, spinsters, childless widows, unwed mothers, factory workers.[9] Through their writing, labor, and articulations, these women model a radical mode of relational self-conception in which political liberation is inextricable from personal cathexis.

A Problem of Reading and Its Objects

An Empire of Touch turns to the symbolic and material labor of women in East Bengal—on which the state-building endeavors of three countries (India, Pakistan, and Bangladesh) have depended—to argue that the life of political commit- ments of women, figural and historical, is captured in material objects of their manufacture. It takes on a basic methodological dilemma of postcolonial studies: despite the centrality of women's labor to anticolonial protest and postcolonial state-building, historiography has struggled with what appears to be an absence in the archive, born of the ostensible division between a public masculine world of politics and a private feminine world of culture, domestic life, and kinship. In this frame, feminized East Bengal and women's political labor are each elided. This book insists on their appreciability, calling for a continually generating archive of presence. In text and object, we see forms of political life that break through the false binaries of self and other; domestic and industrial; individual and collective; affective and material. Navigating what at times feel *knowledge a collective construct between sources & interpretation*

like entirely incompatible hermeneutic discourses—the humanistic and the social scientific—reveals their continuities and the potential interdisciplinary ground opened by their shared use. Fundamentally, this book is engaged in an ongoing struggle to locate a satisfactory vocabulary and paradigm for forms of political subjectivity expressed and embodied by those who, by virtue of gender, nation, class, and empire, have been considered subaltern. When I make a claim for the political character of material and symbolic labor by Bengali women living in the imperial shadow, I identify relational commitment to common good and shared futurity that does not take agency and sovereignty as its determinant. Though it has not always fallen under the sign of the political, this labor is politics in an elemental way; let us call it so.

A guiding question throughout will be how technologies of representation, be they literary, historical, material, or economic, engage forms of political life beyond masculinist projects of individual and national autonomy that undergird familiar conceptions of postcolonial political modernity. Moreover, to what archives do we turn if those of the state appear to foreclose the very basis of this question? *An Empire of Touch* looks to institutional and discursive sites from which the subject of a modern postcolonial political order has been articulated and challenged—law, labor, the psyche, the archive, and the global market—to show how women make their bodies and the objects of their production into signs of political commitment. Each of the objects in this book—archival fragments, photographs, correspondence, handloomed cotton, figurines, novels, ashes, embroidered quilts, jersey knit, artisanal handicrafts—reveals the intimate, tactile, and yet determinedly public and relational practices by which the postcolonial nation is imagined and fabricated into being.

Objects, particularly those manufactured by human hands, are central to the emergence of the autonomous subject in liberal political thought. Lockean distance between made-object and making-person is the stage on which dramas of individual sovereignty, rationality, and subjectivity are played out, particularly in postcolonial contestations over labor and rule. It is therefore in those objects, at these sites of subject-negotiation, that we see how women produce the terms of their own politics and self-conception; we see how the articulation of desire by women makes itself known. The idiom and form of their commitment are not singular. Indeed, the full feature of a deeply relational politics of the self and of the nation begins to emerge through the multiple, sometimes contradictory, sometimes overlapping investments of the figures engaged by this book—from the fictional to the world-historical; from revolutionary women to raped children; from Nobel laureates to wage laborers.

Although the book's historical origin is 1905, it begins *in medias res* with the 1932 death of Pritilata Waddedar, a twenty-year-old schoolteacher who killed herself after leading an attack on the Pahartali Railway Club in Chittagong, East Bengal. In a theoretical gambit to the book's abiding question of the legibility of female political subjectivity, we open by reading Waddedar as a theorist of her own historicity. The first chapter, which constitutes part I of this book, responds to Gayatri Chakravorty Spivak's canonical question of whether the subaltern woman's voice can be heard in the historical archive by arguing that Waddedar, dressed in the cotton garb of a Muslim man, left her body as a sign that was meant to be as legible as the manifesto found inside her pocket which stated, "I boldly declare myself a revolutionary." What comes to be communicated, in her writing and by her body, surpasses the merely mimetic. Beyond representation, there is articulation through touch and intimacy. The problem of reading Waddedar's actions, the ways in which she has been renarrated and unspoken, gets to the crux of the gendered terms of what and who can be political. It is a problem to which we will return in the final chapter in essays written by women currently working in the garment industry, whose continuing labor has been figured on a global stage as unqualified exploitation. In a very different idiom, in a very different historical moment, we see restaged that canonical debate of postcolonial female political subjectivity; articulations of desire make themselves legible outside of the singular framework of liberal selfhood.

If at stake in the encounter with Pritilata Waddedar is a problem of reading historical evidence of feminine forms of political protest, then the two chapters of part II, "The Fetish of Nationalism," turn to the problem of objects and subjectivity, the perceived threat of material overattachment to psychological and political projects of autonomy. Drawing out a broad history of women's political work in East Bengal during the rise of nationalist movements following the 1905 partition, these chapters engage three historical darlings of the postcolonial and Western canon: M. K. Gandhi, Rabindranath Tagore, and Sigmund Freud. When Tagore condemns the Gandhian practice of spinning cotton thread by hand as a technique of postcolonial resistance, he calls the handloomed *khadi* it produces a fetish: a manufactured (made by hand) object that threatens the sovereignty of its maker. Nonetheless, in chapter 2, we see that even in the most canonical examples of Indian anticolonial imagination, the fetish performs an apotropaic magic that enables forms of affiliation and attachment that do not privilege the nation but instead draw together the local and the global in a shared anticolonial project. Feminine labor and its made-objects are herein the grounds of postcolonial possibility. When, in chapter 3, we return to Tagore's critique of nationalism in his 1916 novel *The Home and the World*, we encounter materiality as that which derails the symbolic economy of women as metaphors in psychoanalysis and politics both, Bimala, the young housewife at the center of Tagore's novel, models a politics of affinity and intimacy through an embodied and material identification with rural East Bengal. By following an ivory statuette of Vishnu, given to Sigmund Freud by the Indian Psychoanalytic Society, this chapter traces an emergent bilingualism in which the conditions of anticolonial political possibility were articulated in the patois of a psychological subjectivity.

Cotton cloth, a critical technology for Gandhian *satyagraha* (a program of nonviolent resistance) and the *swadeshi* nationalism born of the 1905 partition, appears again in the final part, "International Basket Case." Now in the hands of two precarious figures of the postcolonial world—women raped during the Bangladesh war of independence and then "rehabilitated" through training as artisanal textile producers, and contemporary female garment workers—fabric becomes the vehicle of a new economic and political order. Returning to the archive with which the book began, chapter 4 traces, through rumors of fire, the calculus of legibility that governs what constitutes feminine political labor. Named war heroines, *birangonas*, by the new republic, women raped in the 1971 war were asked to bear the weight of both a disappearing archive and a nationalist narrative. Like their very bodies, the textile work they were offered as occupational therapy following the war becomes a central example of a new developmental discourse of Third World women's empowerment. In the final chapter, we see how the material kinship between this artisanal manufacture and the contemporary garment work for which Bangladesh is today vilified and undercompensated reveals the imbrication of aesthetics training and tactile labor through which women articulate themselves.

Standing at the scholarly impasse between an ethical project of marking subaltern silence and a historical project to recover women's hidden agency, it is clear that we need new frameworks for feminist and postcolonial analysis. In anchoring itself, even and especially as critique, to a Western paradigm that takes the subject/object divide as epistemological, postcolonial studies has averted its gaze from an extant archive of materiality. Hence, this book follows the historical traces of how Bengali women have claimed their labor, making what has too often been seen as "merely" intimate and domestic into appreciable political acts. What emerges is a landscape of political life marked by interdependence and relationality, offering a narrative beyond that of women's empowerment and independence as the postcolonial enterprise. Across historical time, these women consistently refuse critical and cultural pronouncements of their own subjugation and underdevelopment. Methodologically, this book traverses culture and politics to locate in the mundane stitching of cloth clarion calls of anticolonial resistance and self-articulation; it presses on the theoretical limits of sovereign subjecthood; it looks beyond the rights-based discourse of personhood and possibility; it offers forms of reading that undo the division between agency and articulation; it extends the spaces in which we might go seeking political labor and its traces.

An Empire of Touch is based on the premise that the molecular residue of East Bengal and the political labor of women are always present in our conception of empire and its resistances. Drawing their presence to the surface challenges the foundational postcolonial narrative of what Indian Subaltern Studies historian Ranajit Guha has called the "historic failure of the nation to come to its own."[10] This failure, for Guha and other members of the Subaltern Studies Collective, is both of political imagination to conceive of a truly postcolonial future and of nationalist historiography to account for "the politics of the people."[11] At stake is not the ideological question of whether alternate forms of politics flourished despite their marginalization in elitist historiography, but rather the empirical question of where and in what forms those politics might be located. It would seem that women limn the periphery of the colonial archive, appearing as disruptions, incoherences, and excesses, the nature of their political lives operating in a correspondent but obscured world. I take their appearance as a rupturous announcement: an invitation to broaden our critical field of vision.

From the new perspective of the gathered object-archive of this book, a psychoanalytically oriented form of feminist critique of postcolonial political life is as much about the development of a subject of this order as it is about the production of that subject's structural referent, the nation. Therefore, this book makes a claim for a political and economic life constituted by touch, from a context in which the interdiction against touch, in the form of the social policing of caste and religion, was often the basis of the social. Here, I lean upon, or reach toward, Erin Manning's textured sense of the gestural political possibilities of touch, in which "[t]ouching you, I begin to write a corpus that defies the Aristotelian *polis*. This corpus tells a story, plural but not like-minded, of bodies reaching out toward one another, a story of the separation and sharing of bodies, of the transposition of the being-body, multiple, always in excess of its-self, excribed within a corpus I can never quite articulate."[12] In postcolonial political life, the touch of empire—its material, psychic, epistemological, and political contact—is tattooed into the skin of that corpus. It evinces a form of postcolonial imagination in which the politics of liberation is inextricable from the labors of contact; in which intimate, relational practices of self-articulation are the basis for nation-making.

A Gandhian ideal of purification through tactile labor, weaving a material and metaphoric national fabric out of onanistic self-touching, holds pride of place in a postcolonial imagination. But it is, ultimately, a fantasy that operates against the lived reality of fabric production and use: what we see, entangled in the fiber of textile, is that the touch and labor of its manufacture are communitarian, self-dissolving practices. What we see is a politics of touch that manufactures a body politic through accumulation and contact. To be touched is to be made and unmade in relationship to another, another's body, another's desire, another's trace. Given the profuse character of touch, this book pins itself to three terms as a conceptual framework: *contingency*, *cathexis*, and *desh* (nation or home). Taken together, they help us understand the encounter between bodies and objects as a negotiation with technologies of representation that govern the legibility of political work. Individually, each captures a register of touch: somatic, material, psychic, affective.

The Apparitional and the Ancestral Bengal

At the heart of this book is the apparitional form of a nation whose persistent appearance ruptures postcolonial chronospace. As an apparition, East Bengal comes into being as a political, ideological, material, and aesthetic category through its own negation. Only when Bengal is partitioned and then reunited, and partitioned once more, does East Bengal come into sensuous self-appearance. I continue to refer to East Bengal across the historical arc of this book in order to trace what it reveals in its resurgence and reappearance. Jacques Derrida writes, in *Specters of Marx*, "The specter is a paradoxical incorporation, the becoming-body, a certain phenomenal and carnal form of the spirit. It becomes, rather, some 'thing' that remains difficult to name: neither soul nor body, and both one and the other. For it is flesh and phenomenality that give to the spirit its spectral apparition, but which disappear right away in the apparition, in the very coming of the *revenant* or the return of the specter. There is something disappeared, departed in the apparition itself as reapparition of the departed."[13] East Bengal's becoming, or more specifically, its manufacture, is a double movement by which its appearance and then its resignification disclose the labors that bring the postcolonial nation-state into being and what cannot be compelled into its form. East Bengal connotes, too, all that did not come to pass: speculative futures and forms of life that appear now under the sign of failure—failed states, failed politics, failed subjects. Rather than romanticize absence or rehearse postcolonial melancholia, I want to suggest that the touch of East Bengal across time and space, its ability as an ideal and a material figure to effect and mobilize commitment, and its political force are the invocation of a nation that never was and thus might still be.

East Bengal is the name for a site of inquiry that is both and neither the India-hued Bengal of postcolonial historiography and literary studies nor the Bangladeshi laboratory of postwar international development. Like the partition which, even after being annulled, reappears as object of memory, East Bengal refuses to fall away in the face of postcolonial geopolitics. I call it East Bengal to invoke the incomplete and resurgent becomings of this place and its history, to mark the possibilities and futures that it conjured which did not come to have a material life, to approach it as a speculative vision of political cathexis. *Cathexis*, the term James Strachey translates into English from Freud's *Besetzung*, appears first as an economic concept to describe the quantity of libidinal energy that might affix to an object (which might in fact be an idea, a person, a thing), rendering it meaningful.[14] Through cathexis, objects are manufactured for and by the psyche. If *contingency* is a blasting apart by touch, *cathexis* is a binding together—of subject and object—by investment. By *binding* I do not mean to imply coming coherence but rather the paradox of being undone at the limits of the self. Cathexis, for this book, is the force of attachment that blurs the subject-object divide precisely at the site of that object's making. In this way, the name East Bengal is the name of an apparitional *desh*, whose sensuous self-appearance in material forms (and material itself) reveals the labor and artifice of nation-making. It also carries within its form that originary Bengal, which prior to 1947 was called in Bangla (the language, as distinct from the ethnolinguistic identarian category "Bengali") *Bangla-Desh*.

Desh, which in Bangla connotes home, country, and locality, indexes a range of affective and material attachments and commitments that exceed and predate the postcolonial state.[15] It is, vernacularly, the sign of the local. This is to say, although it adheres to a nationalist imagination and to the very name of the nation, it will consistently, throughout this book, signal the aliveness of local cathexis and affiliation. East Bengal (or, as it is called in Bangla, *Purba Banga*) etymologically and ideologically stands for the originary Bengal, that from which all other imaginations of *desh* arise. Meaning both "East" and "ancestral," *purba* aligns with kinship (*purba-purush*: ancestral men/forebears) and space (*purbadesh*: ancestral home) such that there is an affective tropism toward the East. Bengalis, in whatever scope of diaspora, introduce themselves by their *desh*, rural ancestral territory which they may never have seen but evoke as intimately as affiliative genealogy. When Hindus left ancestral homes in East Bengal during the various upheavals following the 1905 partition (and continuing to the present) to migrate within Bengal, though across a geopolitical boundary, many would eat soil before their departure. Taking into their bodies the land from which they were removed, they would carry the essence of *desh* within them. The deeply local character of *desh*, unbound by the phenomenological limits of the nation-state, is in this way both profuse and diffuse. Thus, this examination of East Bengal unpins itself from the space-time demands of the "state" as an ideological concept and as a phenomenological reality.

Confounding imperial and postcolonial attempts to produce the nation-state as a compelling singular object of political cathexis, a powerfully felt transhistorical transnationalism persists between Bangladesh, its erstwhile neighbor West Bengal, and its historical prepartitioned state. Despite the 1947 partition of British India, in which Bengal was once again cleaved into East and West—West Bengal becoming a part of India and East Bengal incorporated into Pakistan, whose other wing lay some 1,300 miles away—Bengal had been and would continue to be marked by moments of upheaval during which the geopolitical border between East and West would prove to be as porous as the idea of postcolonial sovereignty itself. This was perhaps never more true than in 1971 when, during Bangladesh's war for independence from Pakistan, tens of millions of Bangladeshi refugees flooded across the border into India, drawn not just by spatial proximity but also by a shared linguistic and cultural life that had not died with the creation of two new nation-states a quarter century earlier.

Derrida writes of the apparition that "[w]hen the ghostly body (*die gespenstige Leibhaftigkeit*) of the emperor disappears, it is not the body that disappears, merely its phenomenality, its phantomality (*Gespensterhaftigkeit*). The emperor is then more real than ever and one can measure better than ever his actual power."[16] With the loss of the phenomenological nation, the potency of its sway and the relations of its manufacture come into focus. East Bengal's apparitional form opens up a new archive that is fundamentally rooted in the concept and matter of *desh* and yet, in its local character, reveals the fugitive range that exceeds its location.

Thus, the first three chapters engage figures, historical moments, and texts central to the postcolonial canon; their familiar appearance takes on a new shape in the context of East Bengal. In turn, the latter chapters trace the path from the 1971 independence of Bangladesh to demonstrate the recursive continuity between this nation-state and its prior incarnations, which are never lost, do not disappear, and are never completely disavowed. East Bengal produces a powerful form of public feeling that operates across the sociopolitical, material, and ideational order. Its symbolic and sentimental force refuses to be mapped onto geopolitical borders and their historiography, compelling us to ask: Where does a nation that never was exist? This question is taken literally in what follows.

I posit East Bengal with full awareness that I may be accused of prioritizing cultural referents and terms that are now coded "Hindu." Indeed, in the current frigid geopolitical climate between India and Bangladesh, it may seem perversely asynchronic to turn attention to their repudiated contiguity. But it is precisely this shared disavowal, which points to the incomplete recalibration of affiliations that come with the production of independent statehood, that suggests a productive unsettlement. Tracing figures and terms that traverse the time and space of state-making clears a path through the fantasized rigidity of borders. Rabindranath Tagore, who won a Nobel Prize in Literature in 1913, penned the national anthems of both India and Bangladesh. Though nominally both "Indian" and "Hindu" (the contestedness of these terms for Tagore will become clear in chapter 2 amid his debate with Gandhi over anticolonial imaginations), Tagore remains richly cathected to in the Bangladeshi national imagination. *Mukti Bahini*, Bengali guerilla forces who fought the Pakistani army in 1971, announced themselves by whistling his songs, which became the shibboleth of a nationalist loyalty. Even as relations between independent Bangladesh and India have soured in the subsequent decades with the rise of Wahhabi influence in Bangladesh and anti-Muslim Hindu nationalism in India, the relationship between East and West Bengal, like that between politics and feeling, remains co-constitutive and contingent.

Desh in the truest sense of the word, the Bengal that persists between and within the boundaries of two nation-states, offers a fresh account of their becoming in a markedly local tenor. For this reason, *An Empire of Touch* is organized around possibilities that emerged following three moments of political upheaval in Bengal: the 1905 partition of the state, the 1930 outbreak of anticolonial violence, and the 1971 Bangladesh war for independence. This historical arc is not pinned to the dominant narrative of the subcontinent, in which 1947 serves as the nation- and meaning-making event. Although the catastrophic violence of the partitioning of India and Pakistan, as historical caesura, exerts a powerful magnetic force on political and affective narratives, in arguing that 1947 is not the defining event for East Bengal, this book reorients the postcolonial history of the subcontinent. It ruptures the myth in which a singular political event suddenly instantiated the nation and displaces the singular force of a political future drawn out of Hindu nationalist roots.

As a result, I do not claim to offer a seamless historical narrative of the rise of nationalism in Bengal. Nor do I suggest individual moments as hermetic case studies. Rather, the structure of the book follows from its premise that in eruptive political and historical moments, affiliations and investments come into being: forms of libidinal upsurge in which not all cathexes will prevail but out of which radical possibilities appear in moments of what Émile Durkheim has called "collective effervescence."[17] These moments, which I describe throughout the book as "anti-originary," refuse progressive teleology: they start, stutter, skip, get caught in the groove of the historical record. By calling them anti-originary, I am resisting the romance of nostalgic resignification and the dismay of traumatic repudiation. Implicit here is the conviction that, even as these forms of attachment do not take on institutional lives, they do not die away.

Their appearance as interruptions, excesses, and incoherences illuminates an alternate vision and lived possibility of what constitutes the political.

In this regard, this book is utopian. It sees desire as political and feminine labor as imagining collective life and commitment otherwise. Whereas postcolonial political modernity based on the model of liberalism vaunts rationality as a marker of a fit political subject, this book is interested in what is extruded in the making of this subject, what cannot be compelled into its shape, and what kinds of psychic and material touch come to constitute its politics. As a result, *An Empire of Touch* is shot through with figures, objects, and ideals that collide with one another; *contingency* is a word we might use for beacons to recognize shared political feeling across historical time.

Contingency, from the Latin *contingere* (*con*—together, *tangere*—to touch), is another name for the encounter of shared space, time, and recurrence that asks us to read for articulation in the fragment, presence in the trace. The gathering point of contact, contingency testifies to the power of affiliations and desires that do not map onto the individual, sovereign subject, the liberal political project, or the postcolonial nation-state. Historical contingency, what Walter Benjamin calls the past as it "flashes up at the instant when it can be recognized and is never seen again," breaks open progressive historicism's parable of wholeness and development that has consigned East Bengal and its representative feminine subjects to the waiting room of late capital.[18] Freeing us from the overdetermination of postcolonial failure, contingency makes way for what Eve Sedgwick calls a reparative reading practice, one oriented toward *touch* as accretion, accumulation, and resolvedly still, interruption.[19] For this book, it is an ethical orientation as much as a theoretical one.

What the Archive May Hold

Following the 1857 Mutiny and the establishment of formal British rule in India, the Raj turned to institutions and technologies that leaned heavily on emergent epistemologies of individuality, interiority, and development to construct colonial subjects as objects of governance. Imperial strategies of governance and anticolonial discourses of nationalism joined in this period to produce a common discourse of self-determination that promised the sovereignty and intelligibility of an individual and national subject. Bengal, with the imperial capital of Calcutta and the agricultural abundance of the Ganges-Brahmaputra Delta, was a laboratory for these sciences of subjectivity. Colonial knowledge systems to which we will turn—from political philosophy to psychoanalysis and fingerprinting, from jurisprudence to demography and development economics—show Bengal's significance as a rich object of inquiry and site of intervention for the systemization of knowledge and influence by colonial administration and global governance alike. Out of these epistemological structures, the contours of both a discernible collective (the prototype for some aspect of the national imagination) and individual subject came into form. Here, we can see the legacy of John Stuart Mill's contention that the social collective is but a dilation of the character of the individual.[20] In the frame of law, this individual was constructed as approaching, while never fully inhabiting legal and political equivalence with, his British counterpart: nearly rational, nearly self-interested, nearly autonomous, nearly masculine.

More starkly still, the colonial production of political subjecthood was conditioned by the production of sexual difference: the convergence of institutions of imperial governance and nationalist iconography of Bengal as pervasively feminine and spectacularly maternal. The romanticized image of the Bengali woman as mother/land/goddess became a political force in response to the discursive power of the national ideal. By the same stroke, masculinity was produced as an affective and performative supplement.[21] We will see, particularly in the first three chapters, how this antinomy played out across not just ideological spaces but geopolitical ones as well. For example, as discussed in chapter 3, Bimala, the main character of Tagore's novel *The Home and the World*, is commonly read as a site of seemingly excessive national and erotic attachment who illuminates the limits of a political order rooted in rationalism rather than feeling. But, in fact, Bimala refuses the distance of resemblance offered by metaphor and instead articulates an embodied, totalizing self-identification with rural East Bengal. When chapter 4 turns to women raped during the 1971 partition—designated *birangonas* (war heroines) by the state and offered compensation for their war "labor"—a new vision of the politics of representability comes to light. Following the 1905 partition of the region, which ignited vigorous nationalist movements both within and without Bengal, East Bengal came to be figured as feminine and poetic whereas West Bengal came to be masculine and political. Central anticolonial and postcolonial projects of individual and national sovereignty were, in this way, practices of gendering and of delineating political and material labors.

As a historical referent, the pre-1947 form of the colonial state of Bengal was an administratively bound category that, following 1905 and the subsequent reunification of the Bengal Presidency in 1911, included not just the two Bangla-speaking regional lobes of East and West (*Purba Banga* and *Paschim Banga*, respectively) but also the provinces of Bihar, Orissa, and Assam. The name "Bengal" telescopes to index the ideal of Calcutta as an erstwhile center of colonial governance and as a nexus of nationalist foment. In this way, a layered synecdoche emerges in which Calcutta—urban, majority Hindu, with a significant English-speaking bureaucratic *bhadralok* or "gentleman" class—stands in for the whole of India. In turn, India—partly by virtue of the post-1965 intellectual diaspora, which populated literature and history departments with the early generation of postcolonial scholars, many of them of precisely that class from Calcutta—stands in for the whole of the colonized world. Indeed, the myopia of *desh* so conceived is one way to understand the critique of Subaltern Studies for seemingly ignoring the question of Islam, while focusing so studiously on Bengal where half of its inhabitants are in fact Muslim. For this reason, my reading of East Bengal revises the narrative of political modernity offered by postcolonial studies, which has historically focused on West Bengal as a ur-representation of British empire and anticolonialism. Claims of Bengal's scholarly desiccation miss the originary conflation of the two Bengals.[22] That Bengal of postcolonial studies fame is not one.

In 1905, given that the province's population was greater than that of any other province in colonial India, the presidency of Bengal was an unruly charge for colonial administration.[23] Moreover, it was the site of growing protest among the *bhadralok* class, whose socioeconomic participation in the colonial apparatus was particularly significant, as Bengal was the seat of the Raj's administration. Seeking to disaggregate the urban elite of Calcutta from the ancestral *zamindaris* or estates from which they drew much of their income and status, the partition line drawn by Lord Curzon's government bisected Bengal on the basis of religious difference; the region designated East Bengal had a majority Muslim population, while West Bengal was predominately Hindu. Bengal meted out its communal population in a particular, and historically contingent, manner: along the very axis of rural dependence and urban development. The bifurcation of Bengal produced, on the one hand, vigorous anticolonial protest, largely by Hindu *bhadralok* in East Bengal for whom the partition meant becoming both a political and demographic minority; and, on the other hand, an emergent sense among East Bengali Muslims of political and economic possibility.

David Ludden suggests that the partition of Bengal followed the vectors of capital—limiting as much as possible the bifurcation of *zamindari* estates—in the bureaucratic reorganization of a deeply cherished ideological space.[24] For the Viceroy of India, Lord Curzon, and his compatriots, it created a coherent space bound by the Meghna-Brahmaputra Basin as East Bengal streamlined its river, natural resource, and railway administration, as well as offered the not insignificant benefit of dividing Muslim voices and political demands from the growing cacophony of the anticolonial Congress Party. For West Bengali political thinkers, many of whom derived wealth either individually or culturally from *zamindaris* contained by the river basin, the supply line between the promise of progress and modernity and the nourishment offered by its antecedents was cut. What resulted was the division of longstanding forms of manufacture, production, and consumption between the now-marked Muslim East by the Hindu West, even after the partition was reversed in 1911. Turning to work, bodies, and articulations that have been, by virtue of their feminization, depoliticized and objectified, we see the gendered manufacture of postcolonial political possibility.

Who is the subject of this possibility? It is now, thanks to the work of critical race, queer, and feminist studies, a critical convention to acknowledge that the model of the liberal subject is ill-fitted to many, if not most, of the conceptions of political life and thought.[25] In the postcolonial case, a curious contradiction emerges at the limits of this subject fantasy: articulations that refuse the sovereign individual as locus or telos appear within the context of a struggle for state sovereignty. They are, for this reason, often recoded or elided. Lauren Berlant and Lee Edelman, in *Sex, or the Unbearable*, write that within Euro-American cultures (though unmarked), to encounter nonsovereignty "is to encounter relationality itself, in the psychic, social, and political senses of the term."[26]

 This nonsovereignty is the negation of containment and rationality. But for the subjects I engage in this book—Bengali women under empire—the fantasy of sovereignty has always been unsettled and unsettling. I turn to the language of the nonsovereign mindful of the tenuous claims to sovereign subjecthood which have been the grounds of anticolonial protest and of how women of the Global South have been figured as the limit (if not failure) of liberal, sovereign subjecthood. Perhaps more than any other critical term in this book, it may prove to be inadequate. However, I begin with it out of a fidelity to the language of politics to which women themselves turn: that which emerges from the social text of their own lives. *women*

Swadeshi, the anticolonial program of economic self-sufficiency meaning "country of one's own" that came to prominence in Bengal after the 1905 partition; *swaraj*, the term popularized by Gandhi as the demand for "self-rule"; and *swadhinata*, the word in Bangla and Hindi semantically coded as "independence" but more precisely translated as "self-dependence," unite under the shared reflexive Sanskritic pronoun for the self, *swa/sva*. But this self, to which each of these terms and their confederates refer, is not the self of liberal self-determination, not the atomistic, autonomous self of possessive individualism that undergirds Enlightenment thought. This self is in relation to a greater Self. Bengali nationalist leader Bipin Chandra Pal objected, on these grounds, to Gandhi's use of *swaraj* to describe a negative freedom in the guise of liberal political thought.[27] He writes that *swaraj* is in fact "when the individual self stands in conscious union with the Universal or the Supreme Self. When the Self sees and knows whatever is as its own self, it attains swaraj. . . . The self in Hindu thought, even in the individual, is a synonym for the Universal."[28] Though Pal identifies this self as a character of Hindu thought, the sociolinguistic life of the Sanskritic prefix abides no communal boundary on the subcontinent, and this is the discursive matrix within which a variety of nationalist projects—Hindu, Muslim, and secular alike—operate. The individual as political actor is not the same as the individual as political subject; *sva* carries in it an articulation of the self as subject that is always leaning toward another who is not separate, the continual becoming of a capacious, nonsovereign self. This is the binding work of being undone—not the ecstatic *jouissance* of self-shatter but an undoing that is constitutive of the political subject, an always relational self, an always, then, political self in negotiation with instruments and institutions of power.

To encounter postcolonial nonsovereignty, we can say in echo-distortion of Berlant and Edelman, is thus to encounter a foundational relationality that dynamically shapes the psychic, social, and political registers of life. It offers a way to see the accumulative, communitarian possibilities that appear under the sign of failed individualism. In the case of East Bengal, it further enables us to see why and in what ways this historical place remains such a satisfying and magnetic object of cathexis, of nonsovereign affiliation and binding—the site of a distinctly uncosmopolitan transnationalism.

This book reads material objects—fabric, texts, archives, art—as gathering sites of political articulation and investment. *Articulation* here signifies both the utterance and, to follow Bruno Latour, the orientation of "being affected by differences."[29] It is not a vitalist conception of labor because *things* in this book are neither inert objects nor the object of inquiry themselves: this is a book about the relation between intimate, tactile things and porous, political bodies.[30] A commitment to postcolonial studies and to feminist theory, and to the legacies of imperial knowledge and subject production, means that this book places the human and her lived life of possibility at the fore of its study. *An Empire of Touch* shows how she has never been outside of the world of politics, but through her labor and its touch, offers this world radical possibilities and fabricates them into being. Articulation, for our purposes, restores to affect its sensual and relational quality.

Articulation as the power to affect and be affected shows that the intimate contact of labor makes way for a politics and ethics of accumulation and permeability. Returning to Baruch Spinoza's (by way of Gilles Deleuze) notion of the body's "power to affect and be affected," I take affect to be a capacity and phenomenon that stages the ethical encounter of touch.[31] This is a form of Ranjana Khanna's understanding of affect as "a surplus that questions its boundaries, and a surplus that may manifest itself in affectlessness, it is the porous interface of the skin that marks a relation to alterity."[32] Take, for example, the tradition of *kantha* stitch quilts that appears in chapter 5. Originally objects of a deeply domestic and familial practice, made by the compression of old cotton *saris* and cloth and sewn using thread pulled from *sari* borders, *kanthas* are a form of self-expression for women—in the imagery and design as well as in the corporeal imprint left by their making—not oriented toward the market. Today, however, *kanthas* circulate globally in the fair-trade economy as symbols of women's empowerment through handicraft production. Their new material life, now rotely reproduced on single-layer new cloth to be sold in bulk to commercial merchants in Europe and America as well as to a globalized subcontinental elite, is one which, even as the *personal*-ity of the object disappears, retains the somatic promise of touch, of contact in a newly dispersed economy.

Turning to objects alone, particularly domestic and feminized ones, cannot account for or hope to understand the lives of political labor. The problem of women, for the Subaltern Studies Collective, has been—perhaps more acutely than for any of their other inquiries—the problem of the archive. Partha Chatterjee argues that evidence of women's political commitments is not housed in the colonial archive; instead, "[t]he domain where the new idea of womanhood was sought to be actualized was the home, and the real history of that change can be constructed only out of evidence left behind in autobiographies, family histories, religious tracts, literature, theatre, songs, paintings, and other such cultural artefacts that depict life in middle-class homes."[33] The colonial archive, for Chatterjee, already under pressure to produce evidence of 'subaltern consciousness,' offers only historical hints of women's participation in nationalist politics. More broadly, this problem of the archive—of the material objects by which we conceive a political subject and a political history—is a problem of our conception of the political.

Culture becomes the unreliable boundary of political possibility in a myth now decisively debunked by feminist historians who have produced a rich counternarrative to this claim of the archive's failure, the limited sphere of women's political life, and the material objects of that history.[34] To ask after the form and feature of women's political life in India is now to be afforded a range of primary and secondary material that evinces the dense diversity of this labor. At the same time, this form of historicist rejoinder has been subject to its own critique. Spivak, in "Can the Subaltern Speak?" and in her introduction to the *Selected Subaltern Studies* collection, warns against what she sees as the fantasy of her Subaltern Studies colleagues and other historians: that they can locate evidence of subaltern politics, that agency is an identifiable structure, that the subject of subaltern politics is the individual. It is a feminist deconstructive reminder of the political and psychic projections by which the category of the subaltern is produced; it is the ethical injunction to consider the power of representation.[35]

By neither eschewing the archive's limited vision nor reifying its material form, I have endeavored to follow Spivak's enjoinder to its epistemological limit.

This project, like many others of postcolonial studies, began in the colonial archive. It began at the British Library and National Archives of India, looking for documents about women's participation in anticolonial nationalism. The first chapter of this book in particular owes itself to those archives. Far from being obscured within the colonial and national archives, Pritilata Waddedar's trace is profuse and diffuse, demanding a form of reading for her articulation and the terms by which she comes to be commemorated and historicized that resists hermeneutic mastery and embraces intimate contact. The pressure upon the archive becomes starkest in chapter 4, where the Bangladeshi National Archives incinerate records of women who, having been raped during the 1971 war, will come to be called *war heroines* by the government. Recordkeeping rather than archiving, this postcolonial nation-state orients its historicist practices toward a global aid apparatus which, as we will see in chapter 5, quantifies the quality of life as a measure of postcolonial progress. Neither record nor archive seem able to contain the question at the core of our inquiry: How do postcolonial women, whose labor is the fulcrum of state-making—that well-trod ground of the recognizably political—articulate the terms of their own relational, aspirational commitments?

Within and in between moments of archival buckling, I have turned to a curated archive of objects, texts, and ephemera to locate the insistent mark of women's investment and political commitment in the supplementary movement of texts and textiles. They are bound to one another by a shared confluence of space and possibility, what I call here *contingency*.

Death of a Discipline Foretold

The permeability of touch is not limited to the subjects of this book. In the writing of it, I have endeavored to produce intimacy as scholarly practice. In the latter chapters where my material has come directly from living people—those who volunteered in rehabilitation efforts following Bangladesh's independence, artisanal textile producers, garment workers—the *feeling* of connection and embeddedness became more profound and more ethically vexing. But even in the earlier chapters, those which are "historical," the question of my own limits as a scholar in the encounter with these objects and speaking-subjects has been central. Where do my position in the American academy, my political commitments, the clothes on my own body end and the material of my study begin?

That question has rather insistently refused resolution. In a book about the possibility of a politics of being undone, I have aimed to be open to being worked upon and dissembled—a form of what Spivak has termed "critical intimacy."[36] This is, in part, a matter of scale. Critical intimacy attempts to draw objects near, to engage the local, to be touched. Turning to the local and the intimate, *An Empire of Touch* parses the global life of empire.

Recent disciplinary trends toward the global Anglophonic and planetary, repudiating the postcolonial for what might be seen as its embarrassing overpoliticization, have followed what Terry Eagleton diagnoses as the shift from nation and class to ethnicity, which is "also one from politics to culture."[37] The field, as such, has gone even further, leaning away from cultural critique toward the postcritical and descriptive turns in literary studies more broadly. This has meant a renewed romance with the literary, in which the politics of critique align with the national and the aesthetics of culture align with the cosmopolitan. Although the admonition of postcritical thinkers that the fascination with hermeneutics of suspicion has limited and perhaps even mutated the mandate of literary studies is a salutary intervention to the self-consuming practice of overreading, the disavowal of the political in what used to be called postcolonial studies would seem to throw the critical baby out with the provincial bathwater.[38]

It has become commonplace to proclaim the end of postcolonial studies while simultaneously lamenting its unrealized potential as an inquiry into relations of power. However, in this historical moment, at which neoliberalism's new market convenes alongside growing militant ethnonationalisms across the world, we need more than ever the category of the postcolonial, as a humanistic formation that indicates the shared work of description and critique to understand the interdependence between aesthetics and politics. This is far from an obsolete or extravagant hermeneutic forty years on, when *homo economicus* governs the value of the humanities and its mandate in the university. Against the artful depoliticization of the global, this book is committed to the work of the postcolonial—as a concept and as a hermeneutic—and its politics in the faith that it is possible to be critical, to prioritize the political, while still making room for the textured richness of wonder and rupturous surprise.

This book's account of intimate tactile labor connects flows of contemporary global capital to the material life of politics, demonstrating the corporeal, epistemological, and ideological interconnections wrought by empire and its afterlives. Material intimacies made possible by textiles reorient the critical trajectory by which the figure of the Global Southern woman can be seen as available for rescue or intervention. As we will see in the final chapter, the moniker "ready-made garments" is a grotesque misnomer for an industry deeply exertive and physical. The sleight of hand by which the body of the (young, female) garment worker is disappeared in the market form does not expunge the particulate signature of the object. One "piece" will often come into contact with several dozen bodies over the course of its making—hands, fingers, tongues, lips, teeth, sweat, blood, spit—and it is the nature of cotton, of this organic fiber, to take into itself those leavings and incorporate them just as it will incorporate the bodily traces of its wearer. It is this accumulative contact, this shared body captured within material, that is at the center of this book's story about the labor of women and what we call the political. This is a call for a dilated phenomenology, one in which the trace of touch, borne in the structure of text and textile, abides even and especially in the instance of its apparent effacement. In warp and woof, in captured dust of human remains, cloth gathers global interconnection: not simply the empire of capital, but an empire of touch. Accumulation and contact are the bases of political possibility in which the postcolonial endeavors of individual and national sovereignty are reimagined. In this light, we can see the material coincidence of 2013 with which we began as a battle over what will come to represent Bangladesh in a global market and a postcolonial imagination. Will it be muslin's valorized artisanal labor marked masculine (though always bearing the traces of women's bodies) or the mundane industrial labor of young women?

Although textiles of East Bengal are a particularly resonant and collocated site from which to consider the kinds of political subject life and imaginative worlds opened up through a capacious understanding of touch—its material, corporeal, psychic, and aesthetic dimensions—this book engages a variety of other material encounters to think differently about contact, about historicism, and about technologies of representation. An empire of touch is fabricated with the disciplining contact of governmental surveillance and containment; the purifying contact between individual hands and woven thread, drawing together a common nation bound by its fabric; the absorbing identification with an ideal which transforms the capacity of the body and the sense of the self; the contamination of violence figured as foreign touch that is cleared away by state veneration; the global circulation of intimate objects imbued with the particulate remains of labor.

Given its porosity, cloth retains and absorbs traces of its encounter with the bodies of those who manufacture and use it, militating against the illusion of corporeal or psychic autonomy as it mimics the skin on which it rests; so too, all of the objects of inquiry in this book persistently undo the fantasy of possessive individualism that governed imperial rule and continues to haunt the postcolonial project. I am, in the end, committed to a redemptive quality of text and textile so conceived—not in the terms of access and agency promoted by liberal feminism or fair-trade marketing but as an ethical injunction to read for accumulation and trace of a more intimate nature, to conceive of labor and touch not as being freed into individuated *homo economicus* but set open into relational world-making. Through this local, material history of women's labor in East Bengal over more than a century, *An Empire of Touch* insists that women articulate in their own idiom political desires and commitment; they speak for themselves what constitutes a good life and shared being in the world.

PART I

Reading the Body Politic

1

Virgin Suicides

On September 23, 1932, Pritilata Waddedar, a twenty-year-old school-teacher and member of the Indian Republican Army (IRA),[1] a local chapter of the larger revolutionary group Jugantar,[2] became the first Indian woman to die in the commission of an anticolonial attack in the twentieth century when she committed suicide after leading a raid on the Pahartali Railway Institute in Chittagong, East Bengal. Police found Waddedar's body outside the Institute dressed in men's clothes, with no visible injuries, and they discovered tucked into her shirt several pamphlets of her own writing, including "Long Live Revolution" and "An Appeal to Women."[3] In the latter, she had written:

> Women to day have taken the firm resolution that they will not remain in the background. For the freedom of their motherland they are willing to stand side by side with their brothers in every action however hard or fearful it may be. To offer proof I have taken upon myself the leadership of this expedition to be launched today.[4]

The tract ends with the exclamation, "I boldly declare myself a revolutionary." Her body, spectacularly stilled outside the site of her attack, offers proof of another order. Of what it offers proof, the modes of reading and memorialization it invites, and the afterlives of that body and its articulations constitute the terms of a colonial and postcolonial struggle over meaning-making. At the time, Waddedar's dead body took on a kind of evidentiary status in the prosecution of her comrades, a colonial assertion of authority in the courtroom—a prophecy, perhaps, of how it would come again, decades later, to be the disputed object of historical narrative. Pritilata Waddedar, variously called terrorist, martyr, goddess, and dupe, herself comes to be a kind of contested territory.

What is in a name? *Terrorist*, the watchword of our post-9/11 times, signified for British colonial authorities resistant bodies that threatened to co-opt their claim to sovereign power and ability to decree life and death. Turning to violence to overthrow the British, in explicit repudiation of the program of civil disobedience being popularized by M. K. Gandhi at this same moment, groups like Jugantar appropriated and reversed back onto the state the modes of its control. In so doing, they revealed the antinomianism of the Raj's claim to uncontested power. Some forms of violence—those that are state-sanctioned—are appropriate, rational, justifiable; other forms of violence—those that take the dismantling of the state as their very goal—are savage, chaotic, passionate, excessive. As Achille Mbembe has argued, "The exercise of reason is tantamount to the exercise of freedom, a key element for individual autonomy. The romance of sovereignty, in this case, rests on the belief that the subject is the master and the controlling author of his or her own meaning."[5] Waddedar, and the name by which she and her actions are marked in historical record and in spectral iteration, inaugurate a hermeneutics of legibility, authority, and subjectivity. For these reasons, I call her and her comrades by the name they inscribed upon their bodies and actions: *revolutionary*.[6]

For colonial authorities, the discovery of Waddedar's body outside the Institute ended a months-long search and verified their suspicion that she was involved in terrorist activities following the February 1932 death of a British police officer. Moreover, her body added to the growing cache of evidence against suspected Jugantar leader Surya Sen. At his trial, Waddedar, dead for more than a year, would be resurrected as witness against and indictment of her revolutionary comrades. For those very compatriots in Jugantar and for nationalist historians after them, however, the image of her corpse outside the Institute preserved her as martyr. In the months following her death, a photograph of her face and the text "Long Live Revolution" were printed on red leaflets, distributed throughout Chittagong as revolutionary *memento mori*, and showered onto the grounds of the Intelligence Branch Inspector's compound.[7] She joined the leagues of other rare Bengali women in secret revolutionary groups, such as Shanti Ghosh, Suniti Chowdhury, and Bina Das, and was glorified above them. She gave her life in her act of anticolonial violence, while they lived. As the exceptional sacrifice, her death rendered her exemplary.[8]

Her name became a synecdoche for blazing female heroism: *Agnikanya Pritilata* ("Firebrand Daughter" Pritilata).[9] For nationalists and historians alike, Waddedar's memory has been distilled to the iconicity of a single name, "Pritilata," as she is called in films, recollections, and (consistently) academic texts.

The assumption of a first-name identification represents a claim of intimacy that sits uneasily with my own explicitly feminist approach here, which aims to trace the unstable legibility of a form of political protest that depends on the destruction of life. This is not to suggest that to call Pritilata Waddedar by her last name as a scholarly practice is a recuperative or neutral gesture. Rather, by so doing, it is to insist upon careful attention to the gendered engine of memorialization that produced her as familiar and accessible to our touch across time (distinct from that by which Surya Sen also comes to have a single-name afterlife as "Masterda"). Compounding the authoritative proper noun "Master," which denotes both his career as schoolteacher and his eminence, the honorific suffix *da* ("older brother") familializes but does not familiarize Sen in a professionalized memorial. However, references to Waddedar by her first name serve as a discursive fixing, rendering her at once exemplary and familiar, heroic and ancillary, relic and ruin. This cohering function is made possible by her gender and the mode of her death, a form of representational violence that leaves her open to scrutiny and to narrativization.

I. Curated Fragments

This chapter follows Pritilata Waddedar's body and memory as they are incarnated into legal, historical, and cultural evidence—made to speak, silenced, destroyed, and reimagined—by colonial authorities and nationalists alike. In the particular forms and terms of her sacrifice, Waddedar both augurs and undermines these future rewritings, offering her dead body as "proof" to systems of evaluation that it calculatedly confounds. The chapter traces the development of two legal apparatuses—one concerned with the construction of the female subject under law and the other with the identification and regulation of extrajudicial bodies—to demonstrate the imbrication of imperial technologies of consent and capture against which she made herself known. Cloth, materially and symbolically featured in each of the four chapters that follow, appears spectrally: it is the recalled but untouched envelope within which Waddedar's body is preserved in the archive and opens up a mode of reading surfaces and their contiguities. This chapter keeps at the fore of its attention the materiality of historical encounter with Waddedar, mediated through, and by, the colonial archive; it concerns itself with the artifacts of a revolutionary action and what they reveal about the limits of what can be preserved, narrativized, and imagined of a female political subject. For this reason, it is structured in time with the stops and starts of Waddedar's own archival appearance. It follows both letter and form of Waddedar's articulations in order to argue for the extant expression of her intent and, by the same stroke, against fantasies of her containment and linearity. The legacy of the Chittagong uprising, often marked as peripheral to a nationalist narrative of modern India that presupposes its current form, reorients our conception of an anticolonial imagination because Jugantar's intent to liberate the motherland was as much a local project of imagining Chittagong outside the purview of imperial rule as it was part of a broader program of anticolonial resistance.

The Chittagong Armory raids, like other armed insurgencies in twentieth-century British India, have come to be marginalized in the history of the region by virtue of their apparent failure to produce the goal of independence. It is tempting, then, to position the raids and Pritilata Waddedar in historiographic obscurity, and this as an excavation. But in the 1930s, when the future of an India and a Bengal free of British rule was not yet clear and certainly had not yet taken the form of a Bengal divided between the independent nation-states of India and Pakistan, independence was an ideological and aspirational category of affiliation and community. Bengal was the object of anticolonial insurgency even as a more expansive sense of India as a political figure had taken hold. In the near-century since the Armory raids, their memorialization has largely been partitioned along the lines drawn by Cyril Radcliffe in 1947, while the rhizomatic root system of Indian independence stretches across the territory that would become Pakistan and then Bangladesh. However, in recent years, a renewed interest in anticolonial organizations has drawn the events of Chittagong back across the border to India in the form of historical fiction and three feature films. This is a curious reinscription of a place and a moment outside of Indian national time. Indeed, it must ignore the local fidelities of Jugantar to be retrospectively incorporated into two nationalist histories. Drawing on the colonial, pre-Partition national form of British India, the Chittagong insurgency has become the object of a nationalist etiology that transcends postcolonial nation-states.

In 2010, Indian filmmaker Ashutosh Gowariker released *Khelein Hum Jee Jaan Sey (We Play with Our Lives)*, a Hindi feature film on Chittagong focusing on Sen, who, according to the trailer, "trigger[s] a revolution." The determinedly local violence of the Chittagong uprising in the cinematic retelling is not only a national memorialization but also an origin story for a nation that effectively does not exist. The incorporation of Chittagong back into the body of India reimagines the relationship between anticolonial resistance and postcolonial nationalism, refusing to acknowledge the multiple ruptures by which those two sites have been geopolitically separated from one another. The film capitalizes on resurgent nationalist sentiments and fantasies of an inviolable, transcendent

early stages
beginning

state. While Chittagong might have become part of a separate nation-state, the events of the 1930s can be coalesced within a narrative of incipient Indian independence, their telos redirected *ex post facto*.[10]

By turning to the outbreak of anticolonial violence in Chittagong, the major port of the Bay of Bengal, in a moment at which the popular face of nationalism in British India was that of Gandhi, his salt march, and his hunger strike, this chapter offers a response to enduring questions of postcolonial studies: Who is a revolutionary? And what is a revolution if it brings no liberation? Whither the post of the postcolonial? The apparition of the 1857 Mutiny, in which sepoys in the Bengal Presidency Army raised a revolt against the British East India Company to set off rebellions across north and east India, has been manifested in moments of political upheaval for nearly a century as the anti-originary revolution. As that which ultimately resulted in the transfer of administrative control to the British crown and the advent of formal colonial rule, 1857 is the phantom of possibility to which each iteration of revolution returns, to which perhaps Pritilata Waddedar responded in her final declaration of herself. Waddedar is, for the purposes of this book, both a historical figure and a theorist of her own historicity. She argues, in her writing and with her body itself, for a form of self-memorialization that preserves rather than effaces the illegible and the unrepresentable. In those textual and bodily articulations, she resisted and undermined the very processes by which she has come to be known under the sign of a single name. Nevertheless, she left herself to be read. She declared herself and her political commitment. As she cited the apparitional revolution, let us then read that declaration alongside the terms by which she described her actions and their intent.

In her diary, Waddedar describes Surya Sen's final words to her: "Women, regarded as a race of mothers in the Bengali households, also are enraged now in the display of valour but this chapter of history is yet to be recorded. Let the chapter be composed through your success or through your self-immolation."[11] Waddedar makes the curious counterfactual assertion that her participation in the attack on the Railway Institute and her potential death would be self-immolation. Though she cites Sen for her iteration of "self-immolation" as history-making and community-building, she does not imagine the act of immolation as instructive; hers was instead to be the spectacular offering of her body to their shared cause, a signal flare of community. She writes that, for Sen, whether or not she survived was ancillary to the pedagogical and illustrative potential of her spectacular violence and apparent obedience. Her self-sacrifice was intended to compose a history that the valor of her fellow women could not. It insisted that the destruction of the individual body forms the body politic. It wrote a corporeal history that could only come to be in the absence of Waddedar as living, speaking actor. Waddedar's evocation of self-immolation as a historically self-conscious semiotic practice draws on and resignifies the common form by which female self-immolation is figured: *sati,* the Hindu practice of burning living widows on the pyre alongside the corpses of their husbands. The language of self-immolation, with its attendant specter of the act of *sati,* remarkably appears throughout the writings of women who participated in anticolonial violence of the period. It is a startling departure from the heroic lingua franca of revolutionary communities, as the practice of widows being cremated with their deceased husbands was largely disavowed and vilified in Bengal by the twentieth century. Despite the heterogeneous composition of groups like Jugantar, the women who participated in anticolonial violence in particular were marked by commonalities of background and education. Many, like Waddedar, were well educated, came from progressive middle-class families, and held leftist political views. Within this political community, *sati* was far from a naturalized contemporary cultural phenomenon; rather, it was seen as atavistic and distinctly unmodern. What is it about the language of self-immolation that offers such fugitive possibility for these women? This is a naming that works through negation, an apposite resistance to the questions of agency, modernity, and progress coalesced under its sign.[12]

Pritilata Waddedar was not alone in turning to *sati* as a productive, if uncomfortable, analytic of revolutionary desire. At the end of her seminal 1983 essay "Can the Subaltern Speak?," Gayatri Chakravorty Spivak relates the story of Bhubaneswari Bhaduri, a young woman of sixteen who hanged herself in Calcutta in 1926. Spivak writes:

> The suicide was a puzzle since, as Bhubaneswari was menstruating at the time, it was clearly not a case of illicit pregnancy—the ready and overdetermined solution to the unexplained deaths of unmarried women. Nearly a decade later, it was discovered that she was a member of one of the many groups involved in the armed struggle for Indian independence. She had finally been entrusted with a political assassination. Unable to confront the task and yet aware of the practical need for trust, she killed herself.[13]

Six years before Waddedar's attack on the Pahartali Institute, Bhubaneswari was similarly charged with a task of anticolonial insurgency, the violence of which she displaced onto her own body.[14]

These two women are sisters in arms. By outward appearances, they are remarkably similar: both young women from educated, middle-class families; both members of anticolonial revolutionary groups; both dead before the age of twenty-one. Indeed, both take their own lives and leave their bodies as signs. Their uncanny doubling, however, seems to end with the posthumous lives of those bodies. Bhubaneswari Bhaduri, unable or unwilling to carry out the assassination with which she is tasked, killed herself behind the shuttered doors of her home. From then on, her body and her life are obscured from our view until Spivak encounters her ghostly presence by chance. Waddedar led six men into the Pahartali Railway Institute and emerged with them moments later, having helped to take the lives of three British subjects. She killed herself on the steps of the building, in plain sight of the incoming police charge, her pockets filled with political propaganda. From then on, her body is suspended in our view, the subject of paeans and proclamations and commemorations.

Of Bhubaneswari, Spivak writes that "[her] suicide is an unemphatic, ad hoc, subaltern rewriting of the social text of *sati*-suicide as much as the hegemonic account of the blazing, fighting, familial Durga."[15] In describing Bhubaneswari's suicide as unemphatic, Spivak suggests that her speech, though precise and motivated, is somehow stilled. It is stripped of the illocutionary force of emphasis. Much scholarly attention has been paid to Spivak's use of *subaltern* in reference to Bhubaneswari, a departure from its deployment by the Subaltern Studies Collective for whom the term follows Antonio Gramsci's use of it to indicate groups subject to the hegemony of ruling classes. For most of the Collective, subaltern has been shorthand for a critical positionality from which to consider elite historiography. Subaltern politics, according to Ranajit Guha, is "an autonomous domain for it neither originated from elite politics nor did its existence depend on the latter"; it is an alternative form of political consciousness.[16] In Spivak's hands, subaltern is not an essentialist category of reclaimed agency but rather the site of a contestation of power.

Rajeswari Sunder Rajan argues that Bhubaneswari's suicide is precisely what produces her subalterneity, her spectral place at the margins of memory; her death provides the condition of possibility for rewriting the social script of *sati* and of heroic mother goddess.[17] For Rajan, Bhubaneswari refuses with her dead body the narration of her death under particular terms (illicit pregnancy) and refuses with her silence the narration of her death by other terms (heroism or patriotism). Bhubaneswari's death, when read through her revolutionary affiliations, might have been subsumed within a masculinist discourse of idealized and idolized mythic femininity rather than conjugal misfortune, if not for what Spivak identifies as hermeneutic resistance.

Bhubaneswari Bhaduri, in waiting for the onset of menstruation to hang herself, made her body into a sign. It averred at once her commitment to the nationalist cause and the failure of her mission. It refused the preemptive etiology of her suicide, any attempt at a political or psychological autopsy. This "displacing gesture" destabilizes the processes of signification; her body, so inscribed by intent, cannot be read.[18] For Spivak, this is the condition of subalterneity—being subject to the semiotic violence through which signals can only ever be mis-read, of ceasing to be subaltern precisely in the moment of being read. It is a deft sleight of hand by which *sati* becomes synecdoche for the female subaltern subject and the canonical legacy of the essay trains the contemporary reader to look for revolutionary potential in its wake. This is what Sandhya Shetty and Elizabeth Jane Bellamy have described as "inserting the body (via menstrua-tion) into the question of the founding of postcolonialism."[19] "Can the Subaltern Speak?," inarguably one of the most significant texts of postcolonial studies, opens the archive with and to the body of the colonial woman.

Rosalind Morris, in the introduction to a volume reflecting on the essay and its significance over twenty-five years, writes that "the woman, or more specif-ically, the subaltern as woman, is a figure in whom the question of ideology—as the production of subjects in whom desire and interest are never entirely symmetrical or mutually reinforcing—splits open."[20] In the colonial archive from which Spivak gleans traces of female suicide appearing under the sign of *sati*, the question of desire is always in excess of the modes of reading. This invites the essential provocation from which this book begins: How does the political subjectivity of women, the articulation of a condition of desire, make itself legible? So, let us follow Spivak into the archive, proceeding from her own self-revision in *The Critique of Postcolonial Reason* (1999) that Bhubaneswari had in fact spoken herself as a political subject. Where Spivak produces for Bhubaneswari (with whom her connection is familial) a kinship with women illuminated in the archive through the referent of *sati*, we begin in the archive with a woman who appears first captured in the grip of colonial power. In posi-tioning Waddedar next to Spivak, concatenating their echoes, I hope to suggest the relational nature of women's speech in the postcolonial archive.

Pritilata Waddedar, like Bhubaneswari, made her body a sign. It registered vividly the nature of her protest: a disruptive, agrammatical iteration of resis-tance. But to take seriously the purposefulness of her intent, the figuring of a bodily politics of protest requires that we not rest in the moment of decon-structive ellipsis. It demands that we recognize and register that protest, the signal that has not gone astray in the nearly eighty years that separate us from its articulation. It demands that we also account for the material forms of this encounter. Waddedar's writing, taken from her diary, appears in reproduced fragments as part of police files on the Chittagong Armory raids. The excerpts are those that were entered into evidence by the Crown during the trial of her comrades the following year; the remainder of her diary was destroyed, burned like her body was after its autopsy. Waddedar also appears by way of affiliation: in the writings of Surya Sen used during his trial; in *Chittagong Armoury Raid-ers: Reminiscences*, the 1945 memoir by Kalpana Dutt, the only other woman to actively participate in the IRA, and in Dutt's police file; and subsequently, in the historical nonfiction account *Do and Die: The Chittagong Armoury Uprising 1930-34* (1999), written by Dutt's daughter-in-law Manini Chatterjee, on which two feature-length Hindi films would later be based. Waddedar is curated by colonial authority and intimate memory into archival fragments; our encounter with her words and body is mediated by this relationality. And it is precisely through this relationality that Waddedar offers us a way to read.

Dead outside the place in which she took three lives as part of an anticolonial insurrection campaign, she made her body speak. She rewrote the social text of *sati* to emphatically articulate a form of political protest that recognizes its own futurity. Waddedar uncannily predicted how her actions and intents would come to be narrativized and ventriloquized—that she would become victim and goddess—within familiar narratives of either criminal violence or nationalist sacrifice. Not wife, not widow, not set ablaze, she marked her act as an iteration of *sati* that repeats with a difference its constituent parts, disengaging it from the pyre and grafting it to the body of political protest. Whereas Spivak's essay has become the canonical caution against all that goes unheard, Pritilata Waddedar spoke herself and made way for a circuit of intimate political exchange.

While at times it may be tempting to see Waddedar as a figure imperiled by the violence of the archive, of its curation and its narrativization, she continually slips its hold and exceeds its limits. Her curious archival relationship to Indian independence is symptomatic of the case of East Bengal, in the cultural memory of which she has never been lost or shuttered. In 1932, the motherland that she pledged her life to was not yet the nation-state of Bangladesh; today, her name is one commonly given to daughters by Bengali feminists there.

II. Speaking Otherwise

It is a long way from the romantic commemoration by young (mostly Muslim) women in contemporary Bangladesh who bear the name Pritilata to the woman who set out to exchange the lives of British subjects for the life of a nation to come. It is perhaps an even longer way to the historical image of burning widows on the pyre from the schoolteacher who hoped her own death would invite the deaths of others—British subjects and with them, other Bengali women. However, woven through this feminine genealogy is the prospect of desire as political. Colonial contestation around *sati* was waged both in the arena of social intervention by missionaries and in the courtroom, as the colonial authorities sought to codify it through legal circular and, eventually, in the Indian Penal Code.

Legal consequences turned on whether the woman wanted to live or die, whether she wanted to be saved or forsaken, whether she was subjugated or freed by the act of self-immolation. Whether, indeed, there was a legal self engaged by the act. Thereby, at stake is the ability of the law to determine a woman's (often a dead woman's) agency and desire. Colonial and anticolonial arguments about *sati* have depended on delimiting "native" domestic space and colonial incursion into that space. "Saving" women brought them into the public space of colonial conflict, away from that private space in which they might be said to want to die. On the pyre, private wife was made public goddess.

Though the practice of *sati* existed prior to British colonial presence in India, the discourse of *sati* is a colonial construction.[21] The nineteenth-century codification into law of *sati* as a punishable offense represented a paradigm shift in colonial governance, an incursion into the hitherto inviolable realm of "native tradition."[22] In instituting a juridical index by which the desires of Indian women were to be identified and registered, *sati* legislation prescribed and regulated a new public language of consent. It in turn became the de facto template for the colonial state's logic of what constituted a female subject under the law. In the history of its codification, the consent of women takes on increasingly significant evidentiary status, as the courts negotiate in what ways the desire to die might function as a legal category of analysis. As a consequence, for these anticolonial insurgents of the 1930s, *sati* offered a gendered vocabulary for sacrifice that is always-already political.

Sati, in Waddedar's iteration, is an allegory by which the actions and desires of the present are preserved for future witnesses. Paul de Man writes that "it remains necessary, if there is to be allegory, that the allegorical sign refer to another sign that precedes it. The meaning constituted by the allegorical sign can then consist only in the repetition (in the Kierkegaardian sense of the term) of a previous sign with which it can never coincide, since it is of the essence of this previous sign to be pure anteriority."[23] Temporally and representationally discontinuous, *sati* as allegory of female revolutionary violence offers an illusion of coherence that recognizes itself as illusory. It abides by the distance from the site of the pyre and resists the nostalgic reach of identification toward the widow on the pyre. As an allegory for political violence, it destabilizes that false division as women spectacularly immolate themselves in the name of anticolonialism, nodding to the colonial intervention into the practice of *sati* that cleared this ground in the first place.

Indeed, just months before Waddedar's own planned self-immolation, in May 1932, twenty-year-old Bina Das crossed the stage at the University of Calcutta convocation and, pulling a revolver out from under her academic robes, fired three shots at Bengal governor Stanley Jackson. She missed and was arrested immediately by authorities. In her public statement before the Special Tribunal of the Calcutta Court, she declared, "I only sought the way to death by offering myself at the feet of my country and invite the attention of all by my death as a mark of a most immaculate form of protest against the situations created by the repressive measures of the government, which can unsex even a frail woman like myself, brought up in all the best traditions of Indian womanhood."[24] Das's reference to "all the best traditions of Indian womanhood," as Purnima Bose has argued, is a pointed and intentional allusion to *sati*, to proving ground of Indian tradition in the face of colonial governance.[25] By describing her intended death as an "immaculate form of protest" in the courtroom, Das evokes the specter of the widow on the pyre, whose consent and will were the terms by which colonial authorities sought to legislate and regulate domestic practices. All prosecutions of *sati* were thereby political, the management by colonial forces of a competing system of power. Describing the intent of her political protest in the language of Indian tradition in refusal of the imperial designation of terrorist, Das resexed herself into a new kind of public womanhood; she imagined a rebirth on the pyre.

Recognizing the ambivalences and incongruities between the letter of their utterance and the spirit of its form, women who turn to the historical language of *sati* destabilize the liberal paradigm of consent, offering their bodies as templates for political dissent that is never outside the coercive orbit of power. The evidentiary reaches of the criminal code here overlap uncomfortably with the terms of historical memory. As a consequence, the allegory of *sati* is a situated strategy of naming that also keeps the archive in its sights, drawing upon the resources of the past to make visible, if not entirely legible, a revolutionary action in the present. In particular, Waddedar's re-marking of *sati*, the difference of the repetition, names it as a revolutionary practice and simultaneously reconstitutes the relationship between self-annihilation and protest. It asks, in another tongue, whether and how a woman's death—her choice to die—might come to be read.

Waddedar and other women embedded in revolutionary communities were caught in a representational double bind in which their participation in anticolonial violence served to reify, simultaneously and paradoxically, two competing masculinist, hegemonic discourses. The Chittagong IRA and Jugantar more broadly were conceived by their leaders as having two intrinsically interconnected projects: reclaiming the territorial body of the motherland and subverting the discourse of Bengali effeminacy produced by British authorities, the forces of which we will see more broadly in chapter 3. From the inception of the Dhaka Anushilan Samiti, the secret militant group established in 1902 from which Jugantar and the IRA emerged, Bengal—and East Bengal more precisely—set itself up as the site of a radical, corrective political practice of gender.

Anushilan Samiti, whose very name means "body-building society," deployed its local alibi as a youth fitness organization to train young men in hand-to-hand combat, *lathi* fighting, and shooting. It sought to prepare a cadre for potential battle and broke from the larger coalition of Bengali revolutionary groups after the 1905 partition over its commitment to a program of political violence. Sovereignty and masculinity were, in this way, sutured together by the thread of violence. What is more, the latter incarnations of the Samiti positioned themselves against the vivid image of Gandhi and the Congress Party's growing commitment to nonviolent and bureaucratic resistance. Jugantar, many of whose members went on to join the Communist Party of India (CPI), aligned itself to a very different form of bodily politics than did Gandhi (see chapter 2). Although Waddedar, Dutt, and other women who joined Jugantar were also trained to fight (and build test explosives in the chemistry lab of Bethune College), such training was figured as exceptional rather than essential. Their primary function within these revolutionary communities was ideologically limited by the emphasis on armed resistance as a masculinizing project. As a result, these women recognized an incongruity between their revolutionary insurgency and the conditions of possibility of its memorialization. Seen in this way, self-immolation serves as a cipher for the terms of desire and recognizable intent. It announces the relational nature of itself as an act and what Talal Asad, following Maurice Halbwachs, calls the ritual form by which suicide becomes legible as sacrifice.[26]

In the days leading up to the attack on the Pahartali Institute, Pritilata Waddedar wrote compulsively, justifying to loved ones in letters and to herself (and perhaps a future audience) in her diary the violence she was about to enact. In these writings, she imagines embodying a form of self-negating politics of futurity. This articulation of protest through self-annihilation resurrects the specter of the *sati* debate as a contest over the form and intent of women's lives and deaths. To her mother, she writes, "Mother, did you call me? . . . Pardon me, mother, I have given you great pain. I offer my blood to wipe the tears of the motherland. You bless me, or my desire will not be fulfilled. Forgive me, mother, pardon me today."[27] Here born of two mothers— one who will suffer for the violence to be done and one for whom that violence is to be done—Waddedar constructs an intimate fluid exchange of sacrifice (blood for tears) in need of maternal expiation. The desire in danger of being unfulfilled is elliptical, an unspoken aspiration that nonetheless appears at the horizon of representation as a kind of blessed sacrifice.

What remains of Waddedar's writings is entirely in English. Though she likely also wrote in Bangla, only the writing that was useful to colonial authorities and entered into evidence has been preserved. The preceding excerpt from her diary comes from the criminal case file on her, housed in the imperial archive. The encounter with her declaration that she intends to immolate herself bears that bilingual negotiation and ought to be apprehended through that accumulative translation. Etymologically, the English word *immolation* is the act by which a sacrifice is made holy; it is a meaning-making supplement to an act of violence or loss. From the Latin, *immolare*, to sprinkle with sacrificial meal, "to immolate" is defined in the *Oxford English Dictionary* (OED) as "To sacrifice, offer in sacrifice; to kill as a victim."[28] Self-immolation is making a sacrificial victim of oneself. In Bangla, this is translated either as *atmahuti*, আত্মাহুতি, or more precisely, *atmabalidan*, আত্মবলিদান. Where *huti* is sacrificial fire itself, *balidan* is the offering, *dan*, of *bali*, the sacrificial beast. In both of these compound words, the object of the act is the *atma*, translated as "self," but a self not bound to the physical form of the mortal body. In the Vedic tradition, *atma*, unlike *jiva*, the living being, is an articulation of the self, "I am," beyond the phenomenological. *Atma* sacrifice offers up a self beyond the body, a self-annihilation by which the self cannot be annihilated. To self-immolate, in this context, is to destroy the self at the level of performativity and not materiality. Nonetheless, this is a performance rooted in the body, in its sensation and its corporeality. Let us consider the Sanskrit *vahnipatana*, বহ্নিপতন, meaning self-immolation more generally, and *agnipraveshna*, অগ্নিপ্রবেশন (widow immolation). *Vahni* signifies both fire and desire (curiously though, it in other compound forms means an animal that conveys—like the bullock who might in the Bangla word be the *bali*); *patana* is the collapse into an erotic dehiscence, alighting oneself down. Even the widow, cast onto the pyre as a dissipated remainder of conjugality, is offered in the Sanskrit something of somatic repair, as the holy fire of *agni* contains within it the spacious agnosticism of *praveshna* as entrance, penetration, or sexual intercourse. The destruction of the mortal body upon the pyre strains toward the possibility of pleasure that lacerates the sensate form, an ambivalent recompense.

Mythologically, the goddess Sati, from whom the practice draws its name and whose name it bestows upon its supplicants (immolated widows are offered the appellation Sati Mata, the purified mother), is a manifestation of the divine feminine creative force, Shakti. Born the daughter of Daksha, she defies him to marry Lord Shiva, the destroyer, and is banished. Despite being repudiated by her family, she then returns to her natal home to attend a sacrificial worship to which neither she nor her husband have been invited and endures her father's relentless aspersions on Shiva. Renditions of the story thereafter vacillate between Sati as ashamed or enraged or both, but they all agree that Sati, overcome by her father's attacks, sets herself alight—to punish her father and free herself, with an accompanying prayer that she be reborn to a worthier father. Not mourning widow but blazing wife, Sati's self-destruction is retributive and reparative, spectacular and indicting, setting off its own divine violence. Shiva, undone by grief and rage at Sati's death, slices off Daksha's head (replacing it with that of the goat that originally was to be sacrificed), and with Sati's charred corpse on his shoulders begins his awesome *tandava*, the divine dance of destruction.[29] He reenacts upon the world the violence Sati inflicted on herself—turned outward under the guise of mourning—such that her self-sacrifice is the impetus for his cataclysmic rage. Hers is a ground-clearing self-immolation as she makes possible Shiva's righting of the world with the destruction of her mortal body. Congruently, then, the destruction of Waddedar's body makes possible a revolutionary shift in the colonial landscape of East Bengal.

The double derivation of the word *sati*—the feminized form of the Sanskrit *sat*, meaning true or pure, and the mythological, referring to the goddess—bears witness to the promise of ontological clarity on which notions of feminine power depend. Sati's power as a feminine idol comes from her self-destruction; the unalloyed expression of agency begins and ends with a moment of self-annihilation. Sati is able to choose to die precisely because she is pure; her self-destruction in turn retrospectively validates her worth as daughter and divine consort. A similarly spectacular transformation is at work in the logic of the pyre where the widow, having expressed a form of purity in her ostensible choice to die, is reborn as the immortal and insensate goddess. Translation of myth into ritual, however, participates in its own counterfactual reimagining of the goddess Sati, who was a wife, not a widow. The retributive force of Sati's self-annihilation is translated into a recuperative futurity for generations to come, whose karma has been purified by the widow's sacrifice.

III. Voluntary Culpable Homicide, by Consent

In the nineteenth century, legal debates around the practice of *sati* turned on the ability of colonial officials to hear and to read a woman's utterance and performance of the will to die—or, more to the point, the failure of that representability. The juridical statute depended upon the basic opacity of a desire made public. This is to say that the development and codification of the prohibition of *sati* strained against the bounds of what constituted the agential, desiring, rational subject of law in death. Widow who would be *sati* was the test subject for this experiment in subjectivity in which the terms of female desire and consent emerge simultaneously with the possibility of her death.[30] I briefly trace the history of *sati* regulation in this section to offer a historiographic and epistemological account of how it has come to be such a rich concept metaphor for female political action and why women in carrying out anticolonial violence deploy it as an allegory. The terms by which this legislation regulated the conditions and possibilities of consent for women provide the *de facto* template for the colonial state's determination of what constituted a female subject under the law. In the 1930s, women in revolutionary organizations were still subjects under the surveillance apparatus institutionalized by its regulation. They summon the specter of *sati* in order to revise the seemingly irreducible agon between desire and coercion, legibility and resistance, into a strategic ambivalence that interrupts and frustrates totalizing narratives of heroism or victimhood.

An 1812 circular drafted by the Sadar Nizamat Adalat, the criminal court system created by the 1793 Cornwallis Code, declared *sati*, in the manner of other religious practices, allowed wherever sanctioned by religious officials. This followed the general rule of the Nizamat Adalat to allow, and indeed preserve, the sovereignty of religious practice. However, the circular, responding to growing British anxiety about the possible prevalence of the practice, offered the caveat of a newly erected category of illegal *sati* wherein the woman to be burned was either compelled, intoxicated, pregnant, or had young children for whom care provisions had not been made.[31] Though these are all potentially exceptional cases, the revision introduced into colonial policy a standard of consent, implicitly criminalizing *sati* by naming as its potential victims the unwilling or unaware wife and her children, all rewritten as innocent—indeed, unconscious—victims of a native tradition newly subject to legal scrutiny.

In 1817, the Nizamat Adalat returned to the subject to further amend the *sati* policy to allow for additional government oversight of the act; relatives of the widow were required to give prior notice of intent to authorities and allow them to determine the consent and legality of the intended immolation. The court stressed that, in the case of an "illegal" *sati*, the widow would not be the subject of punishment; indeed, it stated its intention to afford protection to widows who might withdraw from *sati*. The Nizamat Adalat's 1817 stance toward the category of illegal *sati* licensed the establishment of a surveillance apparatus that not only witnessed the act of immolation but also sought to record its attendant affects and intents. This abrupt shift away from a longstanding British noninterventionist policy in matters of "native culture" coincided with a more comprehensive shift in colonial policy toward bodies and health.

A sharp rise in mortality rates in Bengal between 1812 and 1817, due in large part to the first recorded cholera epidemic, implicitly undergirded the second Nizamat Adalat circular on *sati*. The nearly threefold increase in reported cases of *sati* offered colonial officials a warrant to intervene. That the new policy on *sati* included a structure by which colonial bodies might be surveilled and affects rationalized into intent points to the pervasiveness of anxieties about uncontrollable bodies in all facets of colonial policy. The 1829 Bengal Regulation of Sati culminated this regulatory effort by declaring all *sati* illegal and unjustifiable.

The 1829 regulation introduced a new language of paternalism and benevolent oversight into the British colonial vocabulary. In its preamble, Lord Bentinck, the regulation's architect, writes:

> The practice of suttee, or of burning or burying alive the widows of Hindus, is revolting to the feelings of human nature; it is nowhere enjoined by the religion of the Hindus as an imperative duty [and] in some extensive districts it does not exist: in those in which it has been most frequent it is notorious that in many instances acts of atrocity have been perpetrated which have been shocking to the Hindus themselves, and in their eyes unlawful and wicked. The measures hitherto adopted to discourage and prevent such acts have failed of success, and the governor-general in council is deeply impressed with the conviction that the abuses in question cannot be effectually put an end to without abolishing the practice altogether.[32]

Appealing first to a universalized feeling, the regulation suggests a dual logic for the shift in official policy. On the one hand, there is an appeal to culture-driven governance which holds that even Hindus, whose cultural practice *sati* ostensibly is, find it reprehensible. On the other hand, the regulation insists that all attempts to keep colonial policy outside the realm of culture by declaring some aspects of the practice legal and others traditional have proven inadequate to curb it. The regulation enters into nearly uncharted waters by drawing the force of religious doctrine into legal discourse, a quarantine that had hitherto been rather scrupulously upheld.

Lata Mani and Jeannette Herman have both argued that the language of feeling elicited in Bentinck's preamble reveals the true subject of the regulation's force to be not the women themselves, but the idea of Indian tradition (figured here and throughout the historical and scholarly inquiry into *sati* as Hindu) as outside of and impervious to colonial administration.[33] Indian women, long figured in nationalist discourse as the emblems and protectors of authentic native culture, are conceived of Bentinck's transitive logic as already resisting—finding "repulsive"—the act by which their gender is simultaneously being marked.[34] Brahmin pundits and nationalist leaders alike fiercely opposed the dissolution of the tradition law divide recommended by the 1829 regulation, the results of which are evident in the 1837 and 1860 drafts of the Indian Penal Code.

Until the 1837 drafting of the Indian Penal Code, criminal cases in British India were adjudicated by the Nizamat Adalat under a modified English criminal law system and administered by presidencies. The First Law Commission, led by Thomas Babington Macaulay—best known for his 1835 "Minute on Indian Education"—sought to offer a more comprehensive and, indeed, contextualized legal language for a region that was proving ever unrulier for East India Company rule. Though it was submitted to the governor-general of India in 1837, it was not codified until twenty years later, following the Indian Mutiny of 1857, the dissolution of East India Company rule, and the beginning of direct rule under the Crown as the British Raj.[35]

It is not coincidental that this new generation of colonial administration would so insistently enter this hitherto sequestered space. These men were pioneering a language and political ideology of empire based in a nineteenth-century liberal discourse of civilization, espoused so vociferously in regard to India by Jeremy Bentham and James Mill, which sought to expand the logic of British secularism into the empire. While liberal philosophy rationalized the expansion of colonial authority, it was simultaneously consolidated in response to a growing "nativist" conservatism in which the newly judicable crime of *sati*, so tantalizingly splayed along this axis of intervention and preservation, came to be a major site of contention.

The debate around *sati*, however, strained toward others raging beyond the no-longer-impermeable boundaries of the colonial space. Contemporary to the dutiful Indian woman who followed her husband's corpse to the pyre, six thousand miles away in the imperial center, a new kind of English woman was coming into focus. This model of English femininity, characterized by a subservience and service that elevated the ordinary woman to the domestic divine, echoed many of the prevailing tropes of ideal Bengali femininity at the time.[36] Authority over a practice in the colonies—and, what is more, over a population—that seemed to evade similar control in Britain thus served as a kind of mitigating proxy, one that happened to reinforce a logic of increased intervention in the name of a reformist impulse. The rise of a liberal state apparatus in India, implicated so intimately in a nation-building project at home in Britain, was made possible precisely because of the violence of coloniality. Liberal reform measures to codify common law and standardize education that faced such resistance in the imperial center could be enforced with impunity. India was, as Thomas Metcalf puts it, a "laboratory for the creation of the liberal administrative state," one rich in resources for interventionist plunder.[37] Moreover, new colonial governance structure and objectives demanded new objects of control.

While the reformist juggernaut barreled toward the supine figure of the widow on the pyre, converting that ideological mandate into legal dictate required implementing a new language of exceptionalism into a discourse that had depended strictly on universality. Until the drafting and implementation of the Indian Penal Code, jurisprudential policy in British India followed a logic of benevolent containment. Criminal law, executed by the Nizamat Adalat, often recommended turning a blind eye to acts that might undermine its general authority, delegating such cases to the religious authorities. This is among the most significant and lasting effects of the 1857 Mutiny in which revolutionaries gave way to colonial subjects. The new penal code, which was central to the Government of India Act that declared Victoria sovereign of the Raj, enthroned a rule of law uninfluenced by the demands of locality and communality. In its consolidation, the British Raj secularized and centralized the state apparatus and deafened its ear to the protestations of racial and cultural difference. As a result, the Indian Penal Code maneuvered its jurisdiction via cognate, grammatically yoking moral sentimentalism, intended to be reformist intervention, and utilitarian philosophy. Under, and by way of, the law, colonial subjects were to be ushered into a kind of rational personhood.[38]

The 1837 draft of the penal code included, under crimes related to the body, a crime called "voluntary culpable homicide by consent," as a mitigation of the charge of murder. In its title, the statute announces two categories of adjudicated bodies: those who give their consent to be killed and those who intentionally take the lives of the former. The statute states that a crime is "voluntary culpable homicide by consent, when the person whose death is caused, being above twelve years of age, suffers death, or takes the risk of death, by his own choice," and offers four provisions intended to confirm the consent, rationality, and intentionality of the subject upon whom the crime is committed and the attendant culpability of the charged offender.[39] First, the subject of the crime must not have been "induced" by the offender into the act which results in death; second, she must be of the age, rationality, and intelligence to "understand the nature and consequences" of her choice; third, if the subject was indeed induced, then the charged person cannot have known about or participated in that coercion; finally, the charged person must not have withheld information that might have caused the subject of the crime to have changed her mind.[40] If all of these conditions were met, the crime of murder was mitigated and deemed the lesser offense of voluntary culpable homicide by consent.

The only example of voluntary culpable homicide by consent that the statute goes on to offer makes clear that the mitigation of murder is not by "his own choice" but by *hers:* "Z, a Hindoo widow, consents to be burned with the corpse of her husband. A kindles the pile. Here A has committed voluntary culpable homicide by consent."[41] The illustration serves to make explicit the intent of a statute that intervened outside the purported strictures of colonial law, into the arena of culture.[42] Moreover, it renders desire into law as an evidentiary category, the determinate factor of consent. What is in fact being codified into law is the legibility of the desires of Indian women to colonial rulers: the ability of government to recognize and institutionalize self-conscious intent.

The very giving of consent, within the logic of the law, is an articulation of desire ("I want"). Consent must be legible, according to the law, and if it refuses or disappoints that epistemological demand it is invalid. Regulation of the practice of *sati* herein functions as the systemization of a particularly gendered affect, the production of state knowledge about its female subjects, and the pathologization of intent. This lays the foundation for the encounter between colonial law and women in revolutionary organizations a century later.

Translation of the practice of *sati* into the legal condition of voluntary culpable homicide by consent literalizes the logic by which the crime will be adjudicated. The conscious act of giving consent exposes the widow to the scrutiny, and autopsy, of feelings and behaviors not explicitly coded within the law. Macaulay, in the "Introductory Report upon the Indian Penal Code," writes that the penal code "will be at once a statute book and a collection of decided cases. . . . Our illustrations are never intended to supply any omission in the written law, nor do they ever, in our opinion, put a strain on the written law."[43] The illustration of the widow on the pyre serves as a mobilizing supplement to the code itself, tiptoeing a legal tightrope between omission and strain.[44] The practice of *sati* is marked as the object of the spirit of the law while it remains unuttered in the letter of the law—the countersign of an interventionist, civilizationalist state.

Voluntary culpable homicide by consent does more than offer a mandate to regulate a domestic practice; it authorizes the regulation of will itself. Consent is the mitigating condition of the crime—which is otherwise murder—but is never exculpatory. Evidence of consent on the part of the widow to die on the pyre can never exonerate the defendant. However, the punitive difference between the two crimes is substantial. With murder a capital crime, the intelligibility of consent could represent the difference between life and death.[45] Mitigation of *sati* culpability is fundamental to this statute, intended as retributive punishment without any deterrent value.

The retributive value of the statute returns us squarely to the provisions of its mitigation, to the juridical indexes of its harm and its propitiation. The illustration offered of the widow Z on the pyre, assisted by A, toward whom the punitive force of law is aimed, is followed by two illustrations of crimes that do not meet the preconditions of the law: the assisted suicide of a child under age twelve and a suicide brought on by deception. In each of those cases, there is inadequate consent. Voluntary culpable homicide by consent is intended both to offer legal recognition to the act of *sati* and to legislate against the men who participate in it. The language of consent in the very title of the statute serves as a stand-in for a far more complex and ambivalent politics of choice.[46] An evidentiary index of consent's codification into law depends on the legibility of desire; illegible desire is otherwise the marker of nonconsent.

The double "voluntary" and "by consent" in the statute suggest—through redundant disavowal—the impossibility of an act that is uncoerced or uncompelled by another person. The statute avers, in fact, the legal impossibility of female consent, even as it provides a juridical rationale of its failure. The act is committed when the subject, male, induces the victim, female, to "voluntarily" put herself to death. Use of the word *induce*, meaning to bring about an action of the body or will of another, circumscribes the condition of choice. Even in cases where "consent" can be proven, the accused party is still guilty of "inducement," an impingement on the spontaneous free will of the widow—a negation of the possibility of pure consent. The law follows a definition of *consent* wherein it is the "voluntary agreement to or acquiescence in what another proposes or desires; compliance, concurrence, permission."[47] Despite the legislation against *sati*, there cannot be an act of widow immolation in which the subject of the judicial disciplining force is the one whose body is at stake because the woman on the pyre is always-already an indirect object of law. Grammatically, this form of consent cannot exist without another: another's will, another's desire. What one consents to must be outside oneself. By that logic, it stands to reason that the person consented to is the actual subject of juridical intent. The woman who has climbed onto the pyre has died, rendering her outside legal control. Furthermore, the paternalistic rationale of the law, aimed at protecting the widow from her family and religious community, is not designed to punish the body to which harm was seen as being done. Nonetheless, hers is a transitional body in the traffic of the culpable. When Waddedar and her comrades invoked *sati* a century later, they also recognized that their own wills to protest would be read as those of the true subjects of law, their male counterparts. We might think of this as a rejoinder to Spivak's famous formulation of white men saving brown women from brown men.

The assertion of consent as an evidentiary category is something of a red herring; it draws our attention to a possibility of legible desire that is in fact foreclosed. Positing consent as the sole mitigating circumstance of a crime, which might on the surface invite contemporary comparisons to assisted-suicide debates, operated in the case of *sati* as a sanction to determine the impossibility of consent. To put it baldly, colonial officials (like later postcolonial scholars) did not believe it possible that a woman would ever want to die by way of immolation of her own volition. Thus, the colonial official called to witness the *sati* was charged to first determine the explicit consent of the widow; she was asked to speak the words of affirmation and autonomy.

Thereafter, the evidentiary index of her consent shifts from the declarative to the indicative where, after the articulation of the consent to die, the widow had to be scrutinized for any symptom of either coercion or hesitation. The spoken word of consent had to be corroborated by bodily evidence of desire. Defined by the statute as a constative rather than performative speech act, the utterance of "I will" or "I want" required the supplement of demonstration. The body of the woman becomes an evidentiary object separate from the expression of her consent, a queer Cartesian split rendered in the law. The woman's body is here not an envelope of her *cogito*, but a potentially resistant and indicting entity in and of itself. Should she sway or falter on the way to the pyre or, when upon it, cry out in pain, her body would be seen to betray some truth hidden by her utterance of will.

This standard of evidence relies intimately on several interconnected fallacies. The first is that "consent" was ideationally and structurally available to women beyond the act of *sati* itself. Not only did the woman facing the pyre have to be represented as a rational actor in possession of her faculties, she was also expected to have rationalized the act of self-immolation by way of analogy. Positing an equivalence between the singularity of death and the condition of life, this logic suggests that in choosing one, the widow will negate the other. A second fallacy was that coercion, if present, could be identified, individuated, and corroborated. The subject of the statute's punitive force had to be determined as having had both the intimacy and the power to influence the will of the widow. Finally, and most significantly, the coexistence of coercion and desire had to be understood as impossible. The widow could not, in straitened circumstances, still want to die. Not only does this final assumption of the law privilege living as the rational choice, it does so from within a Judeo-Christian tradition of the determination of mortality that predicates itself on a common understanding of the limits of life and the effect of destruction of the body as death.

In the statute, consent is only realized belatedly and posthumously. Assuming that a woman dies the pyre, it is only in her absence that her consent to the burning is rendered meaningful in the context of the legal system. For colonial authorities, the widow on the pyre is a death-bound subject, whereas for the Brahmanic pundits who most vigorously protested the legislation, she is a birth-bound subject. Indeed, she is a subject bound for divinity. Spivak writes, "The Hindu widow ascends the pyre of the dead husband and immolates herself upon it. This is widow sacrifice. . . . The abolition of this rite by the British has been generally understood as a case of 'White men saving brown women from brown men.' Against this is the Indian nativist argument, a parody of the nostalgia for lost origins: 'the women actually want to die.'"[48] We might revise that parody further to say, "The woman actually wanted to become a goddess." In this reformulation, the widow-to-be-immolated is offered a kind of remuneration for her symbolic and physical labor.

This is not to assert that if a woman became *sati* it would be in order to be deified, but instead to refuse the contest of meaning-making over a woman's body and her will as the *only* terms of her consent. Somewhere between wanting to be saved and wanting to die, the woman speaks from the pyre. The key, according to Spivak, is not to ask what she says. Instead, we are to consider how, in the triangulated bodily speech of *sati*, the body on fire that is subject to disputed meaning-making resists the question of agency or desire that is intimately bound to the violences that make it visible. I would expand this invitation for us to imagine, outside the paternalistic fantasies in which the immolated widow is either made goddess or let live, the choices and intents that are called to account for the act of self-destruction.

Sati law's regulating function attempts to make legible the desire of the Indian woman—an insidious violence that, in the guise of benevolence, seeks to make bodies, psyches, intents, and desires available to administration and surveillance. Spivak suggests of *Jane Eyre*'s Bertha Mason—a figure outside the bounds of consent—that the destructive force of the madwoman in the attic, setting herself and the home itself aflame, is in fact creative violence. Bertha's annihilation of self and space clears the ground for Jane's domestic and conjugal fulfillment; what is more, the destruction of the mad and nearly animalistic Bertha births the humanness of her successor. Adaptation—Jean Rhys's rewriting of Bertha in *Wide Sargasso Sea*—offers, for Spivak, a corrective to the violence of human-making. She writes, "I must read this as an allegory of the general epistemic violence of imperialism, the construction of a self-immolating colonial subject for the glorification of the social mission of the colonizer. Rhys sees to it that the woman from the colonies is not sacrificed as an insane animal for her sister's consolidation."[49] I want to suggest that the colonial policy which sought to abolish *sati* similarly depended on the transformative force of allegory, the legislation of the act a speaking otherwise of the construction and limits of the consenting subject. The woman whose living body burned alongside a corpse was herself an object already dead, social agenesis itself. So, too, the performance of rescuing her was a stillborn endeavor, a necromantic politics. The project of abolishing *sati*, assured that there was no human life to be saved on the funeral pyre, constructed an *a priori* subject who might have been saved.

IV. Necromantic Political Feeling

Nearly a century after *sati*'s prohibition in the law, Pritilata Waddedar and Bina Das necromance the widow's body in an allegorical iteration in the service not of salvation but of disruption. This disruption is the discontinuous and incongruous kinship forged between the revolutionary and the immolated widow, a bond that emerges precisely from the gap between sign and substance. It thereby reveals the instability of that sign. The multiple, unreliable, and contested conditions of being a *sati* offer a fugitive referent for the condition of being a female revolutionary. Against that which is intended to secure meaning and to offer a stable referent, refusing narrative and hermeneutic discipline, De Man writes, "Allegorical narratives tell the story of the failure to read."[50] The allegorical narrative tells the story of the insistence on reading as a totalizing epistemology, its failure, and the strategic illegibility that failure might produce. *Sati* comes to serve Waddedar and Das rhetorically as a hermeneutic cloak, imbuing the articulation of political protest with the legacy of always-already disputed female agency and choice, evincing a politics of illegibility that is irreducible from a politics of relationality.

For Waddedar and her female comrades, the willingness to die for the cause of national freedom, or for the cause of a generation of rebels yet to come, was already expressed in a gendered idiom. In "Long Live Revolution," Waddedar writes, "History is replete with plenty of examples of how Rajput women fought with unsurpassed bravery on the battlefield and how they did not flinch a bit from destroying the enemy for freedom of the country and for upholding the dignity of women. Then why should we, the women of present-day India, not join the great war for liberating the country from the chains of slavery imposed by the foreigners?"[51] Unlike Bengalis, who in the colonial imagination are figured as bookish and effeminate, Rajputs symbolize militancy. However, when Waddedar cites the image of Rajput women charging into battle, she collates with it another familiar image of in which women commit *jauhar*, mass self-immolation, to avoid "defilement" from being raped by invading forces. This is a militant female violence, self-directed and self-protective.

The proximity of Rajput women to battle meant that their lives were also otherwise endangered—as was, more to the point, their purity. Accounts of *jauhar* hold that either Rajput women, seeing their men's certain defeat in battle, preemptively kill themselves to prevent becoming the object of sexual violence by their victorious foes, or that they are put to death by their kinsmen in advance of war to similarly prevent the loss of their honor. Unlike its common analogy, *sati*, *jauhar* is represented as an exceptional condition of war and not an indication of social depravity by colonial authorities. *Jauhar* functions within a paternalistic logic wherein harm is mitigated by preventing the possibility of dishonor. But as a trope of female militancy that turns on self-destruction, *jauhar* offers a charismatic and local example for the revolutionary women of Bengal. It is a politicized self-annihilation from within the social text of their lives. Kalpana Dutt, Waddedar's closest friend and only female comrade in the Jugantar, writes of herself and Waddedar, "Sometimes we used to dream of becoming great scientists. Then the Rani of Jhansi fired our imagination with her example. Sometimes we used to think of ourselves as fearless revolutionaries."[52] Laxshmi Bai, the Rani of Jhansi, who led an attack against the forces of the East India Company during the 1857 Indian Rebellion, is perhaps the most famous image of the Indian woman warrior. Killed during the battle, her body later found burned, the Rani of Jhansi is often eulogized as a *sati*, particularly in the oral tradition of Rajput women. Lindsey Harlan argues, "For those women who believe that she must have retreated from the battlefield at the last moment to immolate herself, the Rani of Jhansi is literally a *sati*. For those who know that the queen was slain on the battlefield, she is *sati* by analogy. In either case, her death is adjudged unselfish sacrifice. It manifests her goodness, her *sat*. It therefore accomplishes what self-immolation accomplishes: it validates her *pativrata* status."[53] Proof of the Rani's *pativrata* (sacred wifely devotion) is belatedly offered by her death in battle. *Sati* as a demonstration of purity and devotion, the destroying of one's mortal body as an allegiance to another, is transported from the pyre to the battlefield.

In this way, Waddedar and other revolutionary women drew on two separate but related practices of female self-death, *jauhar* and *sati*. One operates in the economy of marriage—the ostensibly private space of the home—where the other operates in the economy of war and patriotism. A curious tension produces the Rani's radicalism at once intelligible and unnarratable by the fundamentally conservative principle of wifely sacrifice. Her goodness, her *sat*, is that of a proper wife. Though she fights for the people of the principality of which she is given control following her husband's death, the logic of her death belatedly animates her identity as wife, not sovereign. Nonetheless, the Rani of Jhansi's enduring legacy in the national imagination as an image of the blazing female heroine presented an alluring form of revolutionary possibility for Waddedar and Dutt who, at twenty, dreamed of being either scientists or insurgents. With no husband, alive or dead, Waddedar is *sati* to a cause, a nonhuman nonmarriage. In announcing her imminent self-destruction as a form of self-immolation, deploying this allegory as a revolutionary tactic of protest, Waddedar eerily prophesies that she would, in death, come to be memorialized and adjudicated on those very terms.

V. Girl, Believed to Be Mesmerized

In the flurry of newspaper accounts and police records of the attack on the Pahartali Institute in 1932, Pritilata Waddedar's body shuttles in and out of view, its condition, clothing, and position documented, revised, and revisited. A year later, during the trial, her remains are recollected:

> A little later witness found Pritilata Waddedar's body in male attire, some distance west of the Institute. Witness seized the property found on Waddedar's person, namely, printed notices of "Indian Republican Army," three photos of Ramkrishna Biswas, a plan of the Pahartali Institute, three cartridges and a manuscript statement with Ramkrishna's photo, a whistle and a photo of Sree Krishna and a leather belt near her head. . . . Witness then produced the Chemical Examiner's report detecting potassium cynade [*sic*] in Pritilata's viscera.[54]

Her body becomes a part of the inventory of forensic evidence collected and catalogued at the scene.

That body, twenty years old, dressed in a *pajama*, *kurta*, and *chadar*, hair covered with a handkerchief, availed itself by its death to the colonial gaze. When its outward condition failed to adequately narrate the who, what, when, and why of its death, her body was dissected at the district police station in autopsy, her viscera coaxed into offering evidence. By way of its atomization, her body offered the how and when of its own destruction: She died immediately, by ingesting potassium cyanide. The incisive eye of coloniality also determined the identity of the body laid on its morgue slab: Having graduated from Bethune College, Calcutta, that year, her name and age were readily available to authorities seeking to confirm that the body belonged to the woman who had eluded police capture in the June killing of Captain Cameron—two weeks after her graduation with honors in English.[55] Her face was identified by its similarity to a photograph in a Criminal Investigation Department (CID) file that Waddedar had previously verified as "that of [herself] in a sitting posture."[56] The only question left was the why, to which a ready response came in the form of the manifesto pinned to her chest, which begins, "I boldly declare myself as a revolutionary, whose ideal is to liberate *mother* India from the British Rule."[57] In her own hand, Pritilata Waddedar named herself and her actions.

On that dead body, four pictures: three of Ramkrishna Biswas, the Jugantar leader who was hanged earlier that year for the assassination of Inspector Tarini Chatterjee; and one of the Lord Krishna, whose gospel in the *Bhagavad Gita* is that of righteous war. The form of self-memorialization that Waddedar performed is subsequently elided from view by the competing narration of her actions and memory by colonial officials and by her own compatriots. To borrow a phrase from Spivak, Waddedar's allegorical rewriting of the *sati* script is interrupted by competing hegemonic, paternalistic accounts of *sati*—according to the criminal logic of voluntary culpable homicide by consent—and of the "blazing, fighting, familial Durga."[58] An aspect of the Hindu mother-goddess and another form of the goddess Sati, Durga is at once fierce and affectionate, and central to the nationalist iconography of the period. As we will see here and in subsequent chapters, the identification of Bengali women with Durga produced a political goddess and depoliticized women's labor.[59]

In February 1933, five months after Waddedar's death, authorities finally arrested Surya Sen after he was given up by the family in whose house he had been hiding. For three years, Sen had eluded authorities as the suspected leader of the Chittagong Armory raids, an expansive campaign of anticolonial insurgency first carried out in April 1930. Sixty-five young men, led by Ganesh Ghosh and Ananta Singh, captured the weapons depot in Chittagong, destroyed the telegraph services, and attempted the assassination of members of the European club—in a single night. After the raids, Surya Sen and the other members of the IRA hoisted the national flag, declaring a provisional revolutionary government, before British troops forced them to flee into the surrounding hills. The seemingly ragtag group of schoolteachers and high-schoolers managed to keep the much larger and better equipped local British military forces at bay for several days, allowing many to evade arrest. In a pointed response to Gandhi's resurrected *satyagraha* campaign of civil disobedience, the architects of the Armory attack turned to armed resistance to distance themselves from what they saw as ineffective anticolonial strategies and to assert a revolutionary masculinity in their place.[60]

Consequently, the goal of revolutionary violence was a dyadic masculinizing project through which the colonial characterizations of the effeminate Bengali would be dismantled alongside the actual colonial infrastructure.[61] "To the Students and Youths of Chittagong," said a locally distributed pamphlet:

> Brothers, rise up to the occasion, feel the extremely terrible pangs of subjugation, see the sad plight in which your country has been put to, look at the way the students and youths of Germany, Russia and China are directing their movement for liberation and act in the same manner, and enkindle the fires of revenge and retaliation in your hearts. Enroll yourselves as solders in the Indian Republican Army and make an ardent effort to save your motherland from the abyss of misfortune and misery.[62]

A locally lived transnational imagination inoculates the bodies of Chittagong youth against the enervation and emasculation of Gandhian nonviolence with the germ of leftist youth uprisings globally.[63] Pritilata Waddedar and Kalpana Dutt, the only women officially allowed into the ranks of the IRA, came to be included within this masculinist and masculinizing collectivity only after

Ananta Singh, an early leader, turned himself in to the police.[64] Singh, who is consistently figured in terms of his physical strength and virility, guarded the ranks of Jugantar: "He was strongly against taking girls into the revolutionary network—he did not trust us. So much so that he could not trust men who were associated with any girl."[65] Women were figured as contagions, the very association with whom would disrupt the homosocial homeostasis of the collectivity. Curiously, it is precisely this language of sexual affiliation to which the Raj would turn to mount its prosecution of Surya Sen, Tarkeswar Dastidar, and Kalpana Dutt. Though Sen was suspected of being the leader and mastermind of the 1930 Armory Raid and the years of subsequent insurgent violence, the primary evidence lodged against him depended upon his relationship with Waddedar, despite her not having joined the group until more than a year into its insurgency.

Ultimately, the court case against Surya Sen for conspiracy reenacted the juridical script of *sati*; it readjudicated the crime of voluntary culpable homicide by consent. Whereas for Waddedar, *sati* functions as allegory, as a sign that "points to something that differs from its literal meaning and has for its function the thematization of this difference," in the court case against Sen, Dastidar, and Dutt, *sati* was stripped of its allegorical function and instead pressed into service of simultaneity and similarity.[66] The Crown, in calling Pritilata Waddedar as ghostly star witness against Sen, reanimated the evidentiary status of coercion and desire, of mesmerism and control. In so doing, it revealed, on the one hand, the inherent politicization of *sati* prosecution in the nineteenth century, and on the other, the intimate logic of political violence in the twentieth century. If, at heart, *sati* prosecution sought to rein in the influence of a native patriarchal system of governance by coercing the body of the widow into evidence, its spectral reappearance in Sen's trial demonstrates the continuing—indeed, intensified—anxiety over governmental inability to parse or police the desires of women as political actors.

Pritilata Waddedar was multiply reanimated in the court proceedings, as her meticulously kept diary—seized from her parents' home when the police informed them of her death—was atomized into evidentiary snippets to indict the man who authorities claimed was truly responsible for the violence she enacted.[67] Waddedar's death rendered her a particularly efficacious and charismatic form of demonstrative evidence because it destroyed her as a responsive subject and ossified her as a hermeneutic object. Unlike her living comrades standing trial, with recourse to defense and ability to bear witness for themselves, Waddedar's body and her writings functioned within court proceedings in the manner of other evidence, as available to narrative and to scrutiny, spoken for and argued against.

The intimacies that bound together members of Jugantar as a revolutionary community were newly signified in the courtroom as legal liabilities, affective indictments of complicity sharply pronounced during the trial. The court determined the culpability of both Waddedar and Dutt in terms of their relationships to the men on trial. Newspapers covering the trial carried rumors of romance, deliciously sublimated, between Dutt and Dastidar, Waddedar and Nirmal Sen, and, most prominently, Waddedar and Surya Sen. Without some kind of libidinal payoff, the papers imply, these women's actions would be unthinkable, unnatural. We are, in this way, returned to the explanation of Bhubaneswari Bhaduri's death in another light. Sexual cathexis is the default figuration of women's political labor, even in the face of their own articulations.

For its part, the Crown eschewed any explicit inquiry into the nature of the relationships between the men on trial and their female comrades. Instead, it relied on the rhetorical force of implication. The judgment issued against Sen, chronicling the case presented by his attorneys, enumerated the facts of the case to which he capitulated: "He further stated that documents found upon his person at the time of his arrest showed that he had been on terms of close association with one Pritilata Waddedar."[68] The "terms of close association" indicate both Waddedar's culpability and Sen's proximity to her—an association that clearly worked powerfully on her. Waddedar, we are to understand, was seduced. Like the illustration of the widow who is induced to self-immolate in the *sati* statute, Waddedar's will bore the mark of Sen's influence.

On November 11, 1933, on page 22 of the *Times of India*, tucked between a story about a marketplace fire and a before-and-after picture ad for Pepsodent toothpaste, the headline for the coverage of the trial read, "Girl, Believed to Be Mesmerised."[69] Waddedar, dead more than a year, and her suspended autonomy were central to the prosecution's case. In a ghostly ventriloquism, British prosecutors read aloud for the court record words written by a woman who died wearing words that declared her intent "to liberate *mother* India from the British Rule."[70]

[The prosecutor] referred to a document, purporting to be Pritilata's version of the Dhalghat incident. In this document, Pritilata was alleged to have described the occurrence at the Dhalghat in the minutest detail. It seemed that she had been completely mesmerized by this person, under whose control she had come and whom she regarded as some kind of divinity. If this statement were relied upon, it would prove that she and Masterda, meaning Surya Sen, were at Dhalghat, that the shooting did take place, that Captain Cameron had been shot when he tried to go upstairs, and that both the accused succeeded in escaping after the incident.[71]

The conditional construction of evidence relies on her trustworthiness as post-humous witness and her insensibility as living actor. Mesmerized, Pritilata Wad-dedar was made a victim and ward of the very state she opposed with her life.[72] The necromantic suspension of Waddedar's will by this court account rendered her nonagential, compliant with state interests, and susceptible to harm. By way of discursive alibi for how she would be made to speak, diagnosed as having already yielded her consent and her intent to Sen, Waddedar was posthumously availed of the court's protective intervention.

Surya Sen, though ostensibly a mesmerist imbued with power to assert his influence over Waddedar, to make her an instrument of his will, was necessarily paralyzed in the prosecution's case. He was accused not of action, but of influence that is only intelligible through the material and recognizable violence of anoth-er's actions. The accusation of mesmerism, rather than ascribing to Sen super-natural and therefore uncontrollable power, pulls away the wizard's curtain. Charges of conspiracy further allowed the Crown to build a case against Sen based on his influence and the violence it indirectly made possible. In particu-lar, to demonstrate Sen's culpability for the Pahartali attack that Waddedar and six uncharged accomplices carried out, the prosecution entered into evidence an essay that Sen wrote in memoriam. While Waddedar and her accomplices were accused of bodily guilt, Sen was charged with guilt of the will.

Capitalizing on the fortuitous coincidence of Waddedar's death and the annual celebration of the goddess Durga (Durga Puja), Sen's essay takes the holy day of Vijaya as its title and ostensible subject.[73] Vijaya, or Vijaya Dashami, is the final day of Durga Puja, which celebrates Durga's defeat of the demon Mahesha-soora and her return from a brief stay on Earth—figured as her natal home—to her heavenly abode. On this day, statues of the goddess are submerged in rivers, symbolizing her return to her husband Shiva in Kailash. Her temporary earthly form washed away, Durga is at once victorious and vanquished.

The word *vijaya*, which means "victory," carries in it the bittersweet promise of annihilation; it is victory through sacrifice. In the essay "Vijaya," Sen figures himself as the builder of idols, crafting from the clay of national attachment bodies that will fight and be destroyed. He writes:

I am the cause of so many lives celebrating their "Vijaya" farewell from life. I have sacrificed at the altar of freedom the youth who are like dolls of gold and made the bosoms of so many mothers empty. How many, oh how many, have I sent to internment, prisons, exile and life term in islands across the sea? I am the cause of cries of lamentation in household after household. The torture and repression of the government visited the land because of my deeds. How can I absolve myself of the responsibility for all these?[74]

According to Sen, his charisma and commitment to the motherland drove the youths to their deaths; they are not impelled by their own nationalist passions. He takes responsibility not only for their deaths but also for their actions; they are "dolls" and he sacrifices them. By declaring himself the cause of their deaths, Sen nudges the nation out of the frame such that these revolutionaries sacrifice their lives to him. He requires national attachment to function only peripherally to inspire his cadre; they are driven forth to sacrifice by love of him more than anything else. Diverging from the nationalist logic of sacrifice for the motherland, Sen makes himself both cause and source of violence.

In his view, the youths, and Waddedar in particular, work through and for him alone. He is the conduit to both national service and nationalist memorialization. The repetition of "I am the cause" in the first part of the essay functions not only as an admission of his culpability, as the British authorities claimed in their case against Sen, but also as an acknowledgment of his authority.[75] The youths who offer up their lives in the act of revolutionary violence, whom he names at the opening of his essay, are nonetheless relatively anonymous foot soldiers, the cries of lamentation over their deaths undistinguished from one another. His claims of power and responsibility thus presage and invite the authorities' investigation of his guilt. Sen reserves his personalized eulogy for Waddedar, as he "remember[s] most intensely today that beautiful and spotlessly pure idol whom [he] had sent for immersion."[76] Waddedar's memorialization depends on her symbolic reduction into an idol. Moreover, Sen's invocation of Waddedar marks a shift in the tone and direction of the essay. Whereas before he had regretted the cries of lamentation he caused and wondered whether his turn to violence was justified, Waddedar's death reifies, or perhaps justifies, his cause. He writes, "May her unprecedented *self-immolation* bring joy to my mind and make me all the more strong. May her reverence for me make me worthy of respect and never may the sorrow of losing her under any circumstances overwhelm such sense of joy."[77] Waddedar's sacrifice only indirectly serves the nationalist cause, through the bodily conduit of Surya Sen, who, strengthened by her death, might continue his work for the nation.

Sen articulates a particular causal relationship in which Waddedar is not the source of his joy because of her accomplishments. Rather, her accomplishments are preemptively hallowed because of those attributes that Sen assigns both to her and to the goddess Durga—innocence, beauty, holiness. "Vijaya" thus becomes an obituary for Waddedar, for her singular death, which is persistently differentiated from those of the fallen male revolutionaries and her female comrades who did not die in the commission of their own acts of anticolonial violence. The violence they participated in as part of an expressed anticolonial ideology tied them to a larger nationalist collectivity, an affiliation that colored the representation of violence in their writings and conversations and the justification of the sacrifice to themselves.

How do we read this obituary for an idol? Judith Butler has argued that the obituary stands as a key apparatus of nation-building, "the means by which a life becomes or fails to become a publicly grievable life, an icon for national self-recognition, the means by which a life becomes note-worthy."[78] The national object that is reified in "Vijaya" is the image of woman as holy and pure. This is an obituary, then, by another name: obituary as hymn, or anthem of a nation to come. The real woman—inasmuch as we are able to talk about real women—is evacuated from this memorialization, leaving only a shell of exemplarity. Waddedar's death is grievable because of her gender, noteworthy because she might serve as example for others. By invoking the singularity of her death, Sen demarcates the lives that will be counted by the nationalist memory that is being synchronically constructed by his essay.

Unlike the message that Sen intends in "Vijaya," in which he is the source and authority of Waddedar's action, the use of the essay in the trial recentered Waddedar, producing her violence as that which made it possible for Sen to be responsible for and guilty of actions to which he could not be physically tied.[79] Waddedar's death became the site of contested memory, a colonial power struggle over the representational power of a female body. If "Vijaya" is a form of nationalist memorialization through which Sen writes himself into history, the court documents of his trial are the imperial refusal of that account. The documents entered into court evidence are archival traces of a contest, in Spivak's terms, between brown men and white men waged over Waddedar's life, her death, and her memory; a struggle for narrative dominance. Both narratives were invested in, but fundamentally unable to register, the conflicted terms of Waddedar's will to die.

Waddedar's seemingly disjunctive invocation of an obsolete and counterfactual allegorical sign uncannily prefaced its subsequent repetition at trial. The iteration of the legal script of *sati* within the courtroom falters in the face of the evidentiary category of will and its unstable legibility. It falters in the face of a protest that traffics in the language of will while evading the representational discipline of its narrativization. Waddedar's spectral presence in the courtroom suggests the possibility of a resistant female subjectivity within and despite the masculinist economy of discursive mastery.

VI. The Myth of Fingerprints

Nearly eighty years after the trial, Pritilata Waddedar is cinematically resurrected in the feature-length *Khelein Hum Jee Jaan Sey (We Play with Our Lives)*. In it, the apparent failure of the mission to free Chittagong by force is compensated by a retrospective reincorporation into the body of independent India. The film builds an unbroken arc toward the expulsion of the British from Chittagong (though in 1947 that would result in the transformation of those Bengalis into Pakistanis), reproducing along the way a nationalist hagiography of the identifiable members of Jugantar who were active at the time—Surya Sen, Nirmal Sen, Lokenath Bal, Ananta Singh, Pritilata Waddedar, and Kalpana Dutt—as well as the anonymous corps of "teenagers." Surya Sen's role as a schoolteacher spurs on his followers in the film, as it did in the court case against him in 1933. It speculates on the ideological influence and the mastery of Masterda. The young men in the film, like Waddedar and Dutt, are entranced by Sen and willing to sublimate their provincial, adolescent desires for freedom—"We want our playing field back"—into his vision of a revolutionary politics. Political feeling, in this way, is a collective force of disparate desires alloyed by a charismatic individual.

The film represents Waddedar as a willing foot soldier in Sen's army, drawn to its ranks by the allure of its handsome cadre, and as a seductive distraction for Nirmal Sen. In other words, she is made a figure of recognizable Indian femininity. During the attack on Pahartali at the film's climax, Waddedar appears clothed in the traditional white sari with red border emblematic of Bengali womanhood, stripped of the disruptive trace of her bodily articulation. As she waves off her comrades and prepares to take the cyanide capsule by which she will die, Waddedar (played by Visakha Singh) throws her head back and cries into the night, "Nirmal, I'm coming to you! *Bande Mataram* [Hail Motherland]!" The aerial shot of Waddedar taking her cyanide positions the viewer as celestial body, gazing down on what are to be remains of a mortal form. Her body, still upon the ground, appears miniscule, the value of her life and her death reframed by the broad emptiness of the ground on which she lies. In the celluloid reimagining of Waddedar's death, she serves two affective masters: the heterosexual desire for a comrade-husband and the ideological attachment to a nonhuman motherland.

When her body was found in front of the Institute in 1932, Waddedar was dressed as what was variously described as a male, a Mohammedan, or a Punjabi. In each iteration her disguise stuttered interpretative mechanics, standing as a material barrier between the piercing gaze of colonial administration and the wayward body of its oversight. At stake is more than a problem of gender: it is *genre trouble*. Waddedar's historical body posed a problem of reading because the familiar taxonomic structures of race, class, sex, and religion shifted to reveal a disjuncture between interiority and surface. Having thus far read Pritilata Waddedar's enunciation, embodied and inscribed, as a recognition of the law's ambivalent indexing of female desire, I now turn to her remains and their reappearance in film and in the colonial archive to argue that they reveal a form of physical capture that works in tandem with the ideological capture of her as an unconsenting subject. We must understand Waddedar as a historical subject through the technologies and ideologies against which her political articulations were formed and made legible.

Traces of Waddedar in official archives—the India Office Records housed in the British Library, the National Archives of India, and the West Bengal State Archives—are scattered, fleeting. Accounts of her appear throughout the police intelligence and judicial files on a period of insurgency collated under the sign of the "Chittagong Armory raids," folded into a causal and linear narrative of collective action in which her life and death are contiguous with those of her comrades. Her death, though the source of enormous anxiety for authorities documenting the growing anticolonial violence, was never singular in its orientation. It was symptomatic of a larger problem of governance and regulation. In this way Waddedar, in accounts both by her comrades and by colonial authorities, was made recognizable by virtue of her affiliation. Her singularity for Sen was a reflection of his own, her representability for the Crown a transitive culpability. I do not wish to reproduce the historiographic violence of renaming by asserting for Waddedar a heroic or tragic individualism; she inscribed in her own writing and on the crowded space of her body intimacy with a revolutionary community. Despite the profusion of photographs of Ramkrishna Biswas on her body, Waddedar's sense of community was a deeply gendered one, influenced as much by the public act of Bina Das as by quieter forms of resistance offered by women who were not invited into insurgent groups as primary actors. They imagined themselves, in Das's words, "just a tiny part of a vast programme."[80] This is an atomic self-conception that operated in its own economy of political feeling, one in which the individual is not the determinant force. Rather, an alternate affiliative structure developed between these women who neither marginalized themselves nor valorized singular heroism. Their relationship to anticolonial resistance was mediated through an intimate identification with Bengal, the motherland, which was the object of that project. They garnered access to insulated male spaces by way of their symbolic potential, but their sense of political possibility was not limited to it. I want to suggest here that the reasons that the colonial archive and the narratives of Waddedar's Jugantar comrades so struggle against this relational formation converge at the anti-originary moment of the 1857 Rebellion, through which the terms of what constituted a revolutionary subjectivity were negotiated.

Hailed as the first Indian war for independence (and indeed, perhaps by that measure, the only, as India's eventual independence came bureaucratically rather than militarily), the 1857 revolt offered an archetype of heroic resistance even as it gave way to greater colonial governmental authority. Mangal Pandey—who helped incite the rebellion by the Bengal Native Infantry and was hanged for mutiny—and the Rani of Jhansi populated an anticolonial imagination with militant figures whose commitment to expelling British forces from India justified death. In addition to suggesting, by way of its sporadic geographic reach, that such a thing as India might be coalesced without the British, the Mutiny sketched the idiom in which a demand for freedom might be made. Karl Marx wrote in *The New York Daily Tribune* in September 1857:

> However infamous the conduct of the Sepoys, it is only the reflex, in a con-centrated form, of England's own conduct in India, not only during the epoch of the foundation of her Eastern Empire, but even during the last ten years of a long-settled rule. To characterize that rule, it suffices to say that torture formed an organic institution of its financial policy. There is something in human history like retribution: and it is a rule of historical retribution that its instrument be forged not by the offended, but by the offender himself.[81]

Historical retribution is precisely what was unleashed by the events of 1857 and their memorialization, because the efforts failed. The incomplete revolt and the dead heroes came to be cited in each incarnation of subsequent anticolonial protest. Thus, the word *revolutionary* carries with it the touch of that moment of possibility; its memory the proving ground of legible anticolonial political action.

At the same time, as it provided the rationale for the 1858 Government of India Act, the Mutiny was the Siamese birth of formal colonial rule and anticolonial resistance, warranting the development of a biopolitical system based in ethnological taxonomy and sciences of identification to regulate an unruly population. These systems of identification and individuation took colonial Bengal as an early laboratory, in concert with the Raj's own migration from civil administration to governmental body. David Scott has argued that the shift to modern colonial governmentality "came to depend, not merely upon inserting English ideas here and there, but upon *the systematic redefinition and transformation of the terrain on which the life of the colonized was lived.*"[82] Direct administration, unlike the indirect dominion of Company rule from 1757, demanded the construction of a holistic individual and collective subject of rule for whom the very question of what constituted life was to be determined and then regulated. Colonialism produced the terms of life and of subjecthood as its governing methodology.[83] We have seen how the Penal Code attempted to produce a uniform juridical index for the secular legal subject; its effect, however, was broadly entwined with the rise of several imperial sciences that made possible its claim to a recognizable domain of power.[84]

These technologies of capture—photography, ethnology, and fingerprinting—constituted a curriculum designed to help authorities confounded by their apparent inability to tell Indians apart.[85] Faced with a population that was recalcitrant both as a mass and as individuals, imperial authorities constellated taxonomical and identificatory techniques to cohere and contain their subjects of governance. In what follows, I trace this techno-legal assemblage in order to better understand how Pritilata Waddedar and her female comrades were availed to the historical gaze. The paradox by which a subject of governance was compelled into descriptive legibility and refused political subjectivity is particularly vexing in the case of the woman who, having announced her intent to die for her motherland, comes to appear as an enigma. Her apparent unknowability, which in the court case is figured in terms of will, has a material life that comes into view through the archival practices and representational technologies of the newly adjudicating colonial state.

Waddedar's CID file, housed at the West Bengal State Archives, consists of a single document, three pages long. It is a typed statement given by Waddedar on June 19, 1932, to Jogendra Gupta, Chittagong's inspector of police. In it she details her family members: her father's name, occupation, and salary; the names, ages, and schools of her three younger sisters; and those of her four cousins, the Dastidar brothers, including Tarkeswar. Responding to queries by the officer, she accounts for women identified as having sympathies toward anticolonial elements, whether she is acquainted with them, and in what context. It is clear from Waddedar's statement and the CID files of a number of other women involved in anticolonial activities that authorities sought to map affiliation by gender, reproducing a normative homosociality. Women, bound to one another, paced borders of revolutionary communities but did not appear at risk to enter the highly regulated cabal. This expectation clearly worked to Jugantar's advantage, as it could use women to carry out tasks that authorities assumed would be assigned to men recognized as members of the group. At the end of Waddedar's statement to the police, she recalls a conversation between herself and Purnendu Dastidar in which she claims he said, "It is the duty of mothers and sisters to prepare the sons of the [illegible]. You are not to fight with any weapons but only to serve those who sacrifice their lives for the country."[86] Less than two months before she opened fire at the Pahartali Institute, Waddedar turned to the police inspector to add in response, "I did not pay any heed to his words and [he] used to call me 'coward.'"[87] These are Pritilata Waddedar's last recorded words to authorities before she was released from custody.

Caught quite literally in the grip of juridical power, Waddedar rehearsed a common narrative in which, as a woman, her relationship to revolutionary activities at best might be tangential and familial. She eluded the disciplining apparatus by reifying gendered constructions of the realm and form of the political, encircling a world to which she seems to have little claim. Authorities, we might conjecture from the lack of follow-up investigation, were placated in their concerns about her involvement with Jugantar, believing perhaps in Purnendu Dastidar's epithet that Waddedar was a "coward." But, read another way, Waddedar presages her imminent actions in her closing words to Gupta. She does not pay heed to Dastidar's words that the duty of women was to nurture and serve the true agents of anticolonial action. She refuses his prescription of engagement, even as she uses it to secure her release from custody. Conscious that her statement would serve as investigatory evidence and of the expectation that her relationship to Jugantar's continued insurgency in Chittagong was liminal at best, Waddedar resignified the aspersion of cowardice. Rather than individuating herself into heroic visibility, she aligned herself to the private sphere of women, the mothers and sisters she addresses in "Long Live Revolution," and, in so doing, confounded the system of surveillance and identification on which colonial authorities depended.

Throughout the police record on Jugantar in Chittagong, its members are described as "absconders." Other potential and promised criminality notwithstanding, their cardinal threat was their ability to avoid detection, to escape the net of the law. Indeed, the question of how to identify in order to contain the individual was a persistent one for the Raj. Between 1868 and 1875, John Forbes Watson and John William Kaye traveled across India to collate a photographic diary of *The People of India* as a gift for Governor-General Canning and his wife. The eight-volume study of 400 "races" and "types" of people on the subcontinent relied upon the evidentiary promise of photography's reality effect—indexicality the proving grounds of a taxonomic impulse—to produce a typological account of India. Castes, ethnicities, and religions were expressed through marked and classifiable attributes to disaggregate the Indian population into minor masses within which the individual remained indistinguishable. This first move is what Foucault characterizes as "massifying, that is directed not at man-as-body but as man-as-species,"[88] allowing officials to target sites of intervention, such as in the case of the 1871 Criminal Tribes Act (CTA).[89] Leaning on ethnological studies like *The People of India*, the CTA suggested a genetic disposition toward criminality that could be categorically identified.[90]

At the time the CTA was instituted, the Thuggee phenomenon was of particular concern. The existence of what authorities called a cult of murderers and bandits in the thrall of the goddess Kali presaged later anxieties about blood oaths taken by militant groups like the Anushilan Samiti (with which Jugantar had deep ties) in front of the goddess.[91] Thuggees are a lasting shorthand for native populations that are dangerous because of the opacity of their practices and affiliations, their ability to seemingly disappear into an adjacent population, and the approbation with which other Indians viewed them.[92] While one aspect of the CTA concerned itself with the racialized native body, the other turned to sex, legislating the registration and surveillance of eunuchs ("for the purpose of this Act all persons of the male sex who admit themselves or on medical inspection clearly appear to be impotent"), whom authorities suspected of kidnapping and castrating children, committing offenses under Section 377 ("unnatural offences"), and dancing and singing in public while "dressed or ornamented as a woman."[93]

Hijras, now legally recognized in India, Pakistan, Bangladesh, and Nepal as a third gender, are communities of people who occupy a liminal state of gender performance and sexuality. The CTA, in categorizing *hijras* as eunuchs and as an identifiable group, attempted to materialize the sexually deviant body within a juridical frame.[94] Though the fear that *hijras*—unable by their very definition to reproduce—would multiply by kidnapping and castrating children was pronounced, colonial authorities were far more concerned with the public performance of sexual non-normativity. The ability to affect the external trappings of another gender or religion disrupted an imperial surveillance apparatus that had been calibrated typologically—the individual interrupting the categorizing function of the state.

Waddedar's appearance in the colonial record at her death in 1932 invokes the CTA's fixation on the relationship between the visible, public body and the apparently Indian predilection toward forms of being that defied catalog. Vestiges of gender anxiety, where the threat of bodies dressed in the material signifiers of another gender indicted a criminal body and sensibility both, patrol the description of Waddedar's body and clothing at her death. Appearing male, Muslim, non-Bengali, it magnetized concerns about the mutability of the colonized body, its ability to evade the disciplining eye by transforming itself. Police records from the Chittagong Armory case are replete with accounts of members of Jugantar in disguise—Waddedar and Dutt as men, their male compatriots as Muslims.[95] The phenomenon of rebel drag was significant enough that following the Pahartali raid, the Governor in Council amended the 1932 Bengal Suppression of Terrorist Outrages Act, "for the purpose of preventing the movements of and the communication with absconders and terrorists," to include the stipulation that "[n]o person shall wear the garb of any community or sex other than his own, unless he habitually does so in the normal course of his profession or occupation."[96] To appear as another gender or another religion was to politicize the body, offering perhaps a new way to think about why *hijras* were identified in initial construction of the colonial criminal type. The ability of members of Jugantar to "abscond" into the surrounding community in Chittagong suggested an environmental or genetic criminal sensibility attached to the entire township. Though authorities were careful to note their certainty that the anti-government elements were almost uniformly upper-caste Hindus and that local Muslims surely must have been sympathetic to colonial rule, typological distinction between races faltered in the face of the ability of the absconders to don the guise of local Muslims and thus essentially become Muslim. Faced with an elusive insurgency whose motivations were already adjudicated, colonial authorities pressed upon the surface of the body under law.[97]

Colonial authorities revealed in their concerns about clothing a dialectical sense of what constitutes the subject. Like historical sumptuary laws designed to regulate social hierarchies and their recognizability, the mandate against communal and gender cross-dressing sought to still the rebellious traffic of bodies in flight. Habit—the routinization of the body through and for work—was excluded from the legislation because of the promise of repetition and regularity.[98] Through its recognizability, clothing communicated a shared sociality in particularly situated ways in British India where, until the arrival of Muslims in the medieval period brought stitched cloth, Hindus primarily wore only single lengths of cloth.[99] Through the early twentieth century, common logic held that Hindus and Muslims could be distinguished by clothing alone—the division between stitched and draped cloth produced a racialized extension of the body itself.[100]

John Forbes Watson, before he collaborated on *The People of India* series, first compiled *Textile Manufactures of India* (1866) on the range of textiles produced and their ethnological referents across British India to introduce this population as a potential textile consumer group.[101] Of particular interest to Forbes Watson was the way in which Hindu and Muslim populations made different use of local textiles such as the muslins of Dhaka, to which he dedicated three substantial sections of the text. Produced first for the Mughal court, these fabrics, as we will see in later chapters, captured the British imperial imagination as much for their mythical consistency as for their symbolism as a trace of a prior conquest.[102] Forbes Watson insisted throughout that even as Hindu men began to incorporate the hitherto repudiated stitched cloth of the Mughal court into their public uniform, small bodily practices interrupted similarity, such that "the two nationalities may almost invariably be thus known the one from the other, even when the dress, as often happens, is of the same shape and material."[103] Racial difference seeped out of the weave of cloth, marking the body through and beyond its covering.

Reading the surface of the body, double-skinned with both flesh and cloth, is a practice of attending to the visible not as proof of the knowable but as acknowledgment of the limits of what might be known.[104] For the imperial eye cast upon Waddedar's body in the historical record and for contemporary film audiences gazing at her remains on screen, its surface invites fantasy of mastery. To glimpse its surface is to assert dominion over what is unseen beneath it—the psychic and epistemological seduction knowing of what she wanted. But what, as Anne Cheng asks, "can surface (or skin) be or do if it is *not* just a cover?"[105] Waddedar's surface—preserved in document and in photograph—is a lamination. Each article upon it and its very form speak. It is a site of encounter between a subjectivity unavailable to the sway of our knowledge and the multiple modes of hermeneutic disciplining by which she was made subject to governance and scrutiny.

So, let us now make explicit the materiality of this encounter with Waddedar's remains. Let us place their archival life in the context of the governmental structure by which they came to be preserved. If the CTA produced a colonial vocabulary for the categorization of deviant and fugitive populations, the legal system demanded the identification and detention of individual criminals. Identification registers, mandated by the CTA, prompted magistrates to catalog characteristics for which an administrative vocabulary of physiognomy was inadequate. One complained that he "could see no way out of the difficulty except branding this class *on the face* in such a manner as to defy concealment."[106] Asked to describe an individual designated a habitual criminal, the magistrate suggested the solution of collective branding. Each individual ought to bear the mark of both his accusation and his community on the part of the body most associated with individuality, uniqueness, and recognizability. His face alone was not enough; it required the supplemental and indelible mark of colonial touch to prove his identity and encounter with the disciplinary apparatus of the law. Although the magistrate's proposal was not adopted, colonial authorities did institute recording and classification of another mark of the body.

In 1920, fingerprinting and photography would form the backbone of the Identification of Prisoners Act (IPA). Pivoting away from prior legislation on criminality as a genetic and collective phenomenon, the IPA mechanized the eye of a disciplinary state with camera and ink. It authorized the collection of fingerprints, footprint measurements, and photographs of people arrested for or convicted of serious offenses.[107] This biometricism's earliest laboratory was Bengal, where Sir William Herschel, chief administrator of the Hooghly District, built on the work of British psychologist, anthropologist, and eugenicist Francis Galton to develop a technique of registration and identification that would become the basis for modern fingerprinting. Inspired by the practice of *teep shai* (mark of pressure), in which illiterate workers would sign contracts by leaving an ink impression of their finger, Hershel first recorded the palm print of a laborer he called Konai as proof of a labor contract in 1858. He would go on to accumulate an enormous archive of fingerprints, mostly from prisoners, from which he proposed an index of patterns by which the singularity of the print could be determined. The ambitious claim that no two people in the world have ten identical fingerprints telescoped from the promise of distinguishable subjects in Bengal. The singularity of the print thus came to be the sign of singular individuality, the very mark of the identifiable person within the orbit of imperial power.[108] Fingerprints, embossed onto the colonial archive, are a kind of reverse touch.

The touch of colonial power reveals itself through the biometric imprints left in the archive when absconders were brought in for questioning or released from prison.[109] Like the native "types" caught in the frame of the ethnologic gaze—transformed, as Barthes says, from "subject into object, and even, one might say, into museum object"—members of Jugantar were arrested by the disciplinary gaze.[110] Their forms—stilled, contained, and named "terrorist"—came to be preserved as objects of imperial power in the archive and now can be viewed as part of an image galley at the West Bengal State Archives Museum. The photographs identify those represented by birth name and criminal designation. When Gowariker's film positions those images of members of Jugantar (either taken in police custody, or, for several dozen young men who had no prior record but were killed in fighting with police, as corpses) next to a black-and-white still image of the actor playing the part in the closing credits, it inscribes a contemporary audience into the gaze of the police. Fugitive forms are doubly arrested: first by colonial police, who authenticated them as "terrorist," then by a largely Indian audience who affix onto that image the name "hero." Photography's temporality, the past perfect of what has been, is what Barthes calls "a certificate of presence."[111] It authenticates a moment and a person who has passed but for whom there is proof of having been. Reencountering the images of these individuals in the cinematic frame alerts us to the original technology of their capture. The legal and mechanical forces by which the colonial state regulated and contained insurgent subjects allow those subjects, nearly a century later, to be renamed and re-identified. Twice over, these wayward bodies are stilled and contained, first in the postcolonial archive, cataloged under the taxonomical rubric of criminality; and then in filmic archive, reimagined with the heroic title that imperial history denied them. The archive is in this way a repository of imperial law and of imperial gaze. We look in the archive to and through the eyes of colonial rule.[112]

Curiously, Waddedar's CID file contains neither the fingerprints noted to have been taken at the time of her questioning nor a police photograph of her face. Instead, it includes an image authorities already had in their possession, which Waddedar was asked to swear was of herself. This image had circulated in a police notice seeking information about her whereabouts, accompanied by the description: "Miss Prithi Waddadar, daughter of Jagabandhu Waddadar (Baidya by caste), of Dhalghat, Patiya and Jamalkhana, Chittagong town; age 20–21 (looks younger than her age); dark; medium build; short; ugly in appearance."[113] Marked by her father's name, her caste, and the scant adjectives by which an absconding woman might be known, Waddedar is squeezed into the frame of recognizability in this image. In the photograph, she sits on a chair, wearing a dark-colored sari with a white border, her hands clasped on her lap (figure 1.1). It is an image that coheres with the statement she offered authorities, of recognizable Bengali femininity and normative embodiment.

Figure 1.1 Photograph of Pritilata Waddedar, on display at the
West Bengal State Archives Directorate in 2014

It is not an image of her as she has been codified within historical accounts and as she was at her death, dressed in men's clothing. Indeed, to my knowledge, there exists no photographic image of Waddedar as she was attired during the Pahartali raid and at her death. Nor is it the image of her face and the words she bore on her body at her death from the red leaflets that were showered throughout Chittagong and air-bombed into police headquarters (figure 1.2). Those explosive, confounding, and disruptive images are not included in the colonial and postcolonial state's archive of her. Within the pages of her police record and alongside her comrades on display at the West Bengal Archives, she is at once recognizable as a "type" and unrecognizable as the revolutionary she declared herself to be. These two images, which look to have been taken at the same time (one a close-up, the other a wide frame), navigate two scales of proximity to Waddedar and the terms of her recognizability.

Clothed in a sari, the iconic image of traditional Bengali femininity, Waddedar in these images recalls the narrative devices of her memorialization. She frees herself

Figure 1.2 Unsourced photograph of Pritilata Waddedar in the public domain.

from the grip of colonial power by citing precisely the forms of feminine constraint that her clothing should imply. It is because she was dressed as a man, we are to understand, that Waddedar was able to attack the Pahartali Institute; cloth was the vehicle by which she absconded. When police found her body, its recognizability was its disguise. Waddedar hailed the touch of the police through the outward sheath of her clothing and the inner sheaves of paper on her corpse. They found the terrorist they were looking for. But that disruptive form—the unseen image of Waddedar clothed in the garb of a (Muslim) man—of which the archive keeps no permanent visual record, is supplanted by the form in which colonial authority and nationalist imagination would adjudicate her death. Waddedar must be resexed into Bengali femininity in order to be preserved. By stripping her of the cotton *kurta* and disguising (in the original meaning of the word, to change a style of clothing) her in a sari, the Crown made its case for her seduction and her comrades for her singular heroism. Male, she was both culpable and disposable. It thus stands to reason that the bronze bust of her installed in 2012 in front of the ruin of the Pahartali Institute in Chittagong would, even in depicting her only from the torso up, insist on representing the drape of a sari across her shoulder. When, each year, the statue is garlanded in memoriam, the marigold chain looped around her neck and fastened to the post behind reimagines her death as a hanging in the manner of political executions. Other than Surya Sen, none of the other dozen members of the IRA killed have warranted such a memorial. Waddedar's singularity, and commemorability, are reinforced through public gendered disciplining.

That which makes Waddedar appear singular, by the same measure, is that which she insisted bound her to a collective, to other women. In the photographs of her, that she is unmarried is visible from the lack of red vermilion *teep* at the center of her forehead and along the part of her hair. The *teep*, the sign by which Bengali Hindu women announce themselves as wives, is also the word for "mark" and the signature from which Hershel first taxonomized fingerprints. So unmarked and unindividuated, Waddedar was free to immolate herself in the manner of the Bengali widow in the name of the motherland for whom she sacrificed herself and whose female population she hoped to inspire by her act. For example, although her individual file in the colonial police archives is strikingly small, and truncated by her death, she appears systematically throughout the records of other members accused of involvement in the Armory raids, particularly Kalpana Dutt's.[114] Dutt's file consists of nearly a dozen folders, hundreds of pages of surveillance records, typed statements, and news clippings that range from 1932 to 1964, when the Indian government formally ceased its investigation of her. It is so vast because Dutt was arrested by the police weeks before the Pahartali raid and was unable to shake their surveillance to join Waddedar and the others. Her archival trace is rich because she lived. Dutt stood trial with

Surya Sen and Tarkeswar Dastidar in 1933 and, unlike the two men, who were sentenced to death for their part in the Chittagong conspiracy, was sentenced to life imprisonment until Rabindranath Tagore and Gandhi both intervened for her early release in 1939.[115] Bound to one another by friendship and by their unique place within Jugantar, Kalpana Dutt and Pritilata Waddedar are also sutured to one another within the colonial archive.

Throughout Dutt's file, there are reports of found manuscripts and fragments in handwriting that was either hers or Waddedar's. This is an odd forensic uncertainty. Police had in their possession samples of both women's handwriting but repeatedly were unable or unwilling to distinguish between them. In part this is because the writing itself is a repetition. Text that appears to be in Dutt's handwriting in June 1933 is identical to the text found on Waddedar's dead body in September 1932. Faced with the reappearance of the disruptive words, "I boldly declare myself as a revolutionary," authorities annotated the statement's source as enigmatic and indivisible.[116] Like the photograph or the fingerprint, handwriting was called upon to be the signature of the individual, an authenticating apparatus that testifies to singular identifiability. When handwriting fails to tell, it signals a refusal of the fantasy of individuation, the myth of authenticity. Kalpana Dutt and Pritilata Waddedar, despite imperial attempts to disaggregate and corroborate body with act, were indivisible until they were divided and distinguished by Waddedar's death.

The colonial archive that contains traces of Waddedar's presence operates in the fantasy of containment and mastery. Accumulated documents and data stand as signs of the comprehension and control of an administrative region that eluded satisfying management. Indeed, my own encounter with Waddedar is availed by a techno-legal assemblage of capture and its systematic documentation and preservation that is the hallmark of imperial governance and its struggle against the revolutionary violence that Waddedar enacted.[117] Pressed between sheaves of paper accumulated in police investigations, she is captured within the archive. But the substance of what is preserved in that record is itself a play on surface. If allegory abides by the reciprocity between surface narrative and shadow meaning, Waddedar's invocation of *sati* is like her donned male garments. It is a foliated surface, contiguous to the skin. This is not surface and depth; rather, it is surface and surface. We touch the state record of her capture. She herself eludes touch. The cotton *kurta* and pants that rested on her corpse to name it on her terms are not metaphors for illegibility. They are the material signs of a commitment to refusal. So too in her writing also resting on her corpse—text as cloth—*sati*'s force for Waddedar is its refusal of hermeneutic clarity. It is the mark of what we will not know, the accumulation of narrative and observation and regulation in the place of certainty about desire.

VII. Séance of Historiography

Although Waddedar's act of political protest comes prefigured for us as an act of revolutionary violence by her own words, the violence inflicted on her body stands in for additional violence against British bodies.[118] Surya Sen conflated her with the ready images of Bengal and Durga in "Vijaya," but Waddedar, by killing herself immediately after attacking the British members of the Pahartali Institute, suggested that her dead body might signify as another casualty of her own violence. The impossible and false dichotomy between wanting to be saved and wanting to die cannot contain a third possibility of identificatory violence. Rather than, or in addition to, being a spectacular embodiment of Indian female sacrifice, Waddedar's dead body outside the building was a repetition (with a difference) of the carnage inside. Her body, dressed in male attire but unmarked by outward signs of violence, presented an epistemological dilemma for colonial authorities who could not understand why this young woman was dead when her comrades fled unharmed.[119] Once it was discovered that she had died of suicide by cyanide, her death became incorporated into a narrative of revolutionary terrorism. But until the suicide was confirmed, her death could be read as collateral damage. That she inflicted it on herself is, then, even more striking, as it offers up another way to read the body upon the pyre. Her suicide refused the familiar narratives of heroism and self-sacrifice while acting as a reminder of the violence and death she caused, an insistent articulation by a body slipping from the grips of mortality.

At the end of "Can the Subaltern Speak?," Spivak asserts a definitive answer to the essay's title: "The subaltern," she writes, "cannot speak."[120] Since the publication of the essay, Spivak has returned repeatedly to the scene of Bhubaneswari's death, rewriting that suicide script over and over again. In *A Critique of Postcolonial Reason* (1999), she writes that her famous declaration was "an inadvisable remark."[121] The failure, the negation of the title, is not Bhubaneswari's silence but the impossibility of its perception. A dropped signal. Static in the lines of history. The blame for this failed reception, for Spivak, is both systemic and personal: the intimacies of silence that bind Bhubaneswari's female relatives, the curious reader, and even Spivak herself; the older sister to whom Bhubaneswari addressed her suicide note; the great-niece who wears only cotton—suggesting a nostalgic adherence to the Gandhian insistence of material nationalism—and heads a transnational corporation; the female Bengali philosopher whose early work was nearly identical to Spivak's own and who acted as ethnographic go-between. Women, Spivak tells us not unsympathetically, should have known better, done better, listened better. The ethics of violence and silence seep through the enveloping grip of familiarity and femininity. She writes that "the effort

[Bhubaneswari] made to write or speak her body was in the accents of account-able reason, the instrument of self-conscious responsibility. Still her Speech Act was refused. She was made to unspeak herself posthumously, by other women."[122] The curious conjunction of speech act and unspeaking converges in the ethical domain of responsibility. Bhubaneswari acted to give account of actions and inactions, of dying alone hanged from a fan and not dying in the commission of an assassination. It is an enunciation that ought to have been heard, but it is refused. The passive voice condemns us all, even before we are apprised of our complicit violence.

Not only was Bhubaneswari's transmission refused by the historical machine, she "was made to *unspeak* herself." The past-tense passive causative construc-tion of Bhubaneswari's silence performs a double violence on the already dead—zombie self-erasure.[123] She is made passively to do something active to an object that no longer exists. More curiously still, the verb "to unspeak," in reflex-ively indicating Bhubaneswari as subject, suggests a constitutive unbecoming in which the speech act that is refused and reversed was previously an act of self-articulation, of self-construction. Made to unspeak herself, Bhubaneswari is made to retract herself from utterance and from view. Made to unspeak herself, she is unmade. The passive voice, however, is an alibi for the activeness of the violence being performed, Spivak alerts us, by a community of women.

The case of Bhubaneswari Bhaduri, then, becomes not a failure of represen-tation but a particularly gendered refusal of communication. But what kind of communication is possible with the dead? What aural or textual trace is extracted in the being made to unspeak? It may be instructive in this moment to consider the corrective that Spivak offers to the sentence "The subaltern cannot speak." While this is the phrase that has been repeated and disputed in the countless critiques of the essay in the past three decades, Spivak writes ear-lier, and reproduces in "History": "The subaltern as female cannot be heard or read."[124] Foreclosure of the subaltern as speaking subject is a result of the inability of the subaltern gendered as female to be read or heard. There is no signal with-out receptor. In this account, the speech act must take a form that is apprecia-ble, legible, audible. Indeed, it is intended to be understood, read, heard. Spivak is not calling for hermeneutic transparency—quite the opposite, in fact. The essay is a clarion call against mastery as historiographic method. Nonetheless, Spivak believes insistently that Bhubaneswari made her body speak, and that her speech act, though refused by her own relatives, echoes still. She was heard after all: "All speaking, even seemingly the most immediate, entails a distanced decipherment by another, which is, at best, an interception."[125]

We might think of this model of interception as an invitation to be haunted. The séance of historiography requires sitting in wait of the dead in hopes that they will speak, that they will choose to speak through the living bodies gathered there.[126] It is a willingness to be possessed, to be the medium through which the disembodied take form; to be a point of contact, contingent, touched. It is also an act of scholarly identification and, more often than not, incorporation, by which to hear, even interrupted and through static, that which was once refused. Moreover, to agree to be haunted is to take seriously what Abraham and Torok have called the "instantaneous and magical" incorporation of a lost object into the ego.[127] The ghost is the familiar who has returned in an unfamiliar nonform and who refuses the obliteration of mortality's reality-making force. To be haunted is to welcome, however hesitantly, intimacy with spirits on the level of formlessness; it is an intimacy that works in secret, and in protest of the amnesia of biological life. Avery Gordon writes,

> If haunting describes how that which appears to be not there is often a seething presence, acting on and often meddling with taken-for-granted realities, the ghost is just the sign, or the empirical evidence, if you like, that tells you a haunting is taking place. The ghost is not simply a dead or a missing person, but a social figure, and investigating it can lead to that dense site where history and subjectivity make social life.[128]

Spivak admits in "History" that she "pray[ed] to be haunted" by the ghost of the Rani of Sirmur, in search of whom she delved into the colonial archives of *sati* regulation. The Rani's traces appeared so faintly and insistently that Spivak desired to feel across the reach of time some touch of intimacy with that historical subject: "The assurance of transference gives way to the possibility of haunting, it is also true that for us the only figure of the unconscious is that of a radical series of discontinuous interruptions."[129]

This chapter has likewise been haunted: the discontinuous, resurgent, fleeting encounter with Pritilata Waddedar's archival presence carries within it the traces of a prior, unshakeable glimpse of another. I have come to know Pritilata Waddedar, in part, by way of Bhubaneswari Bhaduri, whose eruptive presence in my first reading of "Can the Subaltern Speak?" many years ago I've never been able to shake. The finding, and by that I do not mean discovery, of Pritilata Waddedar was a *refinding*, in fragment and static, of Bhubaneswari and of an ethical model of reading as haunting. Rather than attempt to locate those missing pieces and decipher the garble, perhaps the work of analysis is the recognition of and insistence on reading through intimacy, the straining toward one another across absence and repetition and failure. The kinship that binds us as scholars of the postcolonial to legacies of resistant women and unreadable fragments and unstable narratives also binds us to a feminist genealogy of hermeneutics, one that exists alongside the promise of incomplete meaning and unsatisfied epistemophilia.

This chapter has aimed to follow the lead of a historical subject who, in her writings and with her dead body, insistently refused the iniquitous allure of familiar narratives. Immolated, made subject of her own sacrifice, Waddedar aligned herself within a matrilineal history of burning widows and blazing goddesses but jammed the gears of the hermeneutic system of legal evidence that depends on a juridical index of desire. She performed the static in the gap between the name—whether "revolutionary" or *sati*—and its physical remains. As we see in Waddedar's memorials and in Spivak's ghostly histories, those same evidentiary expectations guide the approaches of historians, those of us looking backward to the past hoping to find proof of consent or desire. We find instead on Waddedar's body a memorial to the politics of illegibility that refuses recognition, that offers an abiding resistance to being mastered—even, and especially, as it demands to be read.

PART II

The Fetish of Nationalism

2

The Fetish Touch

(tout objet historique est fétiche)

—Maurice Merleau-Ponty

From April 1916 to May 1917, Rabindranath Tagore traveled across America and Japan on a lecture tour organized by his American publisher, filling auditoriums with people eager to hear from the first Nobel laureate from India. His audiences might have expected readings of poems from *Gitanjali*, for which he garnered such global acclaim, or perhaps philosophical musings from the man Yasunari Kawabata later likened to "some ancient Oriental wizard."[1] Instead, they got what the *Minneapolis Tribune* called a "$700 per scold" political critique.[2] In these lectures, later published with those delivered during his travels through Japan in the same year as a thin volume entitled *Nationalism*, Tagore suggests a comprehensive yet singular etiological narrative of what he saw globally as the deplorable rise of militarism and decline of humanism: the rise of the Nation. Referring insistently to "the Nation" as a capitalized abstract noun with a definite article in the essay, Tagore emphasizes the ubiquity of its form and the emptiness of its character. The use of the noun rendered proper name, as Foucault writes, "is merely an artifice," promising an unambiguous designation scrupulously withheld.[3] This transformation of an abstract noun ("nation") into a proper name ("the Nation") reflects the singularity of the object and its discursive autopoesis.

The Nation, against which Tagore so steadfastly positioned himself, is a formless concept that simultaneously produces and necessitates a mechanical instantiation. This deterritorialized organization parasitically prospers at the expense of the forms of attachment and cooperation to which Tagore was most committed. Indeed, he insisted that anticolonial nationalism and the empire it opposes are indistinguishable, prostrate in front of the same divine force. He writes, "Not merely subject races, but you who live under the delusion that you are free, are every day sacrificing your freedom and humanity to this fetich of nationalism, living in the dense poisonous atmosphere of worldwide suspicion and greed and panic."[4] A global imaginary confederation of the unfree—those for whom autonomy, however false, appears as reality and those for whom even that illusion is denied—is created by the common daily sacrifice. To fetishize nationalism is to worship at the altar of an abstract object that demands the most intimate of offerings of human subjectivity and sovereignty.

Tagore's accusation of fetishism is particularly damning because, of course, nationalism is itself a discourse of autonomy. By insisting that it is inextricably bound to empire by the shared ideal of the Nation, he upends the liberatory promise of anticolonial nationalism. Freedom is impossible, he seems to suggest, as long as it is sutured to the political form of the Nation. In the essay, Tagore repeatedly returns to a mechanistic language to argue that nationalist labor, like colonial authority, turns people into machine parts, automated and insensate. The pathology of this fetishistic attachment, in other words, voids the workers of their humanity, turning them into things, mere matter.

Between 1925 and 1930, Tagore carried out a public debate in the pages of the *Modern Review* and *Young India* with Mohandas K. Gandhi, whom he considered a dear friend, though the two men—perhaps the most famous of modern Indian history—disagreed fervently not just about the form and function of political protest but about the very vision of what a postcolonial future might look like. As head of the Indian National Congress, Gandhi and his labors of spinning cotton thread at the *charkha* (spinning wheel) became the symbol of a growing nationalist movement and *khadi* (handloomed cotton) the covering for a new nationalist body. *Khadi* was figured as an egalitarian fabric, binding an Indian collectivity through exertion and tactility. Although its popularity and visibility peaked during the 1920s noncooperation movement, *khadi* first announced itself as the material of an anticolonial politics two decades earlier in Bengal with the *swadeshi* movement, a campaign of economic noncooperation following the 1905 partition. This local project, with which Tagore felt a deep affinity, was transformed into a nation-making system: cloth becoming the vehicle of collective and individual liberation. In a transitive substitution that will become increasingly familiar, the Bengali *swadeshi* movement made fabric essential to the postcolonial imagination and to the possibility of an independent India. Tagore's critique of what he saw as Gandhi's instrumentalization of the ideal of self-sufficiency that the *charkha* and the *khadi* it produced represented—what we might call, in Tagore's own idiom, its fetishization—is thus also an objection to the extrapolation of the intimate and local into the prescribed and national.

This chapter takes up the ethical and analytic challenge of chapter 1—how do we read acts and articulations of political protest that strategically elude hermeneutic mastery?—by considering the perceived threat of material overattachment to the twinned psychological and political projects of autonomy that marked nationalist politics in Bengal following the 1905 partition. Through a reading of Tagore's songs, essays, and exchanges with Gandhi, I trace the emergence of a fleeting form of political imagination that refused autonomy of the individual as its telos. Within Tagore's trenchant critique of nationalism, there appears a call to conceive of a *swadesh*, a country of one's own, that is a practice of nonsovereign self-making; this locally rooted global form harks back to East Bengal as a site of poetic, ideological, and material possibility. The site of Tagore's ancestral landholdings, rural East Bengal remains at the fore of Tagore's conception of home and the politics of its postcolonial possibility. Though this and chapter 3 engage some of the most prominent male figures of postcolonial history and influential debates over political modernity, they keep squarely in their sights the labor of women that produced the terms against which a masculinist national sovereignty was imagined. Fundamentally, the negotiation of what constitutes the political is played out in Tagore's writing and on Gandhi's body through explicit self-feminization. Even as Gandhi and Tagore may both be seen as national *patres familias*, it is in their performances of and affinities with femininity that their most radical political visions appear. Indeed, this porous political feeling becomes appreciable in its circuit through the bodies and labor of women—female historical and literary characters as well as the image of Bengal as mother/land.

Quite consciously, this chapter—the first of two in which Tagore is central—situates itself in relation to what might be called "Late Tagore." By the time of his public debate with Gandhi, Tagore had largely retreated to Santiniketan, the village in which he established a collection of institutes that would make up the *Visva-Bharati* university system, and turned his attention to its development. Though his celebrity (particularly in Bengal) remained high, he was at this moment neither the romantic visionary of international acclaim he had been a decade earlier nor the nostalgic icon of pastoral patriotism that he would come to be after his death. Late Tagore is the Tagore of an interregnum in which the seeds of political critique sown during 1905 germinated into utopian visions of a postcolonial future. It is from this moment, then, looking back toward his disillusionment with nationalism, that we can see both the ideational influence of his poetry on a global sense of what constituted the nation and Bengal, and the foreclosed possibilities of that ideal.

Bengal's 1905 partition signals a shift of which Tagore's writings become exemplars, giving rise to a set of nationalisms for which his songs and lyrics become anthems. It gives birth to *swadeshi* as an anticolonial strategy and ideology, privileging the local, material, and intimate as vehicles for conceiving of the national. At the same time, in this unmaking of Bengal, East Bengal is revealed in a host of nationalist texts as well as Tagore's own writing to be a kind of elemental motherland, fount of feeling and authentic object of attachment, even as it becomes obscured as a singular object of political imagination. If in chapter 1 we saw the 1857 mutiny as an anti-originary revolutionary moment, we will in this chapter see 1905 as an anti-originary nationalist moment. The forms of nationalism that developed out of the partition ceased to take Bengal as their telos, transforming it instead into the synecdoche of a larger India. Bengal, particularly East Bengal, nonetheless persists as a sentimental and material force—a kind of apparitional nation whose sensuous appearance in the writings of Tagore and his contemporaries reveals that which cannot be subsumed into the political form of the postcolonial nation-state.

This chapter argues that translation of an intimate affect (*desh prem*, or love of country) for Bengal into the abstraction of political nationalism for India, which Tagore so feared, is never complete. It is stunted by the form of what Tagore called the fetish. There remains the unincorporable, disruptive trace of the rudimentary and organic that so moved the poet in the first place. To locate this trace, to account for its force and its failure—its *touch*, as it were—this chapter moves sensorially. It attends to the senses worked upon by the fetish object and their relation to the problem of self-determination central to both Tagore's critique of nationalism and anticolonial political thought more broadly. Beginning with the sound of the fetish, captured in Tagore's post-1905 partition songs, we then turn toward the sight of the fetish, the embodiment and materiality of Gandhi and Tagore which garner such power; finally, we rest on the touch of the fetish, the hands and bodies at work upon the *charkha* and the accumulation of intimacy upon its surface that seeps into a national body.

The *fetish*, in its most basic definition, is an object that contains in its very form imperial power and promise. It does not operate metaphorically like the deity, pointing toward magic elsewhere. Moreover, as an object manufactured and handled, it is a technology of historicism, preserving on and in its body traces and accumulations of the human and the machinic. This chapter returns the fetish to its colonial origins through a hermeneutics of materiality, a mode of what I call reading fetishistically. For Tagore, the fetish of nationalism manufactures its own material objects, objects that in turn become condensed sites of meaning and attachment and threats to the very self-determination they promise. Fetishistic reading asks us to stay within the form of the fetish object, to account for both the traces of human labor and the enchantment of magic caught within the threads of materiality. It is a mode of reading that does not privilege sovereignty, but rather holds open the possibility that these objects make possible a radical alterity from which forms of affiliation and attachment emerge that draw together the local and the global in a shared anti-colonial imagination.

Coded within this mode of reading fetishistically is a commitment to what Eve Sedgwick calls *reparative reading*, a practice in which the rigid and reactive paranoia that militantly orients the reader toward suspicion of the past is jettisoned in favor of optimism. She writes, "Hope, often a fracturing, even a traumatic thing to experience, is among the energies by which the reparatively positioned reader tries to organize the fragments and part-objects she encounters or creates. Because the reader has room to realize that the future may be different from the present, it is also possible for her to entertain such profoundly painful, profoundly relieving, ethically crucial possibilities as that the past, in turn, could have happened differently from the way it actually did."[5] Of the postcolonial futures that orbited around Gandhi and Tagore's debate in the 1920s, few survived the centripetal force of the nationalisms that would lead to Partition in 1947. Neither Gandhi's hope for a common cause nor Tagore's dream of a humanist ethos mark the life of the modern Indian nation-state. But fetishistic reading and its preservative impulse insist that nothing is ever dead, not even those filaments of political possibility.

I. Fetish History

When Tagore in 1916 used the word *fetish*, what did he mean by it? To what intellectual and material histories was he drawing our attention by describing the immaterial force of nationalism, the philosophy of an abstract noun, in the language of magical embodiment? Marx, before he came to commodity fetishism in 1867 in *Capital: Volume I*, writes of fetishism as "the religion of sensuous appetites" in 1842.[6] For Hegel in 1837, the fetish was symptomatic of African underdevelopment: "the characteristic point is the fact that consciousness has not yet attained to the realization of any substantial objective existence."[7] The ability to "exalt to the dignity of 'Genius'" in objects of apparent valuelessness parallels the African's apparent inability to distinguish between the power of the self and the force of the image, suggesting for Hegel a condition of suspended interior possibility.[8] In 1927, Freud first used the term to describe paraphilic desires in *Three Essays on the Theory of Sexuality* in 1905 and developed his now familiar theory of it as "a substitute for the woman's (the mother's) penis that the little boy once believed in—and for reasons familiar to us—does not want to give up."[9] Let us posit that whether or not Tagore was versed in these invocations, he developed his own idiom of the fetish that specifically parallels our most common theoretical uses of it. Common across these cases is the belief that the fetish turns on a basic (and often strategic) misreading and, in turn, fetishism infuses that "wrong object" with overinvestment. The subject takes an abstraction or displacement and mistakes it for the thing itself.

However, the etymology of *fetish* offers what we might think of as a microcosm of colonial materiality. The *OED* supplements its definition of *fetish* as "[a]n inanimate object worshipped by primitive peoples on account of its supposed inherent magical powers, or as being animated by a spirit" with the coda that "a fetish differs from an idol in that it is worshipped in its own character, not as the image, symbol, or occasional residence of a deity."[10] The history of the fetish as an idea and as novel object, William Pietz argues, traces to sixteenth- and seventeenth-century trading encounters in West Africa. Etymologically derived from the Latin *facticius*, meaning "manufactured," the word became in the Middle Ages the Portuguese *feitiço*, meaning "magical practice." From within an extended cross-cultural, precapitalist encounter, the fetish emerged as a made object of contested and cryptic value.[11] The problem of the fetish here is as much one of social incommensurability as of overvaluation; that is, European traders imagined themselves exchanging (and benefiting enormously from the exchange of) objects of "real" value for those to which the West Africans appeared overly invested or attached. In its various discursive manifestations—psychoanalytic, anthropologic, Marxist—the fetish remains the product of an encounter with power, with the forces of language and meaning-making. In a logic reproduced by Tagore's argument, European traders found the attachments and investments of West Africans incorrect, and the term we have thus inherited speaks not to rational choices but to pathology.

However, we would be wrong to let this this venerable genealogy of pathologization obscure the fact that the fetish in those dark places of the world works by way of translation and preservation; it absorbs the affecting traces of personal memory into the body of a material object that is socially appreciable. Unlike the idol, which is a technology of representation that refers to but does not contain a deity (its value symbolic rather than material), the fetish is force itself, materialized. Quite explicitly, it operates neither metaphorically nor symptomatically. It is powerful in its own right, in its own form. The fetish object is what sutures the particular and passionate feeling of intimate worship onto the form of the appreciable, the tactual. In this way, it is an especially resonant hermeneutic through which to theorize the tactile life of politics.

In the form of the fetish, Pietz writes, "the crisis moments of singular encounter and indefinable transaction between the life of the self and that of the world become fixed, in both places and things, and as personal memories that retain the power to move one profoundly."[12] In order for an object to be made a fetish (manufactured), there must exist a commonly recognizable aspect to its form that nonetheless preserves the power to touch individuals, to move them. The synecdochic fragment embodied in the fetish object, the severed part which accepts responsibility for the whole, must retain the trace of familiarity that touches—strikes or pierces—the individual "in an intensely personal way" and yet remains recognizable outside that cognitive intimacy.[13] The fetish is thus a site of condensation and accumulative meaning, cohering that which is intensely individual with that which is socially significant. This, of course and not coincidentally, recalls the structure of feeling that characterizes anticolonial nationalism.

Though the Portuguese traders could not apprehend in the form of these fetish objects that which rendered them magical, the objects nonetheless cohered a social body by way of their force. Made of material appearing valueless to Europeans, the fetish insistently made its worth known by way of its effect on the West Africans. But the power of the fetish affected not only those for whom it appeared as divine. Its touch operated promiscuously; the traders were absorbed into its economy through their encounter with those under its thrall. As an object within a matrix of exchange and valuation, the fetish reached outside the body of the worshipper and regulated the behavior of unbelieving traders as well. The fetish oaths that they were asked to make before embarking on trade lassoed Europeans into the sensorial and affective practices of the fetish and its worshippers.

More generally, the touch of the fetish is the ambiguous contact between the visible and invisible, the material and the ideal, the sensational and the political. To be touched by a fetish is to be drawn into a representational logic of partial perception, to be touched by something you cannot quite make out but nonetheless feel. Captured by this iniquitous logic, the fetish is vilified, pathologized, and repudiated. The autonomous subject, contained and controlled, falters in the face of the fetish; unimpeachable self-sovereignty is revealed as specious. Tagore, like Marx, Hegel, and Freud, viewed the fetish suspiciously, in terms of what it replaces and vanishes, with its economy of enthrallment, the ways the fixation of overattachment alters the subject-object relation. The dehumanized fetishists/nationalists/laborers, in the Medusan tradition, are turned to stone by their own fascination: materialized.

II. Sing the Body Politic

The power of the fetish to touch—that is, affect—is precisely what motivated Tagore's anxiety about the possibility that a material object might reach beyond the perceptive to disrupt the cognitive and simultaneously construct its own worshipping subjects. In the case of Bengal, which would go on to stand in for all of British India, the object and subject of that magnetic touch are gendered feminine. And though the fetish is manufactured, worked on by hands, it threatens—indeed, promises—to work on us in turn. In *Nationalism*, Tagore writes of the Nation as an enormous, unmanned machine where "those who are mechanics are made into parts of the machine . . . the personal man is eliminated to a phantom."[14] That which is human, sentient, personal is eliminated by an immaterial force and in turn transforms itself into a ghost in the machine. The spirits have been chased out of human bodies to populate an ideological workforce with mindless drones. If British colonialism, under the sign of the Nation, first built that machine in order to govern by as "little [touch] by the human hand as possible," then any political strategy which reifies that technology shows itself suspect.[15]

Particularly aggrieving to Tagore was the anticolonial turn toward the Nation as telos, away from the ideal of *swadeshi* to which he himself had been so committed. The word *swadeshi*, commonly translated as "self-sufficiency," did not connote for Tagore nationalism in any functional way. Even in the most stalwart moments of his critique of nationalism, Tagore never swayed from articulating his attachment to Bengal, which was for him both an ideal and a material category. Its body, in his poetic rendering, was not the impersonal goddess of Hindu nationalist ideology but the familiar and beloved mother whose touch was intimate and congenital. It was this love of a personal Bengal that caused him to so resist the politicization of that attachment and what he saw as the artificial idolization of the nation that resulted. Translation of *swadeshi*'s affective force into political strategy by nationalist figures of the period, for Tagore, defiled and fractured a deeply cherished love object, the motherland. *Banga-Bhanga* (the breaking of Bengal), as the first partition of the state is commonly called, inspired Tagore to write some of his most famous songs and novels mourning the wounded body of Bengal and the dissolution of affinities among her inhabitants.

For Tagore, *swadeshi* was an imaginative practice at once deeply personal and inherently dependent on collective will, on *samāj* (society). He writes,

The certain knowledge that I have a *dés* comes out of a quest. Those who think that the country is theirs simply because they have been born in it are

creatures besotted by external things of the world. But, since the true character of the human being lies in his or her inner nature imbued by the force of
self-making (*ātmásakti*), only that country can be one's *svadés* that is created
by one's own knowledge, intelligence, love and effort.[16]

The distinction between *dés* (*desh*) and *svadés* (*swadesh*), country and my own
country, is located in the imaginative power of the Sanskrit reflexive pronoun
prefix *sva*. The reflexivity of self-making is itself country-making. *Swadeshi* functions as a kind of corrective to the automating technology of the Nation by reap-
propriating its logic of production. Here, the machine does not make matter of the
human; rather, the human makes herself as she makes her world with her "own
knowledge, intelligence, love and effort." This labor is not alienating; in fact, that
which makes the self also makes self-determination. Moreover, it is a deterritorialized vision of affiliation, even as its referent remains local and rooted.[17]

Swadeshi, then, as a self-making project irreducible to a collective formation began as a local vision in Bengal following the 1905 partition and would
come to be exported out to a greater India in the subsequent decades, align-
ing itself with the nationalist form of *swaraj* (self-rule) popularized by Gandhi.
The intersection of these terms, which share the prefix *swa/sva*, marks the subject of the political: this self is not a contained or invaginated figure but one
constantly opening outwards toward the indivisible and nonindividual self of
the *atman*. *Atman* is the self beyond the self in the Vedic nondualist tradition,
which refuses the self-object divide both grammatically and metaphysically.
Thus, the prefix *sva* indicates a subject whose very relation to itself and its
object, whether country or rule, does not reify the boundary between the two.
As a model of anticolonial thought, then, this suggests collective cathexis as
self-making and self-made.

Tagore first came to the phrase *swadeshi samāj* in 1905, as an alternative to
the nation that he had already begun to see as a foreign concept, ill-suited to
Bengal and India. He writes, "India has never had a real sense of nationalism.
Even though from childhood I had been taught that the idolatry of Nation is
almost better than reverence for God and humanity, I believe I have outgrown
that teaching, and it is my conviction that my countrymen will gain truly their
India by fighting that education which teaches them that a country is greater
than the ideals of humanity."[18] Tagore's argument for a global liberal human-
ism promoted a logic by which nations cease to provide the organizing principle of peoples, denaturalizing nationalism as a compelling affective or political
structure. But in refusing the nation's regulative force, Tagore did not reject an
affectively compelling vision of India. On the contrary, Tagore's resistance to
nationalism was figured as a mode of affective attachment that political ideology

would snuff out. Such a nationalist cathexis would re-form "India" according to an imperial structure. The "anesthetic" of nationalism, numbing what Tagore saw as the organic and congenital, produced a national unconscious that relied on diluting and destabilizing the structures of feeling underlying collective cathexis. Quite explicitly, this was not an eschewal of the idea of Indianness as a mode of identification, but rather a recognition that "India" need not refer to a nation; it might be imagined otherwise.

Despite his public distance from nationalist politics, Tagore wrote his most famous songs about Bengal during the six-year long period of the partition. The apparent contradictions of Tagore's turn away from the swadeshi movement, even as he penned some of the most famous songs ascribed to it, may offer evidence of Tagore's anguish at the division of his beloved Bengal and its traumatic traces.[19] In the end, it was not the partition that most affected Tagore but the realization that Lord Curzon's policy of "divide and rule" had proved deeply efficacious, the temporary colonial division of the region becoming a vestigial fracture that would eventually splinter irreparably. The geopolitical fault lines of the 1905 partition were those along which the region would come to be permanently divided in 1947. Tagore mourned Bengal's inability to recover appropriately from the trauma of partition, to reconcile itself determinedly. His commitment to the ideal of a unified and united Bengal was shaken not only by the actual partition of the region but also by what it unleashed.

"Amar Sonar Bangla" (My Golden Bengal), which Tagore wrote in 1906, was intended to rouse Bengalis to protest the division of Bengal by invoking the image of a once-whole mother whose very body was now endangered. The song is replete with images of a pastoral Bengal, her mango groves, paddy fields, riverbanks, and banyan trees. The golden Bengal to whom the song is dedicated is addressed as "Ma" (mother), the apostrophic object of the song who is also the central laborer in an affective and bucolic economy. She elicits powerful feelings not only through the beauty of her landscape but also through her suffering, the division of her form along a Cartesian axis: East Bengal, the idyllic pastoral scene of the "true" Bengal (particularly for Tagore, whose ancestral landholdings, or zamindaris, drew from it both genealogy and wealth); and West Bengal, former colonial capital and outpost of a burgeoning political modernity. Mind was extirpated from matter, men who would become nationalist political actors riven from their idealized mother.

In composing the song, Tagore hoped that both the partition of Bengal and the divisive forces of communal violence might prove temporary. Simultaneously, he confirmed the need for anticolonial strategies that promoted local unity. It is fitting that some seventy years later, Bangladesh, the latter-day incarnation of colonial East Bengal, would take the first ten lines of the song as its national anthem. The decision in 1972 by Bangladesh's first president Sheikh Mujibur Rahman to institute it reoriented the song's subject. Rather than being read as an elegy of a bygone wholeness, the song was redeployed as a celebration and veneration of a liberated and reoccupied motherland. But this was no artificial reimagining of the terms of its lyrics; the song, like its author, was always-already representative of the nation-state that would become Bangladesh. In non-Anglicized Bangla, the word for the region Bengal was, until 1947, *Bangla-desh*—the country of that language. All of Bengal, during Tagore's lifetime, was Bangladesh.

The very name of East Bengal, Purba-Banga, indicates both its directional and ontological orientations: *purba* derived from the Sanskrit *purva*, meaning previous and ancestral as well as cardinal east, from where and when the day begins. Purba-Banga, we might say, is the historical Bengal—the very site from which Bengal emerges, its provenance and its inheritance—redoubling a pervasively feminine and spectacularly maternal imagery. Referred to in the song as *tui*, the most familiar of the three second-person forms of address in Bangla, this is a land drawn intimate. The apostrophic mother of "Amar Sonar Bangla" resides in the rural, progenital East, source of raw feeling and raw material too. Purba-Banga's alluvial soil, nourished by the Ganges, Brahmaputra, and Jamuna rivers, feeds the bodies and machines of the industrializing West. Rice and jute make possible a Bengal to come, its time and space origami-split and then compressed into an easterly past and westerly future.[20] The Purba-Banga of Tagore's song produces a body politic; *feeling* metabolized into protest is that which gives form, physiological and sensorial, to the embodied collectivity gathered under the genealogical sign of "Ma."

When Tagore writes that the scent of Bengal's mango groves, the sight of her rice paddies, the sound of her words, made him "wild with joy," he anatomizes being affected in its most fundamental meaning.[21] His sense perception is altered by the encounter with her material form. But this is more than some fleeting encounter. The poet is worked upon and undone by the sensorial contact. He is touched. The idiomatic exaltation that follows as refrain, "*mori hai, hai re* মরি হায় হায় রে," translated into English in Syed Ali Ahsan's 1972 official version as "ah, what a thrill," is precisely that affect which defies the disciplining structure of language. Thrill can relate to the actions either of material bodies—wherein it is the action of penetration, the piercing of one material body by another—or of nonmaterial forces. There, to thrill is to penetrate in another way, "to affect or move with a sudden wave of emotion; to move tremulously or with vibration."[22] The ejaculatory lexical gap of the refrain "*hai hai*" (which is commonly used as an exclamation of despair) is grammatically bridged in translation so that *thrill* offers materiality to the force of feeling evoked by the pastoral form of Bengal. Material and nonmaterial forces jostle against one another in both the linguistic translation from Bangla to English and in the translation of the individual, poetic intimacy to a collective sung anthem.

What kind of public, communitarian affect is thrill? How does the indefinable ejaculation move between and among bodies in song? Ultimately, this is the crux of Tagore's own recession from the world of nationalist politics and his critique of what he saw as nationalism's exploitation of organic feeling elicited by the motherland into a manufactured object of strategic overattachment. In an October 3, 1912, letter to Harriet Monroe, editor of *Poetry* magazine, Ezra Pound writes that that Tagore "has sung Bengal into a nation."[23] His songs constitute Bengal's nationhood, the present perfect yoking the denomination of Bengal as nation to the moment of Tagore's iteration of it in song. The act of singing Bengal, a nation that never became a nation-state, into being suggests the exteriorization of a deeply personal affect, the sounding of that untranslatable refrain on the world stage. Song, unlike its read counterpart in poetic lyric, at once gathers and reaches outwards. Although Pound imagined Tagore as singular in the performative act of song, the very word *anthem* homophonically and etymologically indicates multiplicity. We hear echoes of "and them" in its utterance as much as the promise of antiphony. The song "Amar Sonar Bangla," an anthem long before it was institutionalized as a national anthem, coalesces the unruly and destabilizing energies of private affect into the body politic. Sung together (among them), the refrain of "*hai, hai re*" resounds in a kind of coherence that the individual ejaculation refuses. The redistribution of that articulation across gathered bodies offers another vantage from which to approach Tagore's abiding anxiety about the translation and simultaneously transformation of personal attachment into public sentiment. Despite the lack of gender pronouns in Bangla, the very gendered construction of society meant that the voice of the poet and the chorus in this anthemic cry were masculine. It is this force that we saw Pritilata Waddedar and her female comrades press against in chapter 1: the muffled cry that Mother Bengal gave birth to daughters, too.

The official anthem of Bangladesh ends in a stanza lamenting Bengal's suffering:

Ma tor bodon khani molin hole / Ami noyon / O ma ami noyon jole bhasi / Sonar Bangla, ami tomay bhalobashi

মা, তোর বদনখানি মলিন হলে / আমি নয়ন / ও মা, আমি নয়নজলে ভাসি / সোনার বাংলা, আমি তোমায় ভালোবাসি

(Mother, if your face is darkened / My eyes / My eyes drown in tears / Golden Bengal, I love you)[24]

Ahsan's official translation leans on the connotation of *molin* as "sadness" that "casts a gloom on [her] face." The constitution of the maternal suffering is thus doubled in the apostrophic line that begins with the conditional "if," in turn producing a somatic response in the singer: "My eyes / My eyes drown in tears."[25] But *molin* also can mean unclean, soiled, darkened, tarnished.[26] In light of the territorial violence of 1905, of Tagore's reparative hopes, and of the potently filial discourse around Bengal as a beloved but beleaguered mother, *molin* is poised to refer not to handwringing commiseration but to retributive outrage.

Tagore's lyrics suggest that the task of *swadeshi* cannot be limited to the inadequate recompense of tears when the face of Bengal itself is marred. The singer then weeps not out of sympathy but out of some more biting and perhaps mobilizing response. As the penultimate line of the anthem—followed only by the bridge, "My golden Bengal, I love you"—the tears that flood the singer's eyes are seemingly superfluous. They offer neither comfort nor redress in the moment of partition, but more than a half-century later appear as patriotic excess. The binding of those tears to the amatory exclamation disguises them with ecstasy. Ahsan's translation of *molin* is calibrated for a new vision of Bengal, one that emerges out of the colonial occupation by Pakistan into a future that does not reconcile East to West but proclaims an extant wholeness. This Bengal, Bangladesh post-1971, is the only one for which this song was ever sung and its anthem cauterizes the wound of 1905 into a past outside the lyric temporality of the nation-state.

The full song—rarely sung now, as it has been supplanted in the popular imagination by the truncated anthem—ends in a very different vein. The final line reads, "*ami porer ghorey keenbo na aar, ma, tor bhushan boley golar phaanshi* আমি পরের ঘরে কিনব না আর, মা, তোর ভূষণ ব'লে গলার ফাঁসি (Mother, I won't buy from a stranger's house a noose for your neck, calling it a golden necklace.)"[27] An abrupt departure from the romantic pastoralism of the previous stanzas, the song ends by pointedly articulating a tactic of *swadeshi* protest. The economic strategies of noncooperation and local production that would become a hallmark of Gandhian *satyagraha* found their first laboratory in Bengal following the 1905 partition. "Amar Sonar Bangla" suggests, in its closing lines, a concrete course of action by which the lamenting poet might, if not repair, at least prevent future harm to his beloved motherland. Those ornaments designed to be artifacts of filial affection are revealed to be a threat in disguise. Golden jewelry, which was often the only wealth to which women could assert singular claim and which in the dowry system was intended to serve as social security for brides, in this case is foreign to the body of the mother who is herself already made of gold (*sonar*).

Most accounts of the place of "Amar Sonar Bangla" in Tagore's corpus of songs focus on its bucolic treatment of landscape as indicative of an affective rather than political engagement with Bengal as *desh* (country or Bengal). It, along with forty-five other lyrics, is anthologized under the category of *"Swadesh Gaan* (Songs of *Swadesh*)" in *Rabindra Rachanabali*, the collected works of Tagore. The collection, compiled and edited by Pulinbehari Sen, employs the term *Swadesh* as a categorical marker of those songs by Tagore that took *desh* as their object, sidestepping the evocation of *swadeshi* as patriotism. Some of the songs thus categorized are explicit in their anticolonial ethos, but "Amar Sonar Bangla," in taking as its object the rural form of East Bengal as national signifier, leans suggestively toward the elegiac. However, the apostrophic address common in these songs, a hailing of Bengal as mother, marks their articulation of expressly political feeling.

The affective force of Bengal, in this way, dialectically fashions a poetic subject, reversing the liberal fantasy of sovereign subjecthood over objects. Barbara Johnson's account of apostrophe in "Apostrophe, Animation, and Abortion" is of a state of ambivalence for the exclamatory figure of address. As Jonathon Culler argues, apostrophe not only transforms inanimate objects into "potentially responsive forces" but also fundamentally queers the I/Thou poetic relationship.[28] Put another way, apostrophe is not an emblem of poetic mastery over the insentient, but rather a figure of address in which the poet engages the limits of his own animation. Johnson writes, "Apostrophe is thus both direct and indirect: based etymologically on the notion of turning aside, of digressing from straight speech, it manipulates the I/Thou structure of direct address in an indirect, fictionalized way. The absent, dead, or inanimate entity addressed is thereby made present, animate, and anthropomorphic. Apostrophe is a form of ventriloquism through which the speaker throws voice, life, and human form into the addressee, turning its silence into mute responsiveness."[29] The addressed object is at once materialized and made subject to the poetic voice, animated but revealed to be a dummy; the thrown voice of the poet is caught in the body of the apostrophized addressee.

What, though, happens to the poet himself in this Pygmalion scene? Tagore's address to Bengal as mother, the possessive *amar* (my) in the song's title indicating Bengal's preciousness like gold (*sonar*) to the poet, personifies and nationalizes it in a fantasy of familial intimacy. Bengal—her very limits as a geographic and imaginary space in the moment of the poem's writing revealed as utterly fungible—is constituted by the demand that she hear, but never respond to, how she affects the poet. The poet throws his voice to conjure her form, but that scene of labor is effaced by her animation. Bengal is made, by voice rather than by hand, an object of poetic speech and of a political imagination that necessarily glances backward into a national ahistoricity. We might call this apostrophic address a poetic intervention that constitutes the poet himself as nation-making, or, to borrow Pound's phrase, nation-singing. Apostrophe simultaneously produces the poet and nation both. Crucially, it does so by displacing the fantasy of the sovereign subject who produces the nation as a vehicle of his own autonomy—a fetishistic function that recalls Tagore's hope that country-making is itself self-making (*swadesh*).

In *Persons and Things*, Johnson describes the work of lyric address as a scene of call and nonresponse in which the poetic address calls witness to that object which is apparently enlivened. "Apostrophe turns toward anything the poet throws his voice to, and in so doing magnetizes a world around his call."[30] In the case of Tagore's anthematic Bengal, apostrophe magnetizes a nation around his call. Although in the year of *Banga-Bhanga* Tagore's *swadeshi* song conjured an intimate and local space, six years thereafter he would sing into being a broader expanse of what might constitute *desh*. In 1911, just before the partition of Bengal was reversed, Tagore wrote "Jana Gana Mana," which would become India's national anthem in 1947. Those lyrics trace the territorial limits of a nation that spans beyond Bengal, enumerating geographical referents of a thing that would be (but for a few cleaved spaces) India as we know it today:

Jana gana mana adhinayaka / Jaya hey Bharata bhagya bidhata! / Panjabo Sindhu Gujarato Maratha / Drabiro Utkala Bango / Bindhyo Himachalo Jamuna Ganga / Uchhalo jalodhi taranga

জনগণমন-অধিনায়ক / জয় হে ভারতভাগ্যবিধাতা! / পঞ্জাব সিন্ধু গুজরাট মরাঠা / দ্রাবিড় উৎকল বঙ্গ / বিন্ধ্য হিমাচল যমুনা গঙ্গা / উচ্ছলজলধিতরঙ্গ

(Thy name rouses the hearts of Punjab, Sind, Gujarat and Maratha, of the Dravida and Orissa and Bengal. It echoes in the hills of the Vindhyas and Himalayas, mingles in the music of Jamuna and Ganges and is chanted by the waves of the Indian Ocean).[31]

Unlike the pastoral body familiar of the Mother Bengal, the ruler (*adhinayak*) of the collective hearts and minds of the people (*jana*, people; *gana*, collective; *mana*, mind or heart) of this lyric is grammatically and spatially at a remove from the poetic voice.[32] *Tobo*, the poetic rather than familiar second-person pronoun of this song, calls forth a national nonpresence. It calls outward, away from the maternal physiognomy, the terrestrial soil, to an imperial sovereign without body.

The ambiguous object of this apostrophe poses something of a hermeneutic quandary, a departure from the pointed direct address of "Amar Sonar Bangla." Who is "the dispenser of India's destiny" to whom the song is directed?

There was, at the time of its writing, speculation that it was written in honor of George V, who was crowned in the summer of 1911. The poetic *thou* adheres in perhaps unsurprising ways to the promise of masculine authority, a sonotropism toward emperor. But the fourth stanza pivots away this expectation, predicating the poetic *thou* as maternal: "*Duhshopno aatonkey rokkha koreley ongkey/ Snehamoye tumi mata* দুঃস্বপ্নে আতঙ্কে রক্ষা করিলে অঙ্কে / স্নেহময়ী তুমি মাতা (You've sheltered us on your lap from nightmare and fear / You, beloved mother)."[33] Here, the poem must do away with the poetic distance of *thou/tobo* and return to the familiar *tumi*. Bangla's ungendered pronouns make room for a national body at once deeply endeared and proximate—the very cradle of nation itself—and magisterial and imposing, bestower of blessings and dispenser of destiny. In a letter to Pulinbehari Sen, Tagore offered a rebuttal of the rumors of this as an imperial song, writing:

> A certain high official in His Majesty's service, who was also my friend, had requested that I write a song of felicitation towards the Emperor. The request simply amazed me. It caused a great stir in my heart. In response to that great mental turmoil, I pronounced the victory in Jana Gana Mana of that Bhagya Vidhata [God of Destiny] of India who has from age after age held steadfast the reins of India's chariot through rise and fall, through the straight path and the curved. That Lord of Destiny, that Reader of the Collective Mind of India, that Perennial Guide, could never be George V, George VI, or any other George.[34]

The song offers an alternate conception of sovereignty, one unenforced by the structures of either nation or empire, one uncontained by the temporal limits of monarchical genealogy. The apostrophic "Lord" works in a very different affective economy than the intimate "Mother" who appears so ephemerally in the complete verse and is excised entirely in the truncated official anthem. That "Lord" makes possible a timeless India and collectivity united by a more expansive power than the nation. It enables a nonsectarian collectivity, a particularly important feature of an anthem intended to unite the various religious groups of India. The ambiguity marks the nation not as an object with onto-geographical priority; instead, the nation is made relational and offered a kind of personhood, if not embodiment.

While the localness of *desh* was poetically transformed into a nation with geospatial boundaries in the moment of *swadeshi* agitation, there was an imagistic shift to accommodate the expanding contours of what might constitute a national body. In the same year that Tagore wrote "Amar Sonar Bangla," his nephew, Abanindranath Tagore, rendered in watercolor an image of a national figure around which a popular imaginary would quickly cohere. The sepia-toned painting depicts a four-armed goddess clad in a saffron sari, holding a string of prayer beads, a fistful of rice grain, a sheath of palm-leaf manuscript, and a white cloth.[35] These are ornaments of an indigenous national imagination, distinctly rendered Hindu. The white conch *shankha* bangles on her wrists and the vermilion daub at the part of her hairline signal Bengali wifehood, as her hands grip artifacts of local tradition and the terms of national feeling. The painting, it turns out, emerged out of a very local body; originally, Abanindranath Tagore had titled it "Banga Mata," a vision of the Bengal cleaved in the year of its painting.[36] The transformation of Banga into Bharat in the painting's title recalibrates the range but not the effect of the image. It also presages the subsequent relocation of imperial capital from Calcutta to Delhi. A synecdochic struggle between Bengal and Bharat reveals itself both geographically and denominatively in the obscured, or perhaps unmarked, move. Put another way, the 1905 partition of Bengal provided the imagistic and poetic material for a broader nationalist sensibility in which particularity and local affect are redeployed in a project of cultural condensation. This split the region into two manufactured new objects, which, in Tagore's own idiom of fetishism, became animated outside and beyond the local aesthetic imagination from which they emerged.

III. Homesickness for the Far Away

For Tagore, to imagine collectivity outside the form of the Nation meant that "man will have to exert all his power of love and clarity of vision to make another great moral adjustment which will comprehend the whole world of men and not merely the fractional groups of nationality."[37] Rather than espousing utter nationlessness, Tagore instead promoted an ethical community in which the spatial markers of the nation-state are replaced by a common spiritual engagement—a greater India where "inner truth" would make possible organic anticolonial ideologies rather than poor mimicries of Western nationalism.[38] The rise of militant nationalisms in Bengal signaled for Tagore the deterioration of both humanist ideals and local affiliations. In 1908, sixteen-year old Khudiram Bose, a member of the Jugantar and thereby somewhat kin to Pritilata Waddedar, was hanged for attempting to assassinate Magistrate Douglas Kingsford. He became a folk hero as stories of him dying with a smile upon his face circulated through the region. Tagore writes, following Bose's hanging, that "[t]hough I may stray from it out of weakness, let me never have the temerity to tell my faith to go to hell and instead come to regard my country as supreme, as a cause worthy of stealing, robbing and doing wrong. Patriotism cannot be our final shelter; my refuge is humanity."[39] This is a sentiment he would repeat throughout his 1916 novel *The Home and the World*, which is examined in chapter 3. Turning away from the unbearable sight of a young man's public martyrdom in his travels across Western Europe, North America, and Japan, Tagore began to articulate most emphatically his vision of an affective, deterritorialized political collectivity. Deeply committed to the local—a fungible, expansive localness not limited by physical geography—Tagore aligned himself with a greater India that was unbound by the geopolitical insistencies of borders. It relied not on the dictates of the state as the organizing principle but rather on *samāj*, an ethico-political collectivity drawn together out of intent and possibility.

In this way, Tagore's muscular critique of nationalism emerged as much out of local upheavals in Bengal after 1905 as out of a more global landscape of war, revolution, and imperialism. Just as he wrote, "Neither the colourless vagueness of cosmopolitanism, nor the fierce self-idolatry of nation-worship is the goal of human history," neither cosmopolitanism nor nationalism can fully account for the affective structures of Tagore's anticolonial imagination.[40] These, however, have been largely the dichotomous terms in which Tagore himself and his work have been read: either in a markedly local register, as the man whose words gave lyric voice to the Bengal he so loved; or, alternately, in a universalist vein, as the urbane and fêted poet whose writing now stands at the canonical center of that ever-capacious category, *world literature*.[41] Contemporary conceptions of world literature, tied in the academy to the currents of global capital, have been of an aesthetic category distinct from the politicized legacy of postcolonial studies.[42] Tagore himself, in a 1907 lecture to the Jatiya Shikhsa Parishad (National Council for Education) that was to be on comparative literature, suggested that the essential nature of literature is universal, of the world (*Visva Sahitya*, world literature). This is not a cosmopolitan claim but rather an ethical one, in which literature opens up the possibility of radical relationality.

I want here to mark the difference between this notion of world literature and that of current institutional shifts toward the global, transnational, and Anglophone. Let us read Tagore's plea for world literature in light of his growing anticolonial and antinationalist sentiment. He writes that,

> [We must] view literature as a temple that the universal man (*vishva-manav*) has built; writers have come from all times and all nations to work as labourers in that project. The plan of the building is not available to us, but whatever is wrong is immediately demolished; every labourer has to use his natural competence to integrate his own composition into the whole and thereby complete the invisible plan. In this is expressed his power and the reason why no one pays him a pittance like an ordinary labourer but respects him like a maestro.

In this way, he makes a claim for literature as the method and the symptom of decolonization.[43] The ethical project of world literature is imbricated in a broader project of self-realization (what Tagore calls sadhana), that which is at the heart of swadeshi. By insisting on the political, postcolonial life of Tagore's vision of world literature, I am following his own richly textured sense of the forms of freedom to which we might aspire in both art and politics.[44]

Tagore shot to global fame when he became the first Asian Nobel laureate in 1913, awarded the prize in literature after the publication of Gitanjali, a collection of devotional poems.[45] In the prize citation, the committee remarked that it had given the prize to Tagore "because of his profoundly sensitive, fresh and beautiful verse, by which, with consummate skill, he has made his poetic thought, expressed in his own English words, a part of the literature of the West."[46] The committee had not felt compelled in the case of any of the previous thirteen laureates to mention the words "English" or the "West" in their citations; the Nobel committee, it would seem, was acutely aware of Tagore's non-Westernness and the fact that Gitanjali was originally written in Bangla. It lauded Tagore for his ability to convey that foreignness in terms comprehensible to the Western literary imagination and implicitly eschewed any suggestion that the translation of the Gitanjali could be attributed to anyone but Tagore, even as the effect of W. B. Yeats's introduction and editing of the text remained a subject of controversy.[47] Indeed, the phrase "expressed in his own English words" would haunt Tagore for the rest of his life, not only on the global stage onto which the prize thrust him but also in his personal relationships, especially with Yeats. Even as a man of the world, having won the Nobel Prize and been knighted, Tagore would remain for his entire life forever in translation.

Yeats's influence on the published English editions of Gitanjali was much debated, by their contemporaries and between Yeats and Tagore themselves. In a letter to Edward Thompson in 1913, Tagore writes:

> The Gitanjali poems are intimately personal to me and the pleasure I have of polishing their English versions is of a different nature [from] that of an author revising his works for publication. Every line of these should be as closely my own as possible though I must labour under the disadvantage of not being born to your language. In such a case I have been guided by my instinct, allowing it to work almost unconsciously without being hindered by more than casual suggestions from outside. I think the method that Yeats followed while editing my book was the right one in selecting those poems that required least alterations and rejecting others in spite of their merits.[48]

Despite these assertions, rumors persisted that Yeats had in fact written Gitanjali—evidence, perhaps, of racist perceptions of the linguistic and literary abilities of an Indian—even one born under the linguistic sing of the British empire. Controversy over authorship aside, the English *Gitanjali* that the Nobel committee read was a markedly different text than its Bangla counterpart. Translation, in this case, was not revision but re-creation, repetition with difference. In the English translation of *Gitanjali*, Tagore produced a new text, one that sought to remain faithful to the original and yet came perilously close to disappointing that bid for fidelity. The translated text is his own, "intimately personal" and yet foreign. Tagore's prescriptive similarity between the two texts—"Every line of these should be as closely my own as possible"—suggests the indissoluble difference between the Bangla and the English, a difference born of both the impossibilities of translation and the liminality of the colonial condition.[49] We might see this in consonance with his abiding anxiety about the translation of feeling and attachment into political maneuver by which the fetish of nationalism emerges. Choosing to translate only those poems that required the fewest alterations to be intelligible to a Western audience, those which emphasized the universal over the particular, Tagore identified certain forms available for consumption and marked others untranslatable. Tagore's enigmatic mediation between the English and Bangla versions of the *Gitanjali*, rather than recommending a populist politics of translation, embraced dexterous modes of concealment. Although some of the most prominent modernist icons of the time sought him out and developed congenial acquaintance with him, they remained unable to access many of the poems of the *Gitanjali* even after it won arguably the most global of literary prizes.

Tagore's mystical foreignness, too, which was seen as distinctly Oriental, was as much a product of the way his supporters in the West wanted to imagine him as a product of his intentional self-fashioning. As a cultural commodity (himself perhaps a fetish object), Tagore's spirituality and its vivid "Easternness" garnered enthusiasm among the community of modernist scholars and writers in which he found himself. At a dinner arranged in Tagore's honor in 1912, William Rothenstein and Yeats "asked Rabindranath to sing 'Bande Mataram', Bengal's nationalist song. He hummed the tune but could not remember more than a few words. Then, in succession, Yeats attempted the Irish anthem, Rhys the Welsh national anthem and Rothenstein 'God Save the King.' Each stumbled. 'What a crew!' said Rothenstein."[50] Tagore's refusal to perform for this group a ritual of the nationalism simultaneously orientalized him—performing the untranslatable kernel of his own Bengaliness for an admiring group of modernists—and distanced him from national politics of Bengal.

Political feeling, for Tagore, was a private affect. The translation of himself as national symbol and of intimate attachment to *desh* into nationalism were objectifications, cleaving away at what Tagore would call a personal relationship to the Bengal he loved. In April of 1918, just before his daughter Bela's death from a protracted illness, Tagore wrote to his close friend Amiya Chakravarty, "The fires of destruction are burning throughout the world. History is to be made anew—at this moment I too have some deeds to do, I can no longer remain here in my little corner."[51] Tagore's personal losses are here sutured to the violence taking place around the world, marking the moment as one of simultaneous destruction and renewal. Writing at the end of World War I and on the heels of the Irish Easter Rebellion of 1916 and the Russian Revolution, Tagore expressed a measure of hope for the cleansing potential of that destruction, the possibility for regeneration. Tagore's desire to leave India at that moment—what he in a letter to Rothenstein just days later called "a homesickness for the far away"— was constituted as an uncanny grief.[52] The fires ablaze in his own home made the call of international tumult appealing in contrast. That destruction might result in some change for the better, whereas the loss of his daughter never could. The *unheimlich* homesickness that drew Tagore away from the site of his own loss figures here as a locally rooted globalism, neither cosmopolitan nor nationalist.

Contours of Tagore's globalism are not a matter simply of travel or engagement but rather of affect. In 1919, stunned by the Jallianwala Bagh Massacre, in which British soldiers opened fire on a group of unarmed pilgrims in Amritsar, Punjab, Tagore renounced his knighthood, a symbolic renunciation also of his global acclaim, of a kind of being in the world. Unable to bear the deaths of his countrymen at the hands of the imperial soldiers and buffeted by his own tragedies in his family, Tagore retreated into himself even as the world continued to seek him out. His decathexis of that life abroad, his repudiation too of that "homesickness for the far away," drew him back to Bengal even as he recognized that the pastoral idyll of the motherland he so loved had also been irreparably altered by the forces of colonial and communal strife.[53] His public debate with Gandhi in the subsequent years carried within it the traces of this ambivalent asylum.

Ultimately, he was no more content to simply be at home than he was to completely immerse himself in the Western literary world. His antinationalist stance alienated him from those around him, including Yeats, with whom he had shared such closeness during the war years. Even the Bengali public that so valorized and (despite his own stance against idolatry) idolized him grew impatient with his refusal to endorse a mainstream nationalism, including the Gandhian project of *satyagraha*. An editorial in the Bangla-language daily *Ananda Bazar Patrika* blasted, "The *charkha* movement has been revealed to the poet's intelligence as a hoax. . . . Only an extraordinary genius can say such an extraordinary thing. The ludicrous opinions of the poet may appeal to those who live in a dream world, but those who are grounded in the soil of this country will feel that poet's useless labours are sad and pitiful."[54] Tagore's rarefied intellect, his stature and status as the poet of Bengal, are here indictments of his political imagination; his is not a vision of the world as it is but a fantasy divorced from the very land he so cherished.

Buffeted by personal and public strife, Tagore turned inward to the university he inaugurated, *Visva-Bharati* at Santiniketan, which he hoped would be the "world centre for the study of humanity."[55] But the promise of universalist pedagogy would also go unrealized, as it never became the global center of knowledge on the scale he had hoped.[56] Able neither to eschew an attachment and commitment to his home, to the Bengal to which he wrote odes, nor to reconcile his humanist values with the chauvinism of nationalism, Tagore instead developed a critique of Gandhi's *satyagraha* movement, suggesting it to be a particularly charismatic and specious form of political imagination.

IV. The Fetish Form

The terms of Tagore and Gandhi's public debate from 1925 to 1930 turned on the possibilities of anticolonial affiliation and community. Central to Tagore's critique of the *charkha* as object of nationalist fetish is a problem of autonomy and attachment that haunts the historical invocations of the fetish more generally. As an isolated object, the *charkha* posed no danger; Tagore himself financed the establishment of a handloom-training center in his *zamindari* of Kushtia in East Bengal during the *swadeshi* movement to support it as an artisanal and indigenous practice. Nor did Tagore object to the analogization of spinning to governance. He writes in 1916:

> Before the Nation came to rule over us we had other governments which were foreign, and these, like all governments, had some element of the machine in them. But the difference between them and the government by the Nation is like the difference between the hand-loom and the power-loom. In the products of the hand-loom the magic of man's living fingers finds its expression, and its hum harmonizes with the music of life. But the power-loom is relentlessly lifeless and accurate and monotonous in its production.[57]

When he cites those foreign governments that operated in harmony with their subjects, Tagore draws not on the image of coarse, irregular weave that would mark the product of the Gandhian handloom but of the product of a prior handloom, for in Bengal in particular "handloomed cotton" has long been synonymous with the ethereal muslin from Dhaka.

Though produced by human hand, *Dhakai* muslin, among the most valued objects of the British and Mughal empires both, from the seventeenth to the nineteenth centuries, has an aura of magic. Its fineness, translucence, and airiness defied the calculus of material to technology. Where *khadi* bears the mark, in its coarse and irregular weave, of the crude and therefore highly reproducible means of production and the apparently unskilled laborer, *Dhakai* muslin appears denuded of its manual origin. The hypernatural names of that muslin—*bafthawa* (woven air), *abrawan* (running water), *shubanam* (evening dew)—suggest that nature alone might produce objects so ethereal. A product of the Mughal court, these fabrics were generically known as *mulmul khas* (imperial cloth). They anointed the wearer and, as Bernard Cohn points out, incorporated him into the body of the Mughal ruler.[58] This form of national fabric, artisanal and luxurious, is precisely that against which the Gandhian *khadi* image was developed. Indeed, Gandhi situated the courtly prestige of muslin as a marker of its incongruity to a newly sovereign national body. Describing how Sarala Devi Chaudhurani, Tagore's niece, eschewed her own *Dhakai* saris for ones made of *khadi*, Gandhi writes, "To me *khaddar* [the Punjabi word for *khadi*] is any day more artistic than the finest Dacca muslin, for its association. *Khaddar* supports today those who were starving. It supports women who have been reclaimed from a life of shame or women who, because they would not go out for work, remained idle and quarreled among themselves for want of occupation. *Khaddar* therefore has a soul about it."[59] The association that warrants *khadi*'s aesthetic value is of labor as the uplift of poor, quarrelsome women. *Khadi*'s soul manifests not in the threads of its weave, transcendent like muslin, but in its transformation of the weaver herself.

Here is the crux of the debate between Gandhi and Tagore about *khadi* and the *charkha*: Gandhi believed in, and indeed premised an entire political program on, the metamorphic force of materiality, of labor, of touch.[60] For Tagore, *charkha* and *khadi* had themselves been transformed into objects other than machine and cloth. As an "emblem of deliverance," the *charkha* threatened, for Tagore, the autonomy it claimed to offer.[61] The "cult of the *charkha*," as Tagore described it in 1925, raised the object to the level of a deity and discursively endowed it with the mystical force beyond the power of any human individual. It gathered around it a worshiping body—a group coalesced by rituals oriented toward a singular object that offered meaning to both its organization and its practices—that eroded individual subjectivity and replaced it with anesthetized and mechanized stupor.

For Tagore, *samāj*, or society, effectively offered a nonstatist alternative to the nation, one in line with his sense that the governing force of any collectivity ought to be spiritual (his is an idiom of the Vedic tradition) rather than material.

Samāj was a collectivity that could travel, that would find its inspiration internally and yet produce itself in a larger world. But *swaraj*, the ideology of self-rule (though its Sanskrit root *sva* points as much to the self-restraint that so marked Gandhi's embodied politics as it does to ideal of independence) advocated by Gandhi and other nationalist figures, was a very different machine indeed. In the Gandhian project, this self-rule is achieved through *satyagraha*. Commonly translated as "passive resistance" or "nonviolence," the word derives from the Sanskrit *satya*, meaning truth, and *agraha*, meaning force or effort. Although Gandhi, in his English writings, used the term *soul-force*, we might usefully consider the double meaning embedded in the prefix *satya*, which refers back to *sat*, meaning pure. The work of *satyagraha*, the process by which self-rule was to be established as well as the ideology by which a new India was to be ruled, is the illumination made possible only by the work of self-purification. This force is not, as so often believed, a lack of violence, but in fact force turned inward. It is suffering as a form of purification.

Despite becoming the shorthand of a mainstream nationalism in India—the freedom movement—*satyagraha* was premised on a conception of sovereignty distinct from the hallmark of liberalism. Ajay Skaria argues in *Unconditional Equality* that it worked in service of freedom that is relinquishment instead of liberation. In fact, unlike both the politics of anticolonial nationalism and the piety of Tagorean spiritualism, Gandhian *satyagraha* did not work toward an object (material or otherwise). Rather, it aimed for the abnegation of the self as its telos. According to Skaria, "Surrender without subordination and freedom without sovereignty, as inseparable as two sides of a coin, strive to accomplish th[e] impossible—the pure gift."[62] At its heart, *satyagraha* is a politics and practice of nonsovereign commitment to an ideal of equality that does not reify autonomy and agency. Skaria's reading restores to *satyagraha* its radical potential, rescues it from co-optation as romantic passivity. We can see in this a model of refusal and resistance that does not authorize limited sovereignty of the individual subject or even imagined national collectivity. Here, the resonance with Tagore's critique of the nation-form and the ideological violence of citizen-subject construction reveals the possibility of an anticolonial politics that does not map itself onto the form erected and upheld by imperiality. This is a vision of the political in which the self and its object cohere, opening up new ground on which to think about what postcoloniality might look like if not channeled through the figure of the individual, rational (masculine) subject and his governing body of the nation. However, within the lifeworld of anticolonial politics in the 1920s, this radical possibility blurred into a barrier between two men who had once been drawn to one another as visionaries.

Tagore saw *swaraj* as a political strategy that privileged the material, in the form of the handloomed cotton woven on the *charkha*, over the spiritual—an overvaluation and fetishization of an object at the expense of the human subject. He writes,

> Our country is the land of rites and ceremonials, so that we have more faith in worshipping the feet of the priest than the Divinity whom he serves. . . . This reliance on outward help is a symptom of slavishness, for no habit can more easily destroy all reliance on self. Only to such a country can come the *charkha* as the emblem of her deliverance and the people dazed into obedience by some specious temptation go on turning their *charkha* in the seclusion of their corners, dreaming all the while that the car of *swaraj* of itself rolls onward in triumphal progress at every turn of their wheel.[63]

The spinning *charkha* wheel can no more produce liberation, Tagore suggests, than it can move a vehicle. Its motion is hypnotic rather than progressive, and its product, too, merely matter, merely thread. Curiously, the *charkha* as a material object of nationalist cathexis works in the same way as the Nation as an abstract object. Like the Nation, the *charkha* transforms subjects into mechanical parts but of a machine itself in disguise: the wheel of the *charkha* is not the wheel of the car of *swaraj* because it gathers no momentum, gains no ground. Instead, the phantom of the machine absorbs the human into its emptiness. The logic of fetishism is reversed, then, materializing men—turning them into matter—as the fetish object is abstracted and idealized.

The mesmeric force of the *charkha* is made possible, for Tagore, by India's (read here: Hindu) already slavish attachment to idol worship and ritual. As a member of the Brahmo Samaj, Tagore had sworn off all forms of idolatry. By extension, to transform something so intimate as one's *desh* to an object of worship, the ceremony of which constituted the ceaseless spinning of thread, was to pervert not only the object of worship but also its supplicant. The Brahmo Samaj, a Hindu reform movement begun by Ram Mohan Roy, laid out in its 1830 Trust Deed several precepts that vividly echo Tagore's critique of the nation-form and *charkha* as object of its manifestation. One of the ten tenets of faith enjoins that "followers shall not adore any created thing, thinking it to be the Supreme One; no object animate or inanimate that has been or is or shall hereafter become or be recognized as an object of worship; and no sacrifice offering oblation of any kind or thing shall ever be permitted."[64] The language of delusory sacrifice and false worship that Tagore turns toward anticolonial nationalism emerged from within a particularly privileged and elite world of scholars, activists, and social leaders committed to excising what they perceived as the malignancy of socio-religious atavism around them in Bengal.[65] When Tagore correlates the slavishness of idol worship to the practice of spinning on the *charkha*, he points to what he sees as a broader failure of political and spiritual realization.

The atomic sovereign self of liberal political theory is not the building block of a Tagorean political imagination. That coherent, limited, nucleated individual is birthed by the Enlightenment. It is crafted to bear the weight of narratives of rationality and agency that undergird the nation-state and empire both. Tagore's critique of nationalism is thus at the same time an objection to its elemental concept of the self. That self is an illusion. He writes in *Sadhana* (1914):

> This is the reason why the separateness of our self has been described by our philosophers as *maya*, as an illusion, because it has no intrinsic reality of its own. . . . Imagine some savage who, in his ignorance, thinks that it is the paper of the banknote that has the magic, by virtue of which the possessor of it gets all he wants. He piles up the papers, hides them, handles them in all sorts of absurd ways, and then at last, wearied by his efforts, comes to the sad conclusion that they are absolutely worthless, only fit to be thrown into the fire. But the wise man knows that the paper of the banknote is all *maya*, and until it is given up to the bank it is futile.[66]

The savage, from whom Tagore borrows the fetish in his critique of nationalism, misapprehends the value of the material object before him as metaphor for the misapprehension of human materiality as real. Rather, the true self is like the banknote rendered ash. In its disintegration from its appreciable form, it is loosed from the limitations of its contours and thus liberated. Exchange value destroyed, the autonomous self and the banknote both now operate in other economies altogether. For the banknote, this is in its reorganicization as detritus and waste, its reappearance as something of actual value in flame and warmth to the savage whose handling of those mere trinkets offered no comfort. For the self, it is in its union with God. The limit of the sovereign self is destroyed into the body of the limitless form of the divine. An attachment to materiality—individual self, banknote, spinning wheel—is a fruitless grasping, clinging to that which can be touched in lieu of that which essentially and unrelentingly pervades.

While in Japan delivering the lectures that would come to constitute the latter essay in *Nationalism*, Tagore foreshadowed the fine weave of autonomy and aesthetics that composes the terms of his opposition to the *charkha*. In "Nationalism in Japan," he writes,

> But the danger lies in this, that organized ugliness storms the mind and carries the day by its mass, by its aggressive persistence, by its power of mockery

directed against the deeper sentiments of the heart. Its harsh obtrusiveness makes it forcibly visible to us, overcoming our senses, and we bring to its altar sacrifices, as does a savage to the fetich which appears powerful because of its hideousness. Therefore its rivalry to things that are modest and profound and have the subtle delicacy of life is to be dreaded.[67]

The reappearance of the fetish in this moment points to Tagore's abiding concern that the Nation and its associated fetish objects erode aesthetic sensibilities and possibilities. Themselves unbeautiful, these fetish objects imperil the ability of the supplicant, rendered by way of analogy and pathology savage, to appreciate the production and discernment of art, which Tagore sees as the aspiration of humanity. The joint language of beauty and civilization does not operate here in the developmental logic of modernity, but rather recalls an orientalist fantasy of Japanese aesthetic practice as liberatory. Tagore constructs an economy of aesthetic valuation, of individual dread and collective slavishness. The organized ugliness of the modern nation produces the savage, the desensitized, the enthralled. There can be neither beauty nor love in the Nation because the object to which the savage offers his sacrifice exercises its force by its hideousness, the terror and loathing it conjures. Describing the power of the fetish as causally determined by its hideousness mimics the colonial language of grotesquery and abjection used by Europeans. The fetish is powerful precisely because it invites and simultaneously repels the hand and the gaze.

When Freud in 1927 wrote of the fetishist who reveres and desires a shine on the nose, "the *glance* at the nose," he engaged the sensorial effect that critically underpins the fetishistic relation: the inexorable interdependency between touch and sight.[68] Glance is at once fleeting contact and reflected light. It is that which slips away, either from sight or from touch. Freud's fetishist "endows" that which is visible to, but insignificant for, others with the power to arouse in him both desire and fear.[69] Although the materiality of the fetish object—its thingness—first may suggest tactility, its power lies in its visibility. The very vocabulary of Freudian fetishism is that of sight; the fetish is a material referent of a moment just prior to the traumatic visual encounter with the mother's lack of penis: not hideous, in fact, but recuperative. Rather than destroy the fantasy of the maternal phallus, the fetish preserves the beloved possibility imperiled by the sight now repressed. This preservative function of the fetish echoes Freud's description from a decade earlier in "Mourning and Melancholia" of the identificatory process by which the violence of normal mourning is suspended: "So by taking flight into the ego love escapes annihilation."[70] We might then say of the fetishist that, by glancing at the nose, love escapes annihilation. The love of the mother, the child's identification with her as primary love object, is rescued by the sight of a substitute that insistently reaches toward but never touches the moment of repressed trauma—preservative synesthesia. Fetishism's ocular orientation is deceptive because the fetishistic attachment persists precisely because it evades the scrutiny of others. It appears valueless to everyone but its supplicant, its apparent pathology shielded by its mundane quality. Nonetheless, for Freud, like Tagore, that object indicates not an emancipatory affect but servitude to a moment of horror and disgust.

Freudian psychoanalysis offers a sensorial sedimentation of sight, touch, and recoil. His oeuvre is replete with images that invite and then repel and are manifestly or latently feminine. Freud's reading of Medusa, her hair acoil with serpents framing a face from which one cannot look away and, having looked, must cease to do anything else, finds like-minded company in Tagore's abhorrence of Kali worship, the local tradition from which an anticolonial political imagination drew such force in Bengal in the early twentieth century. Indeed, Tagore's repudiation of Kali worship dovetailed directly with his critique of an emergent nationalist discourse. Kali, like Medusa, is beautiful in part because she is awful. Rather than bearing a fossilizing mane of snakes, she wears on her neck a garland of decapitated heads of men she has slain. They are evidence of prior violence and a promise of the retributive horror to come. Still, she is venerated as the awesome force of feminine *shakti*, maternal benevolence turned righteous violence. Tagore writes in 1915, "It is absurd to imagine that you must create slaves in order to make your ideas free. I would rather see them perish than leave them in charge of slaves to be nourished. There are men who make idols of their ideas, and sacrifice humanity before their altars. But in my worship of the idea I am no worshipper of Kali."[71] So much comes to be sacrificed at the altar of the lesser gods of an idolatrous nationalism. This is language to which Tagore returns repeatedly in his critique of nationalism more broadly and particularly of Gandhian practices. Kali's cult, grotesque and beguiling, to which many of his Bengali compatriots belonged, offered for Tagore the most suspect and treacherous model for a strategy of sovereignty.

Fetish as an incorrect object in the Freudian and Tagorean idioms is both an obstacle and inadequate substitution for a more productive and satisfying cathexis, the kind of attachment that produces conditions of conceiving freedom. Freud and Tagore, in this pathology of paraphilic objects and misdirected sacrifices, orient their suspicion toward the work of the fetish in its original conception as the impossible translation of magical object into exchangeable commodity. The failure on the part of European traders to witness the magic of the fetish object did not in any way limit its force. Cast outside the frame of exchange and recognition, the fetish is free to work on its supplicants and skeptics both. Only when approached by way of the fantasy of rational choices and transferable accounts does it appear not to function. But the fetish is not intended to be exchangeable. It does not travel between economies of magic and meaning. It operates anti-imperially, evading by way of its mundane or dreadful external form the disciplining of its nonmaterial life. Unloved, unvalued, the fetish object—whether trifle or laboriously manufactured piece—refuses the affinity to a universal aesthetics, a well-trained sensibility. Let us then say that the fetish object is one of fugitive possibility. It refuses to be made into an object worthy of the violence of being ruled. Herein we glimpse how handloomed cotton and the simple machine upon which its thread is produced, beyond the Gandhian project of purifying repetitive labor, gesture toward an anti-imperial imagination of a different order, one which does not repudiate Tagore's insistence on labors of spiritual emancipation but rather weaves the mundane and material into the transcendental.

V. Labors of Untouchability

Tagore writes of the temptation of what he calls Gandhi's "*charkha* cult" to describe his ultimate resistance, turning to a language of reason and calculation. "How often have any personal feelings of regard strongly urged me to accept at Mahatma Gandhi's hands my enlistment as a follower of the *charkha* cult, but as often have my reason and conscience restrained me, lest I should be a party to the raising of the *charkha* to a higher place than is its due."[72] Tagore's aversion to the *charkha* cult is causal, in that the reason and conscience that come to supersede his personal affection for Gandhi are those that make possible a personal affect. They have not been chased from his body by cultish attachment. However, the body rests on unstable ground; the hands of Gandhi extended toward Tagore are the hands that spin the *charkha*; the body of Gandhi is the body around which the followers gather. Gandhi's body, publicly displayed and politically mobilized, insistently corporeal, sits in opposition to Tagore's rarefied reason and feeling, the dematerialized presence of his conscience. To have acceded even to his own attachment and loyalty to Gandhi, the touch of his outstretched hands, would have been to participate in an economy of overvaluation, to give more than what "is its due."

In fact, the public fissure between Gandhi and Tagore turned in part on the visibility and materiality of the political body. Tagore carefully cultivated a public persona that, while spectacular in its performance of a kind of ancient or timeless monasticism, remained insistently cerebral and disembodied. His politics too were oriented around the cultivation of a humanist ethos, unbound by the limits of state sovereignty. The public and private relationships between Tagore and Gandhi curiously codeveloped by way of an augmentative naming that made one man pure intellect and the other gross body. The honorific by which Gandhi is now so commonly called that people often mistake it for his first name—Mahatma—means the highest realization of the soul, a name given him by Tagore. Gandhi in turn called Tagore "Gurudev," meaning great teacher, coded spiritually. One might expect Gandhi's denominative to suggest a kind of sloughing of the mortal, material form to render him intangible to the outstretched hands not only of his intimate Tagore, but also to the bodies that walked alongside him, to the bodies that crowded train platforms to reach through compartment windows to touch his skin and his draped *khadi dhoti*. Instead, the Mahatma became, as Shahid Amin astutely points out, an avatar. He was divinity brought close, availed to the human touch by way of *darshan*, the gift of seeing the holy.[73] Rather than shuttle the body of Gandhi away from access by the masses, the honorific exalts and ritualizes the embodied relationship between the Mahatma and his disciples.

The *Mahabharata* posits as exemplar of the relationship between teacher and pupil Eklavya's offering of the thumb of his right hand to Drona. Having had Drona refuse to teach him archery, the low-born Eklavya builds a shrine to the absent master and teaches himself to shoot. Once Drona discovers his exceptional skill, Eklavya—in the manner of self-effacing humility prescribed by the text—credits him, the empty form of his statue, as his guru. Unable to allow such a rival for Arjuna, the great and noble-born archer, to exist, Drona asks Eklavya for *gurudakshina*, a payment in acknowledgment of and gratitude for his teachings, in the form of the digit on his hand that allows him to grip and release the bow. Exchange of thumb for blessing, statue for teacher, leans upon the physical distance and necessary untouchability between master and pupil. While Tagore, "Gurudev," demands from no one the amputation of a digit, his determined distance and mediated disembodiment cite a tradition of obligation and mastery without physical intimacy. Indeed, Tagore expressed deep discomfort even with the custom of *pranam*, the taking of dust from someone's feet and touching it to one's own forehead in a show of respect. That glancing touch of stooped obeisance before him chafed against his insistence on a horizontal structure of spiritual kinship. He writes, in a postscript to C. F. Andrews's secretary W. W. Pearson in 1920:

> You have gotten into some conventional habits such as calling me "Gurudeb" [sic] and making *pranam* to me. Drop them. For I know there are occasions when they hurt you and for that very reason are truly discourteous to me. You know I never care to assume the role of a prophet or a teacher; I do not

claim homage from my fellow-beings, I only need love and sympathy and I am merely a poet and nothing else.[74]

Tagore protests against a variety of affectations congealed in the acts of hailing and bowing, but fundamentally expresses resistance to being manufactured into a kind of intersubjective intellect or spirit. The poet, unlike the prophet or teacher, needs not touch but feeling.

Gandhi, in contrast, embodied not just the nationalist cause but the very terms of its political strategy. His emaciated form, toiling away at the handloom during his many hunger strikes, grew in ideological prominence inversely to its corporeal degeneration. Gandhi's spectacular suffering, the performative ritual of his physical self-abnegation, conjured the abstract body of the Nation that suffers under colonial rule. It is a bodily politics that depended on Gandhi's exceptionality, his capacity and willingness for self-sacrifice singular in its visibility and its effectiveness. Thus, the cult that Tagore lambasted worshipped two figures: the *charkha* and the man whose hands drive its wheel. Gandhi's body and the touch of his hands come to be symbolically fused to the *charkha* itself, a shared materiality between man and machine, their touch producing material itself. *Satyagraha* as political project also depended on the ability of the masses gathered around him to access him, to touch him and in turn be touched by him. Indeed, Gandhi responded to what he saw as the hypermasculine violence of colonialism with an explicit self-effeminacy, an identification with the mother in motherland. Engaging icons of women's household labor as the mode of self-determination, Gandhi produced an idiom of gendered protest and marked women as fit vehicles of political protest. The hunger strike, which would become the spectacular sign of *satyagraha*, recoded an intimate act of domestic protest as political. Referencing the familiar sign of women's refusal to eat as resistance to familial conflict—disengaging from the object over which they had definitive control—passive aggression is transformed into militant passivity. In effecting this transformation, Gandhi also invoked a gendered economy wherein forms of feeling associated with the maternal body—sympathy, love, nurture, sorrow—are markers of the political, simultaneously rupturing and reinforcing the dualism of masculine rationality and feminine affect. This made way for a new political subject whose material labor would be as useful to the cause of independence as her affective labor.

The material produced by that labor, handloomed cotton, is also figured as an object of national futurity. Rebecca Brown argues that photographs of Gandhi with the *charkha*, particularly the Margaret Bourke-White image (figure 2.1) made so iconic on the pages of *Life* in 1946, carefully position the body of Gandhi and the machine of the loom so that he does not actually spin or

Figure 2.1 Mohandas K. Gandhi, January 1, 1946.
Photo by Margaret Bourke-White. The LIFE Picture Collection, Los Angeles, CA.

even touch the loom, but rather sits proximate, "reinforc[ing] the iconic nature both of the spinning wheel and of Gandhi-as-object: they sit near each other, sharing the space but not interacting."⁷⁵ The unmoving and untouched loom in Bourke-White's photograph stands in the foreground, its spokes and filaments leading the eye to the photo's emphasis, which is Gandhi's body in the background of the image, one hand gripping letters, the other wrapped around his own foot. He touches himself twice over in the image—hand to foot and hand to correspondence in his name but touches neither machine nor thread.

The shared space of the photograph constructs loom and Gandhi as related but distinct. The *charkha* defers the image's focus to Gandhi, man supersed-ing even the imagistic force of the machine. "At 76," the caption reads, "the Mahatma is in good physical condition. He weighs 110 pounds, but is not so frail as he looks."⁷⁶ Image and text collude to focalize and buttress the body of Gandhi as the unflagging engine of the anticolonial project, whose seemingly ener-vated form belies his ability to labor, at the loom and for the nation to come. In the public, international imagination curated by *Life*, M. K. Gandhi the man is manufactured as the Mahatma who is machine, his human form central to the charismatic possibility of Indian anticolonialism. *In that issue of Life*, a sartorially colonial Muhammad Ali Jinnah, head of the Muslim League and future first Governor General of Pakistan, in a crisp Savile Row suit and natty spats, or even Jawaharlal Nehru, who would become the first Prime Minister of India, in his sumptuous high-thread-count *khadi* vest and "Gandhi cap," appear starkly foreign in their garb to the nations they will come to lead. Gandhi's nearly bare body, the *dhoti* and occasional shawl a truncated smear of white across his form, stands in for indigenous postcoloniality, untouched by either fabric or fashion of the foreign body to be disgorged from that nation-space to come.

Thus, it is not what Gandhi wears but the ways in which his body exceeds that cloth that is supposed to be its determinant. The frailty of his physical body in the Bourke-White images is strategically figured as superhuman. It leans, touches, relies upon the vigorous embodiment of those around him, but is their ideological prerequisite. One photograph is captioned: "Surrounded by his adoring disciples, Gandhi goes walking each morning. Here he is supported by his granddaughter Sita (left) and daughter-in-law Abha (right)."[77] Those adoring disciples do not gaze lovingly at him or reach toward his form. Instead, he reaches out to stretch his arms across the shoulders of two young women, eyes downcast. They are his crutches, bearing the weight of his emaciated frame across their bodies rendered at once modest and maternal. That he leans upon women rather than any of the far more robust-looking men in the crowd suggests Gandhi's conscious self-identification with the body of reproductive femininity but also, perhaps more cynically, that the nationalist project itself made women catalysts but not actors. Gandhi's proximity to young women proposes a relationship between purified nationalist imagination and the promise of futurity in which Gandhi is architect but not actor. Curiously, this reveals how the production of Gandhi as symbol trafficked in the spectacular subjugation of his body as a thing disappearing and disappearable. Part of the promise of this logic was that the Gandhian project could outlast and surpass the limits of his mortal form because his personality—the other cult with which an Indian public might be said to be enthralled and of which Tagore was deeply suspicious—did not require such corporeality. The materialist bent of *satyagraha*, the very material of its production, already had absorbed into its thread the traces of the immaterial force of Gandhi.

Handloomed cotton produced on the *charkha* was valued because of its contact with the human hand, as the very artifact of tactility itself touchable. Gandhi writes in 1929,

> When the other parts of the globe did not know the use of cotton, India set the aesthetic standard and supplied the rich nations of the West with the finest

fabrics in a variety of colours. And the present evolution of *khadi* shows that slowly but surely it is day by day reaching the aesthetically inclined people. After all, true art can only be expressed not through inanimate power-driven machinery designed for mass production but only through the delicate living touch of the hands of men and women.[78]

Aesthetic value here is inexorably sutured to the touch of hands. It is precisely this effort and contact between body and fiber that also renders the act of spinning and the object of its labor, cloth, an object of desire and of regeneration. The value of *khadi* reveals itself by way of its touch. Unlike machine-made cotton, *khadi*'s texture—coarser, with broader warp and weft, and insistently irregular—does not resemble the skin on which it lies, its artifice exposed by its manufacture. This texturally conspicuous and tactilely aggressive *khadi* of the twentieth century may have sought to distinguish itself from its contemporary milled cotton, but in so doing revealed a larger historical discontinuity between it and a prior indigenous handloom: the muslin of which thirty yards was said to weigh less than three ounces and fit neatly inside a matchbox, which was loomed at an unthinkable 1,800-thread count.[79] This fabric, far more diaphanous than the skin upon which it rested, is only in the most base ways recalled by even the nineteenth-century power-loomed cotton that came to utterly eradicate it both in the market and as a technology.

If Manchesterian cotton comes to be the doppelgänger of human skin to which Gandhian *khadi* refuses to aspire, *Dhakai* muslin is the spectral trace that haunts the possibility of what fabric might be. It has, by way of deep material colonial violence, come to be lost as a practice and technology. William Bolts wrote in 1772 of the financial policies of the British East India Company in Bengal, whereby weavers caught in impossible structures of remittance "have been treated also with such injustice that instances have been known of their cutting off their thumbs to prevent their being forced to wind silk."[80] The grotesque mimicry of Eklavya's *gurudakshina* is here a sign not of gratitude or veneration but of colonial servitude and debt. There is no more fabric of woven air in East Bengal, but its promise and the lingering traces of its touch on flesh haunt the fibers of cotton spun relentlessly in the *satyagrahan* imagination, as does perhaps the stain of amputation's blood. Handlooming as indigenous practice comes to be expressed as rudimentary rather than artisanal by way of the future anterior tense: it will have been that *khadi* is some imperfect replica of skin and cotton both, its tendons severed from the touch of muslin thread.

Although Gandhi insisted in his writing that *khadi*'s value as an aesthetic and commercial object was growing in the early part of the twentieth century, it proved itself a difficult commodity because of the market forces that followed cotton away from Dhaka to Manchester. The very aspect that rendered it valuable to the *satyagrahan* imagination—traces of human labor upon it—is what Tagore saw as its basic incongruity with the needs of the poor whom it also sought to uplift. The expense of *khadi*, in both energy and money, rendered it impossibly expensive for the rural poor, and its appreciable irregularity—a marker of its technological primitivism—rendered it undesirable for an urban elite whose sartorial affinities were with a global and imperial economy. Today, of course, *khadi* has secured a niche market for itself in India as vouchsafe of bourgeois nationalist taste—particularly in its curation by retailers like Fabindia which traffic in upscale indigenous handicrafts for domestic and foreign consumers. That old muslin, woven by Muslim artisans, derived its value in the global marketplace from the ways its material characteristics seemed to exceed and eclipse the technology and labor that produced it. This is to say that the body of the artisan did not render the cloth valuable; rather, its value obscured the body that labored in its production. Unlike Gandhian *khadi* and the contemporary artisan handloomed fabric that I will examine in later chapters, the desirability of *Dhakai* muslin was displaced from the manufacturing body of the weaver. The gossamer thread needed to weave *Dhakai* muslin is a far cry from the coarse yarn band produced under the conditions of the box *charkha* and the imperial dictates of cotton crop. Those who chose to wear *khadi* in the nationalist period appeared to do so in defiance of the terms of beauty, comfort, and work normalized by coloniality and its widely limned global interdependencies of economy and aesthetics.

For Gandhi, the labor of spinning cloth by hand at once drew together a national body—in an Andersonian logic—through the shared work, shared touch of hand to fabric, regardless of class or caste; it produced a common uniform to lay upon that national body; and it performed a ritualistic purification, a self-purification by touch. This is the vision of a project that does not require the other's touch (here rendered colonial, machinic). It holds onto the ideal of autonomy as a kind of self-touching. This cotton cloth, unadulterated by contact with either foreign hands or foreign machine, is itself pure. The purification by touch works simultaneously: the tactile labor of fabric production and the contact between that pure material and the purified body. Masturbatory labor, a deep—if unspoken—pleasure derived and fulfilled by one's own hand and touch, turns the conventional nationalist narrative inward, away from the reproductive motherland whose feminine body is the condition of future possibility and toward the touch between hand and cloth, the skin of the self to manufactured skin. Tagore's resistance to the materialist project of *satyagraha* spinning rooted itself in an insistence that objects could not facilitate spiritual liberation. For him, it was not a return to a pure state in the form of a pure material, an unalienated labor and unadulterated object. Rather the emphasis on touch, self-touching, produced man as machine—even, and perhaps particularly, a machine as simple as the spinning wheel.

The *charkha* as fetish object worked not in the service of man, as a proper machine ought, but rather worked on man himself. Tagore writes, "It was a great day for man when he discovered the wheel. The facility of motion thus given to inert matter enabled it to bear much of man's burden. This was but right, for Matter is the true *shudra*; while with his dual existence in body and mind, Man is a *dwija*. Man has to maintain both his inner and outer life."[81] The *shudra*, or untouchable, is mere matter. It is the twice-born *dwija* who is human, possessing both intellect and body, mind and matter. Drawing on the Hindu caste vocabulary of untouchability, Tagore responds explicitly to Gandhi's other project of social uplift, that of caste reform. The *charkha*, instead of offering the liberation from caste and colonial oppression that Gandhi insisted on, deprives the spinner of that which makes him human, the development of that "inner life" which Tagore sees as real freedom, beyond simply that of politics. The political life of soul-force is a bodily one in which the body produces that which it might bear. On the one hand, we have the onanistic logic of *khadi* production, purifying by touch and by effort (where the *agraha* is most pronounced); on the other hand, we have Gandhi's project of untouchable uplift which aims to break though the interdiction against touching—skin upon skin, skin upon human waste.

Tagore reinforces his argument for the cultivation of intellectual, aesthetic, and spiritual capabilities as the practice of true liberation by inverting the logic of caste interdiction. Matter, that which is sensorially apprehendable, is untouchable. Tagore's own affiliation with the Brahmo Samaj shared with Gandhi a critique of caste untouchability but, unlike Gandhi, who sought reform and uplift, believed in its complete dismantling. Untouchability in that context is proof positive of the perils of Hindu ritual fixation. However, in Bengal the question of untouchability fundamentally skewed not toward Hindu caste but across religion. Touch prohibition, the bodies cast beyond the stretch of hand, posed a much more intimate problem for observant Hindus and their Muslim neighbors. Indeed, we can trace hints of this concern back to the 1871 census, which collated population density with religious identification and gave rise to the image of teeming bodies leaning into one another yet unable to touch. To be rendered untouchable is to be forced outside the bounds of what constitutes not only the human but also the bearable. The untouchable exceeds the primary conditions of somatosensoriality. Skin is not, in the state of untouchability, the possibility of encounter but the very promise of its absence. In a place as dense with bodies as Bengal, the interdiction against touch is a particularly acutely-repeated social violence.

Brahmanic regulations against contamination are so rigid that even the shadow of a forbidden body, whether lower caste, Muslim, or widow, can be polluting. But how, in such very close proximity, can we imagine an uncontaminated life in the world? The very fabric of social life already bears the trace and touch of those bodies marked taboo, formed and maintained by labors of the untouchable. Though a variety of occupations have historically been the purview of out- and low-caste Hindus, in East Bengal, whose labor force was demographically majority Muslim, weaving and laundry were two that were most crucial to the economic and political landscape and to the proximate dangers of worn cloth.

Bengal weavers—officially all men, though women's work was essential to production—who spun gossamer thread and loomed the diaphanous *Dhakai* muslin were Muslims, clothing Mughal court and Hindu *zamindari* alike. Particulate remnants of bodies whose shadow was verboten resided in the most intimate surfaces. Though some Hindu scripture suggests that artisanal craft is untainted, that "the hand of the artisan is always pure," the communion between fabric and flesh cleaves the language of purification and containment.[82] No encounter of such proximity is untainted, nor can it be sanitized. In the pantheon of laborers whose bodies were beyond the pale of touch but whose touch was necessary, laundry or *dhobi* workers sit at the other end of the spectrum. Weaving as highly venerated artisanal craft produces its own economic language of exoneration, as its object is one of beauty, of value, of use. *Dhobi* work is the vilified but essential labor that maintains and makes possible the material life of cloth. C. A. Bayly writes of the exchange relationships of the *dhobi*, "In the case of cloth, the act of washing temporarily brought it into society once again as a kind of commodity. But it was not a neutral process; the very act of washing transferred the accumulated dirt and pollution of the individual cloth to the *dhobi* who cleansed it, with ambiguous consequences for his social standing."[83] We might expand this transferral in the other direction to point out how the process of cleaning cloth is the perfect vehicle for the transfer of traces of the *dhobi* body into the fabric. The porosity of cloth promises that it retains and absorbs the skin and sweat of laboring hands that caress it and ensures that it carries back those residues to rest on the skin of its nominal master. For this reason, in the nineteenth century the technical term used in English by tailors for wrinkles caught in cloth was "memories": proof that it had been inhabited by human form, that cloth preserves its encounter with the body.[84]

Khadi, meant to lie upon the Indian body, forms an indigenous common skin. Rather than a border or limit of the self vis-à-vis another, skin, the largest organ of the human body, is that which makes possible the encounter that undoes the apparent sovereignty of the individual body. Skin is an accumulation of the insides of an individual and the traces of the world outside. Cloth as second skin is thus the ideal vehicle not of touch turned inward in purification but of refusal of the possibility of purification. Cloth catches in its very fiber the traces of that which it touches, which in turn comes to constitute it. The fantasy of spinning as purifying self-touch is in fact the reification of intimate contact. Thread and cloth manufactured on the *charkha* are contaminated, in ways that foreign cloth of the power loom are not, with the immutable and ineradicable traces of a prior contact with the human form. Embedded in the warp and weft of cloth is the possibility of a radical alterity that comes of contingent contact between bodies making world and nation anew. We might, then, think of cloth as the vehicle of an intimate politics in which freedom comes not from ideological expulsion and repudiation but from fleshly accumulation and propinquity.

The Gandhian project of *satyagraha*, as it was deployed with a distinctly nationalist telos, promised labor toward sovereignty, toward liberation. Tagore, unable to abide the fixation on the object—cotton and spinning wheel both—sang of an imaginative force of will that undid the very division between the self and the other, creating in its place a new form of being together in the world, one in which the individual did not constitute the terms of the polity. Neither man as theorist of postcolonial possibility conceived of an encounter between body and material in which the certainty of contamination, the guarantee of never being free of the traces of another, might constitute the terms of liberation itself. Nonetheless, their visions of freedom for India emerged out of a shared sense, if not a shared vocabulary, of deep local intimacy and abiding affiliation. Each critiqued the imperial fantasy of autonomous subjectivity, the presumption of an individualized and isolated self as political actor. Indeed, they reached toward one another, toward a shared sense of the future of an independence to come.

When we speak of the fetish—commodity, sexual, or ritual—we dismiss it as threat and pathology. We pronounce it with dread. The fetish is an object with too much and too obscure power. What we perceive as its form is not its content, is not its effect. It threatens, by its touch, our autonomy and the limits of our personhood. Peter Stallybrass writes that "what was demonized in the concept of the fetish was the possibility that history, memory, and desire might be materialized in objects that are touched and loved and worn."[85] The fetish refuses the distinction and distance between object and abstract value; it does not operate by materializing and memorializing the mundane, but garners value and power by the traces it preserves of that which affects us most. It materializes in objects that which should ordinarily exceed mere objecthood. The transformative magic of the fetish works on the most powerful of abstractions, capturing something of their essence in the body of that which is ordinary. As an object of cathexis, the fetish demands more than ought to be its due.

For these reasons, the fetish is often described as a kind of ghost, a memory function that by the same stroke erases the scene of labor that produces it—whether the means of production or the child's sight of its mother's genitalia. As a technology of preservation, the fetish retains the traces of the past, of that in the past which has touched us and the touch of which we still long for, in a material vehicle. Michael Taussig writes,

> Like the Nation-State, the fetish has a deep investment in death—the death of the consciousness of the signifying function. Death endows both the fetish and the Nation-State with life, a spectral life, to be sure. The fetish absorbs into itself that which it represents, erasing all traces of the represented. A clean job. In Karl Marx's formulation of the fetishism of commodities, it is clear that the powerful phantasmagoric character of the commodity as fetish depends on the fact that the socioeconomic relations of production and distribution are erased from awareness, imploded into the made-object to become its phantom life-force.[86]

The fetish appears through what it erases. The ghost is not just a trace of a past life or an expired way of being; it is the ghost of an erasure, a sacrifice. The fetish outlives the form of life it has erased, but goes on to live (undead, Taussig seems to suggest) a new one that is tactile, regular, ordinary.

What, it forces us to ask, are the everyday lives of these ghosts? What kind of presence do they have in our material, human lives? Because, whether the abstract form of the nation or the woven form of a garment, they could not be more intimate, immediate, and quotidian. While for Tagore the fetish objects of the Nation and the *charkha*, those mechanizing and dehumanizing phantom objects of overcathexis promise no true liberation, their touch nonetheless lingers. It is touch that orients the fetish object toward the future, that suggests the possibility of a life of the material and accumulative. As an object endowed with the trace of a past just prior to traumatic erasure, the fetish becomes a bridge over the moment of loss, from attachment and affection to repair. In the anticolonial imagination, fetish objects of national possibility perform an apotropaic magic, even as that future moment toward which they gesture remains imperceptible. Ultimately, what Tagore objected to in the fetish is that it demands sacrifices that undermine the sovereignty of the individual as sentient and sentimental. If we dislodge the fantasy of that subject, forever in the condition of becoming under imperial governance, we see how a liberatory politics of nonsovereignty accrues upon the body of anticolonial thought and possibility.

The fetish, a material object of colonial life, is a technology of historicism, making visible socially embedded histories of violence and valuation.

Masculinist conceptions of the fetish and the self—Freud, Marx, Tagore—each resist the nonsovereign force of the fetish, the ways it threatens to undo the limits of the individual subject. The fetish fails, by design, in its apparent promise to erase the trace of what came before, but in so doing announces the possibility that true freedom comes in the form of the embedded and inerasable traces of that which preceded it and the remnants of which abide. In the fetish form, histories and future possibilities of worlds made out of touch—human contact and trace remains—are caught. It is therefore perhaps fitting that Tagore, who so resisted the material draw of the object, would come to be the voice of postcolonial India and Bangladesh both—singing them into nation— while Gandhi, who so hoped that the labors of touch might make for a more just and free nation, would give form to postcolonial India's flag. At the center of that tricolor *khadi* fabric, in between the strip of saffron and green, is the image of the *charkha*. India, as it will come to pass, will have been made into a nation of spinsters.

3

Oceanic Feelings

I n honor of Sigmund Freud's seventy-fifth birthday in May 1931, the Indian
Psychoanalytical Society (IPS) commissioned the fabrication of a nine-
inch-tall ivory statuette. This, along with two copies of an address to Freud
in Sanskrit printed on silk, three copies printed on paper, and three copies of the
meeting's proceedings, was sent by Girindrasekhar Bose, the first psychoanalyst
in India and then-president of the IPS. Bose and Freud had been carrying on a
sporadic correspondence for nearly a decade. Upon receiving it, Freud wrote
immediately to Bose: "The statuette is charming. I gave it the place of honor
on my desk. As long as I can enjoy life it will recall to my mind the progress of
psychoanalysis, the proud conquest it has made in foreign countries and the
kind of feelings for me it has aroused in some of my contemporaries at least."[1]
In its "place of honor," next to Freud's collection of antique figures from Greece,
China, and Egypt, the ivory Vishnu served as a referent not just of the dissem-
ination of psychoanalysis outside of Europe, but also of the networks of affiliation that travel made possible. Like its neighbors on Freud's desk, the Vishnu
was at once artifact and art object, a relic of an ancient age, though it was itself
newly made.

Of the mystical quality of commodities, Marx writes that "the existence of
the things *qua* commodities, and the value relation between the products of
labor which stamps them as commodities, have absolutely no connection with
their physical properties and with the material relations arising therefrom.
There it is a definite social relation between men, that assumes, in their eyes,
the fantastic form of a relation between things."[2] Human relationality is that
which is abstracted, despite that it is by the material touch of human body to

inanimate object that the commodity is manufactured. In the case of that statuette, the enigma of its force, the "ideas embodied in" it, is an abstraction into metaphor that comes at the expense of the social world—the world of capitalist empire—that psychoanalysis and colonialism both would disappear. Against effacement, then, I suggest we commit to the sensuous materiality of Vishnu, to rematerializing the extant presence of human labor, the touch of the human body, by which it circulated in networks of imperial interdependency. In so doing, we come to see not just a history of contact between the geographically far-flung sites of colonial Bengal and Vienna but a far more intimate and embedded convergence between the discourses of psychoanalysis, colonialism, and anticolonial nationalism than Freud's hope of "proud conquest" could ever convey.

Uneven and unequal, the encounter between psychoanalysis and colonialism in Bengal stretched beyond the clinic into a literary imagination and onto the public stage of politics. For Freud's students in Bengal, who were subjects of the British Raj, psychoanalytic paradigms of interiority, subjectivity, rationality, and development were not simply hallmarks of their clinical practices but the ideological vocabulary of their time. Started in 1922, only three years after the establishment of the British Psychoanalytic Society, the IPS came into being while the fitness of the Indian to rule himself was foremost on the minds of colonial subjects and governmental bodies alike. Freudian psychoanalytic thought did not simply offer a diagnostic of native underdevelopment, as historians of science have argued it did in parts of North and Sub-Saharan Africa, but in the hands of Bengali and British practitioners came to offer a malleable and capacious hermeneutic of the psychic life of coloniality.[3]

Revisions of its central paradigms—Oedipal desire and developmental sexuality—by members of the IPS to privilege the primacy of the mother at the height of anticolonial nationalist movements in Bengal point to a new bilingualism in which the conditions of political possibility were articulated in the patois of a psychological subjectivity. Analysts training themselves and each other in the early days of the IPS took up the internationalist, universalizing project of psychoanalysis in good faith—and in their practice found that this science which has so frequently faced claims of provinciality and rigidity spoke directly to the demands of a postcolonial imagination. By this I do not mean to claim a liberationist ethos for the colonial life of psychoanalysis. But we would be wrong to ignore how the IPS as an institutional structure and psychoanalysis as an extant vocabulary in Bengal participated, perhaps unintentionally, in the creation of a relational, political self at the threshold of analytic knowability. That material reality has been abstracted, much like the Vishnu on Freud's desk. The colonial context, in fact, authorizes a retelling of the possibility of psychoanalysis itself at the autochthonous tension between manifest and metaphoric.

For this reason, this chapter follows three concentric abstractions, central to psychoanalytic theory, taken up in Bengal: from the Oedipal structure which, when armed with a new mythopoetics, reveals political potential of maternal power; to the interpretative mechanisms by which desire is understood when it is materialized rather than metaphorized; and finally to the phenomenon of the feeling at the mists of psychoanalysis, beyond the drive, which upends the limits of knowability. Critical to each of these interventions is that which is also critical to Bengal writ large at this moment: the figure, symbolic and real, of woman and of female desire.

In chapter 2, we saw how the *swadeshi* movement begun in Bengal, from which the Gandhian freedom movement would draw its strategies of economic noncooperation, made cloth central to the nation and, by the same stroke, made the labor of women essential to the project of conceiving postcolonial futures. There, Tagore's critique of anticolonial nationalisms turned on the dialectical abstraction of material objects of use ("emblems of deliverance") and materialization of intimate ideals (*swadesh*, a country of one's own making) into mundane objects (the "fetish" of the Nation).[4] The coincidence—the shared time and space—of *swadeshi* nationalism and Freudian psychoanalysis in Bengal offers us a new way to read one of the most famous novels of the postcolonial canon in which the desire of a woman is commonly understood as a metaphor for the violences of nation-becoming. Set in a village in rural East Bengal following the 1905 partition, Tagore's 1916 *The Home and the World* follows Bimala, the young wife of the Bengali landlord, or *zamindar*, Nikhil, as she is drawn out of the feminine space of the *zenana* (which literally means "of women," and is the inner apartment of the home in which the women live) out into the larger world, represented both by Nikhil's friend Sandip, with whom she begins an affair, and the *swadeshi* movement of which Sandip is a charismatic leader. Evoking Tagore's own *zamindari* in Kushtia, East Bengal, the village in the novel stands in for all of Bengal and India as well as, paradoxically, that which must be left behind in the progression to independence. In figuring the novel's young housewife Bimala as a site of transgressive national and erotic attachment—her insistent self-identification as the embodiment of Bengal—Tagore reimagines Freud's "dark continent" of female sexuality not as the limit of psychological knowledge but as an alluring threat to the homosocial rationalism of political modernity in the guise of nationalism. *The Home and the World*, so often read as a paradigmatic novel about the emergence of postcolonial political modernity, is in fact a manifesto for the subsumption of self into radical identification and cathexis as the basis of politics.

At the convergence of these two discourses' shared disavowal—that of the woman as desiring subject—and their shared traffic in the trope of metaphor,

Bimala appears a startling alternative to what Tagore saw as the mechanizing and abstracting autopoesis of anticolonial nationalism. I mean *desire* here in the broadest psychoanalytic sense as that which, through the force of libidinal cathexis, constitutes the terms of its own recognition.[5] Desire, Jean Laplanche and Jean-Bertrand Pontalis note, does not fully overlap with Freud's use of *Wunsch* (wish), the impulse to re-experience a foundational satisfaction that correlates both to an internal landscape and the search for that memory-trace in the world, and through Jacques Lacan "appears in the rift which separates need and demand; it cannot be reduced to need since, by definition, it is not a relation to a real object independent of the subject but a relation to phantasy; nor can it be reduced to demand, in that it seeks to impose itself without taking the language or the unconscious of the other into account, and insists upon absolute recognition from him."[6] So, when I argue that the desire of Bengali women disrupts the psychopolitical language of the *swadeshi* period, I do so to point to how, in delimiting recognizable objects and orientations, colonial psychoanalysis and anticolonial nationalism simultaneously produce the terms of their own counterimaginations.

Dipesh Chakrabarty writes that during the Bengal Renaissance, "[n]ationalist thought was premised precisely on the assumed universality of the project of becoming individuals, on the assumption that 'individual rights' and abstract 'equality' were universals that could find home anywhere in the world, that one could be both an 'Indian' and a 'citizen' at the same time."[7] The individual subject under governance was rarely, and then only contestedly, ever conceived of as other than the modern, bourgeois, male subject—in Bengal normatively marked as upper-caste, educated, and Hindu. Bimala's profound identification with a nonhuman ideal that she refuses to abstract demonstrates the artifice and construction of two ideologies unable to speak to the majority of the people of the nation to which they claim access and, in so doing, ruptures the metaphoric economy of nationalism. Of course, feeling and rationality have long been unequally distributed along the axis of gender, and I do not here seek to recuperate a "natural" affinity between women and embodied feeling. Rather, Bimala's socio-somatic experience of being *affected* by the idea and the materiality of the nation is *affect* in its most basic sense. Her very capacity to be is transformed by the encounter with Bengal, her personal nation. Bimala demands, like the Vishnu on Freud's desk, a mode of reading that will not transform the body into abstraction, and so this chapter, in its commitment to sensuous materialism, takes Bimala's feeling of oneness with Bengal as an experiential reality. In a curious reinscription of Tagore's own commitment to *swadesh*, which we saw in chapter 2 imagined nation-making to be a self-making practice, Bimala expresses what I call an *oceanic political feeling*, an indissoluble bond between nation and subject in which political liberation is inextricable from cathexis. Against the tide of nationalist calls to placidly embody the virtues of the motherland for which men will fight, Bimala makes herself the motherland who will not be a mother, imagining anew the feminine labor of *swadeshi*.

I. Adjustment of Oedipus

The 1905 partition gave rise not just to a powerful form of anticolonial nationalism in its model of *swadeshi*, but also to the idea of a motherland in a particular form. It gave birth, we might say, to a feminine and maternal Bengal. While *swadeshi* slogans made the body and the name of the mother objects of political resistance and the symbolic litmus test of freedom—in freeing the mother, her sons will have freed themselves—she was also the object of philosophical interest for clinicians and lay members of the Indian Psychoanalytical Society. Theirs was, of course, an almost singularly male community and most of their patients middle-class, Bengali men like themselves, though the IPS hoped to attend to a broad need for psychological care. Bose writes, in a 1923 account of the IPS to *The International Journal of Psychoanalysis*, that "in India, psycho-analytic investigations were very likely to yield very fruitful results both from the scientific and therapeutic standpoints. The mental cases practically went untreated and the immense variety of social and religious customs, some of them of extremely ancient origin and others comparatively recent with the people existing in different grades of civilization from the most primitive to the most modern, offered an immense field for the psycho-analyst."[8] Cases that hitherto had been outside of the European purview of psychoanalysis could, Bose hoped, expand and enrich its therapeutic methods and theoretical terms.

I will not offer here an exhaustive account of the IPS, its members, or their contributions to psychoanalysis: Christiane Hartnack and Ashis Nandy (among others) have already done an admirable job thereof. Rather, I turn briefly to the work of three early members whose encounters with Freud evince some of the rich entanglements that bound psychoanalysis to colonial Bengal.[9] Postcolonial examinations of the IPS have categorically cast Bose as the hero of this narrative encounter, the empire analyzing back as it were. Indeed, Bose seemed to take seriously the "international" character of the International Psychoanalytical Association and its journal as a mandate to use his own case studies to revise psychoanalytic paradigms, reimagining the scope of what its claim to universality might imply. He may have been a student of Freudian thought but Bose did not imagine himself a provincial acolyte; a shared vocabulary and commitment to the Freudian principle of "remembering, repeating, and working through" constituted a genealogical intimacy for Bose, a claim to inheritance and fidelity that sanctioned even his revision of the most central Freudian concepts. It is this enthusiastic appropriation of psychoanalytic thought, translated across language, across space, and across "culture" that drew Freud's attention to Bose and maintained their largely genial correspondence over almost twenty years. Writing to Bose's literary agent in support of his monograph *The Concept of Repression*, Freud expressed his "great and pleasant surprise that the first book on a psychoanalytic subject which came to us from that part of the world (India) should display so good a knowledge of psychoanalysis, so deep an insight into its difficulties and so much of deep-going original thought. . . . Dr. Bose is aiming at a philosophical evolution and elaboration of our crude, practical concepts and I can only wish psychoanalysis should soon reach up to the level to which he strives to raise it."[10] Bose's philosophical evolution of psychoanalysis would be one committed to preserving its fundamental promise of the territorial conquest of the ego over the domain of the id, while effecting a perspectival shift in what it as an analytic could bear.

Freud's primary interlocutor in the group, Bose was the first Indian to be trained in psychoanalysis, and his revisions of the Oedipus complex for the Bengali subject reimagined its constitutive terms, providing a historio-cultural rationale for what he saw as the fundamental differences between the Western subject of Freud's analysis and his own Bengali *bhadralok* (literally meaning "respectable person," and signifying upper-class, upper-caste) patients. Trained as a physician at Calcutta Medical College, Bose's interest in hypnosis and mesmeric magic drew him to psychology and to Freud. In his 1929 "The Genesis and Adjustment of the Oedipus Wish," Bose argued that the castration threat so prominent in Freud's case studies is rarely witnessed in male Indian patients because of a desire on the part of the Indian man to *be* a woman, because the Bengali mother stands in for both mother and father. He writes:

> With the advent of ego-identity in the father-mother relationship, sympathy for the woman from the standpoint of the man develops and the Oedipus complex is adjusted. The Oedipus wish thus does not succumb to the threat of castration but to the ability to put the ego in the position of the mother in the father-mother relationship and to the ability to defy the father and to castrate him, i.e., to make him into a woman.[11]

Sympathy, the condition of shared feeling, is a mechanism of identification by which the Bengali son aligns himself, and feels himself in common, with the mother. He therefore does not need to repudiate his desire for her; rather, in order to love the father, the son gives him the gift of castration. Bose's claim that Indian men have a primary identification with, and desire to be, the mother staunchly refuses the Freudian developmental narrative whereby the male child's affection for the mother transforms into castration-fear at the realization of sexual difference, making the father the primary love object and object of identification. In Bose's theory, the ability of the male child to castrate the father supplants the fear of castration in Freud's archetypal male child and makes possible an alternate conception of the place of Oedipal desire and a different account of its pervasiveness in Indian literary and cultural discourses.[12] However, like Freud's complex, Bose's theory of the Indian boy's "desire to be female" still spares little room for female desire.[13] Like the language of nationalism that avows identification with and desire for the feminine motherland as a conduit of a particularly indigenous masculinity, Bose's theory of the psyche traffics in the metaphoric rather than material function of women's bodies and desires. It fails to imagine the relationship between women and the feminine ideal and how the cathexes of women who might wish to be women condition the social fabric. While for Bose the nature of attachment to the mother and maternal ideal was a therapeutic concern, the psychic arrangement of his theory had, in fact, a governmental life. The significance of maternal primacy, in the form of mother-goddess worship in Bengal, resonated beyond the confines of the psychoanalytic settee, well into the sphere of nationalist politics.

Though most of the members of the IPS were Indian practitioners, two of its early affiliates were British officers in the Army. Owen Berkeley-Hill, staff physician, came to India in 1907 and in 1919 became the first Superintendent of the Ranchi European Lunatic Asylum, the only facility in British India to cater exclusively to Europeans. Berkeley-Hill had, by the time the IPS was established, struck up a friendly if limited acquaintance with both Freud and Ernest Jones through his father, a noted British physician. Claud Dangar (C. D.) Daly started out as a captain and, between tours in India, underwent analysis with Freud, Jones, and Sandor Ferenczi in turn. Unlike Bose and the other Indian analysts who sought to mold the contours of psychoanalytic thought to their environment, Berkeley-Hill and Daly translated their psychoanalytic training into a mode of cultural analysis, seeking to understand through the normative paradigms of Freudian thought the behavior and lifeworlds of Indian colonial subjects. Psychoanalysis, in this way, came to be a governmental epistemology. Their "findings" may not have directly influenced colonial policy, but as administrative bodies within that structure and with the purported scientific expertise of psychoanalysis at their back, Berkeley-Hill and Daly relayed a totalizing psychic theory of Bengalis to the Raj and to a larger psychoanalytic reading public. In addition to *Samiksa*, the journal of the IPS, members of the IPS submitted essays to *The International Journal of Psychoanalysis*, circulating the analytic insights of colonizer and colonized among a global community.

Daly is mentioned periodically in correspondence between Freud and Jones as a figure of annoyance and sometimes ridicule, as having "foolish character traits, conceit and inferiority, slightly hysterical, rather an ass but easy to manage,"[14] being "a bore and an ass,"[15] and tedious. None of the polite equivocations Freud offered Bose were directed at Daly, though Freud cited his essay on menstruation and Bengali women, "One Aspect of the Mother Complex," in a brief footnote in *Civilization and Its Discontents*. Despite his marginalization as a thinker by his analysts, Daly persisted in his attempts to understand the psychology of the Indians around him, particularly in the period of growing anticolonial violence, which included Pritilata Waddedar's attack on the Pahartali Club that was examined in chapter 1. Daly writes in his 1930 article, "The Psychology of Revolutionary Tendencies," that "the Indian revolutionary identifies himself with Kali, the mother who successfully rebels against and humiliates the father, and condones her criminal tendencies. For the mother, like himself, was tyrannized over by the father during his childhood. We may here suspect also a deep-seated castration wish against the primal mother, possibly having its final source in the oral sphere."[16] Daly cites accounts of secret societies like Jugantar and the Dhaka Anushilan Samiti swearing oaths in front of images of Kali with a pistol in one hand and the *Bhagavad-Gita* in the other, as well as the popular image from Bankimcandra Chatterji's 1882 novel *Anandamath* in which initiates vow to give up their domestic and familial attachments in front of a Kali statue that stands in for India: "The Motherland is our only mother. Our Motherland is higher than heaven. Mother India is our mother. We have no other mother. We have no father, no brother, no sister, no wife, no children, no home, no hearth—all we have is the Mother."[17] Daly's account makes Kali the powerful figure of rebellion; the nominal son identifies with the powerful warrior mother-goddess who vanquishes the father. Hers is a self-retributive violence; this mother waits for no son to fight on her behalf. Instead, he follows her example against the father, though unable to fully overcome his own violent wish toward her.

For Daly, an entrenched conflation of nation with mother, as it incited nationalist fervor, could only be symptomatic of a pathological attachment and inchoate psychological development. He goes on to write that "[i]n the Bengali, we have a psychology that differs considerably from the European, its equivalent with us being found only in pathological cases. *They are a race who fail in their rebellion against the father, and as a result of this failure adopt a feminine role with feminine character traits.*"[18] In this model of rebellious desire, the father figure's centrality is at once reified and eschewed. The un-deposed father is never identified, even while Hindu subservience to the British authorities is corroborated in the language of father worship. Having repressed his aggressive instincts after failed rebellion against the patriarchal figure of Freud's primal horde, the Bengali survives by way of self-feminization.[19] In order to properly Oedipalize and develop, then, Bengalis were in need of an appropriate paternal figure through whom disavowal of the mother-goddess/land could begin. "It is only by a deep study of the psychology and needs of the Indian peoples, and the application of the knowledge obtained by psychological research, that the British Government can hope to continue to rule them to their best advantage in the present, and perhaps guide them to final liberation from their psychological fixations in the future."[20] Gender training, supported by paternalistic administration, figures a state of suspended animation where rebellion hovers on the horizon as threat and aspiration. Benevolent colonial administration was in this way directed toward affective care. The goal of liberation was then not political—as the nationalist rebels misrecognized it to be—but psychodynamic.

Daly, whom Freud concluded had "got[ten] down to the deepest layer of his deposits and grasped his passive attitude to his father, that is the *wish* to be castrated," spent nearly twenty years among a people who, according to himself and Bose, shared with him this essential wish.[21] They remained for him objects of analytic and administrative curiosity but were kept, in both his phylogenetic imagination and diagnostic sensibility, afar. Owen Berkeley-Hill, Daly's British compatriot in the IPS, in contrast, married an Indian woman and, as administrator of the Ranchi Asylum, committed to understanding not just the sociological characteristics of Indians but also the effects of intimate contact between them and the British. His collected writings, which include essays on femininity and anal eroticism in Hindus and a speculative inquiry into the prophet Mohammad's psychosexual development, were banned in Bengal for fear that they would incite communal riots.[22] Freud worried less about the political backlash than the possibility that this reflected poorly on psychoanalysis in the eyes of the British authorities, even as he admitted that Berkeley-Hill's work was "interesting enough for publication, although it shows that he can do no more than apply what he has got out of his reading."[23]

Freud's response to his interlocutors in Bengal—aside from a few brief expressions of enthusiasm for Bose's work—was markedly tepid and rendered their contributions to psychoanalytic thought marginal. It may have been the quality of their analysis; or it may have been the vast geographical distance that gaped between Bengal and Vienna; or it may have been that the sociopsychological lifeworld of their work in which culture and politics adhered to an undisguised attachment to and identification with the mother exceeded the limits of his psychoanalytic theory and view of the world. Even then, though, Freud remained curiously unwilling or unable to eschew the adjustments to core psychoanalytic concepts raised by Bose and his colleagues. He wrote to Bose in 1933 that though he found Bose's theory of the opposite wish "flat," "I am not ready to stand up for my own objections. I am still bewildered and undecided."[24] Maybe this tells us more about Freud's own hesitation to double down on the universalist bent of psychoanalysis than about his skepticism regarding Bose's work. Indeed, in his final letter to Bose in 1937, Freud seemed to remind them both that "psychoanalysis is as yet imperfect and in many points still uncertain."[25] It may be that the "proud conquest" of psychoanalysis that the Vishnu statuette recalled to Freud when it was placed at the center of his desk in Vienna and then London signified also the incomplete and impossible translation of Freud's own ambivalent father-worship in the land of mother goddesses.

II. Of Mother Goddesses and Motherlands

Even before the advent of the study of psychoanalysis in India, the Raj inaugurated its rule over Indian subjects by way of what Ashis Nandy has described as "the homology between sexual and political dominance" and "the homology between childhood and the state of being colonized"—the Oedipalization of colonial subjects.[26] A political language of maternal intimacy was itself an extant vocabulary to be deployed in nationalist discourse. As the imperial imagination constructed Indian, but especially Bengali, male effeminacy as pathological, underdeveloped, and homosexual, anticolonial discourse contrapuntally produced *Bharat* and *Banga Mata* (Mother India and Mother Bengal) as a distillation of the relationship between mothers and sons. *Swadeshi*'s anthem, the call and response of its gathered bodies, named the object of its desire not in the cartographic or environmental terms of Tagore's *swadeshi* songs that would go on to be the national anthems of Bangladesh and India, but in the name of its most intimate object: *mata*. Bankimcandra Chatterji's "Bande Mataram (Hail Mother)" was the song of a nationalism constituted by the mother. The intimate relationship between woman and nation has commonly been figured in terms of exemplarity: the image of *Bharat/Banga Mata* derives from the women who populate the imaginative space of the nation, who by resemblance vouchsafe an ideal that will be catalyzed into ideological action. But if we invert this correspondence, we begin to see how the symbolic object coerces gendered labor into being. The romanticized image of the spectacularly maternal Bengali woman that was so important to the *swadeshi* movement and broader nationalisms thereafter comes into legibility as a political concept in the enforced absence of women who cannot and will not aspire to it.

Prior to its bifurcation, Bengal connoted a shared linguistic tradition with diverse, and deeply localized, cultural and political worlds. When it was made, by the hand of colonial governance, into two separate regions, Bengal became an organizing political principle. Alongside Tagore's lyrical rendering of its bucolic abundance, Bengal was produced by *swadeshi* discourse as expansive rural homeland and Hindu nation both. The nationalist discourse that was Hinduized during the nineteenth-century Bengal Renaissance and catalyzed by the 1905 partition traced its roots deep into a history of worship of maternal Hindu deities such as Durga and Kali. "Bande Mataram" roused *swadeshi* followers into the service of an embattled but fierce motherland, its origins as a hymn to the nation as Durga haunting its every articulation. Bankimcandra Chatterji's *Anandamath*, in which the song first appears, allegorizes British imperial violence through the 1771 Sannyasi Rebellion, in the midst of the shift from Mughal to British East India Company administration. In *Anandamath*, both Muslims and the British are figured as foreign rulers, reinscribing an authentic Hindu national identity.[27] The projection of Bengal onto India thus enables the translation of India into Hindu, the language of the motherland imprinted with the shadow of the mother goddess. It suggests that the sons of that land are also the devotees of that deity, demanding a population loyal to both nation and religious ideology.

Though the historiography of the region, and of India more broadly, has focused on political formations that yoked themselves to the battle cry of "Bande Mataram," that discourse as much as the partition itself gave rise to rich alternative political imaginations, not least of which were those tapped into by the emergence of the Muslim League in 1906, which in the region laid the foundation for the terms of Bangladeshi independence nearly a century later. It was, in part, the marginalization of other voices, the exclusion of other Bengali bodies, from *swadeshi* nationalism that drove Tagore's repudiation of it. In a concern that we see repeated in *The Home and the World*, Tagore recognized that the creation of East Bengal as a Muslim land that also provided poetic and material resources for a Hindu nationalist politics in West Bengal was untenable. Bengali nationalism could not in the same breath declare East Bengal to be the ancestral (indeed, maternal) homeland and disavow the presence of the laboring bodies that populated it as foreign.

The translation of goddess worship into Hindu nationalist iconography was mediated by a structure of political hierarchy in which the stakes of this iconographic conversion were not limited to an anticolonial aim alone. Partha Chatterjee writes:

As with all hegemonic forms of exercising dominance, this patriarchy combined coercive authority with the subtle force of persuasion. *This was expressed most generally in the inverted ideological form of the relation of power between the sexes: the adulation of woman as goddess or as mother.... This spirituality did not, as we have seen, impede the chances of the woman moving out of the physical confines of the home; on the contrary, it facilitated it, making it possible for her to go into the world under conditions that would not threaten her femininity. In fact, the image of woman as goddess or mother served to erase her sexuality in the world outside the home.*[28]

The idealization of woman as goddess in nationalist discourse allowed for a coterminous desexualization of domestically incorporable women and delineation of restrictive standards of behavior. Good women—those who might fit the mantle of mother or goddess—embodied the pure and spiritual nation. By transforming these good women into mothers and goddesses, toward whom sexual desire was proscribed, nationalist discourse sought to desexualize the space of anticolonial politics. This moreover participated in the ideological project of remasculinizing the Bengali male nationalist. Mrinalini Sinha identifies how the notion of the Bengali *babu* was constructed as a perverted form of masculinity within a discourse of conquest and empire mobilized by British authorities.[29] The construction of the effeminate Bengali in popular culture developed alongside the British cult of masculinity in the nineteenth century, as part of a project to reify and bolster the image of the virile Empire.[30]

Empire, in order to function efficiently, needed the discursive project of identifying Bengal, and its residents, as at once dutiful and innocuous. Thomas Macaulay, in his biography of Lord Robert Clive (1840), referred to Bengalis as

the race by whom this rich tract was peopled, enervated by a soft climate and accustomed to peaceful employments, [who] bore the same relation to other Asiatics which the Asiatics generally bear to the bold and energetic children of Europe. The Castilians have a proverb, that in Valencia the earth is water and the men women; and the description is at least equally applicable to the vast plain of the Lower Ganges.... There never, perhaps, existed a people so thoroughly fitted by nature and by habit for a foreign yoke.[31]

Unlike the martial races of Northern India who struggled against the vicissitudes of climate and conquest, Bengalis are figured as an effeminate race made weak by abundance and peace, in relation not only to the British but also to the other races and peoples in India. The popular colonial construction of the effeminate Bengali man turned on the familialization of affect, in which an overweening attachment to the mother, whether human or national symbol, derails masculinist progress. In this way, gender—femininity in particular—became the crucible of political subjectivity. Jasodhara Bagchi argues, "The colonial intelligentsia had to accommodate the public image of the foreign rulers into an unmistakable indigenous sign that would mark a colonial Bengali man as distinct from the alien rulers. 'Bengali mother' was such a sign, and its force increased as the experience of colonialism began to make itself felt and Bengali society entered its nationalist phase."[32] A genealogical nation emerged through the political remasculinization of its population.

Swami Vivekananda, Hindu revivalist monk and disciple of the Bengali mystic Sri Ramakrishna, traveled across India, the United States, and Europe to lecture on Hinduism and India between 1893 and 1902, articulating a pointed response to the colonial conflation of the Bengali/Hindu and effeminacy. Unlike his guru, who embodied and embraced an ecstatic union with femininity and forms of the feminine divine, Vivekananda sutured a message of physical, spiritual, and cultural strength to a nationalist call. He closes an essay entitled "Modern India" (1899), which critiques the economic imperialism of Britain through the analogy of Hindu caste, with the prayer, "O Thou Lord of Gauri, O Thou Mother of the Universe, vouchsafe manliness unto me! O Thou Mother of Strength, take away my weakness, take away my unmanliness, and make me a Man!"[33] Though an appeal to both Shiva and Jagat Janini, the name for the feminine aspect known as the Mother of the Universe, Vivekananda's prayer for masculine potency is a markedly feminine appeal. He does not directly name Shiva, whose aniconic abstract symbol is the phallic *lingam*, but refers to him by his conjugal designation as Lord of Gauri, the manifestation of Durga. Even the most masculine aspect of the Hindu iconography is, in this case, a proxy for the feminine. It is to them, this female-dominated parental divinity, that Vivekananda makes his plea for manliness. It is the mother who can make him a man, who can make him strong, not in her service but through her aspect itself.

Catalogued under the imagistic constitution of nation was the fertile, reproductive woman who was also associated with verdant images of the pastoral, the destitute and exploited mother whose one-time abundance had been defiled, and the invincible mother goddess who would slay all in her path to protect her children.[34] The image of an abject mother who is also an omnipotent goddess conditioned a masculinist nationalism wherein virile men both protect a weak and infirm mother and ascribe to the goddess a seemingly limitless religious energy that fuels their nationalist project—responding explicitly to their emasculation in the imperial imagination. At the same time, this economy of maternal metaphor guarded itself against the incursion of women as political actors.

"Bande Mataram," the first two verses of which are written in a Sanskritized Bangla that would render it particularly mobile across the Indo-Sanskritic regions of north and east India, prostrates a particularly male singer before a mother named in turn Lord, Durga, and Lakshmi. *Bande*, commonly understood as "to worship or adore," was translated by Sri Aurobindo Ghose as "I bow to thee."[35] (Ghose, once a member of the Anushilan Samiti from which Jugantar and the IRA to which Pritilata Waddedar belonged would emerge, was arrested in connection to the Alipore Bomb case; he later renounced this public political life to become a spiritual teacher.) But *bande*, from *bandan* বন্দন which is "song of praise," shares a telling root with *bandi* বন্দি which is "captive." To be in praise of, to exalt and worship, is to be bound by and held in the sway of that which is exalted and worshipped: the abdication of one's freedom in abiding attachment. This is a remarkable sentiment prowling the echoes of a cry of resistance and a demand for freedom. Striking too is the double life of the phrase's other word. *Mataram*, the Sanskritized form of *mata*, is first and foremost the proper noun of Mother. That *mata* in Bangla is also a verb meaning "to go mad, to be intoxicated, to be thrown into excess" hints, homophonically if not semiotically, at the affective potency of the noun form. In song, "Bande Mataram," its call and response, is in fact an articulation of being bound in ecstatic, even excessive, love. The anthem of *swadeshi* announces a political imagination in which the goal is nonsovereignty itself.

Bhupendranath Dutta, the younger brother of Swami Vivekananda, member of Jugantar and first editor of its eponymous newspaper, wrote that his fellow revolutionaries during the *swadeshi* movement were *deshpagal*, crazy for the nation.[36] Their willingness to die for the abstract concept of the nation, he contended, was understandable through an intimate substitution of birth (small) mother for national (large) mother.[37] Himself a member of a secret society that demanded blood oaths and committed itself to violence as a means of resistance, Dutta conceived of *desh* as an object with the power to infect and affect. We might revise his psychological diagnosis into *deshmata*—the intoxication of *desh*, which is itself a system of symbolic substitutions. *Pagal* names a condition of madness decidedly singular, noncommunicable, and etiologically self-directed. *Mata's* double valence parses what appears as the excess of nationalist feeling, through a displacement whereby attachment to the human form of the mother is oriented toward an object endowed with characteristics that recall her in the shared word of mother and madness. *Mata* creates a communion of bodies under its sign, the contagion (the Latin *contagio* a variant of *tangere*, from which we get touch and contingency both) of its affective force.

This affective power, translated by way of myth into political practice, testified to a psychosocial commitment to the figure of femininity as world-making. Seven years into their correspondence, Bose sent Freud a copy of his Oedipus essay, along with a collection of other writing. Freud replies,

I have read all of your papers, the popular ones as well as the more important scientific ones and I am impatient to see them published in books as you promise.

You directed my attention to the Oedipus Wish especially and you were right in doing so. It made a great impression on me. In fact I am not convinced by your arguments. Your theory of the opposite wish appears to me to stress rather a formal element than a dynamic factor. I still think you underrate the efficiency of the castration fear. It is interesting to note that the only mistake I could discover in your popular essays relates to the same points. There you say that Oedipus kills himself after blinding which he never did. In the scientific paper you give the story correctly. On the other side I never denied the connection of the castration wish with the wish to be a female nor that of the castration fear with the horror of becoming a female. In my 'Passing of the Oed. Complex', I tried to introduce a new metapsychological possibility of destroying a complex by robbing it of its cathectic charge which is led into other channels besides the other idea of repressing it while its cathexis is left undiminished.

But I confess I am by no means more convinced of the validity of my own assumptions. We have not yet seen through this intricate Oedipus matter.[38]

Having called the feature of the Oedipal wish "universal," Freud resists Bose's "adjustment" even as he admits to not being fully compelled by his own account.[39] The "great impression" is the fingerprint of skepticism, apparently inspiring Freud to search out potential weaknesses and potential errors in Bose's account. He is willing to ignore what appears to be Bose's failure at cultural fluency: in misrelating the myth in the essay, Bose reveals to Freud his citational distance from it. But that there may be other myths of Oedipus seems more than Freud is able to warrant.

Asserting that "the castration threat is not the essential factor in Oedipus adjustment" in his Bengali patients, Bose delinked the relationship between sexual development and the primacy of the father as an object of desire, effectively intervening in the abiding colonial homology.[40] In a letter to Freud discussing his modifications to the Oedipal theory, Bose writes, "The Oedipus mother is very often a combined parental image and this is a fact of great importance. I have reasons to believe that much of the motivation of the 'maternal deity' is traceable to this source."[41] Like Freud's Oedipus complex, which finds its narrative logic in the Greek myth, Bose's reconceptualization turns to the place of the maternal deity in Bengali cultural imagination—translating myth into symptom. Where an Abrahamic patrilineality formed the spine of Freud's clinical, philosophical, and intimate practices, the local maternal deities who could, with their clay forms, be touched and seen were the parental images around which Bose's conception of psychic life orbited. But despite the profusion of mother goddesses, the IPS did not send Freud a sculptural representation of any of those deities so significant and prolific in Bengal—not Kali, not Durga. Instead, they chose Vishnu.

III. Vishnu Manifest

The ivory figurine appears elliptically throughout American poet Hilda Doolittle's (H.D.'s) *Tribute to Freud* (1956). In her first encounter with it, she describes the statuette on the crowded desk in detail, wondering if its centrality in the organization of Freud's other statues was "a place of honor," as Freud had promised Bose; an indication of its precedence; or a product of aesthetic preference. Of the object itself, she writes, "Though I realized the beautiful quality and design of the ivory, I was seeing it rather abstractly; the subject itself did not especially appeal to me."[42] The Vishnu appears dematerialized; its latent content partially obscures its manifest presence, "the extreme beauty of this carved Indian ivory which compelled [her], yet repelled [her], at the same time."[43] Indeed, its referential and symbolic force, for H.D. and for Freud when he first received it, determines its value. It is significant because of what it points to, whether conquest or repressed memory, but its physical form carries within and upon it a material history afforded barely a glance.

In the space of Freud's office (figure 3.1), the Vishnu is an object of interpretative possibility. The modes of its inquiry, H.D. suggests, are multiple but nonetheless insistently refer to something other than the thing itself:

> Did he want to find out how I would react to certain ideas embodied in these little statues, or how deeply I felt the dynamic *idea* still implicit in spite of the fact that ages or aeons of time had flown over many of them? Or did he mean simply to imply that he wanted to share his treasures with me, those tangible shapes before us that yet suggested the intangible and vastly more fascinating treasures of his own mind?[44]

Objects on Freud's desk embody—that is, give form and stability to—ideas, which move and change and thrive. However, that metaphorization of objects, figured as speaking otherwise about "intangible and vastly more fascinating treasures" elsewhere, works at the expense of the thing itself. But what might the object itself have to tell us? As a souvenir (from the French word, of course,

Figure 3.1 Sigmund Freud's ivory Vishnu statuette.
Courtesy of the Freud Museum, London.

for memory) of the encounter between psychoanalysis and colonial Bengal, the statuette bears a history on its form that cannot simply be dispelled into abstraction. If we return the body of the statuette to itself, rematerialize the statue and restore to it its surface, and refuse its transformation from thing to idea—holding in abeyance the psychoanalytic impulse to mine obscured content from an object that, when emptied of that symbolic meaning, is discarded as a shell—something of the mystical and mundane character of this art object and commodity makes itself known. That is, the Vishnu, installed in the office of a man for whom the fetish is a preservative technology by which a beloved and necessary fantasy of maternal endowment persists in the face of its material absence, might be a "token of triumph" over the effacement of the social relations and labor by which it came into being.[45]

When the Indian Psychoanalytic Society conceived of a gift to send Freud, they in fact could scarcely have chosen a more appropriate symbolic object than the figure of Vishnu. An aspect of the supreme in the Hindu *trimurti* system, Vishnu is the preservative aspect of the threefold divine (the others being the creative Brahma and destructive Shiva, whose consort Parvati took the form of Sati, as related in chapter 1).[46] Though each aspect retains its own characteristics and devotional traditions, each is simultaneously synecdochic of the others. Thus, they are rarely worshipped in the form of the trinity, as in Christian traditions. Rather, the worship of Vishnu or Shiva in the Vaishnava and Shaivite traditions incorporates the inextricability of the *trimurti* while exalting the manifestations and attributes of the particular god as Brahman, or the Absolute.[47] Vishnu, especially, is regarded as the aspect that encapsulates all three: described as having made of his own body Brahma from his right side to create the world, the aspect Vishnu from his left to preserve it, and from his middle Shiva to destroy it.[48] Alain Danielou describes the force of Vishnu as "the name given to the cohesive, or centripetal, tendency known as the *sattva* quality. All that in the universe tends toward a center, toward more concentration, more cohesion, more existence, more reality, all that tends toward light, toward truth, is the Visnu[49] tendency."[50] Having made the world, he preserves it as he rides upon the coiling serpent of time. In Vishnu's four hands, he holds a lotus, a mace, a discus, and a conch. The Preserver holds a curious number of destructive objects, pointing first to the inextricability of destruction from preservation and second to the symbolic condensation of the attributes of all three aspects of the *trimurti* who emerged from Vishnu's body into what he carries on that body. The conch, from which the first sound of the universe emerged, is creation and existence itself; the discus, spinning on the end of Vishnu's finger, the limitlessness of the mind; the lotus, so often that upon which deities stand, proffered forward by the statuette as if to beckon toward the unfolding universe of its petals; the mace, hanging loosely against his folded thigh, is the power of knowledge.[51]

Consolidated onto the body of the figurine, then, are some of the most prominent characteristics of the Freudian psychoanalytic practice, its inquiry into the mind, and its abiding faith in the preservative promise of destruction. As a symbolic object, the Vishnu seems to fit perfectly among the collection. But as a material object white against the dark of the table, it disrupts the spatial landscape, drawing attention to its form and, if we refuse to remain in the symbolic realm alone, its origin and extraction too.[52]

It is something of a paradox that metaphor's potency for a field like psychoanalysis lies in its ability to conjure what has been covered over, but that this representational consolidation elides modes of substitution. De Man calls this *disfiguration*, "the repetitive erasures by which language performs the erasure of its own positions."[53] What metaphor effaces, de Man suggests "figure" might recall. The materiality we encounter through a promiscuous and contingent reading practice reveals that with which metaphor cannot contend, the modes by which it disciplines relationality, and, in this way, that which escapes its grasp. If metaphor works by transforming objects into referents, transubstantiating the material into the ideal, the reading practice I am espousing here abides in the substantial.[54] Moving beyond de Man's conception of the figure as theoretical, we might say that accumulated meaning adheres onto the material. Where metaphor's contact is a form of erosion toward abstraction, the physical figure gathers traces of touch that materialize its representational history. Like Gandhi's handloomed *khadi*, which was to be the metaphor of a national labor of purification but the fabric form of which was a collection of inextricable bodily intimacies, materiality militates against the masterful forgetting of metaphor. This mode of reading objects and texts is a determinedly feminist one, set against metaphor's gestures toward sovereignty and containment. Approached in this way, the ivory Vishnu statuette is a material object on which histories of aesthetics and epistemology converge through circuits of imperial exchange, not simply as a symbol of "the proud conquest" of psychoanalysis. It evinces a material history of the encounter between psychoanalysis, colonialism, and nationalism, each a disciplining apparatus of desire that traffics in the trope of metaphor, so that we may see in turn what remains: what survives the violent stabilization of attachment to meaning, desire to use; what exceeds and thus reveals the limits of those mechanisms of control and narrative.

Aesthetic, political, and intimate entanglements emerge not by accident but through touch of contingency on matter itself. What this means is that we repeatedly encounter what appears to be coincidence in this heuristic of intimacy and embeddedness. A metaphoric reading of the statuette produces one itinerary of modern coloniality and its governing apparatuses, an abstracted recollection of the myth of progress and civilization it promised. Materially approached, however, that statuette propels us onto a path strewn with traces of encounter, conquest, construction, and ornamentation. Tactile histories embedded within the body of the Vishnu reveal themselves along this route. To arrive at Freud's office in Vienna, the Vishnu likely traversed three continents, limning the contours of an expansive imperial network of labor, trade, and governance.[55] Bengali linguist Suniti Kumar Chatterji, who visited Freud in 1935, took note of the Vishnu and offered an account of its arrival there, writing:

> Among the images of ancient Egypt, Greece, China on the table I saw another image which was known to me beforehand. It was an almost half a cubit high ivory image, of Mahavishnu seated on coiled Shesnag—the body of the coiled Nag (Serpent) formed a throne, the expanded hood of the serpent was like an umbrella over the head of four-handed Vishnu on the throne. The image was made by the artisans of Travancore. Once, in the course of our tour to South India, we went to Travancore; there we saw such an image being made. I placed an order for one which was despatched to me later on. Such a big sized ivory image was rarely made in Bengal. Girindrababu and others from Calcutta sent it to Freud as a present for his seventy-fifth birthday celebration. They bought it from me, as something befitting the occasion would have to be presented. The original image was a bit plain, so it was decorated further by a skilled artisan from Murshidabad, the base was made of sandalwood on which a Sanskrit inscription was done. Freud was very much pleased to have it. And that he was pleased was proved by his keeping the image among the selected items from Greece, Egypt and China in a clearly visible place.[56]

The Vishnu catches Chatterji's eye not just because of its familiarity but because it stands out on that crowded desk. The desk's surface is crowded with figures, mostly of bronze and dark stone, nearly all shorter than the nine-inch-tall Vishnu that sits on a sandalwood base nearly as high. Vishnu's sharp white outline cuts across the deep patinas, onyxes, terra cottas, and crimsons of the desk. The coiled serpent on which he sits arcs its five hooded heads over him in canopy. The *shesha-naga* (Shesnag) on which Vishnu rests, often called Ananta, is king of all the *nagas*, primordial serpents, whose coiling is said to initiate the time of the universe and its creation. *Shesha*, Sanskrit for "remainder," is what remains when all else ceases to exist; the serpent king promises to be that which exists when the universe whose creation his motion set off is finally destroyed. Vishnu is usually depicted reclining upon the *naga* while the serpent floats in the churning cosmic ocean, though in the statuette he sits upright, as in the reliefs of the Badami caves in Karnataka, South India.[57] Chatterji's re-encounter with the statue, years after he purchased it in Travancore while on tour with Rabindranath Tagore, offers a partial itinerary for the Vishnu. But the material life of the Vishnu begins before its initial carving in Travancore, in another British imperial holding altogether.

From the nineteenth century, trade routes carried new, "green" elephant ivory from the British protectorate of Zanzibar—historically the source of three major imperial goods of spices, ivory, and slaves—across the Indian Ocean to Bombay, which was a center of ivory carving and an international port. Raw material, dead animal matter, and living human matter departed from the port of Zanzibar into divergent circuits of colonial travel, but were nonetheless still bound to one another by the ideological labors of being made useful and formed into objecthood.[58] The 1895 *Statement of the Trade of British India with British Possessions and Foreign Countries for the Five Years* noted the curious relationship between Zanzibar and British India, as cloves and ivory left the island to be reshipped from Bombay to Europe. "This trade has risen and fallen according to the supply from the mainland, and that supply has to a great extent depended on the success or failure of the operations of slave hunters."[59] Well into the height of imperial dominion, global demand for the goods of East Africa fueled the traffic in slaves. Traces of slave bodies, the extractive violence of their forced labor, were carried on the ivory and spices that circulated to India and then to Europe. Ivory was, then, not just an artifact of human violence against the animal but also one of human violence that renders some humans animals as well.

Between its departure from East Africa and before its arrival in Vienna, the ivory object would be curiously nationalized, clearing space for what it would come to mean on Freud's desk. From Bombay, that ivory circulated among major sites of artisanal manufacture in the west and south of India: Delhi, Mysore, and Travancore. Craftsmen in Murshidabad, Bengal, and Moulmein (now Mawlamyine, Burma) largely worked in Burmese ivory, which was less desirable on the international market but geographically more available and significantly cheaper. Travancore ivory carving was seen as the very best of the empire, in part because of the quality of the African ivory with which artisans there worked. They and the ivory carvers of Murshidabad routinely traded off prizes for best carving at imperial exhibitions held throughout India, despite the general sentiment that their raw materials were of vastly different quality. Sir George Wyatt remarked in *Indian Art at Delhi in 1903* that "the purity, opacity and stability of the Travancore ivories when compared with the flimsy brittle goods of Murshidabad, are doubtless largely due to the superiority of the green ivory invariably employed by the workers in the former, over the old brittle ivory of the latter, locality."[60] The Vishnu statuette condensed into its nine-inch form traces of three highly valued sites of British imperial labor—of the touch of artisanal and anonymous hands—each contributing to the manufacture of an object that would ultimately travel with Freud to London, metropole and imperial center, where it is now housed among his antiquities and his archive in the Freud Museum.

The relatively local travel of the Vishnu within British India, from Travancore in the south to Calcutta in the east, slightly north from there to Murshidabad, and back again to Calcutta, produced a joint accumulation of detail and value on the body of the statuette. As first manufactured from raw material into aesthetic figure in Travancore, the Vishnu required, according to Bose by way of Chatterji, additional decoration to be appropriate to the occasion of a gift for Freud. Put another way, the statuette required a richness of detail before it was fit to be sent to a man for whom the accumulation of detail (a kind of thick description) was his very methodology. Ornamentation added in Murshidabad palimpsestically affixed local—that is, Bengali—elements to an object that stands in for the whole of India in Freud's office, demonstrating that a Freudian commitment to descriptive opulence permeated even its aesthetic sensibilities.

H.D., having assumed that the Vishnu's centrality on Freud's desk indicated it as his favorite, writes, "He said, barely glancing at the lovely object, 'It was sent to me by a group of my Indian students.' He added, 'On the whole, I think my Indian students have reacted in the least satisfactory way to my teaching.' So much for India, so much for his Indian students. This was not his favorite, this Oriental, passionate, yet cold abstraction."[61] Rendered an abstraction again, the figurine's coldness is less the touch of its material form and more its apparent inability to move Freud, by reference or orientation. The Vishnu, it turns out, was not evidence of psychoanalysis's proud conquest of the world but rather of Freud's "least satisfactory" pedagogical encounter. He dismisses the statuette and those who sent it, affording them "barely" a glance (look and touch both), but the Vishnu's place of prominence on his desk suggests a more complicated relationship between Freud and the statuette and, indeed, between his discipline of psychoanalysis and the colonial site from which the Vishnu was sent to him.[62] The material objects of Freud's collection evince a history of desire and disavowal that intimately frame his encounter—and the limits of his engagement—with the IPS and the India for which it stood in his mind in the unreconciled association between materiality and maternity.

When Freud moved to London in May 1938, he ensured, by way of Princess Marie Bonaparte, that his collection of nearly 3,000 antiquities and figurines from 19 Berggasse in Vienna would meet him in his new study on Maresfield Gardens.[63] It did—unscathed—though more than half of his books remained behind and were confiscated by the Gestapo.[64] The objects that he had so carefully carried with him into exile—the bronze Athena who had lost her spear, the painted Osiris, the Chinese terra cotta warrior[65]—he had begun to collect in 1896, in the months following the death of his father.[66] His favorite of these objects, Athena, goddess of weaving, wisdom, and war, is said to have been born fully formed from the forehead of her father Zeus. Metis, her nominal mother, having been swallowed by Zeus, is incorporated and disappeared into the body of the father; Zeus, in carrying inside of him both Athena and Metis, is then father and (non)mother both. As Amber Jacobs points out, for Freud, Athena is "perfect," "precisely because she represents the triumph over the mother yet simultaneously erases the nature of that triumph. In loving Athena, Freud will not know Metis."[67] Bereft of the man whose specter so marked his own psyche and psychoanalytic practice, Freud began to gather antiquities and newly manufactured objects that harked back beyond the time of his own history. Freud filled his office in Vienna, his desktop and glass-front cabinets, with these material referents of ancestries other than the paternal that slipped from him. When they went with him to London in those last years of his life, they filled what would be his final analytic space.

By most accounts, the objects in Freud's office had a kind of life to them, an auratic force that transformed clay and metal and wood into objects of interpretative and communicative possibility. For his patients, they were an associative mechanism, a vehicle for their own reflective processes. For Freud, too, they were more than art objects, though their function may have been more commemorative of loss than of recovery. The falcon-headed Horus he bought in 1931 perhaps recalled the childhood dream from *The Interpretation of Dreams* thirty years before:[68]

> I saw *my beloved mother, with a peculiarly peaceful expression on her features, being carried into the room by two (or three) people with birds' beaks and laid upon the bed.* I awoke in tears and screaming and interrupted my parents' sleep. The strangely draped and unnaturally tall figures with birds' beaks were derived from the illustrations to Philippson's Bible. I fancy they must have been gods with falcons' heads from an ancient Egyptian funerary relief.[69]

The dream, which Freud describes as a "true-anxiety dream" and thus one which derives its content primarily from sexual sources, laminated the German slang for sex, *vögeln*, and the word for bird, *vogel*, in the face of the falcons onto the image of his mother's expression.[70] Although in his analysis he claims that the fear of her death was secondary to an extant anxiety, "to an obscure and evidently sexual craving," the description of the birds as funerary haunts the Horus bought the year after Freud's mother's death.[71] In the system of metaphoric substitutions of mother for bird for falcon-headed god for sexual desire, the gross materiality of Freud's remembered fear of the loss of his mother is effaced.

Horus, created by his mother Isis out of the dismembered parts of her brother/ husband Osiris and a self-fashioned golden phallus, alludes to the memory of a dream in which Freud's beloved mother's face was peaceful in a death to which birds carried her away from him, and held the promise of his own future release. He wrote to Sandor Ferenczi of the sense of freedom brought on by her death: "I was not free to die as long as she was alive, and now I am. The values of life will somehow have changed noticeably in the deeper layers."[72]

Freud did not attend Amalia Freud's funeral, instead sending his daughter Anna to "represent" him there.[73] Anna stood in, as symbol and substitute both, for an absent father and liberated son; she again became Antigone, whose very name means both against and in place of generation and whose very purpose was to bury the dead.[74] Horus is a reminder of death foretold, Freud's and his mother's both. His refusal to participate in her burial, a keeping alive of her through disavowal, suggests a less complete entombment to memory than that which he ascribed to his father through his analytic practice and art collection. That so many of the objects of Freud's collection were funerary befits their commemorative purpose. He would die in his study in London, surrounded by those objects, a year later of a lethal dose of morphine injected into him by his personal physician, Max Schur—in a tomb of his own curation. Freud died in the mausoleum he built for his father and the museum his daughter would build for him, albeit in a different place than where the intergenerational commemorative project began.

Indeed, the night before the Freuds fled Vienna, fellow psychoanalyst August Aichhorn arranged for Edmund Engelman to photograph Freud's study so that, "as Aichhorn envisioned it, the home of psychoanalysis might be painstakingly recreated as a museum after the impending war."[75] As Diana Fuss and Joel Sanders note, "Engelman's photographs dramatically capture what . . . a century of Freud commentary had overlooked: the location of the analytic scene within the walls of a crypt. When patients arrived at Freud's office, they entered an overdetermined space of loss and absence, grief and memory, elegy and mourning. In short, they entered the exteriorized theater of Freud's own emotional history, where every object newly found memorialized a love-object lost."[76] Of course, the interplay of memorialization and preservation is central to the psychoanalytic project. Indeed, the oft-cited archaeological metaphor of psychoanalysis, which so vividly repeats in the objects of Freud's collection, operates by the principle that loss is never complete, that in ruin and fragmentation the past might be resurrected if not repaired. Psychoanalysis as an excavatory endeavor abides in the space between what is absent—repressed, lost, repudiated—and that which recalls it. Thus, we might rethink the funerary fixation of Freud's collection in light of its commitment to grief and loss as well as to memorialization and return. Its association with the remains of death is precisely what recalls life to it and to Freud—at least, so it seems in the space of 19 Berggasse.

The collection, static though its contents were, underwent a transformation in its relocation to London. If the consulting rooms Engleman captured show a theater of a history of loss and return, the study in Maresfield Garden is a simulacrum of that still image. The objects, which would be placed in as close a likeness to their place in the Vienna consultation room as Freud's housekeeper's memory could enable, froze somewhere in their travels across the continent.[77] The promise of her perfect tactile muscle memory, suspicious to anyone of a Freudian disposition, faltered in the face of Freud's own decline. He writes, "All the Egyptians, Chinese and Greeks have arrived, have stood up to the journey with very little damage, and look more impressive here than in Berggasse. There is just one thing: a collection to which there are no new additions is really dead."[78] It was not just that the physical space of the rooms was different in London; Freud himself was changed, his orientation now determinedly toward his own death. The collection of objects which had over forty years grown to spill off of his desk and shelves onto surfaces throughout his chambers in Vienna ceased to be a living, growing organism in exile. Their accumulation was imbued by a kind of life force, even as the objects themselves were often symbols of the afterlife. In London, not only did his collection not grow, it came to be contained. Though the figurines on the desktop, of which the Vishnu is one, were (re)arranged in mnemonic fidelity by the woman who, in paid labor, had dusted and cleaned and handled them most frequently and intimately, the rest of the collection, which had in Vienna splayed itself across the surfaces of the examination rooms, in London was captured into cabinets and shelves. To encounter this space now as a contemporary museum is to see the collection of objects from behind velvet rope, thing-ed. Bill Brown suggests that "we begin to confront the thingness of objects when they stop working for us."[79] In the analytic space, the work of the objects was one of referentiality. Transforming the space of Freud's office and the site of his death into a museum stilled the objects of his collection; they were demetaphorized. Without the analyst as transferential conduit, they became just things. Eva Rosenfeld, on visiting Freud in his new home, remarked that nearly everything was as it had been in Vienna. Freud's prescient response: "Everything is here, only I am not here."[80]

IV. Feeling Oceanic

In 1926, five years before the Vishnu statuette arrived in Vienna, Rabindranath Tagore and Sigmund Freud met briefly in a Vienna hotel. There is little archival trace of this encounter, aside from two photographs (figures 3.2 and 3.3) and Freud's remarks in a letter to Anna von Vest: "Tagore invited us to pay him a visit on 25th October. We found him ailing and tired, but he is a wonderful sight, he really looks like we imagined the Lord God looks, but only about 10,000 years older than the way Michelangelo painted him in the Sistine."[81] While Tagore's flowing white beard and hair may indeed have resembled that of Michelangelo's depiction of God on the ceiling of the Sistine Chapel, hand outstretched toward Adam's, racial and representational differences are accounted for by Freud's caveat that Tagore looks older than that image designed to look eternal and ageless. Tagore's Oriental foreignness appeared to Freud a relic even more ancient, speaking as much to Freud's imagination of the India that Tagore came to represent as to the actual man who stood before him in Vienna. Tagore's performed Asiatic spirituality embodied for Freud the unknown and unknowable spiritual depths of the East, even as he reminded Freud of a seminal image of Western religion.

The encounter between these two men—poet and doctor—illustrates a confluence of aesthetics and epistemology of which the ivory Vishnu statuette

Figure 3.2 Meeting between Rabindranath Tagore and Sigmund Freud, Vienna, October 25, 1926.
Photo courtesy of the Rabindra Bhavan (Institute of Tagore Studies and Research) Archives, Visva-Bharati University.

Figure 3.3 Meeting between Rabindranath Tagore and Sigmund Freud,
Vienna, October 25, 1926.
Photo courtesy of the Rabindra Bhavan (Institute of Tagore Studies and Research)
Archives, Visva-Bharati University.

would remind Freud when he received it five years later. Freud's description of Tagore's apparent antiquity was uncannily repeated on his office desk, where the Vishnu—which Chatterji commissioned while traveling with Tagore—came to be taxonomized among "real" antiquities.[82] The translation of Freud's office as clinical space into museum after his death was proleptically availed by the terms of modern science and its relationship to imperialism. On Freud's desk, as objects of analytic reference, figurines were organized into a language of subjectivity. The Vishnu, like Tagore before it, was rendered ancient before its time, metonymically evoking the timelessness of India in the orientalist imagination.

For Tagore, who was at least familiar with the basics of Freudian psychoanalysis by the time the two met, psychoanalysis was part of a larger imperial project of knowledge production: the attempts of science and rationality to plumb the depths of the self, to understand what Tagore saw as the limitlessness of the spiritual being. Despite the fact that they did not meet until 1926, there is evidence in his writing that Tagore was aware of psychoanalysis as early as 1915, when he wrote to W. W. Pearson: "The dream had affected me so deeply that I had been discussing it with several persons trying to probe the mystery of psychology that could create such a vivid vision and intense feeling out of nothing, never suspecting that this dream came to me through the medium of infinite mind that lies between individuals. It gave me the truth for a moment that in reality your suffering was mine."[83]

A fundamental problem with the psychoanalytic paradigm, Tagore suggests, is the dissonance between its intersubjective analytic methodology and its epistemological insistence on individual subjectivity: "How can the world created by an individual in his own mind be understood by another individual having a different mind?"[84] In contrast, the Hindu-reform Brahmo movement offered Tagore a vocabulary of shared relationality, a common submersion in the limitless Brahman through the "worship and adoration of the Eternal, Unsearchable, Immutable Being who is the Author and Preserver of the Universe" that rendered the language of psychoanalysis pale and brittle.[85] Though this was the primary frame of his spiritual life, Tagore turned in his writings to a variety of local traditions of devotion to describe an intimate and yet impersonal relationship to the divine. He even appears to have attempted, in conversation with Anil Kumar Basu and Sarasi Lal Sarkar, to understand the force of psychoanalysis that had gripped their thinking.[86] But by 1931, Tagore's patience had run out and he wrote scathingly to Sarkar,

> I do not want to intrude upon the field of *psychoanalysis* [in English in original]. This is in the early stages of becoming a science, still undeveloped, thus providing a perfect excuse for people to chatter as they please. Furthermore, there can be no better opportunity for giving vent to unhealthy thoughts than this form of scientifically approved scandal. In this so-called branch of science anyone can assume the role of a scientist, there is no need to pass a stiff examination to be selected as a competent practitioner. In Bengal, psychoanalysis opens a further door for throwing insults at people; those with a taste for this will be delighted.[87]

Psychoanalysis, this imported pseudo-science, had for Tagore neither verifiable heft nor cultural nuance. It spoke to what he saw as the lowest impulses of the individual and of Bengali society both—ill-fitted to this new soil, though for markedly different reasons than Freud's hesitation about its importation to India. Even before Freud met the Indian poet in Vienna, around the time he began his correspondence with Bose, he entered into a decades-long epistolary relationship with Romain Rolland, French novelist and Nobel laureate, with whom Tagore too shared a long intimacy. In 1929, in the opening pages of *Civilization and Its Discontents*, Freud writes of a friend who, upon receiving from him a copy of *The Future of an Illusion*, shared a "peculiar feeling" described as real religious sentiment. "It is a feeling which he would like to call a sensation of 'eternity,' a feeling as of something limitless, unbounded—as it were, 'oceanic.' "[88] Freud goes on to say, "I cannot discover this 'oceanic' feeling in myself. It is not easy to deal scientifically with feelings."[89] The letter to which Freud refers, sent to him in 1927 by Rolland, came as both men were in the midst of writing: Freud his *Civilization and Its Discontents*, Rolland his three-volume set on the lives of the Bengali Hindu revivalist figures Sri Ramakrishna and Swami Vivekananda. In that letter, Rolland writes of an eternal sensation which "may very well not be eternal, but simply beyond perception, like the oceanic."[90] What was this feeling? And why did it so trouble Freud, who would write later to Rolland that the letter on the oceanic feeling had "left him no peace"?[91]

For two years, Freud wrestled with this sensation, which Rolland not only said he was never without but also that he was convinced was shared by millions of others. In *Civilization*, Freud sidestepped that which beckoned from beyond the perceptual and physiological, ultimately consigning the feeling to a primitive state of infantile narcissism—a frank disappointment when it comes to analysis. However, as is often the case with Freud, something irradiates out of this containment. Freud offers, before turning to the psychodevelopmental, the possibility that Rolland meant what Hannibal meant when, in Christian Dietrich Grabbe's play, being betrayed by his former patron, he exclaims as he takes poison rather than be captured, "We cannot fall out of this world."[92] For Freud, this is an identical "consolation." Although the individual may face death by his own hand, by his own will, he is still bound to some broader relationality under the sign of the "world."

Freud calls this "an indissoluble bond, of being one with the external world as whole."[93] It is being found by being bound. But his seemingly willful translation of the Grabbe from "we shall not" to "we cannot" undermines his subsequent insistence—and indeed, a cornerstone of psychoanalytic theory—that the ego as an enclosed sense of self is that which we know most certainly. The predictive modality of "shall not" is replaced by the impossible "cannot." Kaja Silverman points out that unlike infantile narcissism, in which all the world is contained within the self, Freud's recapitulation of Grabbe inverts the self-world relation so that it is in the experience of finitude rather than of megalomania that the self is expanded.[94] Even as he seeks to pathologize the oceanic feeling, he opens space for it as identification that shatters the envelope of the self.

Perhaps Freud's difficulty with this concept of limitlessness came from what he intuited was its source, the ancient Oriental world of India, of which Michelangelo's God and Tagore the poet would remind him. He writes, finally, to Rolland, "I shall now try with your guidance to penetrate into the Indian

jungle from which until now an uncertain blending of Hellenic love of proportion, Jewish sobriety, and philistine timidity have kept me away. I really
should have tackled it earlier, for the plants of this soil shouldn't be alien to me;
I have dug to certain depths for their roots. But it isn't easy to pass beyond the
limits of one's nature."[95] Proportion, sobriety, and timidity, racially and reli-
giously marked, prevent the mixed-metaphor immersion in the oceanic feeling and excavation of fertile roots. Though Freud does not seem to have gotten
very far in his horticultural expedition, we glimpse in his sense of the oceanic
feeling—this indissoluble bond—a model for radical politics, for affinity and
intimacy that are determinedly and radically nonsovereign. However, this oceanic political feeling sits uneasily with the Freudian psychoanalytic project and
the very constitution of the post-Enlightenment subject.[96] Recall Frantz Fanon's
insistence that the colonial intellectual on the path to decolonization must
unlearn the concatenation "of a society of individuals where each is locked in
his subjectivity, where wealth lies in thought."[97] While colonialism and nationalism took the individual "thinking" subject as the monadic unity of political
thought, they could not account for the deindividuation of feeling. Nor could
Freud's psychoanalytic thought, though at the end of Freud's life he struggled
with the possibility that the dissolution of the self into a whole may indeed be
the goal of all life.

A decade earlier, in *Beyond the Pleasure Principle* (1920), Freud had written that
"the aim of all life is death."[98] For Freud, this death is the thermodynamic state
of zero excitation. It is extinguishment. In this way, the loss of the self gives way
to nothing else. Freud's inability or unwillingness to incorporate Rolland's conception of a lived nonsovereignty, a continual experience of oneness with that
beyond the perceptual, becomes clearer to us in light of his teleological figuration of the aim of all life. Given Rolland's immersion in the life and teaching
of Ramakrishna and his engagement in Hindu mysticism, he likely references
a common story told by the mystic of the experience of *samadhi*, the state of
complete union in the limitless Brahman.[99] "Sometimes God effaces even that
trace of 'I.' Then one experiences *jada samadhi* or *nirvikalpa samadhi* (ecstasy
without form). That experience cannot be described. A salt doll went to measure the depth of the ocean, but before it had gone far into the water it melted
away. It had become entirely one with the water of the ocean. Then who was to
come back and tell the ocean's depth?"[100] In this longer anecdote, which Freud
would have encountered if he had read the volume of *La Vie de Ramakrishna* that
Rolland sent him, there are startling resonances between the salt doll and
Freud's reading of Grabbe's *Hannibal*. The salt doll, made of one of the very substances into which it will be submerged, originally believes itself external to the
ocean. Its encounter with the ocean reincorporates it into the substance from

which it originally came and which even in its solid state it still resembles. In its finitude, it realizes its true essence. That is the experience, the sensation, of knowing the universal and essential—not indissoluble so much as utterly dissolved, unremovable, and indistinguishable. This is for Rolland, reading Ramakrishna, one model of self-knowledge.

Rolland's salt doll story is, however, a strange version of the parable which Ramakrishna often repeated; moreover, the parable itself is a strange diversion from Ramakrishna's spiritual oeuvre. In *The Gospel of Sri Ramakrishna*, and in its Bangla original *Sri Sri Rāmakrishna Kathāmrita*, the collected accounts of the mystic, the salt doll appears nearly a dozen times. The majority of those renderings do not expatiate the ecstatic union with the infinite of *jada samadhi* as that from which one does not return but rather as the state of which one cannot tell—except for the few who, like the sage Shankaracharya, "retain the 'ego of knowledge' " so that they may return to teach others.[101] Thus we might say that for Rolland, this oceanic feeling is the ego overcome; for Freud, this feeling that gave him no peace is the ego imperiled; for Ramakrishna, it is the ego transformed, as the salt doll becomes awareness itself so that the subject/object divide vanishes. In his own spiritual practice, Ramakrishna's expressions of this state are inextricable from the figure of the maternal deity. As a young man, he was the priest of the Dakshineswar Kali Temple and maintained throughout his life a powerful affinity with femininity. In an account in *The Gospel*, he says, "I spent many days as the handmaid of God. I dressed myself in women's clothes, put on ornaments and covered the upper part of my body with a scarf, just like a woman. With the scarf on I used to perform the evening worship before the image. Otherwise how could I have kept my wife with me for eight months? Both of us behaved as if we were the handmaid of the Divine Mother. I cannot speak of myself as a man."[102] As the handmaid of the Divine Mother, Ramakrishna avows a fundamental identification with her and utilizes a performed similitude as a shield against the baser desires of carnal passion. It is this association with femininity that makes possible a self-effacing union of another order.

Although Tagore explicitly distanced himself from the Hindu revivalist traditions of the Ramakrishna Order, the language of spiritual ecstasy and union with Brahman was central to his conception of life and reality.[103] In 1935 he even penned a brief poem in honor of Ramakrishna's birth centenary: "Diverse courses of worship / From varied springs of fulfillment / Have mingled in your meditation. / The manifold revelation of Joy of the Infinite / Has given form to a shrine of unity in your life / Where from far and near arrive salutations / To which I join mine own."[104] Tagore identifies the centripetal force of Ramakrishna's teachings, commingling tantric, Vaishnava, Vedantic, Bhakti, Sufi, and Christian citations, as the "manifold revelation of Joy of the Infinite." That which

Ramakrishna calls the ocean of bliss, Tagore calls Brahman. Indeed, the two men shared a sense of syncretic spiritualism that pervades Tagore's writings and presages his critique of a burgeoning Hindu nationalism in *The Home and the World*. While the nationalist ideology fermenting in Bengal, which crystallized following the 1905 partition, harnessed itself to the metaphor of nation as mother and goddess both—the vivid imagery and idol spectacle of Durga—Tagore repudiated the transformation of personal god into collective icon. Goddess as nation manufactured a devotional body whose encounter with both ideals had to flow through a singular circuit, forestalling the possibility of unmediated devotion and ecstasy.

For Tagore, the goal of life was the liberation of self-knowledge, but not in the forms offered by a psychological sense of self, a revivalist ecstasy, or a political vision of freedom. He writes,

> This "I" of mine toils hard, day and night, for a home which it knows as its own. Alas, there will be no end of its sufferings so long as it is not able to call this home thine. Till then it will struggle on, and its heart will ever cry, "Ferryman, lead me across." When this home of mine is made thine, that very moment is it taken across, even while its old walls enclose it. This "I" is restless. It is working for a gain which can never be assimilated with its spirit, which it never can hold and retain. In its efforts to clasp in its own arms that which is for all, it hurts others and is hurt in its turn, and cries, "Lead me across." But as soon as it is able to say, "All my work is thine," everything remains the same, only it is taken across.[105]

This model of spiritual liberation is at once deeply individual and essentially nonsovereign—in this sense, quite different from the oceanic feeling. Desire to be united with the infinite remains unsatisfied as long as the devotee imagines himself separate from it to begin with and, in attaining access to it, attempts to make it his own. The infinite, ocean of salt and bliss, is never not present or availed to the devotee. Realization of oneness, with the infinite and therein with all else in the universe, is the goal and method both. Thus, it cannot be transubstantiated into material form; its very nature exceeds figuration. It is, perhaps, then not surprising that Tagore would articulate so staunch a critique of the nationalist metaphor of goddess as nation, and in turn object of worship, that traffics in a liberationist ethos. As I argued in chapter 2, Tagore was convinced that attachment to material objects came at the expense of precisely the self-knowledge that ought to lead to true freedom.

Both psychoanalysis and nationalism orient themselves to material objects, not for the objects themselves but for their metaphorical value. Whether a statuette in Freud's clinical space that "helped stabilize the evanescent idea, or keep it from fleeing altogether" or the hymn "Bande Mataram" that constituted the nation as Durga, the mother goddess, material objects fix relationality, channelizing desire and rendering it visible.[106] Tagore's vision of spiritual and political liberation, mirrored in Freud's troubled encounter with the "indissoluble bond" of oceanic feeling, refuses the disciplining apparatus of mediated desire and knowledge. But this freedom and self-knowledge, conditioned so closely to the body and mind of the poet, remains a masculine project. Women, we will see, engage a very different relationship to nonsovereign liberation indeed. We might say, following Freud, that if "it is not easy to deal scientifically with feelings," it is not easy to deal politically with them either. Attempts to rationalize and mobilize feeling into relational structures are foreclosed as a failed project.

Not long after the Vishnu arrived in Freud's office, he noticed hairline cracks forming along the base on which it stands. He writes, in his personal diary, "Can the god, being used to Calcutta, not stand the climate in Vienna?"[107] Read metaphorically, the cracks symbolize the unassimilability of the Vishnu, as representative of India and an Indian psychoanalytic project, to the analytic space of Freud's office and mind. The Vishnu is marked by its failure to thrive. We might see those cracks otherwise, if we approach them through their tactile material life. Ivory—calcified tissue—like cloth, carries upon its surface and into its structure the traces of human contact as much as climate. Oils and skin cells penetrate it, traces of the human body seep into its pores and force them open; cracks and discolorations are proof of its manufacture and its manipulation. They are not in this way a mark of inadequacy and failure but rather the accumulation of contact and intimacy. In *The Home and the World*, Tagore distills his most incisive critique of the fetishization of *swadeshi* products: There, ivory reappears as an unsubsumed remainder and reminder of another colonial materiality.

In the novel, Bimala is drawn out of the inner apartments of the home by the call of the *swadeshi*. Her husband, Nikhil, though opposed to the political project of nationalism, supports a variety of local *swadeshi* ventures. The *swadeshi* strategy of replacing foreign goods entirely with local products, as Tagore suggests in his debate with Gandhi (which I examine in chapter 2), depends on valuing objects for their symbolic rather than material value. Bimala, who is moved to burn all her foreign clothes as the *swadeshi* fire takes hold of her body, remarks of the Bara Rani's objects of desire, "Her 'brother' bubbles up as usual, and the Bara Rani's room becomes littered with all kinds of awful sticks that go by the name of *swadeshi* pen-holders. Not that it makes any difference to her, for reading and writing are out of her line. Still, in her writing-case, lies the selfsame ivory pen-holder, the only one ever handled."[108] Ivory, distinctly *bideshi* (foreign), is what is loved and valued, touched and—though not used for writing by a woman for whom literacy is not available inside the *zenana*—handled. The accumulation of *swadeshi* objects is a placeholder for the impossible intimacy and affection from Nikhil, but ultimately an unsatisfactory local artifact.

The ivory pen-holder, originating like the ivory Vishnu perhaps across the Indian Ocean in another holding of the British Empire, draws to it the touch of the Bara Rani's hand; it too, despite its foreign origins, bears the mark of home. Its object value engages a broader aesthetic and ideological economy, even as it accumulates the traces of longing and loss upon its surface. For the Bara Rani, having never left the confines of the home—neither *zenana* nor village—the ivory pen-holder is the world brought close. It has traveled far to arrive in her hands and compels that touch by its foreignness. The fictional ivory pen-holder and its historical Vishnu counterpart are objects rich in symbolic value, drawing our eye toward their latent content and diagnostic possibility. But they are also objects made by and for the touch of the hand, accumulating in their bodies traces of labor, desire, and violence. The matter of the ivory statuette, its substance, is the palimpsestic history of encounter that bound the imperial and the intimate. The cosmopolitan travel by which we trace the ivory Vishnu, transacted between prominent men, is haunted by objects that follow its path of manufacture to end up in the hands of a Bengali woman who has never left the inner apartments of a rural household in East Bengal, the profits of whose rents fund nationalist politics in the former imperial capital. *Swadeshi's* ideological discourse, the valuation of the local over and at the expense of the foreign, founders in the private market space of the inner apartments. Widowed, illiterate, *purdahed*, Bara Rani ventriloquizes through her touch resistance to a *swadeshi* political imagination that would ignore the local desire for and attachment to *bideshi* objects. *Swadeshi* nationalism's purifying project is undermined by the traces of global contact: not, then, the home and the world, but the world already inside the home.

V. From Home to World

Despite the discursive antiquating of Tagore in Freud's description, by 1926 Tagore and the India of which he was seen as representative, despite his own avowed commitment to the localness of Bengal, were locked in an inescapable embrace with the very notion of modernity and its nationalist incarnation. In the novel, there are two models of the nation and two associated affective structures. One, which Tagore marks as organic, is embodied by the passion that Bimala feels so deeply toward Bengal and that Nikhil far more sedately expresses toward a larger humanity. The other, which Tagore portrays as a manufactured facsimile, is represented in the novel by Sandip's politicized and jingoistic Hindu nationalism. By setting at the forefront of the novel Bimala, a woman filled with a *swadeshi* spirit like that which once also moved him, Tagore concedes and even celebrates the affective force of the image of the nation of Bengal as woman (mother, which is the first word of the novel, lover, and goddess) while he bemoans that image co-opted, reimagined, and endowed with new meaning in service of a particularly partisan nationalist discourse. Bimala's articulations of unbridled feeling toward Bengal, which she sees as a twin of herself, ruptures the ideological impasse between Nikhil and Sandip, each of whom conceives a relationship to Bengal by way of logic and strategy. Bimala's desires splay broadly, refusing the disciplining logic of either vision of politics. If *swadeshi* nationalism purported to mobilize a nation in service of the motherland, this novel shows how the centrality of the mother in that discourse elides women and their labor. It asks, what happens in the libidinal economy of women and political feeling when no one is or aspires to be a mother?

Rarely read as a novel about East Bengal, *The Home and the World* has been given pride of place in a postcolonial canon as a novelistic hinge between a colonial India marked by its perpetual antiquity and a modern nation marked by its embryonic potential. It evinces the synecdochic substitution of romantic East Bengal for political West Bengal for postcolonial India. By attending to its localness through Bimala's sensorial identification with a landscape she sees from the home but never touches, forms of commitment and imaginative possibility come to light that challenge the gendered division of political and affective labor that comes to be naturalized against the geographic division of the two lobes of Bengal. We catch glimmers, too, of political futures that do not come to pass in the form of the postcolonial nation-state but will not fall away.

In *The Nation and Its Fragments*, Partha Chatterjee argues that nationalists sought to resolve "the women's question" in Bengal by identifying domestic space as an ideological battleground upon which to wage their anticolonial struggle. He writes that, to the nationalist, "the world is the external, the domain of the material; the home represents one's inner spiritual self, one's true identity. The world is a treacherous terrain of the pursuit of material interests, where practical considerations reign supreme. It is typically the domain of the male. The home in its essence must remain unaffected by the profane activities of the material world—and woman is its representation."[109] Bengali nationalism attempted to redirect the issue of women's rights and advancement into a patriarchal discourse of protecting the "essence" of culture. The consecration of the domestic space in Bengali nationalist discourse removed it from the purview of colonial politics and gave it a patriarchal form that reified traditional notions of domesticity.

If nationalist politics resolved the unruliness of the presence of women by containing them within the space of the home, orthodox psychoanalysis relegated them to the very limits of its hermeneutic quest. In *The Question of Lay Analysis* (1929), Freud famously remarks, "We know less about the sexual life of little girls than of boys. But we need not feel ashamed of this distinction; after all, the sexual life of adult women is a 'dark continent' for psychology."[110] Sexual desires of women are cast as the epistemological limit of psychological knowledge; comparing female sexuality to the racialized impenetrability of Africa, the "dark continent" (the phrase appears in English in the original), Freud delimits what the European science of psychoanalysis can know, about women and about those people who populate the colonialized world.

Braiding together female sexuality, scientific knowledge, and imperial conquest, Freud's claim demarcates a broad geographical and epistemological space of unknowability that is at once dangerous and seductive. As a concept-metaphor, the dark continent recalls the constitutive truism that we cannot conceive of the projects of empire, anticolonial nationalism, and political modernity without the production of sexual and racial difference.[111] Like the psychic lives of primitives, female sexuality, for Freud, is not simply unknowable; both represent an ontological failure and epistemological challenge for a field of inquiry that aims to construct a universal theory of the psyche.[112]

In the figure of Bimala, Tagore offers an alternate vision of Freud's "dark continent": the desiring woman as a wellspring of affiliative and identificatory feeling. The language of civilization in this modern novel is caught up with larger questions of colonial rule and the potential for independence—distinctly gendered. To read Bimala either as driven purely by instinct and feeling or as childlike and susceptible to manipulation would be at once to reify the imperialist discourse of "native" psychic underdevelopment and to ignore how Tagore positions her relationship to Bengal in the terms of an organic and often pure—if markedly libidinous—identification. He writes in *Nationalism* (1917), "The very psychology of men and women about their mutual relation is changing and becoming the psychology of the primitive fighting elements rather than of humanity seeking its completeness through the union based upon mutual self-surrender."[113] Psychic primitivism is not a gendered diagnosis for Tagore, but rather a symptom of a modern disease. When the nation is the organizing logic for community and affiliation, Tagore suggests, its sectarian magnetism deprives men and women of their basic humanity—figured consistently in his writing not as the sovereign individual of Enlightenment tradition but of an ethical relationality, an encompassing intimacy on the level of the spirit. Nationalism, for Tagore, is the basest form of idolatry, replacing the possibility of radical intersubjectivity with a desubstantiated image, "one of the most powerful anesthetics that man has invented."[114] For these reasons, I want to suggest reading the novel's ambivalence toward Bimala's rapturous and seemingly excessive desires as part of a larger critique of the embeddedness of nationalist politics and embodied feeling.

Tagore's critique of nationalism as "self-idolatry" in *The Home and the World* manifests through relationships marked by degrees of impossibility and reproductive failure, each of which provides an alternative imagining of the relationship between the home (the family, the local, the nation) and the world.[115] Thus, another future of identification with and attachment to the motherland emerges, one that does not reproduce the imperial structure of the nation, positing instead an anticolonial imaginary that looks beyond the nation form even as that possibility is violently foreclosed upon. This is not to suggest that Bimala is represented as the heroine of the novel, or that the novel does not produce a trenchant critique of the "covetous self-love" that marks both her and Sandip's articulations of nationalist attachment. Rather, I am arguing that, while the novel cannot incorporate or condone Bimala's conflation of the erotics of nationalism with conjugality, her insistence on a personal relationship with the nation in which they disappear into one another offers a vision of radical political possibility.

In the face of Sandip and Nikhil's visions of politics that, though in conflict, are each rendered recognizable as such, Bimala's intimate and insistent identification with Bengal reveals how discourses of rationality and subjectivity, echoing colonial rhetoric, undermine alternative imaginations by delimiting the space of "real politics." Bimala's powerful feelings for the nation she sees at once as and like herself are only excessive, irrational, and destructive if we believe that hers is a misrecognition. But if in fact there is no boundary between her and Bengal, if she is actually that which the concept-metaphor of the nation as woman figures symbolically, then the calculus of excess is upended. While nationalist rhetoric deploys the metaphoric relation to uphold its masculinist and masculinizing project, Bimala reveals its limit and intimates that which asymptotically appears on the horizon of possibility. Even and especially as she is disciplined for it, she articulates a politics deeply and personally felt. Recalling here the various forms of oceanic feeling that Freud fretted about and was himself unable to understand or experience, in Bimala we witness a fluid feeling of another order, one in which the dissolution of the self is the ego reinforced. Covetous self-love that is a collectivizing affect makes for a form of political feeling that indexes Tagore's ideal of a *desh* of one's own that is itself self-making. Because the novel is set in East Bengal—its central landscape feature in poetry and environment its confluence of rivers—Bimala's might as well be called a riparian political feeling as an oceanic one. It is that which both upholds the banks of the life-giving rivers and, in its force, threatens their stability.

The move from home to world in the novel is a move from the provincial to a postcolonial world. It is not only Bimala who moves from the *zenana* to the outer apartments, but an image of Bengal herself that is projected onto a wider plane of affiliation. Bimala shuttles between inner sanctum of the home and politicized outside world, negotiating a division between what she comes to mean to Sandip as an image of the nation and her own self-conception as Bengal's mirror image; she is at once symbolic object and desiring subject. She says of her transformation, "So long I had been like a small river at the border of a village. My rhythm and my language were different from what they are now. But the tide came up from the sea, and my breast heaved; my banks gave way and the great drumbeats of the sea waves echoed in my mad current. I could not understand the meaning of that sound in my blood. Where was that former self of mine? Whence came foaming into me this surging flood of glory?"[116]

A seemingly minor displacement, the move out of the inner apartments is actually a traumatic breach both for the logic of the domestic space and for Bimala herself. She enters the *zenana* of Nikhil's house as a wife and is expected to remain there for her whole life, or all of his. Her transgression out of that space takes her on a path that, under other circumstances, she would follow as a widow. In the novel, Bimala is acutely aware of the compendium of losses compressed into the act of traveling from the inner to the outer apartments, but offers a caveat: "Only some personal sacrifice, I felt, could help me to bear the tumult of my exaltation."[117] Her sacrifice in the name of nationalist tumult is to tread a path of virtual widowhood, leaving behind the space in which her existence is defined by and through her husband's life.

In Satyajit Ray's 1984 film adaptation of Tagore's novel, *Ghare Baire*, Nikhil accompanies Bimala down the long hallway into the outer apartments where his closest friend, the charismatic nationalist leader Sandip, awaits. She and Nikhil walk together down the hallway that takes her from the gendered sanctum and into a space previously populated only by men; Bimala is thus compelled into the world, at his insistence, and by the charisma of Sandip's words during the rally as she watches from behind the bamboo screens of purdah. When he speaks, she is physically pulled closer and closer to his image until her forehead rests against the screen that separates her and the other women of the household from the rally. Cinematically, Bimala's nationalist ardor follows her lust for Sandip, sexual desire prior to the working of political feeling.

However, in the novel, the boundaries of the marital space are infringed upon long before Sandip's entrance. A nonhuman object of desire disrupts the conjugal home. Bimala says, "My sight and my mind, my hopes and my desires, became red with the passion of this new age. Though, up to this time, the walls of the home—which was the ultimate world to my mind—remained unbroken, yet I stood looking over into the distance, and I heard a voice from the far horizon, whose meaning was not perfectly clear to me, but whose call went straight to my heart."[118] The "new age" that breaks through the once inviolable space of the home touches Bimala; a contagion, it physiologically and psychically taints Bimala's lifeworld even as it remains ontologically nebulous. This call, drawing Bimala out from behind the protective walls of the domestic space, is a yet unrealized promise, able to move and fire Bimala despite still being indistinct. Its effect is at once destructive and constructive; it shatters Bimala's world, the *zenana*, but also avails her of a much larger world in which she might exist. This new age is a nationalist age, and the voice at the horizon might as easily be Bimala's own as Sandip's. The source of the voice is subsumed by its ability to move Bimala beyond the inner apartments and beyond what she knows of herself. She has been touched by a call she hears which colors her sight: Bengal, which she will insist is nearly her identical, synesthetically announces herself to Bimala through a sensorial colonization. Even before Sandip offers up a political vision of nationalism for Bimala, she already *feels* in her body the power of its logic.

This is because Bimala is already intimate with the purported object of Sandip's politics—the feminized land that appears under the sign *mother*. Before Sandip woos her with the metaphor of woman as nation, Bimala has already self-identified as the figure of Bengal, its "sole representative," with "the *Shakti* of the Motherland manifest in" her.[119] Political feeling, we might say, is an affective incitement in the Deleuzian sense—a becoming, transforming the capacity of a body in the world through the engagement with the powers of other bodies, of becoming the body politic that is at once somatic and psychological. This is affect in both its registers: that of being worked upon by an encounter with an object (here, unseen), and of the psychosomatic experience of change by way of that encounter. In this language of embodied affect, Tagore draws on a ready discourse of gendered feeling. The affective excess, which turns Bimala's "sight, mind, hopes, and desires" red—the color of blood and of the vermilion *shindoor* slicing through her hair part to signify her marriage—manifests physically and cognitively. It alters the very state of her senses, obscuring her vision and her sensibility.

When Freud locates the sexual desires of the adult woman psycho-geographically in the dark continent of unknowability—which exceeds the epistemological structures of psychoanalytic theory—he removes female desire from the sight of analysis. But Bimala knows precisely what it is that she wants, even if "its meaning was not perfectly clear," and that cognitive rupture is bridged by a "call," ideational rather than aural, whose meaning is perfectly clear. This form of feeling disrupts the channelizing force of knowledge, just as it will ultimately elude the artifice of the nationalist machine.

Nationalist politics traffics in the reproductive metaphor of nation as family, and in the case of Bengal, its most visible and venerable attribute: the mother. But Bimala, strangely childless despite a decade of marriage, seeking a personal relationship to the nation, refuses to be fully subsumed by a mediated and carefully formulated metaphoric relation. Bengal, she insists, "is a woman like [herself], standing expectant. She has been drawn forth from her home corner by the sudden call of some Unknown."[120] Bimala's wanton identification with her country, of which she has seen nothing more than her parents' home and as far into the East Bengal village as is visible from the windows of the zenana, disrupts the metaphoric function of the mother in motherland. She desires and claims for herself a singular intimacy with what, in the nationalist metaphor, is a collective object. Her country, who is like her: a woman who is not a mother; who has no waiting children, no militant sons. What she waits for is Unknown, not the child as future to come. Metaphor has no space for the intimacy Bimala seeks; it cannot accommodate her radical identification with this country that leaves little room for maternal fervor. In this materially felt relation, the nation can be freed of its metaphoric valorization as goddess and matriarch to be just a woman like Bimala, waiting to hear a call beyond the perceptual that might draw her into an indissoluble bond with that which she both is of and is made into. Not salt dolls dissolved in the ocean, salt is here drawn out by the ocean for the call of independence.

Bimala's intimate, unruly feeling for the political is set in opposition to the contending but inextricably bound masculinist rationalities of Nikhil and Sandip: Nikhil's constructive, Sandip's constructed. But no such manufacture touches the contours of Bimala's politics. She says, "As soon as the swadeshi storm reached my blood, I said to my husband: 'I must burn all my foreign clothes.'"[121] Nationalist desire's storm within her manifests itself in an impulse of destruction; the swadeshi movement has literally taken hold of her, infiltrating her very blood, demanding she destroy the foreign-made second skin that rests upon her body. The contagion of swadeshi's storm operates jealously, unwilling to share somatic space with another foreign body. Skin, Michel Serres writes, "is a variety of contingency: in it, through it, with it, the world and my body touch each other, the feeling and the felt, it defines their common edge. Contingency means common tangency: in it the world and the body intersect and caress each other."[122] Bimala's skin, making contingent contact between the swadeshi fire inside and the foreign cloth outside, intervenes between those worlds—the storm of nationalism inside her veins as much an alien presence as the epidermal Manchesterian weave.[123]

When Bimala articulates the instantaneous compulsion to destroy that cloth, she is refusing to allow her body, her skin, to so intervene. Indeed, the watery (plasmic, even) storm inside demands burning outside. That which has rested so intimately at the margin, marking the limits of her body, has to be destroyed so thoroughly as to eradicate the traces of that contact, in a ritual of self-purification. Ultimately, Bimala's need to burn that cloth—and the reason that Sandip urges his own swadeshi workers to do the same to foreign cloth sold by the Muslim merchants in the village bazaars—refers back to cloth upon skin as a suturing of the foreign touch.[124]

The satyagrahan project of handweaving as self-touch (which I discuss in chapter 2) the masturbatory labor of disinfecting, is refigured in Bimala as the desire for the touch of swadeshi, at once self-identificatory and communitarian. When she is unable to convince Nikhil that her "destructive excitement" will "give us the energy to build" to garner his support for her sartorial bonfire, she demands that he evict Ms. Gilby, her English teacher, from the home.[125] The storm of swadeshi looks inward for objects of desire and attachment, inside her blood and away from the foreign touch of English education or cloth. Over the course of the novel, Bimala describes the effect of the idea of Bengal on her in terms of burning fires and flooded rivers within her, the nation becoming an object to be felt bodily and manifested environmentally. "When, like the river, we women keep to our banks, we give nourishment with all that we have: when we overflow them we destroy with all that we are." Interrupting the symbolic triangulation through which women are kept at a representational remove from the motherland—they may resemble the mother, or they may recall the land—Bimala mixes metaphors, so to speak, to uncanny end. She dissolves the divisions that hold the representational structure of metaphor in place, not through effacement as de Man suggests but, at its limit, through radical figuration.

Nationalism's phenomenology is distinctly gendered; both men in the novel articulate their relationship to Bengal in terms of rationality and politics. Nikhil, on the one hand, with "his fanaticism for truth," refuses to subscribe to a patriotism that is steeped in partisanship, drawing a connection between the self-idolatry of Sandip's nationalism and tyranny.[126] Sandip, on the other hand, for all of his passionate words about nationalism, does not feel the storm of swadeshi in his blood like Bimala; he calculates and formulates an ideology of nation-worship that puts him at its center. The power of Sandip's message is rooted in its ability to capitalize upon a pre-existing metaphor of mother-love and affiliation to a feminized image of nation. Tagore, so opposed to the apotheosis of Bengal as an object of nationalist worship, counterpoises the seeming organicism of Bimala's embodied affect with Sandip's calculated strategy. Though it appears ultimately destructive, this force reveals the limited ability of any political strategy to satisfy the feeling of a woman who sees herself not as agent of the motherland but as its very incarnation.

Even Sandip, who imagines that he has created Bimala as the image of a national goddess, admits in the end that he cannot contain the consequences of this creation. He says, "In my leave-taking today your worship stands out the biggest thing. Goddess, I, also, set you free today. My earthen temple could hold you no longer—every moment it was on the point of breaking apart. Today I depart to worship your larger image in a larger temple. I can gain you more truly only at a distance from yourself."[127] While the call of *swadeshi* draws Bimala out of the inner apartments into the outer world, the world of nationalism provided by Sandip proves itself inadequate to the force of feeling Bimala has for Bengal. This is, we might say, what happens when a material figure is mistaken for a metaphor.

The worshipful excess with which Bimala views Bengal and *swadeshi* cannot be contained by the limits of nationalism made available by Sandip, nor can its forces be "mastered" by the epistemological frames made available by colonial discourses that understood nationalist affect as pathological. "I was the giver of light, of life, of Shakti, of immortality—in that belief, in that joy, I had burst all my bounds and come into the open."[128] Identification eludes the enmeshment of those nets of desire. We might also think of it as the rupture out of bounds into the boundless, into the riparian, the oceanic. By offering herself willingly and limitlessly to the service of the nation with which she so intimately identifies, Bimala disrupts a political system that would exact from her just that, but would call it compulsion rather than choice. Her service takes on a host of forms, from the inspiration she imagines she offers to the *swadeshi* workers, to her wedding jewelry, which she offers up in a moment of marital sacrifice. She widows herself from her domestic world to serve the nation that she so loves.[129]

VI. Worshipping Objects

The calculus of Bimala's desires appears critically imbalanced from the vantage of a nationalist politics that centered on the rational, masculine subject whose relationship to the nation is metaphorical rather than unmediated. In this view, Bimala's desires are excessive and misplaced. However, if we take Bimala seriously as a political actor who intentionally articulates a deeply felt horizontal affiliation, we begin to see not just the radical possibilities of nonsovereign attachment but also a fatal flaw in nationalism's model of cathexis. The channelizing mechanisms of nationalist politics through which collective desire and investment are translated into an abstract figure of the state fail to contend with the vibrant and insistent life of feeling as political. Sexual desire, politics, and a language of religious worship are inextricable from one another in the novel; Tagore binds Bimala's coming into the world to her becoming an object of her own devotion. She reflects, "When, in Sandip's appeals, his worship of the country gets to be subtly interwoven with his worship of me, then does my blood dance, indeed, and the barriers of my hesitation totter . . . I feel that my resplendent womanhood made me indeed a goddess."[130] Bimala's desire is twofold: to participate in this collective worship of the motherland and to be the object of that collective worship. As the embodiment of Bengal, in her own eyes and in Sandip's, Bimala is both the awe-inspiring goddess Durga and the fertile soil of the Bengali landscape, to be worshipped and coveted. Having spent her married life seeking an object of worship, Bimala is seduced by the power of being the worshipped, effectively disappearing Sandip, the devotee. As goddess, Bimala takes center stage in her own narrative for the first time, having thus far relegated herself to role of supplicant, forever seeking benediction from Nikhil, lord and husband.

Not insignificantly, however, the goddess with whom Bimala, like the swadeshi movement, aligns herself is Durga, rather than her fierce aspect, Kali. Durga is the mother of the "mother goddess" image, benevolent and beloved. Unlike the black face of Kali, who wears around her neck a garland of decapitated heads as proof of her insatiable bloodthirst, Durga's face is the illuminated beauty of the good wife and devoted daughter. As I discuss in chapter 1, the annual celebration of Durga, Durga Puja, culminates in the submersion into water of clay representations of the goddess. Hers is the body that is hallowed as it is eradicated, whereas Kali is the feminine force of destruction itself. Kali is an unruly goddess; the wide-eyed faces of slain men that adorn her bare breast—skin upon skin upon skin—hint at our own potential annihilation as much as they promise the divine force of protective rage.

At the novel's start, Bimala laments her dark skin, shyama, which is the other name for black goddess Kali; her transformation into a goddess of swadeshi distances her from Kali and from her own mother, from whom she inherits her complexion. Bimala and Sandip agree that the condensation of Durga as public goddess and Bimala as domestic goddess produces the image of nation at once familiar and formidable, with ready narrative and referential frame. Sandip says,

> Do you not know that I come to worship? Have I not told you that, in you, I visualize the *Shakti* of our country? The Geography of a country is not the whole truth. No one can give up his life for a map! When I see you before me, then only do I realize how lovely my country is. When you have anointed me with your own hands, then shall I know I have the sanction of my country; and if, with that in my heart, I fall fighting, it shall not be on the dust of some map-made land, but on a lovingly spread skirt—do you know what kind of skirt?—like that of the earthen-red sari you wore the other day, with a broad blood-red border.[131]

Sandip's version of *swadeshi* depends on a distinctly Hinduized image of the nation; more than just a desirable woman, Bimala is also a manifestation of *Shakti*, a divine feminine power which is at the heart of all creation in Hindu mythology and the ideological stem from which Kali and Durga each emerge. The "blood-red border" of Bimala's sari demarcates the borders of Bengal that will be drawn in the blood of nationalist sacrifice. Sandip's nationalist ideal is a desirable and limitlessly powerful woman for whom the *swadeshi* supporters ought to be willing to offer their lives. In calling her a goddess, Sandip attempts to reify his own power: he has the ability to name her, harness her power, have her sanction. The Bengal for which he fights is a nation made in the image of a goddess to whom he has primary access. Nikhil describes this in terms of both Bimala and Sandip as a "covetous self-love," driven not by a sense of the public good but by a kind of masturbatory instinct.[132]

The world, for Bimala and her love of Bengal, is not enough. "I have my desire to be fascinated, and fascination must be supplied to me in bodily shape by my country."[133] The desire to be "fascinated," held under the sway of something other than herself, for Bimala, is a longing for an erotic of self-abrogation that neither Sandip nor Nikhil can offer. She describes her mother as the ideal of womanhood, made exemplary by her unflagging devotion to her husband. This is the ideal against which Bimala imagines herself, seeking to become a model of femininity through the worship of her husband who, though he loves her, cannot accept her subservient adoration. Nikhil seeks a modern woman to be his companion, while Bimala seeks an object in which to invest her libidinal energies. This worthy object is not Sandip, who, unlike Nikhil, not only accepts but also welcomes reverence, while proving himself duplicitous and weak.[134] The only ideal that merits Bimala's true passion is Bengal, which she sees as her double. The *Shakti* within her is the same *Shakti* of Durga in the hymn "Bande

Mataram," and so her fervor for the nation is itself a reclamation of what is for Bimala a primary and primal affiliation: between mother and land, between woman and nation. Bimala aligns with *mata*, the mother, and gives herself up to *mata*, madness. The repetition of "Bande Mataram" is then self-hailing and its displacement.

The darkness and impenetrability of Bimala's insides are ever darker in the novel next to the electric-light artifice of Sandip's nationalist project. "Ignorant men worship gods. I, Sandip, shall create them."[135] Sandip sees himself as producing Bimala as goddess for the worship of ignorant men, co-opting ready religious and national sentiment. Nikhil's view of anticolonialism, often read as the ventriloquization of Tagore's own, offers a third option of identification. His humanist universalism, a model of affiliation unaffected by the coercive forces of sexual and violent desire that mark both Sandip and Bimala's nationalist engagements, appears in the novel as disaffected and enervated. Indeed, the affair between Sandip and Bimala is made possible by Nikhil's apparent impotence, which is sexual as much as ideological.

In Ray's 1984 film adaptation, Nikhil is distinctly desexualized, falling asleep in their marriage bed while Bimala gazes longingly at herself in the mirror—foretelling that he can no more prevent the fires of the *swadeshi* movement from razing the homes and businesses of his Muslim tenants than he can satisfy his wife's desires. Bimala "is no mother. There is no call to her of children in their hunger, no home to be lighted of an evening, no household work to be done. So she hies to her tryst, for this is the land of the Vaisnava Poets."[136] Doubly released into the world of desiring possibility by her lack of children and her status as Rani of the household, waited on by women within the *zenana* whose lives depend as much on Nikhil as on her, Bimala rushes off to a tryst not with Sandip but with the vision of the nation as herself: she is Krishna of Vaishnava poetry, seducing the *gopis* with his flute. Vaishnava tradition in Bengal is rooted in the propinquity of desire and devotion, the ecstasy of losing oneself in union with the divine in the form of Krishna. It, like other Bhakti traditions, promises radical nonsovereignty as telos, the profit of which is liberation beyond the individual, the sentient, the rational.

Strikingly, Tagore turns frequently in the novel to invocations of Bhakti traditions, alongside Shakti and Durga worship. Whereas nationalist discourse made Durga into national metonym to produce a singular and pseudo-monotheistic ideology of nation worship, Tagore's critique of nationalism actively sought out local models of affiliative community and communion. Gaudiya Vaishnavism, emerging in East Bengal in the fifteenth century, resisted the dualist character of Shaktism, positing instead divine and devotee as of a shared substance. Andrew Sartori notes that while the tantric tradition was central to nationalist discourse, many prominent nationalists—like Tagore—had connections to the Brahmo Samaj. Others still, like Bipin Chandra Pal, sought to incorporate Vaishnava forms into nationalist discourse. Sartori writes, "This was because, whereas the Shakta allegedly sought to realize God through the single medium of one human relationship—the child's love for his mother—the Vaishnavite sought the sublimation of all human relations and affection into a spiritual connection with God, leading not only to a richer repertoire of spiritual practice but also to a vision of 'the Spiritual Being manifested in or as Man.' "[137] Though the rhizomatic structure of Vaishnavism did not ultimately come to be incorporated into nationalist discourse, it is for Bimala, in *The Home and the World*, one way to conceive of her devotional relationship to Bengal beyond the mother-child metaphor demanded by *swadeshi* nationalism.

Traces of Vaishnavite Bhakti in the novel are unsurprising given that Tagore, in 1915, translated and published *One Hundred Poems of Kabir*, the fifteenth-century mystical poet of the Bhakti tradition. More locally still, the syncretic mystic tradition of the Bauls limned Tagore's language of worship and Bhakti. From the Sanskrit *vatula*, meaning "mad," Bauls are a minstrel community whose folk songs, often performed on the single-stringed *ektara*, draw together Vaishnava and Sufi forms and profoundly influenced Tagore's poetry and songs. Indeed, the phrase "*moner manush* মনের মানুষ (person of my heart)," which appears throughout Tagore's writings, is the name by which Bauls describe the divine. This is a very different form of self-knowledge than that of the Bengali vision of psychoanalysis espoused by Bose and his compatriots in the IPS—one of Bose's most famous essays, "*Manusher Mon* (The Minds of Men)," tellingly inverts the term. Lalon Fakir, perhaps the most famous Baul singer, as contingency would have it, lived and died on Tagore's *zamindari* in Kushtia. Lalon has come to be, with Tagore, sanctified as the indigenous poetic voice of East Bengal. His songs about seeking out communion with his *moner manush* are insistently localized in the pastoral spaces of Bengal, enabling the retrospective figuration of him as the voice of a Muslim Bangladesh.[138] In the same year he translated *One Hundred Poems of Kabir*, Tagore also began publishing songs by Lalon and other Bauls in *Prabashi*. It seems that Tagore, as he turned away from nationalist partisanship, gravitated toward these local, syncretic ideologies as alternate visions of devotional attachment to the nation. The voice of these attachments, in the novel, is Bimala's. Hers is the language of worship and longing for self-abnegating communion. Hers is the voice that erupts from between the rationalist discourses of the two men who stand in for home and world both.

Fundamentally, the novel upends the promise of reproductive nationalism in all of its figured relationships, none of which are able to perform the heteronormative function of state consolidation. Bimala's self-love illuminates the forces of cathexis that uphold, even as they are eschewed by, the structures of nationalist politics and humanist philosophy. Mirroring each other but always seeking to differentiate themselves, Sandip and Nikhil often are read as foils for one another: Nikhil's rationalism against Sandip's emotionality; Nikhil's love against Sandip's carnality; Nikhil's rootedness against Sandip's itinerancy.[139] But theirs is also a relationship of intimacy that defies a name. It is not simply a relationship of friendship or of patronage but an affective attachment that lingers even in the face of eruptive betrayal.

Despite the betrayal of his friend's seduction of his wife, Nikhil is clearly unwilling to be apart from Sandip; he will send Sandip away from Bimala, but not from himself. And, even as Sandip denies Nikhil's influence upon him, he appears at the novel's end to return the sovereigns Bimala has stolen for him and to make amends. He says, "Don't you mistake me, Nikhil. You must not imagine that contagion of your company has suddenly turned me honest; I am not the man to come back in slobbering repentance to return ill-gotten money. But . . ."[140] Directing his unspoken and unspeakable compunction only to Nikhil with the doubly directed "you" and "Nikhil," Sandip can bring himself neither to leave nor to apologize. Hovering just beyond language in the potentiality of the ellipsis, veiled in the realm of unutterability, lies the desire that so resolutely bonds men as brothers, rivals, and (never quite) lovers.

In a novel of impossible loved objects and failed desires, Sandip and Nikhil's relationship too is propelled by what we can only apprehend through the catachrestic category of friendship. But the homoerotic desires that animate their friendship haunt the narrative periphery, serving as a reminder of the centrality of homosocial bonds in a society in which heterosociality is denied and demarcated by the very division of home and world. In the home, men are only availed relations with women sexually unavailable to them (except, of course, after marriage), and so move out into the world to express and enact affective intimacy toward other men.[141] Sandip and Nikhil's relationship has a psychic life far beyond that of heterosexual competition, but remains just outside the bounds of the narrative, unable to name or locate itself where it will not fade and die in the face of overwhelming heteronormativity. Indeed, were it not for the communal violence that erupts in the village—had things played out as Nikhil seemed to expect, with his uprooting himself from his ancestral land and moving to Calcutta—he would have been accompanied by Sandip, not Bimala. They would have moved into the world together, leaving behind the home now populated only by childless women. In setting out to protect the Muslim peasants who live on his land, Nikhil consigns that future to the realm of impossibility.

Triangulated desire between men is, of course, also the paradigmatic structure of affect for psychoanalysis. In an Oedipal logic in which the desire for the mother is circuited through and made legible by the governing principle that the true object of desire for all men is in fact the father, Sandip and Nikhil jostle for the power position. However, if we consider Bose's revision of Freud, the resonant force of attachment to the motherland and of the muscularity of attachment between men that is not simply competition illuminates political and erotic desire anew. From this vantage, Bimala and Bengal are not transitional objects in an Oedipal triangle but structuring elements of the intimacies that make possible private and public life. What Freudian analysis, as engaged by colonial authorities in this period, would have diagnosed as the failure of masculinity and psychic development plays out in Tagore's own local idiom as the crisis between a public world that demands the abstraction of attachment to the maternal ideal and a private life that enshrines it.

At the end of the novel, Nikhil's decision to leave East Bengal for Calcutta is more than just a move away from the rural to the urban. Rocked by Bimala's and Sandip's betrayals and the eruption of communal violence, Nikhil, so equivocal and judicious in the face of *swadeshi* fire, doubts for the first time the solidity of his role. The riots force him to realize that "as master of the house [he is] in an artificial position—in reality [he is] a wayfarer on the path of life," releasing him from the bounds of home and setting him adrift into the world.[142] In an echo of Bimala's move out of the historically and relationally determined space of the inner apartments into an unmoored expanse of the larger world, Nikhil prepares to leave his *bhitte mati* (the physical land that connects him to his ancestors), uprooting himself from his native and inherited soil.[143]

Within the seemingly synonymous travel between the home of *bhitte* to that of *basha*, (diasporic homes established away from ancestral soil) is condensed a matrix of affiliations and obligations that bind Nikhil to a sense of home beyond physical space or conjugal structure. In Bengal, where villages are often named for the *zamindars* who rule them, the *zamindar* or—as Nikhil is called—*rajah* (king), is the symbolic manifestation of the land. To cut ties with it, as Nikhil prepares to do, is to relinquish more than property; it is to recognize the end of a longstanding and community-structuring form of patronage and imperial political imagination. Dislocated from various incarnations of home and belonging, Nikhil "hears the true voice of home"—not from Bimala or the poor Muslim tenants he sets off to save from Sandip's *swadeshi* mob, but from his sister-in-law, the Bari Rani, already widowed from the forms of intimacy and rationality Bimala loses over the course of the novel.[144] Though she has not left the house or the *zenana* since her arrival at the age of nine, the Bara Rani prepares to join Nikhil and Bimala in Calcutta. The relationship between Nikhil and the Bara

Rani, often read as a thin fiction of Tagore's own relationship with his sister-in-law, Kadambari Devi, presents a vision of home and belonging oriented around kinship and desire rather than physical space.

Their relationship, like so many others in the novel, has no appropriate name and no commensurate vocabulary. Nikhil says of the Bara Rani, having previously described her as widowed and childless, that he

> could see at once that the little differences she used to have with Bimala, about money matters, did not proceed from any sordid worldliness, but because she felt that her claims in regard to this one relationship of her life had been overridden and its ties weakened for her by the coming in between of this other woman from goodness knows where! She had been hurt at every turn and yet had not the right to complain.[145]

A catachrestic closeness between childhood playmates directed through conjugal obligation, the terms of their affection are neither fully sexual nor completely filial. Neither Nikhil nor the Bara Rani can lay claim to one another or demand recognition of their relationship. Unlike his marriage to Bimala, which at some point surely was expected to produce children, Nikhil's relationship to the Bara Rani is made barren by her marriage to his brother and by her widowhood. At the end of the novel, however, as Nikhil invites the Bara Rani to go with them to Calcutta, there is a brief glimmer of hope for a reunited domesticity of which she can be a marginal part. Indeed, any hope for the home, which has been so battered over the course of the novel, rests upon the possibility that Nikhil might survive his heroic attempt to rein in the communal violence in the village.

Nikhil's destruction, though only strongly implied in the closing lines of Tagore's novel, is made fantastically visible in Satyajit Ray's 1984 film adaptation in a moment of spectacular loss and metamorphosis at the end. The film is bookended by flames, which the audience only understands at the end to be those of Nikhil's funeral pyre and of the communal riots. The novel ends with uncertainty, if not despair: Will Nikhil live? Will Nikhil and Bimala be able to reconcile, something that is only possible in Calcutta, in the world, so to speak? In the film, in contrast, there is definitive closure. There will be no children, no possibility of a future, as Bimala becomes a widow before our eyes. Nikhil's death manifests through a series of overlaid dissolve shots which transform Bimala from wife to widow; removing the vermilion in her hair part in one; her jewelry in the next; her colored sari in another; and shearing her head in the last, so that she is left the mirror image of her widowed sister-in-law. But Bimala is not the primary love object of Ray's cinematography, making the scene of the palanquin bearing his body, viewed through a window at a distance, so startling a loss. Nikhil's death is a traumatic blow not only to Bimala but also to the audience, which only fully learns of it through Bimala's transformation and from whose gaze his dead body is withheld.

Throughout the film, Ray remains largely loyal to Tagore's plot and characterizations—until this moment of fantastic loss and metamorphosis at the end. In the years between Tagore's and Ray's imaginings of nationalism and desire in The Home and the World, there was a foundational restructuring of the nation of India and of Bengal. The 1947 Partition of British India into India and Pakistan, splitting Bengal into two nation-states, cleaved open new ground on which the film figures the possibilities of an anticolonial imagination. Samir Dayal suggests that "Nikhil's voice should properly be heard not as a voice 'crying in the wilderness' but as a dispatch from a possible, better future."[146] Despite his deep disillusionment with World War I, Tagore remained hopeful for a productive anticolonialism emerging out of the liberal humanist ideals for which Nikhil stands in The Home and the World, though it seems necessary to leave Bimala by the wayside. The novel's elliptic end keeps open the possibility of reconciliation and futurity, but at a price. We are forced, by constraints of nationalism and demands of psychoanalytic structures of desire, to choose between male homosociality in the world and reproductive heteronormativity in the home; we cannot have both nation and wife, goddess and mother. Within the novel there persists the possibility of that better future that may survive if Nikhil does. Bimala's redemption can only come to pass if Nikhil lives to see out his promise of reconciliation. In violently foreclosing upon that possibility in the film, Ray lays bare the failure of both of those possibilities.

Nearly forty years after the 1947 Partition that permanently divided Bengal, Ray acknowledges that Tagore's hope for a reunited Bengal—for an anticolonialism that reconciles its factions and looks beyond its borders for solidarity—will not come to pass. Bimala cannot participate in a reproductive futurity because the possibility of reconciliation in The Home and the World has already failed in wake of the partition of the subcontinent. The dream of a reunited Bengal is shown to be stillborn in the final scene of the film, where it becomes clear that there is no salvation or regeneration for the woman who sees herself as embodying Bengal. Even Tagore, who in 1916 had perhaps a modicum of hope that Mother Bengal might live to birth sons and daughters, composed an elegy to a part of Bengal no longer incorporated into the body of India. The matri bhumi, the motherland, is an amputated remainder elsewhere. The pastoral village in which Nikhil's funeral pyre burns is now a historical referent of the ancestral homeland of East Bengal, cut off from Calcutta and the national future of India to come. When the novel serves as an allegory for postcolonial India, it is about excessive desire and its repercussions. But when it is a story about East Bengal in particular, it draws to the fore what gets lost in the move to the nation-state but does not fall away.

In Ray's 1984 India, Bengal has been partitioned and, in his film, the woman whom Tagore figured as its embodiment becomes a childless widow. This is also the death of the *zamindar* family, as the Chowdhury name will die out with the Bara and Chota Ranis. For both of them, in the *zenana*, Nikhil is the home and the world. With his death, the home and world both disappear. The world of the *swadeshi* movement seeps into the once-insular *zenana*, disrupting what once seemed to be the balance between inside/outside, female/male, domestic/political. The entrance of nationalism—an affective and often carnal desire for Bengal—exposes the primacy of some desires and the impossibility of others. Those unproductive, illicit, and failed desires simultaneously expose the fissures within the *swadeshi* movement. We might read the novel's ending as a punishment of Bimala's transgressive desires, with reconciliation and familial futurity brutally foreclosed. But perhaps the only future possible for the Bengal of the novel is one populated by childless widows. Tagore, witness to the infectious hold of nationalism in Bengal and India more broadly, seems to admit that the walls of the home have been irrevocably breached by *swadeshi* as much as by a more global network of objects and ideas.

So, then, let us not consign Bimala to the flames of failure and destruction. She offers something quite remarkable in this novel so often read as a critique of a political imagination that she seems unable to comprehend. Unlike the purported hero Nikhil, the rational humanist who wishes for communal peace with his Muslim dependents, from whose labor he funds Sandip's Hindu nationalist project, Bimala is clear-eyed. Though the idyll of the home is destroyed, another nonsovereign form of belonging is imagined in its place, in the form of a radical contiguity between Bimala and Bengal, rivers breaching their banks in a kind of limitlessness. The home must be destroyed because it can contain neither the political nor the erotic desires of the woman who is its representation. Bimala may lose her home, but she cannot fall out of this world.

PART III

International Basket Case

4

Archive Asylum

By 1916, when Rabindranath Tagore finished his novel *The Home and the World* and set off on the lecture tour that would produce *Nationalism*, the partition of Bengal had been revoked by George V at his Coronation Darbar in Delhi in 1911, during which time he also announced the moving of the administrative capital of British India from Calcutta to Delhi. The reunification, of course, was temporary—voided permanently in 1947 when British India came to be divided into the independent nation-states of India and Pakistan. Much of what was East Bengal became the province of East Pakistan and then, in 1971, Bangladesh. Much, but not all. By this I do not mean the territorial transactions that shaped the physical boundaries of the new nation-states—though those are telling of political ideologies that superseded linguistic nationalism—but rather an unincorporable remainder that refuses, as Tagore in 1916 hoped and prophesied, the translation of *desh* into nation. This remainder, which is and is not Bangladesh, which cannot fully be reconciled into the nostalgia of an undivided Bengal, is that which came first into being at the 1905 partition during which region, religion, and resources were meted out across new political lines.

The first three chapters of this book are set in that former Bengal and its historio-literary world. The two final chapters move away from historical and figural women and their articulations of political desire toward contemporary women whose lives and labor produce the terms of postcolonial possibility. For this reason, the tone, orientation, and objects of inquiry for this and chapter 5 shift to the oral and embodied. At the same time, the chapters in this final section are bound to the previous chapters by the common thread of materiality and touch. Cotton fabric reappears in the hands of two liminal figures of the postcolonial neoliberal world: women raped during the Bangladesh war of independence and then "rehabilitated" through training as artisanal textile producers, and contemporary female garment workers.

At the end of chapter 3, we were left in rural East Bengal facing a home—and potentially a world—filled with childless widows, the threat of postcolonial nationalism figured as barren and forestalled reproductive futurity. That chapter traced the lineaments of possibility that emerge in the intimate encounter between personal cathexis and collective freedom to account for the power of attachment as a political labor and to insist that this affective formation is curiously and necessarily gendered. Chapter 3, along with the previous two chapters, engaged the question of women's political subjectivity from within a colonial archive and a postcolonial canon, looking backward toward the life of East Bengal, which, with the 1947 Partition of British India, would take on a new form. These chapters have benefited from a long and rich tradition of scholarship on anticolonialism, subalterneity, and nationalist politics. They have also laid the groundwork for the examination of the new life of East Bengal and the uncanny reappearance of the symbolic and material labors of its women, startling in their repetition, after the independence of Bangladesh in 1971, in the final two chapters of this book. In East Bengal a half-century later, we begin with a nation filled with raped women and unmarried mothers, the lineages of postcolonial nationalism figured as the mobilization of a newly unreproductive labor.

A note, then, about methodology in this chapter: Throughout my research in Bangladesh, my interlocutors all assumed that I would seek out interviews and oral histories with people who were associated with the war effort or with rehabilitation projects. Indeed, recent scholarship on the 1971 war has leaned heavily on personal interviews, with researchers either taking ethnography as their primary method or turning to conversations with individuals to supplement and illuminate historical material. In so doing, these scholars have built a rich human archive around the war and around issues like rape that they argue have been systematically excluded from official accounts. My own research is indebted to that work but explicitly pivots away from the production of oral history as a counterhistorical mode, an analytic model that recalls the broader social scientific ethos of scholarship around Bangladesh. In the face of what appears to be a disappearing state archive and fractious political landscape, the field of contemporary Bangladesh studies—across disciplines—has been marked by a positivist commitment to knowledge production, to serving as a corrective to state and global amnesia.

As a literary scholar in the American academy, my investment in the aftermath of this war is informed by a commitment to humanistic inquiry and its potential, to borrow Spivak's phrase, to offer "an uncoercive rearrangement of desires."[1] This is to say that, although I was often encouraged to seek out women who were "widely known" to be *birangonas*, I have chosen to focus instead on how that term has been deployed and what forms of life and memory have not been and cannot be folded into its purview. When I met women who were subjected to sexual violence during the war, I endeavored to engage their experience through their particularity rather than through the generalized and hollow signifier of *birangona*. My hope was to understand what other narrative organizations might emerge without the prescribed vocabulary of harm, shame, prevalence, bravery, or heroism that attends the term *birangona*. Refusing to condition their accounts through the semiotic disciplining of that state-rendered term, I militate against the impulse of naming itself in the hopes of clearing a space to articulate narratives of violence, of repair and its failure, that do not conscript women's lives and bodies into nationalist labor. I have also endeavored here, more than in any other chapter in this book, to highlight the question of my own "archive fever," my epistemophilic impulse. For this reason, this chapter abides by an ethical commitment to query how my own desire is imprinted in my relationship to this material—human, textual, and fabric.

I. Tea and Sympathy

It is over tea on my fourth visit to the office of the Research Director at the Bangladesh National Archives that I begin to suspect that I am being stalled. With each visit, the tea has been brought out more promptly, the accompanying biscuits have become more elaborate, and the list of verifying information I will require to get access to material related to Bangladesh's 1971 war for independence has gotten more convoluted. I am doing research on women raped during the war, their designation by the government as "war heroines" (*birangonas*), and the state-sponsored rehabilitation efforts toward reincorporating them into the body of the newly formed nation. That project consisted of multiple interconnected goals related to the body of the woman and the domestic space: providing gynecological care (including abortions), arranging adoptions, setting up marriages, and/or returning women to families from which they had been separated. The material is highly classified and will require approval from the Ministry of Cultural Affairs. It is sensitive in particular because the International Crimes Tribunal—begun in 2008 and as of 2018 still nominally ongoing—is prosecuting "persons for genocide, crimes against humanity, war crimes and other crimes under international law." Archival holdings are so secret that they do not have a public catalog or index.[2] So while I sip tea and wait for my documents to be approved, I do not know what it is I cannot see. What I do know are the rumors of what mobilizes this bureaucratic politeness.

When I am not drinking tea in various administrative offices throughout the Secretariat, furnishing proof of identification and letters of introduction, I am meeting with people for whom the 1971 war is recently lived experience. Some fought as Mukti Bahini, the term for the Bengali guerrilla and paramilitary forces, during the war; some volunteered in the rehabilitation efforts in its aftermath; most have inscribed their lives to the memory of a war which was not yet a half-century ago. These individuals who do not work for the government each tell me the same thing when I tell them I am waiting for access to the Archives: *Those records don't exist. They have been burned.* It is a startling iteration every time—a remarkably consistent statement from individuals who offer significantly disparate accounts of almost everything else. In each iteration, the method and outcome are the same: The files have been completely destroyed by fire. The person responsible changes in the various tellings of the rumor: some say it was the first Prime Minister Sheikh Mujib himself; others avow that it must have been his successor General Zia; yet others promise it was done by General Ershad after him. The lives of these incarnations, which I will trace in this chapter, nonetheless attribute archival fire to directive by the head of state; it was a sovereign decree. Rumors of fire in the archive are material instantiations of Derrida's *mal d'archive*, the death drive that stalks archival desire with its "silent vocation [to] burn the archive and to incite amnesia."[3] The very constitution of the archive, according to Derrida, is the memorialization that in the same stroke threatens a radical forgetting. Mesmerized by the repetition of the rumor of fire destroying files in the very place built to preserve them, I find myself repeating it to people I meet in Dhaka. I press upon its iterability by proffering it to government officials, administrative figures, to the archons themselves.

Sharif Uddin Ahmed, now a history professor at a private university in Dhaka, was director of the National Archives from 1997 to 2007. When I test out the rumor on him, he offers a striking response: When he took over the administration of the archives, he found a man in Old Dhaka who dealt in bulk scrap paper. In his possession were kilograms upon kilograms of bundled documents from the Central Secretariat. Janitorial staff and clerical peons, having noticed that these roped stacks of paper were growing dusty with disuse in the basement collection, had begun to sell them off to the dealer, who would have pulped them. It was impossible to say how much material had already been destroyed. Dr. Ahmed's account of the anachronistic encounter between men who valued government documents for their paper weight, the intervention by the preservationist force of the archive, the discharge of responsibility for care and for destruction onto bodies marked by their subalterneity, was meant to reassure me that whatever the fate of the documents about women raped during war might have been, the sovereign as state was not to blame. What is noteworthy about the anecdote that he offered in response to my rehearsal of the rumor is at once the lack of denial that records had indeed been destroyed, the oblique possibility that their demise came through mundane neglect of dust and pulp, and the attribution of destruction to a lack of understanding and minor greed. The rumors that I had been hearing were pointed in their causality and culpability of the head of state who ordered that the records be irrevocably destroyed because of what they represented to him: protection, shame, atavism. In Ahmed's telling, archival violence was accidental, banal, and undirected. The disrepair of the archives and the possibility that the files that I had petitioned to see might not exist at all were, according to him, products of a postcolonial condition. It would seem that independent Bangladesh—unlike British India, which depended intimately on the production and preservation of administrative data about its subjects—is a recordkeeping but not archiving state.[4]

This chapter examines the record of Bangladesh's archive fever around women raped during the war by tracing the lives of the rumor of fire. The repeated and unattributed claim that governmental documents about wartime rape have been burned is what Foucault has called "an incitement to discourse," clearing the ground for a prolific and public accounting of war violence and its memory.[5] Scholarship on rape during the 1971 war, especially that which has examined the place of violence and the representations of women in national memory, has consistently described it as a secret—a public secret, but always an utterance under concealment.[6] This chapter argues that, in fact, there is no secret. There is an exuberant proliferation of discourse about rapes during the war and about *birangonas* that is constitutive of the idea of Bangladesh itself. What appears as muted—in the whispers of the rumor, in the academic claims that women cannot articulate their experiences as *birangonas* because of shame—is the disconnect between the figure of the *birangona* and the particularity and nationalization of narratives of sexual violence during and after the war. This is to say, *birangona* is a socially empty category.[7] There is no secret because there is no interior subject position that belongs to the *birangona*.

To be clear, I am not contending that women were not raped during the war, or that some women did not accept compensation from the government under its rehabilitation policies, or that some women do not publicly utilize the term to describe themselves. Rather, I argue that the apparent difficulty of locating narratives of *birangonas*—inside the burning archive and out in public spaces—is best understood through the technologies by which this term came into being and by which accounts of violence against women circulate. By creating a political category stripped of social referent, the state avows the abstract existence of women who were raped during the war—and who thus labored for the nation—and dissolves the need for any particular woman to claim that name. It absolves a national public from having to recognize sexual violence as nonheroic and non-sanctioned labor and from having to engage its intimate and familiar presence. The immateriality of the unseen archive and circulating rumor also thus evinces the power of this category; it shows that there is no need to mark that which has never been under threat of eradication.

The archive, Derrida reminds us, is not an object oriented toward the past. "It is a question of the future, the question of the future itself, the question a response, of a promise and of a responsibility for tomorrow. The archive: if we want to know what that will have meant, we will only know in times to come. Perhaps. Not tomorrow but in times to come, later on or perhaps never."[8] Prolepsis, the anticipatory figure that conjoins a present moment to a future instantiation, is the condition of both the archive and the rumor. Rumor and archive are here co-constitutive: the fertile space opened up by rumors of archival violence by the state engenders the proliferation of compensatory and counter narratives by the polis. For this reason, I read rumor together with oral accounts, government documents, and a documentary film to argue that the representational force of rumors and unverifiable stories is intimately linked to subsequent state and nongovernmental organization (NGO) rehabilitation efforts aimed at "displaced" women. For Gurudashi Mondal, the woman at the center of the 2005 documentary film *A Certain Liberation*, a personal account of the war and of being raped and held prisoner at a military camp is subsumed by public accounts of her heroism and her purported madness. This contestation over national and individual narratives reveals the structures of feeling that mediate the nascent nation-state's production of its own history while war crimes trials are readjudicating harm, complicity, and narrative as a nation-making project. This chapter engages the forces by which the lives and narratives of women raped during the war come to be treated by the preservative and destructive technologies of the newly postcolonial state writing itself into being. Rumor is, in this way, a syntactical hinge of the absent, incinerated archive which, in the conditional past perfect tense of incipient possibility, might have been called upon as narrative evidence. Instead, the social category of *birangona* is mobilized by the state in its place; the word is itself an absent archive.

Postcolonial studies has had a cherished relationship to the archive since the early work of the Subaltern Studies Collective. Its new historiography, which sought to excavate the subaltern from obscurity, nonetheless privileged the colonial archive as the site from whose gaps and fissures traces of subalterneity could be gleaned.[9] At the same time, the commitment of the Collective to tracing multiple forms of subaltern expression drew on rumor as a tool of peasant insurgency. As a corrective to the sedimentation of the archive, rumor, in Ranajit Guha's famous deployment, went where other recorded speech could not; it was dispersed in its circulation and drew together collectivities in its effects.[10]

Thus engaging two of postcolonial studies' most privileged paradigms of expression and epistemology—archive and rumor—this chapter considers the modes of reading that these forms invite and the modes of memorialization that they make possible. In the space between rumor and archive, we find articulations that challenge the normative frames of legibility and the capacity of the state to account for violence upon and narratives by women during the war. This chapter responds to a broader question of subaltern and postcolonial studies: In what forms does political labor come to be preserved and recognized? Pointedly, here, I return to the question of chapter 1, and an abiding theoretical commitment of this book, to ask again how women's bodies are captured by state narratives that cannot account for them except through the frame of heroism or victimhood. Although the appropriation of labor by the state is hardly a condition exclusive to women—the material and symbolic work of soldiers, for example, upholds state narratives of sovereignty—women's labor here curiously makes them ideological objects rather than political actors. Therefore, in this chapter, I show how women fabricate alternative political imaginations from within these representational structures. Rumors of the archives' destruction are a form of semiotic discipline that determines the limits of what can be known, by whom, and how that knowledge might circulate. I want to inquire into the oxygen of rumor's fire, that which feeds its circulation, and the traces left in its wake.

In the end, women's bodies bear the weight of an archive that the state will not house. After many months of petitioning and pleading, I was given provisional access to the material on the Bangladesh Liberation War at the National Archives. The collection consisted only and entirely of Bangla- and English-language news dailies, moth-eaten and water-stained. These same newspapers are cataloged and freely available for examination at the Bangla Academy. Whether there is a shadow state archive with material redacted from public view, I do not know. But in the spirit of this book's commitment to the life of contingency, an archive did open itself to me eventually.

Upon my return from Bangladesh, I contacted a woman who, in *The Spectral Wound*, Nayanika Mookherjee's examination of ethnographic, textual, and visual representations of *birangonas*, is credited with a photograph of a group of women at a rehabilitation center, huddled around a sewing machine.[11] Not even sure that the person I wrote to was the photographer, I was gratified to be able to hear of Jill Sabella's time in Bangladesh during the war, accompanying her first husband, who was a *National Geographic* correspondent. I was then stunned when a week later a box arrived—not from Dhaka but from Colorado—containing Sabella's photographs, collected accounts, official correspondence with the Rehabilitation Board, extensive notes, and annotated news accounts: an *archive*. Material traces that I had imagined were consigned to ash. Although Sabella's collection of documents and photographs certainly cannot expiate the state's avowedly empty archive, it illuminates a critical technology of memorialization around 1971. Private material, accumulated scraps and ephemera that individually may not meet the epistemic standards of formal archival practices, aggregately points to the rich life of alternative archival spaces and their narrative possibilities.

II. Archive Fire

During the nine months of Bangladesh's war for independence from Pakistan, March–December 1971, rumors of systematic rapes circulated locally and in the international press. Articles in the *Guardian*, *New York Times*, and *Times of India*, among others, carried reports of widespread rape and indiscriminate killings of Bengali civilians by the Pakistani army. Despite the historical commonplace of rape in wartime, correspondents were struck by the regularity and brutality of the stories. "The Rape of Bangladesh" became a familiar lede in international dailies.[12] On the ground, there were repeated accounts of truckloads of young women and girls being taken away by the army, of soldiers entering villages to single out women to be raped in their own homes. But there were also stories of neighbors who informed the army where women were being hidden or who forced families from their homes by threatening or carrying out rape. These stories were intended to shock the system, to demonstrate by way of what was thought of as the most heinous act the extent of broader atrocities for an international audience looking to a war framed as a civil conflict in South Asia. Rumors of sexual violence were the currency of the war's ideological impact.

By the war's end, estimates of its toll ranged between three hundred thousand and three million dead, eight to ten million refugees, and between two and four hundred thousand women raped. Though the war statistics have all been subject to debate, none has been more so than those quantifying the rapes.[13] Wartime chaos, compounded with lack of reporting mechanisms and stigma around public recognition of sexual violence, meant that rape estimates drew largely from anecdotal evidence and extrapolation from the numbers of women who were offered assistance and aid by the Rehabilitation Board. The estimates operate under the shared assumption of the amplitude of rumors and the scarcity of official reports by the Bangladeshi government. Sarmila Bose, for example, in her controversial book *Dead Reckoning*, argues that given the lack of official documentation, the overemphasis on anecdote, and the relatively small Pakistani military force, the prevalence of rape reported by the Bangladeshi government is impossibly high. Following claims by the Pakistani army that its soldiers were not complicit in the rape of civilians and that, when rape did occur, it was committed by local Bengalis, Bose's argument stands in sharp contrast to the narrative espoused by scholars and activists sympathetic to the Bangladeshis in the war.[14] In some—limited, theoretical—ways, she is correct. Lack of administrative archive material regarding sexual violence *does* open both the government and national memory up to exaggerated claims. The symbolic and political significance of the claim that scores of Bangladeshi women were raped by Pakistani soldiers upholds the central narrative of Bangladesh's national identity: that its independence was also a triumph over military genocide by Pakistan. When that becomes the crucible for examinations of sexual violence during the war, its impact, and its memorialization, the conditions of hermeneutic possibility are radically constrained. For this reason, several ethnographic studies of women raped during the war, including Yasmin Saikia's *Women, War, and the Making of Bangladesh*,[15] Mookherjee's *Spectral Wound*, and Bina D'Costa's *Nationbuilding, Gender, and War Crimes in South Asia*, seek to intervene in this contestation over prevalence and the science of reliability.

At stake is not just accounts of the prevalence of sexual violence during the war but also comments on what the quantification of harm tells us about national narratives. Scholars like Mookherjee, D'Costa, and Saikia turn to the personal and ethnographic for a qualitative understanding of the experience of sexual violence and its politicization. In so doing, they depart from both the governmental narrative of unbridled Pakistani barbarism and the apologist claim of hysterical exaggeration. They consider the texture of harm and its adjudication: violence by Bangladeshis toward Urdu-speaking Biharis, intimate betrayals by neighbors, the limits of the state as an administrative force. These studies also implicitly reveal the limits of the forms of representation of rape, even as they each deploy the term *birangona* as an aggregate moniker for a variety of forms of sexual violence.

The origins of the term *birangona* to designate women who had been raped during the war and thus would be hailed for their "service" as "war heroines" are unverified. Some scholars cite its use in a December 22, 1971, declaration by Home Minister A. H. M. Kamruzzamman on behalf of the newly formed government; others avow that *Bangabondhu*[16] Sheikh Mujibur Rahman, the country's first president and prime minister, routinely used the term.[17] Despite consensus that it originated, either officially or unofficially, from government sources, the word *birangona* does not appear on any official documentation for compensation or identification following the war. Rather, it becomes a political envelope around a government project of repair and valorization of women's bodies that resignified a variety of forms of violence into evidence of heroism. The word *birangona* বীরাঙ্গনা is the feminized and conjugalized form of *bir* বীর, for "heroic" or "valiant"; it is at once heroine and wife of hero. Indeed, the lexeme *angana* অঙ্গনা in this copulative compound means not just "woman" but the body of a beautiful woman, her graceful physique. While the masculine prefix is an affective category, its compound form is corporeal. The body of the woman is at once beautiful and valorous, or perhaps beautiful enough to draw the desire of valor to it.

In Bangla, the word *birangona*, which had minimal public and literary usage prior to 1971, is stalked by the unfortunate but linguistically rational near-homonym *barangona* বারাঙ্গনা, which means prostitute. There, the alluring feminine body is sutured to the prohibition of *bara* বারা. Hers is a body from which you are to avert your gaze, the touch of which is forbidden. The most generous reading would suggest that it was a remarkable oversight on the part of government officials to adopt this term in lieu of other readily available feminine portmanteaus. Nonetheless, this distorted echo of a name appears throughout claims that contest the accounts of women who have come forward about having been subjected to sexual violence during the war. To call them prostitutes is to assert the limits of what can be grieved and what can be incorporated. Moreover, to suggest that the women consented and were compensated is to forestall the possibility of their bodies being recoded as those of national heroes. In the name *birangona* and its echo, the sanitizing celebration of violence against women as acts of valor is conspicuously undercut by its proximity to the repudiated female body. Perhaps officials believed the term to be a transitional one, a bridge to a national future in which traces of trauma have been shed from the symbolic feminine body. Perhaps, too, they hoped that the designation would go unpeopled, that no one would come forward to give a face and a name to the title.

We need only look to Kamruzzamman's announcement, the only recorded official utterance of the term *birangona*, to begin to see how economies of legibility immediately governed the state's ability and willingness to even utter the name of sexual violence. On the same day that Sheikh Mujib was released from prison in Karachi and transferred to house arrest, Kamruzzamman told reporters that "all young girls and women who have been subjected to inhuman torture by the occupying Pakistani army in the last nine months will all be accorded full respect as *birangonas* of the Bangladeshi liberation struggle."[18] Coalesced under the sign *birangona*, then, were several interconnected imperatives of the state. Kamruzzamman says neither the English word *rape* nor its Bangla cognate *dhorshita* ধর্ষিত; instead, the circumlocution "inhuman torture" resolves an undefined but acute harm for which women and girls will be "accorded full respect." On the one hand, "inhuman torture" suggests a broad range of injuries inflicted on women and girls during the war, harms that the state has offered to recognize: imprisonment, kidnapping, rape, assault, deprivation. On the other hand, it is clear that the state does not intend to engage more intimate, mundane kinds of violence separate from those "tortures" committed by the Pakistani army: not murder of families; not rape by Bengali collaborators who were often neighbors, friends, or local officials; not forced expulsion from property. To be accorded the respect of a *birangona*—its content not yet articulated—women had to have been subjected to forms of harm for which the state had already determined a narrative and for which it would offer them an economic and ideological compensation. In this way, the term *birangona* is a framing device that represents, without naming, sexual violence.

Building on Kamruzzamman's announcement, the government of the new republic set to work with a plan for the rehabilitation of women (*nari punorbashon* নারী পুনর্বাসন) who were raped or displaced from their families, that would consist of camps for the displaced, medical care, and vocational training. I discuss the rehabilitation project more fully later in this chapter, but for now it is important to note the alacrity with which officials took to the task of rehabilitating women under the banner of national reparation. Attending to the harmed bodies of Bengali women was the symbolic work of cleansing and healing the body of the nation itself, for Bangladesh in 1971 asserted itself as at once a new nation-state and an old national form. *Banga Mata*, Mother Bengal, who in 1905 called men to her service to resist the mantle of British colonialism, reappeared nearly a century later to call a new generation of Bengali men to the service of her repair. The body of the woman, so long intimately symbolic of the nation, now had to be central to the project of building a new Bengal from the wreckage of war and decades of Pakistani rule. This labor of repair, modeled in significant ways on the rehabilitation efforts undertaken by India and Pakistan following the 1947 Partition, was intended to valorize the body of the Bengali nation while preparing its representatives to be reincorporated into that nation. But the constitutive differences between the Bangladeshi project in 1971 and those undertaken a quarter-century earlier tell of the development of a particularly Bengali nationalist model of repair.

Feminist historians have built a significant cache of scholarship around the practices and policies of the women's rehabilitation and recovery in India following 1947.[19] Less well documented and studied is the parallel project undertaken in Pakistan. Whereas scholars like Urvashi Butalia, Ritu Menon, and

Kamala Bhasin have supplemented the bureaucratic record held at the National Archives of India with oral histories and collected narratives, the Pakistani story is largely available only in its administrative incarnation.[20] Those records are stored at the National Documentation Centre in Islamabad, where many of the official documents related to Partition and to state policies of repair have been digitized, and in part at the National Archives of Bangladesh, where material related to Partition migration, resettlement, and property disputes is housed. This material, meticulously organized and indexed, is a telling rarity at the Bangladesh Archives. While it is true that material from the British era is also well maintained in Dhaka, it is sparse. The majority of the holdings were transferred in 1947 to the India Office at the British Library, the National Archives of India, or the Pakistani National Archives—to national capitals from the capital of a new state within Pakistan. Material from the Pakistan era, however, unlike that of latter years, has been carefully organized and bound in objects of imperial value—held between sal-wood boards, bound with jute rope. The material life of those documents draws our attention to the archiving commitment of the Pakistani state, in stark contradistinction to the Bangladeshi state, which will maintain the archive but not commit to adding to it.

Of primary concern to the 1947 programs in both India and West Pakistan was, on the one hand the recovery of women who had been "abducted" during Partition, and on the other hand the redistribution of property among newly arrived refugees. In the case of Bangladesh, the vast majority of refugees who returned after the war were Bengali and returning to their own homes. Property redistribution occurred under the auspices of the Vested Property Act. Itself a Partition-era policy, the 1948 act—more commonly known as the Enemy Property Act (EPA)—enabled the government of Pakistan in East Bengal to confiscate any property belonging to "evacuees," who became, in the law's 1965 incarnation, "enemies." These laws coded Hindus as marginal citizens whose loyalty to the state was undermined by what was understood as their communal sympathy toward India; during the 1965 Indo-Pak War, they were suspected enemies within the state. When the new republic reinstituted the terms of the EPA as the 1972 Vested Property Act, it consolidated property belonging to Hindus and other religious minorities who had fled during the war. Hindus, unable or unwilling to return to a state in which they had been particularly targeted for violence, now faced the extra burden of being unable to return to ancestral homes that had been confiscated. This law effectively undid in Bangladesh the effects of the 1793 Permanent Settlement Act, which installed *zamindaris* as the most significant organization of land rights, establishing the tenancy of Muslim peasants under a largely Hindu population of *zamindars*. An independent Bangladesh, though politically secular, was in this way reclaimed as a Muslim homeland.

If the Vested Property Act sought to reconfigure the spatial form of Bangladesh as a nation, the project of women's rehabilitation administered to its symbolic and reproductive form. The post-Partition recovery and rehabilitation programs identified the presence of disruptive female bodies within the bounds of the new nation-states as a necessary vehicle toward expressed sovereignty. It is estimated that between eight and ten million people crossed the borders in Punjab and Bengal in 1947, the vast majority in Punjab where there was a nearly equal transfer of population—five million Muslims to Pakistan, five million non-Muslims into India.[21] Partition in Bengal, though significant, does not hold the same cultural or ideological force that it does in Punjab for several reasons, the most critical being that between 1905 and 1971, the region saw several significant communal conflicts that resulted in the displacement of Hindus into India from East Bengal. The border remained porous to the traffic of bodies and to fantasies of return. Moreover, the project of recovery focused on restoring women to the nation to which they "actually" belonged—Muslim women to Pakistan, Hindu and Sikh women to India—regardless of what they identified as their homes. They became vested property of another order. In the case of India in particular, the stakes of retrieving Hindu women from Pakistan and from Pakistani men, who were figured as their captors, were enormously high. A national masculinity was on the line. Urvashi Butalia writes, "If Partition was a loss of itself to the 'other,' a metaphorical violation and rape of the body of the motherland, the recovery of women was its opposite, the regaining of the 'pure' (and this purity had to be constantly re-emphasized) body of the woman, essential, indeed crucial for the State's—and the community's—self-legitimation."[22] Sexual violence during Partition, for India, was figured as a matter of honor and purity. Even feminist historiographic accounts of the rehabilitation process note that although there is far less anecdotal and historical information about what happened to Muslim women who were "returned" to Pakistan, it all points to a far less agonized process of integration. They suggest that in addition to Islam's tolerance of women remarrying, the bodies of those women were not seen as adjudicating a national masculinity.

In case of Bangladesh in 1971, recovery was not an abiding concern. Though women had been displaced from their homes and families, this was a domestic rupture. What had to be restored to Bengali women was their purity, not as Hindus but as the bearers of national futurity. Later in this chapter I look more closely at the somatic and psychological regimens of the project that sought to prepare women for this aspirational goal. Broadly, rehabilitation efforts for displaced women were aimed at providing them useful skills so that they might become economically productive. It is worth noting that relatively few women availed themselves of the government's program; largely it was only those who were found in encampments, rescued by Mukti Bahini or volunteers, and pregnant. Thus, the program's other normalizing goal of marrying off these women to reduce the social stigma and, indeed, visibility of their harmed bodies comes into focus. If the word *birangona* and the offer of compensation for war "labor" compressed sexual violence and military heroism into a recuperative national femininity, valorized and sanitized, the double connotation of the word echoed the work of rehabilitation centers to simultaneously shift women out of camps back into the domestic sphere and/or the realm of economic productivity.

For women who would agree to come forward and register themselves as having been subject to "inhuman torture" by Pakistani forces, the government issued an official citation that would serve as proof to furnish for benefits earmarked for those who participated in the war effort. The citation reads: "Having been inspired by love of nation, you have participated in the struggle to liberate your motherland and have suffered at the hands of Pakistani soldiers serious harm [*ahota* আহত]."[23] Nowhere in this notice does the word *birangona* appear, nor does any reference to sexual violence. However, this abstention does not necessarily signal a silence around the rapes of women or its conversion into a secret. I want to suggest that official government correspondence attempts to make good on the broader promise of the rehabilitation process that the specificity of harms incurred during the course of war (harms to be physically and psychologically repaired) could be subsumed into a narrative of nationalist labor. So, then, let us pose the pivotal questions: What are these women being compensated for? What is the nature of their labor and the measure of its value? Where the government established public sector quotas to hire Mukti Bahini and a subsequent pension plan, funneling their voluntary military service into salaried employment, the compensation for *birangonas* necessarily interweaves work with loss. It is, in this way, more precisely intimate indemnification coded as nationalist labor. By this logic, *birangonas* are not paid for the "use" of their bodies so much as for the losses to which that use gives rise and the suggestion that the harm (*ahota*) they suffered at the hands of the Pakistani soldiers limits their future labor potential for the motherland.

Within the space of the rehabilitation center, oriented toward domestic reparation, the conjugal title of *birangona* is at once euphemistic and aspirational, much like the colonial construction of *sati* described in chapter 1. Wide is the gap between *birangona* as a descriptor of body and relationality and the words by which masculine war labor is known: *mukti bahini* (those who literally bear freedom) or *mukti juddha* (those who battle for freedom). If the designation *birangona* was intended to make legible, to governmental structures and to a national public, personal harm as political labor, it was coded as a passive denominative. For this reason, as the state moved away from the early work of rehabilitation toward a more active stage of nation-building, the use-value of *birangona* as a political sign diminished. It was meant to be a transitional condition, one from which both women and the nation would evolve into reproductive futurity. From this vantage point, then, the state's archival drive to preserve material relating to sexual violence during the war appears constrained from its inception.

Bangladesh, unlike Pakistan and Britain, does not orient itself to archiving. Files from the Central Secretariat, despite official ordinance that all records be transferred to the Archives after twenty-five years, are rarely delivered and are even more rarely available for study at the Secretariat Library. In part this is a response to the demands of a more contemporary imperial structure. The global aid apparatus, from which Bangladesh has received such significant support since its birth—nearly $50 billion in less than fifty years—demands record-keeping as an accountability measure. Those records, manifest as reports, survey results, and external evaluations, enable donor agencies to monitor and evaluate efficacy and future need. But there is not an attendant requirement for archiving by the Bangladeshi state—a condition that shapes many of Bangladesh's domestic practices as well. Records do not have to be preserved or narrativized when they are not oriented toward an archival impulse. We might also see this through the prism of postcolonial resistance: in its state-making practices, Bangladesh has eschewed the forms of knowledge production, preservation, and narrativization that its colonizers relied upon to uphold their relationship of dependency. While I do not claim that this is a conscious move on the part of the Bangladeshi government, it nonetheless appears as an assertion of self-determination.

Materially, the state heralded its anarchival intent from the earliest days of the postwar efforts. When women were brought in to the rehabilitation center, many were unable or unwilling to speak, even to say their own names. As a result, the authorities instituted a system of numbered identification; women and girls were thereby anonymized and quantified. This system further promised the spatial and temporal containment of the rehabilitation process. Life before, after, and outside its bounds could bear another name altogether. Moreover, it could be redacted. Intake forms at the center were filled out in pencil, inscribing accounts in a medium designed for impermanence.[24] Pencil made it possible to record, over and over, stories that changed and details that appeared. In lieu of recording accumulative, potentially contradictory, and nonlinear accounts, penciled forms were infinitely changeable, leaving little to no trace of the rescinded narrative. While this may have resulted in final accounts that were more lucid and orderly, it also excised the memory of silence and incoherence that so signified the condition of many of these women when they arrived.

Even in its recording, the rehabilitation process aimed to rationalize and compel the experience of violence into legibility—and to make it possible for it to disappear altogether as the need to keep the social secret of rape came to be replaced by the public force of the term *birangona*.

Rumors of fire in the archive that continued to circulate in Bangladesh in 2015 were anticipated by the modes of record keeping established in 1971. On the one hand, it would appear that the state did not intend to archive this material at all. An archive of its war for independence could bear the mark of women's war labor—the grievous harm, *ahota*, they suffered at the hands of the Pakistani army—but would not absorb the particularities of pencil-written accounts. On the other hand, variants of the rumor suggest that the supposition of an archiving intent is central to the narrative work of recounting the archive's destruction. In each iteration of the rumor, there is a claim to the rightful stewardship of this material and its relationship to the nation. The destruction, in this way, points to a political pivot by the state toward writing a new history in space cleared by fire.

III. Rumors of the Archive

The most common version of the rumor that I was told speaks as much to the demographics of those who prominently work on histories of 1971 as to a register of believability. Many either aligned with the Awami League, the party founded by Sheikh Mujib, or the now largely politically defunct Communist Party, but at the very least almost singularly opposed the Bangladesh Nationalist Party (BNP), the party founded by General Ziaur Rahman. This version of the rumor insisted that General Zia, who came to power following the 1975 military coup and the assassination of Sheikh Mujib (along with all of Sheikh Mujib's immediate family except his daughter, Sheikh Hasina, who is currently prime minister of Bangladesh, and her sister), ordered that all the records from the Women's Rehabilitation Board be burned. He found the files unsightly. Trailing the aura of this rumor is another: General Zia's wife, Khaleda Zia—who has headed the BNP since her husband's assassination in 1981 and twice been prime minister—was said to have been found in the cantonment during the war. "Found in the cantonment," in 1971 discourse, directly indexes military rape. Throughout the war and in the weeks following the Pakistani surrender, volunteers would venture into the cantonments across Bangladesh to free women who had been held there and raped for days, sometimes months. *Cantonment* was shorthand for the violence to women that could be talked about publicly, that was an approved official narrative because it signaled the legible war crime of Bangladeshi women being raped by Pakistani soldiers. Unlike the accounts of women who were held in makeshift Razakar (the name for Bengalis who collaborated with the Pakistani army) camps or assaulted by civilians, women "found in the cantonment" were coded immediately into a recognizable frame.[25] The rumor that this is where Khaleda Zia was found is uttered alongside the rumor that her husband ordered the archive of women burned. In these proximate rumors, causality is held in abeyance. The grammatical structure of the rumor in circulation does not demand that one utterance directly affect the subsequent. Indeed, it is precisely the lack of immediate causation between these two rumors that gives them such purchase as unsubstantiated claims.

Side by side, the rumors uphold but do not explain one another. The rumor that Khaleda Zia was found in the cantonment—indeed, that when Mukti Bahini went in to escort her away from where Pakistani soldiers (as her husband had been before his defection) and their families lived, she replied, "*Ami ekhaney besh achhi* (I am doing just fine here)"—does not presume that she was raped.[26] Rather, the rumor sets Khaleda Zia's experience of the war apart from the atmospheric threat of sexual violence, from those of other women found in the cantonment who could be incorporated into a nationalist narrative. Moreover, by way of this rumor she stands in for the threat of Pakistani allegiance, a greater loyalty to military affiliations than nationalist ones. The rumor that General Zia ordered the files destroyed reinscribes the figure of the *birangona* as central to a vision of the early republic, but now as a vehicle of rewriting that account. In a different light, it solicits Zia's administrative focus on women; his ascendance to power coincided with the declaration of the UN Decade of Women, and Zia established a Ministry of Women's Affairs to oversee his Women in Development (WID) program. His relationship to Bangladeshi women is framed as a very different form of paternalism than that of Sheikh Mujib, the purported Father of the Nation. Thus, at stake in the rumor that Zia was responsible for the archive fire is not a question of conjugal loyalty but the very origin story of Bangladesh's birth into statehood.

At midnight on March 26, 1971, negotiations about who would assume the prime ministership of Pakistan broke down between President Yahya Khan and Sheikh Mujib, whose Awami League had won a majority of seats in the Pakistan general election. Sheikh Mujib sent a telegram to party leaders in Chittagong declaring independence. Later that day, Awami League leader M. A. Hannan broadcast a version of Mujib's declaration over Swadhin Bangla Betar Kendra (Independent Bengal Radio) and to the Associated Press. On March 27, General Zia, who was the commander of the East Bengal Regiment, broadcast on the radio two subsequent declarations attributed to Sheikh Mujib. In the first,

Zia declared himself temporary head of the new republic, while Sheikh Mujib was imprisoned in West Pakistan. This announcement—unlike the March 26 announcement, which was plagued by static—was broadcast clearly and heard across Bangladesh. Zia then was forced to correct that statement over the radio later the same day, pronouncing,

> Major Zia, Provisional Commander-in-Chief of the Bangladesh Liberation Army, hereby proclaims, on behalf of Sheikh Mujibur Rahman, the independence of Bangladesh. I also declare, we have already framed a sovereign, legal government under Sheikh Mujibur Rahman, which pledges to function as per law and the Constitution. The new democratic government is committed to a policy of non-alignment in international relations. It will seek friendship with all nations and strive for international peace. I appeal to all governments to mobilise public opinion in their respective countries against the brutal genocide in Bangladesh. The government under Sheikh Mujibur Rahman is the sovereign legal Government of Bangladesh and is entitled to recognition from all democratic nations of the world.[27]

Zia's rise to power five years later echoed his first declaration of himself as sovereign. As the International Crimes Tribunal was convened in 2009 to adjudicate complicity and sedition during 1971, contention by the BNP (with Khaleda Zia as its leader) that it was General Zia who in fact declared Bangladesh independent connoted disloyalty to the nationalist narrative espoused by the ruling government, the Awami League. In that version of history, there cannot be the birth of Bangladesh without its father, Sheikh Mujib. If General Zia declared Bangladesh's independence, then he supplanted Sheikh Mujib's paternal power.

Consequently, the rumor that General Zia ordered that the files be burned conjures a broader archival threat, suggesting that foundational stories of nationhood are constantly under threat of erasure. This is what Derrida calls the archival drive. The rumor of Zia's decree cultivates a fertile ground for strengthened calls for excising narrative accounts that diverge from state-sanctioned ones. It is a strikingly different response than that invited by the rumor's other incarnations. Less common is the rumor that Sheikh Mujib himself ordered the files from the Rehabilitation Board to be destroyed. In this telling, Sheikh Mujib feared that material evidence of women having been rehabilitated, if not of having been raped, could not be safely contained. The archive could not be trusted to safeguard women's identities and accounts of what had happened to them, threatening their future prospects and the state's claim that the rehabilitation process could be totalizing and therefore unmarked. This rumor suggests that the project of rehabilitation—wherein women who were raped by Pakistani soldiers could be offered compensation by the state for the violence they experienced recoded as labor—was designed to be outside of national time, a bracketed condition from which new national subjects would emerge. Sheikh Mujib's variant of rumor upholds the common image of him as *paterfamilias*; the decree to destroy the files is coded as moral rather than opportunistic, as in the case of the Zia rumor. It is perhaps, then, not surprising that this rumor circulates with less enthusiasm, less force than the other. Against the backdrop of the tribunal, this rumor is tinged with a nostalgia that is particular to the cult of personality around Sheikh Mujib.

Convened by Sheikh Mujib's daughter, Sheikh Hasina, the International Crimes Tribunal attempts to resurrect the populist force of "Mujibism" with the four tenets of Sheikh Mujib's early policies: nationalism, secularism, democracy, and socialism. In the latter Sheikh's hands, those foundational principles have been distilled into an increasingly autocratic nationalism that feeds on an unsatisfied bloodlust for collaborators from the war to be brought to "justice." In this way, 1971 remains an open wound. It draws to it the aspirations, frustrations, and aggressions of a nation that continues to identify itself by the losses of the war. Sheikh Mujib's failure to carry out war crimes trials and his eventual granting of general amnesty in 1973 to collaborators and Pakistani soldiers has come to be seen as a source of Bangladesh's struggles. Returning to the scene of war nearly fifty years later becomes a way to offer irresolute recompense to the generation of Bangladeshis for whom it is memory, as well as the latter generations for whom a nation to come is yoked to its memory. Popular support for the tribunal holds that if those who collaborated against Bangladeshi independence in 1971 can be identified and punished, then the losses of war that are seen as having hindered Bangladeshi socioeconomic and cultural development can be put to rest. It is as though reanimating the war in the realm of law will enable a return to the promise of independence, to the possibilities of freedom and futurity that it represented.

Bina D'Costa identifies a third incarnation of the archival rumor, this one implicating bureaucratic rationale and a conditional sovereign. General Hussain Muhammad Ershad, who came to power in 1983 after the assassination of General Zia and a military coup, invested deeply in Zia's WID project and consolidated the Women's Rehabilitation Training Foundation (WRTF) with the Women's and Children's Affairs Ministry. Caught in the grip of significant foreign investment in gendered development initiatives, the Ershad administration merged the American dollar-driven endowment of the WRTF with state bureaucracy. D'Costa quotes Maleka Khan, a social worker who had been one of the earliest volunteers in the rehabilitation process: "We may have many faults, but we dreamt of a free country. It hurt to see our history was being destroyed. I heard that the files were burnt with kerosene. Shamsunnar Begum, the chairperson at that time, told me they had no other option."[28] The rumor offers no explanation of why the history of sexual violence against women had to be utterly removed from the state archive at this juncture, but suggests that the developmentalist state courting foreign aid dollars needed a new foundational myth of the Bangladeshi woman. This image of the Bangladeshi woman as the darling of the international aid apparatus (which I examine in chapter 5) could not be reconciled with the image of the violated female body whose repair would recommend the success of the state.

Embedded in all these rumors is the trace of another colonial violence. While birangonas are an abiding signifier of the intimate casualties of war, the most publicly mourned losses of the war are represented by the figure of the buddhijibis বুদ্ধিজীবী (intellectuals, literally those "who live a life of thought") massacred on December 14, two days before Pakistan's surrender. Earlier that year, on March 25, Pakistani soldiers rounded up and shot a number of Dhaka University professors with machine guns on the campus—an ominous portent of Pakistan's intentions toward civilians, particularly of a certain class. A confidential telegram from the American consul in Dhaka to the State Department on March 27 reported, "Academics met since military crackdown fearful for safety and in hiding. They believe they are subject to elimination. Systematic destruction of academic records at university suggests campaign underway to erase all traces current 'trouble making' generation at Dacca University. Figure of thousand dead at university nonetheless strikes us as exaggerated, though nothing these days is inconceivable."[29] On December 14, the culmination of this project came when more than two hundred Bengali academics, journalists, doctors, and artists were rounded up and murdered. In the waning moments of the war, the Pakistani army annihilated what it saw as the prospects of the nation, an uncanny but intentional repetition of the forms of violence aimed at women's bodies as the reproductive vessels of national futurity.[30]

Targeting academics, journalists, and activists as instigators of the unrest was only part of the Pakistani army's rationale; embedded within this military operation was a longer-standing effort on the part of the central government to reallocate intellectual resources away from East Pakistan. Over the course of twenty-five years, the massive educational disparities between East and West had inverted; whereas in 1947, 70 percent of university enrollment in Pakistan was in the East, by 1968 it had fallen to 45 percent.[31] Yet more stark was the decline in primary education in East Pakistan. Drawing in part on the common trope of the bookish Bengali versus the militaristic Punjabi, the Pakistani government shifted resources away from education in the East to isolate its use-value into raw material resources. We can then see the killings at the university in March and December as the end-game of a concerted strategy of intellectual and structural decimation. Bangladesh's independence had been secured, but its future would be maimed by the eradication of several generations of the cultural and social classes that would have led it. Here, too, there are shades of an earlier colonial policy: that of the British, who produced a division between East and West Bengal in which the East was denuded of all but raw material.

In this light, anxieties about safeguarding the memories of Bangladesh's independence appear as constitutive fears about the nation's ability to produce its own historiography. Indeed, this is central to the work of rumor and to the proliferation of public narrative in Bangladesh about a variety of violences and losses gathered under the sign of the war. These public discourses work in staccato and in stereo against the fear that, having lost these scholars and thinkers who would have chronicled, narrativized, and taxonomized Bangladeshi national becoming, the foundational account of the state as independent is in peril. Moreover, the eradication of this intellectual generation has meant that the historiographic practices of Bangladesh are stalled between the past of the colonial archive of British India and the future of development discourse. Whereas the term *birangona* is a transitional one, done away with at the end of the war's repair, *buddhijibi* holds out the promise of a preserved past and possible future. Their loss is the loss of a nation's ability to tell itself into being, the lost echoes of Tagore's hope that Bengal might be sung into nationhood.

In a similar vein, each incarnation of the rumor of archival fire predicates sovereign decree as intentional narrativization. Mujib, Zia, and Ershad each write, through the ordered destruction of archival material, a history of the nation, its birth, and its future inextricable from the bodies of women. Taken together, these rumors do another kind of narrative work altogether. They circumscribe the possibility of official discourse around sexual violence during the war and incite the proliferation of public accounts that operate indirectly. Rather than traffic in positivist identifiability, these accounts produce sexual violence as at once ubiquitous and obscure. The "open secret" of sexual violence—everyone knows that women were raped during the war—is in fact a transitive condition in which everyone knows *of* someone, proximate but not intimate, who was raped during the war. Those women are not referred to as *birangonas*; rather, the violence done to them is named. They are *lanchita* লাঞ্ছিত (disgraced and sullied), or *nirjatita* নির্যাতিত (oppressed and tortured). *Birangona*, as a discursive category, is empty of the descriptive particularities recalled by the language of violence and disgrace; it comes to be the name of and for women everyone knows.

There is, of course, a small group of women who came forward and are referred to publicly as *birangonas*, most of whom did so following the 1992 establishment of the Gana Adalat (People's Court), a mock trial convened by writer and activist Jahanara Imam during which charges were brought against people accused of being collaborators. Though the trial had no legal standing, it inaugurated a new period of interest in identifying war criminals and victims alike. Herein, the figure of the *birangona* is resignified away from its original claim of war labor toward the material instantiation of the claim of genocide. Atrocities of war are glimpsed through the violence done to noncombatants, to the symbolic image of the nation itself. The production of narratives by and about women who are identified as *birangonas* in this period catalyzed a romanticization of nationalist labor that coincided with the 1991 elections, the first legitimate and free elections since 1973. Widely seen as a return to the democratic ideals of the early state, the elections birthed a renewed interest in completing the unfinished task of prosecuting war crimes. Twenty years after independence, Bangladesh turned its sociocultural, if not political, attention to identifying elements within the nation—signified by the term *Razakar*—that had during the war, and tacitly in the period since, worked actively against the original and abiding interests of the nation. Though the official narrative holds the Pakistani army culpable, the question of violence against women became a litmus test of the nation's ability to reconcile itself to the past.

Nilima Ibrahim's 1995 Bangla-language narrative *Ami Birangona Bolchhi* (*I Am Birangona, Speaking*), the most famous work on *birangonas*, consists of fictionalized stories of five women based on those whom Ibrahim encountered while running early state rehabilitation efforts. It has become the script for public accounts of *birangonas*. Each story features a woman who has embraced the term *birangona* and found some measure of normative success in life; the popularity of Ibrahim's text attests to a broad desire to see war violence as reparable and the term *birangona* as psychically and socially fulfilling its political intention. By fictionalizing the stories, Ibrahim renders them capacious: the details are at once particular and familiar enough to engage the economy of identificatory equivalence; the repeated self-declaration of the title "*Ami Birangona* (I am a *birangona*)" promises a collective utterance; the heterogeneous composition of characters suggests the commonsense conclusion that if such varied women were raped, then any woman might have been raped. Indeed, though *Ami Birangona Bolchhi* is now often misdescribed as nonfictional, fictionalization makes possible its social impact.

Fragments of the narrative have become so familiar that they circulate as a kind of protean rumor themselves. For example, in the first story of Tara Banerjee/Mrs. Thomas Nielson, her father comes to visit her at the rehabilitation center following the war. Tara expects that he has come to bring her home, but he demurs, promising that because of the money that has come in—alluding to state compensation for her—they are building a new house in which she will have space all to herself. He does not return for her again. This story is commonplace in 1971 discourse, recounted as proof of the failure of an older generation to participate properly in building a nation and its narrative. As fiction it is enormously potent, enabling a purifying distance and a patriotic self-satisfaction as Tara's father's failure—his abandonment of his daughter—is repaired both by her subsequent happiness elsewhere and by the nostalgic frame of valor. Though he could not recognize her heroism and sacrifice, the contemporary reader can, proving such readers the true stewards of Bangladeshi independence. The popularity of the text attests to the sentimental satisfaction it affords.

Moreover, Ibrahim's account, like other public rehearsals of experiences of women who came forward to be recognized as *birangonas*, stages a paternalist apotheosis for Sheikh Mujib. He, the father of the nation, accepts its ravaged women even and especially when their biological fathers will not. A common story that circulates in public discourse (a riff on an anecdote in *Ami Birangona Bolchhi*) describes Sheikh Mujib's visit to the rehabilitation center. Inquiring as to why one of the young women has not filed her paperwork for war compensation, Sheikh Mujib is told that though her father came once to see her, he never came back. How, she is said to have asked Sheikh Mujib, could she fill out a form that required as primary identification her father's name? To this Mujib is famously said to have embraced her and shouted, "*Lekhe dao tor babar naam Sheikh Mujib!* (Write down that your father's name is Sheikh Mujib!)" This story builds on an image of Sheikh Mujib as benevolent protector, whose literal and figural touch transforms violence intended to dishonor women into their familiar inclusion as maternal signifiers of the nation. The use of *tor*, the most familiar form of address in Bangla, produces the linguistic intimacy of home, the affectionate informality of family. In his speech at the Ramna Racegrounds on January 10, 1972, upon his return to Bangladesh after his imprisonment during the war, Sheikh Mujib recalled the sacrifices of people from all parts of the nation for the war effort but singled out the *sangram* (battle) of "*amar maayera, amar boneyera* (my mothers, my sisters)." Their war effort, like the farmers and soldiers also cited, birthed the Bangladesh to which he victoriously returned.

As the authoritative father figure, Sheikh Mujib demarcated the form and limits of the new national family. Just as he welcomed women and girls who had been raped into the sphere of his paternal protection, he would not brook the inclusion of what he saw as evidence of Pakistani touch in the pregnancies and children resulting from war rape. Ibrahim writes of a conversation with Sheikh Mujib in which he says (referring to the government's rescinding of the ban on adoption, which enabled Mother Teresa's Sisters of Charity to coordinate international adoptions of "war babies"), "Send away the children who do not have their fathers' identity. They should be raised as human beings with honor. Besides, I do not want that polluted blood in our country."[32] Rehabilitation, as a nation-building project, necessitated ethnic cleansing. Traces of Pakistani violence on the bodies of the nation's representatives had to be eradicated, either biologically erased or physically removed. The powerful conflation of the woman's body with the Bengali nation is a long-standing formation (the early nationalist incarnation of which I trace in chapter 3) that reemerges in this period as a corrective to the ideological violence not just of war but of decades of colonial rule by Pakistan. Women's bodies are asked to bear the weight of the state's indemnifying project.

IV. Scraps of Sari

Maleka Khan, inspired by her training as a social worker and as a lifelong Girl Guide to help in the rehabilitation efforts in the days following the end of the war, recalls traveling through Dhaka, tracking rumors of women being held in makeshift encampments by either the Pakistani army or local collaborators. Having heard throughout the war of women and girls being taken from their homes or separated from their families as they fled and whispers of what was being done to them—rape, torture, imprisonment—Khan and the other volunteers anticipated what they might find. Ranging from the prepubescent to the elderly, the women came from across Bangladesh; they were middle class and poor, rural and urban, Hindu and Muslim. They were often moved from encampment to encampment, their captors dogged by the Mukti Bahini forces. By the end of the war, some had been held for months.

When Khan, accompanied by one or two Mukti Bahini for protection, would hear—usually from rickshawallahs and others whose manual labor rendered them highly mobile through the city—of some locked room or guarded enclosure from which the sound of crying had escaped or the sight of a woman was glimpsed, she would go armed with little but her own cotton saris and her commitment to the Girl Guide oath to serve her country and help others. She recalls, "We did not know what we would find there. We did not know the need. I would bring my old cotton saris and rip them into pieces. I could not offer them a whole sari, but I would wrap the pieces around them to cover their bodies as we took them out."[33] Those saris, worn soft with age and use, were the first thing the women and girls rescued would wear upon their bodies. It was the touch of her cloth, bearing the traces of her body, that was the first touch of safety for these women and the bridge of care to the outside world in which a newly independent nation existed. For these women who had been confined to spaces of touch that intended to offer no comfort, some of whom had been continually raped for nearly a year, contact with cloth as familiar as Khan's cotton sari was an encounter with the past of their own familial lives. It was the touch of a Bengali woman like them. Khan's saris and her presence ruptured the container of the camp as a circumscribed space of violence and subjugation. In handing out strips of the cloth that once lay upon her own body, Khan reoriented the bodies of the women away from the dehumanizing practices of their imprisonment and toward the simple task of getting dressed. This act recalls one of the earliest embodied practices of Bengali womanhood: learning to drape a sari, the muscle memory of a matrilineal world. And so, a kinship emerged between them—Khan and these women. Their bodies, hers physically untouched during war and theirs assaulted, were bound together by the local textile of Bengal *taant* (cotton).[34] And the cotton that lay between them heralded the tactility that would mark the rehabilitation program.

Taant saris are instantly geographically recognizable. Woven only in Bengal, the nearly translucent cotton, named for the word "loom," is stiffened with starch to give it enough body to be dyed and ornamented. Over time, with repeated washings against the *dhobi* (washer) rocks, the fiber loosens and yields a fabric that clings softly to the body. *Taant* is an intimate technology. Produced on handmade looms, of thread spun from reused cotton scraps, *taant* emerges from the bodies of the women who spin, cut, and starch it. Unlike its artisanal cousins, muslin and *jamdani* (flowered muslin), with which it shares basic technological characteristics and common epistemological heritage, *taant* is an egalitarian fabric. It is cheap enough that even the poorest woman can afford it and durable enough to last her a lifetime. Indeed, *taant* is a life-giving textile for the poor. For centuries women used old *taant* saris, folded repeatedly, as water filters. This cloth filtration method once had extraordinarily high rates of effectiveness against waterborne pathogens such as cholera (up to 99 percent).[35] However, as cotton quality declined and the common short-staple cotton indigenous to Bengal was replaced by imported American cotton, rates of cholera and other waterborne diseases spiked. The new, looser weave of cotton, economically valued for its immediate softness, no longer had the fiber structure to do the daily labor of filtering out plankton and bacteria.[36] A prized material signifier of Bengal that is beloved as much for its beauty as its ubiquity, the touch of *taant* fabric is the touch of the particularly Bengali, the markedly feminine—a touch by and for the labor of women. *Taant* is, in many ways, the transitional fabric between the coarse handloomed *khadi* cotton of Gandhian *satyagraha*—fabric the making and touch of which was to purify a nation—and *Dhakai* muslin of imperial nostalgia, as handwoven cotton that recalls at once the skin on which it rests and the limits of materiality.

Taant saris materially and symbolically adduce the local character of Bengali identity. For this reason, when the Bureau of National Reconstruction, established in 1962 by Ayub Khan to facilitate a unified Pakistani economic, political, and cultural program, delineated elements of East Pakistani life that were too Sanskritic or Hindu to be incorporated into the nation-state, it targeted in particular the sari. It also banned the *teep* (a red bindi worn by women—also the word, you'll recall from chapter 1, for a fingerprint impression) and the songs of Rabindranath Tagore examined in chapter 2.[37] Saris draped on the bodies of young women recalled images of Bharat Mata from the early nationalist period and served to remind the Pakistani government that, despite the attempt to unify two wings of Pakistan under the banner of a single nation-state, Bengalis remained insistently attached to cultural formations and productions that appeared to fall under the sign of foreignness. They were infected by India—not the modern nation-state but its colonial antecedent.

The amalgamated image to which the central government responded was that of young women during the 1952 *Bhasha Andolan* (Language Movement), who took to the streets in cotton saris, hair braided with flowers, singing from Tagore's corpus of *swadeshi* (patriotic), *prem* (love), and *puja* (worship) songs alike.[38] Articulating a national cultural identity, the *Bhasha Andolan* began as resistance to attempts to unify Pakistan under the single banner of Islam and what the government claimed was its lingua franca on the subcontinent, Urdu. At its heart, however, it was the first enunciation of anticolonial resistance by the Bengalis, for whom the idea of a nation was inextricable from language and its cultural life in poetry, music, literature, and habitus. In this way, Tagore's "Amar Sonar Bangla," the pastoral hymn he penned following the first partition of Bengal, became the poetics of a political resistance. The Bengal of which he sang was resignified as the Bengal pressing against the limits of its renaming into East Pakistan. What is more, during the war the song would be the shibboleth of safety for Mukti Bahini, who would whistle it to identify themselves. To know Tagore was to announce yourself as Bengali. Indeed, the idiom of nationalist resistance from the turn of the century reemerged as patriotic songs of a unified Bengal were adopted to express a new linguistic nationalism.

This linguistic nationalism—a primary adherence to Bengali as way of being, as an entrenched quality of cultural practice—mobilized a prior idiom of patriotism and rootedness to the physical space of Bengal in service of an independence movement against the deterritorialized vision of Muslim unity. This is in part because Bengalis, in the eyes of the Pakistani government, were Muslims of another order, whose spiritual lives and social practices had not yet been sanitized of traces of other ritual forms. Though Islam had been introduced to the region in the eighth century, the Pakistani government saw Islam as practiced by Bengalis as having preserved vestiges of local traditions, a syncretic figuration that gravitated toward Sufi mysticism.[39] Thus, to assert Bengaliness as the oppositional term to Muslim nationalism was to insist on an alternate history of religion on the subcontinent and the very forms of what an Islamic life might look like. Bengalis did not imagine that this commitment aligned them to India. The declaration of an independent Bengali nation-state—which American officials feared would incite West Bengal to secede from India and form a unified Bengal—was a mandate on the communal terms by which the 1947 Partition disregarded the potency of local affiliation and tradition.[40] Bangladesh's independence made a case for intimately shared cultural and social imagination (*desh*) as an organizing vehicle of the modern nation-state. Its subsequent failure in recent decades toward religious and linguistic minorities within its borders, then, repeated precisely the violence its independence movement sought to escape.

The 1952 *Andolan* prefaced the emergence of a Bengali political formation that insisted upon an unapologetically provincial conception of nation. During the *Andolan* and in the years thereafter, during the central government's crackdown on dissent, a new politico-cultural identity developed to account for the possibility of an independent Bengali state. It sang the songs of Tagore, Atulprasad Sen, Rajani Kanta Sen, and Mukunda Das and announced itself in the Sanskritic cry "*Joy Bangla* (Victory to Bengal)," while nonetheless affirming the ways Muslim identity cut through the history and the formation of Bengal itself. During the war, the Swadhin Bangla Betar Kendra interspersed its war news broadcasts with live performances by artists who offered the soundtrack of a nation being born. Those songs, all in Bangla, announced the sociocultural paradigm of the nation. Moreover, the image that accompanied that aural signifier was that of young men and women singing, their bodies announcing a racial identity as their voices produced a linguistic one— another Bengal sung into nation.

Tareque Masud's 1995 documentary *Muktir Gaan* uses archival footage shot in 1971 by the American filmmaker Lear Levin of a traveling troupe of young performers called *Bangladesh Mukti Shangrami Shilpi Shangstha* (Association of Bangladeshi Artist Freedom Fighters). Composed of what was intended to be the representation of the nation that fought to free itself into being—young, energetic, "modern" Bengalis who were both Hindu and Muslim—the troupe traveled up and down Jessore Road, which was made internationally recognizable by Allen Ginsberg's poem "September on Jessore Road" (1971), performing for refugee camps and Mukti Bahini training sites. The men of the group stood in strapping contrast to the starving bodies of the refugees, embodying the optimism of the Bangladesh to come. The women took center stage as a corrective to the vision of the violated woman. They were healthy and unblemished, repeating that familiar image of young women in white saris with red borders and braided flowers in their hair marching through the streets of Dhaka in 1952, singing the songs of Tagore and Nazrul Islam. While international newspapers carried photographs of starved bodies and raped women, groups like this evinced hope of what the war might bring about, challenging a general pessimistic fear that even if Bangladesh defeated Pakistani forces, it would be critically maimed and unable to establish itself as a productive nation-state.

It is by this logic not surprising, then, that the Pakistani army stripped young Bengali women of their saris to presage rape. As a general practice across these encampments, the women were stripped of their clothes and shorn of their hair. The rationale was highly functional, because women had taken to hanging themselves by their saris or, naked, by their braids.[41] But the choice also divested the women of markers of precisely that which rendered them targets of rape in the first place: the symbols of their Bengaliness and their femininity both. It is crucial here to note that Hindu women were particularly targeted as objects of violence, the effect of raping them twofold: to defile their bodies—and in so doing cause them to lose their caste/religion (*jaat hara*)—and to intimidate their families into fleeing.[42] If the systematic program of rape drew its ideological inspiration from the abiding metonymic identification between Bengali woman and nation, taking away the saris exposed the body of the woman to the violence of rape and the moralizing economy of "dishonor."[43] Cutting off the braids of the Bengali women and girls rehearsed another vivid image of Hindu Bengal incompatible with the Muslim nation-state: shorn, the women were turned into the vision of widows.

Hindu widows, somatically and sartorially denied access to the pleasures of conjugal life, were shaved as a reminder to themselves as much as the men around them that they were no longer within the purview of domestic femininity and desire.[44] Women and girls held and raped by Pakistani soldiers and Razakars were themselves forced into a kind of widowhood as their imprisonment removed them from the course of regular life, disengaging their diets, their hygiene, and use of their bodies from their familial histories.[45] One cannot but be struck, in photographs of them from the rehabilitation camp, by how hauntingly they look like widows. The image of a young girl (figure 4.1), hair cropped short, wrapped in a plain white sari, could as easily be of a child widow. Indeed, for many, having been raped effectively cut them off from the possibility of future domestic lives, policed by cultural norms of purity not dissimilar from those that proscribed the behavior of Hindu women. Where Pritilata Waddedar, unmarried and dressed as a man declared herself a *sati* at the moment of her self-death, where the Gandhian dream of purified cotton thread

Figure 4.1 Young Bengali women, with shorn hair and white saris.
Photo by Jill Sabella. Private Collection.

made a nation of spinsters, where Bimala who saw herself as the embodiment of Bengal becomes a childless widow, the girl in Sabella's photograph appears as widow between her aborted pregnancy and future marriage. Here, the aspiration and the failure of the rehabilitation program's effort to return these women and girls to their families or, by marriage, to offer them new ones comes into stark light.

The rehabilitation program undertaken by the state had several interconnected, normativizing goals, chief among them marriage. However, that would come later in the process. Of first-order concern in the days and weeks following the end of the war were the bodies of these women and girls. Those rescued by Khan and other volunteers, as well as those who were brought by Mukti Bahini and neighbors to the rehabilitation center set up at 20 New Eskaton Road, arrived with a range of medical needs. The government would not officially take over the rehabilitation efforts until January 7, 1972, when it established the Bangladesh Central Organization for Women's Rehabilitation (*Kendriyo Mohila Punorbashon Shongstha*), attempting to streamline the grassroots efforts of Sufia Kamal—with whom Maleka Khan was associated—and Nilima Ibrahim. While the government scrambled to provide official assistance to the effort, volunteers raced against what they saw as the clock on saving women from dying of infection from venereal diseases, committing suicide, or being forced to carry unwanted pregnancies to term.

Merle Goldberg, an American journalist and abortion rights activist, had been following news accounts of the rapes during the war and coordinated with the International Planned Parenthood Federation (IPPF) to send a contingent of volunteer doctors to Dhaka to render gynecological care.[46] Dr. Geoffrey Davis, an Australian doctor who was part of the delegation, estimated that four hundred thousand women and girls had been raped, though only the merest fraction of them found their way to the makeshift clinic that the IPPF, in collaboration with the newly formed Ministry of Planning, set up in Dhanmondi. Rates of venereal disease were overwhelming, and many of the women were suffering from infection and complications from abortions performed by laypeople. Davis and Dr. Malcolm Potts estimate that though they performed several hundred abortions within the first few weeks, tens of thousands of other women sought out local methods.[47] Most of the patients they saw there were brought from rehabilitation centers and ranged from those too young to have developed pubic hair to those in late menopause. Potts describes how many would lie, unmoving and unspeaking, in the hospital beds "still as logs" as they awaited their "procedure."[48] At the camp, too, they were *boba* (mute). Khan recalls, "They were struck deaf and dumb, but so were we."[49] The toll of war, of mass casualty and migration, of systematic culling, stripped language from the women who were subject to that particular violence and those tasked with their care as well.

In the rehabilitation center, which had very few trained mental health professionals, social workers and volunteers did not privilege talk therapy. Instead, they sought to keep the bodies of the women occupied. Tasks that were somatically and culturally familiar—cooking, sewing, weaving—allowed the women to touch a prior life, to recall familial traditions, without needing to identify themselves or that life by name. After what was for some of the women months of imprisonment, the rehabilitation process began with bodily retraining structured by the elements of the most common experience of women and girls in Bengal before the war: domestic labor. Until the rise of industrial garment work in the 1990s, which I explore in chapter 5, most Bengali women did not formally enter the labor force. Indeed, the rehabilitation program's emphasis on vocational training to offer women the possibility of economic independence was a drastic departure from traditional gendered labor. But it presciently recognized that the new nation would critically depend on the female workforce to drive its economic future. The training and therapy offered through the rehabilitation program was broad, but particular emphasis and value were put on *shelai*—stitching. This was labor both nostalgically familiar—that of mothers and grandmothers, echoes of the fantasy of domestic idyll that was supposed to have preceded the war and the violence upon their bodies—and proleptically valorized. It was artisanal rather than industrial, the work of "good" women rather than the fallen ones who might not be saved within the discourse of heroic valor. In this way the project of rehabilitation critically linked what Sheikh Mujib figured as ethnic cleansing with the psychological care necessary to build a new domestic subject.

An unintended consequence of this gynecological state intervention was the radical transformation of women's reproductive health care in Bangladesh. International NGOs and development agencies pressed the point of population control, while local organizations recognized that contraceptive access offered women new possibilities in both their intimate and economic lives. The Women's Rehabilitation Board partnered with the Directorate of Training, Research, Evaluation, and Communication of the Bangladesh Family Planning Association to provide contraceptive resources for women at the center as well as locals. Several board members of the Bangladesh Family Planning Association and the IPPF collaborated on the Bangladesh Women's Emancipation Programme (BWEP), a plan to mainstream family planning services and support women who had been subject to sexual violence during the war. The February 1972 proposal called first for emergency medical assistance across Bangladesh to supplement the IPPF's efforts in Dhaka and a media campaign to draw attention to the prevalence of sexual violence and reduce its social stigma. Subsequently, what the BWEP called the "Rehabilitation and Emancipation" phase focused on economic productivity. While this followed the logic of the National Rehabilitation Board, BWEP insisted, "Women's emancipation, besides contributing directly to social and economic uplift in Bangladesh, will also give a new and positive direction to our country's family planning efforts. It is a well known fact that birth rates go down as women's emancipation goes up."[50] BWEP prophesied the determinant link between the reproductive health of Bangladeshi women and the neoliberal discourse of empowerment that has so structured international aid policies since 1971. The production of Bangladesh as a site of intervention and surveillance by donor countries continues to depend on the gynecological life of women, originating with women who were subject to sexual violence during its war for independence.

Without the stigma of pregnancy—whether ended through abortion or adoption—women who stayed at the center practiced forms of domestic life to which they might, in the program's ideal, return, as well as developing skills oriented toward making them wage earners. The center, after all, was intended to be an intermediary space between the harms of war and the life afterward. We might, then, see the program as having the two imbricated goals of exigent care for physical and psychological trauma and of reincorporation into socio-economic life.

Women who were identified as suffering from persistent and acute mental health issues were sent to the state mental hospital in Pabna, with the implicit hope that if they were unable to be helped they could remain incarcerated there. Rehabilitation efforts relied on the visibility of reparable bodies to mobilize a broader rhetoric of new nationalist possibility. Women in the program were the litmus test of the state's ability to provide for its subjects and to recover from the losses of a war designed to incapacitate it. It is important to point out that the state's policy discourse and the material practices of the volunteers and workers at the rehabilitation center did not necessarily follow one another. The focus of the rehabilitation center bore the mark of proximity augured by the first touch of Khan's old saris on the bodies of women found in camps: familiar, safe, but nonetheless apart. The staff especially feared that the women at the center would become dependent on them and on the program for its affective and social protections.[51]

Recognizing far more quickly than the government that chances of women's returning to their families were often quite slim, staff at the rehabilitation center sought to offer their wards as much training for a new version of life as they could. Outside of the familiar work of stitching and weaving, women were given vocational training in clerical and technical fields; the state's economic landscape would have a high demand for skilled labor. But even with a focus on professional skills and economic independence, something of the domesticating project continued to characterize most of the training and care the women received. Khan recalls taking a group of women to the Red Cross orphanage in Dhaka, so that they might be hired as nurses and caregivers to the war orphans waiting to be sent to Scandinavia, England, and the United States.[52] This is a heartbreaking irony. The same rehabilitation program that made possible abortions and adoptions supplied the international organization that would disseminate children of the war around the world with temporary, impersonal mothers from that very program. It reveals the intense patrolling of women's bodies and labor as symbols of the nascent nation.

Indeed, among the initiatives funded by the state for the Women's Rehabilitation Board was essentially a dowry system that incentivized Mukti Bahini to marry women from the center. Issues of consent here are perhaps unsurprisingly opaque and recall long-standing questions about the terms of women's desire and choice that I examined in chapter 1; given the exceptional sociocultural position of a single woman and the pressures to normalize after the war, many women agreed to the marriages. Prospective grooms would be given 1,500 *taka* (approximately $190 at the time) and, as the women would also receive war compensation, couples would have a shared income as evidence of their war effort. However, few men came forward, and the program was quietly ended after several recorded incidents in which women were abandoned immediately after the marriage. Though the program did not have much success, it solidified a broader political project. The linguistic nationalism of the 1952 *Andolan* had been supplanted by a racial nationalism in which the body of the Bengali woman purged of traces of contact with Pakistani bodies was figured as the symbol of national possibility. This transformation was structured by a model of the family in which the nation's father, Sheikh Mujib, erected genealogical borders to uphold new geopolitical ones. Indeed, the life of the women's rehabilitation process is almost entirely sutured to Sheikh Mujib's, as his death in 1975 marked the end of the official program. His death, and the end of his political cult of personality, was a turning point for Bangladesh's relationship to its own historiography.

V. Something Like Liberation

Even though the official and affective project of rehabilitation ended with the death of Sheikh Mujib, its unfinished aspirations echo throughout Bangladesh decades later. The open wound of the war gathers into it the formative energies of a nation that can neither forget its toll nor recover its losses. Gurudashi Mondal, the subject of Yasmine Kabir's riveting 2005 documentary *Shadhinota (A Certain Liberation)*, walks through the bazaar of Kopolmoni, a small town in Khulna, cursing at passersby, pretending to strike men with her walking stick, and exacting from their pockets small sums of money. She cuts a striking figure as one of the few women in this space and the only one constantly in physical contact with men. Reaching, touching, grabbing, Gurudashi—or "Mashi" (maternal aunt), as she is consistently called—abides no distance between her body and those of the men she encounters. The first half hour of the thirty-seven-minute film consists of largely of men—acquaintances from the bazaar, local officials, children—making themselves available to her playful violence, describing it as *ador* (affection), and insisting that her madness (*matha kharap*, literally "of ill mind") has a clear etiology and outcome: She is the mother of Mukti Bahini; having lost her sons in the war, she went mad; there should be a memorial for her. Gurudashi agrees vehemently, if obliquely. "I am going to die here in Kopolmoni; if there is a memorial here, these boys will have somewhere to go."[53] So vividly alive, Gurudashi attempts to forestall her own vanishing from the physical space of the town. Although the young men suggest a memorial to her now, hopscotching the normative arc of memorialization that follows from death, she seems to recognize the danger of a future in which her visceral, disruptive presence will not be there to remind people of the moment of which she has become representative.

What does it mean to demand a memorial for a living person? Freud likens memorials to mnemic symbols, external markers of a past loss that enable moving forward.[54] By calling for a memorial of that which is not yet gone, the men of the bazaar admit an asynchrony between themselves and the war, between the physical presence of Gurudashi and her symbolic value. Her life, severed from normative domesticity, is in some way already over. Their romantic identification with her sons, who died with the most hallowed term available within the national consciousness, makes Gurudashi a conduit to a heroic masculine past, an artifact of the war's success, even as she herself is a figure of misfortune. They articulate an investment in her as a symbol of the nation that is familiar to them. Recognizing in the claims of her madness that she herself cannot be "repaired," these men seek to fix her in space, materially. But Gurudashi is no ghost. Her haunting of Kopolmoni is a corporeal interruption of national time as she keeps 1971 alive by inhabiting forms of freedom that are inextricable from their legacy of violence.

Throughout the film, Gurudashi is described as free. Paramount to the documentary are questions of what it means to be free and who bears the cost of freedom. The nuanced English translation of the film's title renders the Bangla word *shadhinota* (from the Sanskrit *svadhin*, and of a shared root with the nationalist terms *swaraj* and *swadesh* that we examined in earlier chapters) as "A Certain Liberation," implying that Gurudashi's liberation is, on the one hand, far from complete and, on the other hand, deeply subjective and yet still definitive. It connotes the constitutive losses and violence that have brought Gurudashi to the streets of Kopolmoni, losses that are situated both individually and nationally. Promotional copy for the film makes explicit the national context of Gurudashi's "madness," even as it refuses to articulate the nature of its etiology: "Gurudashi Mondal gave herself up to madness in 1971."[55] Exact contours of the trauma remain necessarily blurry, while the instantiation of that madness is offered a national corollary. She does not *become* mad in this formulation; she allows herself to be consumed by the ineluctable logic of madness, her "liberation" into madness conjoined to the newly born nation. The promotional copy goes on to say, "In her madness, she has found a strategy for survival. In Kopolmoni, Gurudashi has attained near legendary status. Through her indomitable presence, she has kept the spirit of the Liberation War alive." Her pathologized state—the sickness she embodies—is figured as preservative, of herself and of a historical moment made visible by her inability to leave it behind. She serves as a persistent and incisive reminder of national and personal trauma. Her "madness," made liberation in the film, expresses, produces, and preserves remnants of violence played upon both her body and the fledgling nation with which her madness is twinned.

For men who encounter her in the public bazaar, she is an alluring, if amusing, anomaly who poses no threat to them or to the hermeticism of masculine spaces. She is shielded by that apparent madness. For women like the one with whom she lives, Gurudashi skirts the bounds of what is possible and reveals the dangers of overreach. They see, far more acutely than the men in the bazaar, the cost of her freedom and the calculus by which it exceeds the possibilities of their own desires. One says, "If I wandered the bazaars, would anyone come to marry my daughters? Even if I am poor, there is such a thing as *samāj* (society)."[56] Gurudashi's liberation from the ties of conjugal life enables her to move in ways that reinforce her unincorporability back into *samāj*. The catastrophic loss she expresses—that of her children—is what ties the women around her to the domestic space, a space that is both historically and socioeconomically marked in Bangladesh as being one of containment and limited possibility.

What these women do not explicitly express is a conception of how Gurudashi comes to her ambivalent freedom. Whereas the men of the bazaar justify her behavior through the loss of her sons, the women recognize but do not speak of violence on her body. Gurudashi is the subject of the documentary not because of her madness but because of what is proleptically known by the audience as its cause. She accedes to the stories that the men in the bazaar tell about her, not offering the corrective that she later shares, alone on a boat, speaking directly into the camera: Her children were not Mukti Bahini, but rather during the war were so young that she was still nursing them when the soldiers came to demand that her husband work for them. At his refusal, they shot and killed him and the children and took Gurudashi to a camp, where she was held until she was freed by Mukti Bahini. From there she was taken to the Pabna Mental Hospital, from which she escaped so frequently that she was finally released. There is no secret to what happened to her, but she refuses the name by which she is made subject of the film: Gurudashi is not a *birangona*.

An account of the violence she has experienced and the losses she has incurred, in the narratives offered by the men who insist she deserves a memorial or in her own sharply lucid recollection, cannot be incorporated into the symbolic category *birangona* because Gurudashi's life and losses are inexorably social. The frames of recognizability erected by the word *birangona* ensure its subsumption back into the domestic sphere in which *birangonas* are either the women who can be married off to Mukti Bahini because they are war comrades bound by heroism or they are the subjects of whispered accusations of sexual disgrace and dishonor. Gurudashi, despite potentially having received from the government compensation from the war, affixes herself to an entirely relational space.

Her familiar sobriquet, "Mashi," is a sign of family, care, and respect that stands apart from *birangona* as a sign at once of heroism and taint. The touch of a *birangona* is the trace of the touch of military confinement, of "Pakistani" hands. Gurudashi's body is maternalized rather than sexualized, eliciting none of the whispers of disgrace that envelop the idea of *birangona*. Indeed, she claims a language of impropriety—"*Ami meye ta bhalo na* (I am not a good woman)"—that her neighbors refuse.[57] They refer to her instead by familial terms and honorific pronouns. Where she marks her non-normativity, the danger that a single woman roaming the streets ought to present, the community around her insists on her innocuousness.

Identified as a maternal presence, rather than by the ambivalent sexuality of the *birangona*, Gurudashi is sanitized by the losses that avail her to the public space. She marks her somatic presence in town by wet-nursing, often without the consent of their parents, infants with whom she comes into contact. So, when the people in the bazaar refer to her as "*Banglar Ma* (Mother of Bengal)," it is at once a romantic and functional description, which of course repeats the early nationalist image of Bengal that was designed to actuate anticolonial revolt. Stripped of her own children by the war that made Bangladesh, she performs the intimate labor of impersonal motherhood in uncanny sorority with the women from the Rehabilitation Center. We might think here, too, of Mahasweta Devi's short story "The Breast Giver," in which Jashoda, who is forced into "professional motherhood" when her husband loses his feet, wetnurses the children of the wealthy family whose car ran over those feet. Having secured her family's prospects, she finally succumbs to breast cancer and, despite "see[ing] her milk-sons all over the world," dies alone.[58] Gurudashi, perpetually aware of her own radical finitude, leaves traces of herself all over Bangladesh. Though she is confined to Kopolmoni, she claims that all of the children of Bangladesh are hers. She says, "I am an abnormal woman; these children make me normal." In the stark knowledge that there will be no actual memorial for her, she insists on a most intimate form of memory transmission.

Gurudashi is disruptive to the landscape of a postwar Kopolmoni in several registers. In the markedly Muslim space of contemporary Bangladesh, Gurudashi recalls prior forms of social life that largely disappeared with the mass exodus of Hindus from Khulna and other rural areas from 1905 onward. While she demands that passersby call her "mother," she also supplicates in front of the Mother Goddess, Kali. Dakshinakali, the form of the goddess that is worshipped throughout Bengal, is the vision of the fierce and fearsome

mother whose comfort resides in the promise that she will vanquish all enemies, proved in the garland of men's heads she wears around her neck. It is
not difficult to see why Gurudashi finds such comfort in this image and why
inside the temple she can express grief and despair that transform into playful
violence in the outer world. With Kali, she is with the feminine figure most like
herself—and the one to whom the plea for protection, though perhaps decades
too late, might still be made.

Gurudashi's identifiable Hinduness curiously conflates with her declared
madness. I have thus far insisted on describing her madness as "apparent" and
"declared" in order to draw attention to the discursive work that the claim of
madness does for Gurudashi and the community, even and especially in the
face of her remarkable lucidity. Madness is the form by which the violence
and losses she has borne are made socially intelligible. It screens a narrative
of her that enables her transgressions into masculine spaces and onto masculine bodies without recalling explicit sexualization and obscures articulations
that might disrupt her tenuous incorporation into the social world. When
Gurudashi says anything that breaks the script of the public account of her
losses, her madness is a ready social remedy. It gives the men in the bazaar
license to produce her at once as a figure of familiarity and of national significance while disregarding the materiality of her trauma. Fragments of recalled
violence, like the machine-gun-like noise she makes while striking people with
her stick or her claim that Sheikh Mujib broke her leg but bought her that stick,
are read as incoherences of madness rather than as ruptural remainders of
lived harm. Moreover, the claim of her madness constitutes the terms of her
freedom. She moves freely because she is mad—a curious inversion of the historical confinement of the mentally ill.

The mental health infrastructure in Bengal, other than the Ranchi Asylum
for Europeans, established by Owen Berkeley-Hill (whom I discuss in chapter 3)
to provide psychiatric treatment for British officers, consists almost entirely
of lunatic asylums. The Pabna Mental Hospital, to which Gurudashi was taken
after her release from captivity, is the only public behavioral health facility
in Bangladesh. It was established in 1960 by the Pakistani government on
grounds seized by the local spiritual leader Sree Sree Thakur Ankulchandra
who, like many other Hindus of the area, migrated to India during the 1947
Partition. Under the auspices of the Enemy Property Act of 1948, the first
Bengali hospital aimed at treating rather than incarcerating the mentally ill
was set up. Indeed, until the mid-1990s, the records of former patients were
routinely transferred over to the temple on the property where the Hindu
priest stood as guardian and archon. Those records were apparently destroyed
in a fire some years ago.[59]

When Gurudashi was found by Mukti Bahini at a camp, a male relative relates to the camera, she was taken to Pabna. Her repeated escapes, her refusal to be enclosed within the institution, are not figured as effects of her insanity but as glimmers of her prior self. Before the war, he says, she was a solitary (*neebhrito*, নিভৃত) person from a solitary place. She is pulled toward a home as isolated and solitary as she was before the incursion of violence onto her body and life. That she now derives her life entirely from her immersion in public social places is a mode of survival that he analogizes by way of Tagore's 1865 poem "*Dui Bigha Jomi* (Two Units of Land)," in which Upen, a poor farmer, is forced off his tiny plot of land by a greedy landlord. As he leaves the land that has been in his family, but because of Permanent Settlement has not been owned by it, for generations—his *bhitte mati*, ancestral land—Upen says, "*Monay bhabelam, morey bhagaban / rakhebe na mahagortey, tai lekhey deelo bishwanikhil/dui bighar poribortey* মনে ভাবিলাম, মোরে ভগবান/ রাখিবে না মোহগর্তে, তাই লিখি দিল বিশ্বনিখিল/ দু বিঘার পরিবর্তে (I thought to myself, my Lord will not confine me to this pit of illusion, so he inscribed for me the whole universe, in lieu of two bighas)."[60] Compensation for the loss of Upen's connection to his ancestral home—the very foundation of his patrilineal heritage and his claim to a motherland—is the arrival of a personal god who gifts him all the world. For Tagore, this circuit of exchange is bittersweet but ultimately amended by spiritual freedom beyond the material. But the poem's redeployment to describe Gurudashi's liberation in madness brings into sharp relief the irreparability of some losses.

Gurudashi's freedom comes at the cost of the most intimate material signifiers of home and belonging. The loss of the motherland is represented by refugees during the war as a fundamental psychic trauma in a particularly Hindu idiom, as to leave one's *bhitte mati* or *vastubhita* (foundational home) was to extirpate oneself from a familial history and its protection. Dipesh Chakrabarty describes how Hindu refugees fleeing to West Bengal during Partition and after understood their displacement:

> For the ability to maintain connections with one's *vastubhita* across generations is a sign of being fortunate, a fortune that itself owes something to the auspicious blessing of one's ancestors. This idea of "home" was extended during the course of the nationalist movement into the idea of the "motherland" where Bengal became the name of part of the world made sacred by the habitation of the ancestors of the Bengali people. To become an *udvastu* was thus to be under some kind of an extreme curse.[61]

Unmoored from this foundational home, refugees faced the loss not just of a present material stability but also of a transhistorical refuge and protection.

East Bengal's soil is generative and life-giving, through its agrarian bounty and through the lineage and familial history it offers. Accounts of refugees eating soil from their homes before fleeing are common in Partition and 1971 narratives; when unable to physically inhabit ancestral land, they would take traces of it with them, within their bodies, corporeal preservation. For Gurudashi, the loss of home is parceled together with the loss of family. Her freedom comes from being *udvastu*—unhomed. A certain liberation indeed.

Inextricable from the film's question of what constitutes freedom is the attendant question of how grief and loss can be borne—by individuals and by a nation. Gurudashi's desire for a memorial for herself and her children recalls a wider demand for mechanisms of fixing the memory of 1971, in the form of war crimes tribunals and cultural representations. But figuration of her madness as the vehicle of her liberation is telling, too. Her freedom bears the cost of what she cannot fully articulate, what exceeds narrativization. She says, "When I think about it, a wave breaks inside of me." Beyond the limits of speech is a somatic trace of her profound loss. Narrative accounts of her experience of war, like those of the war more broadly across Bangladesh, are what can be spoken of when the full extent of loss eludes language and its frames of representability.

The disappearing archive with which this chapter began abides by the impossible fantasy of preserving remnants of the past in the face of inevitable destruction. The wish of a woman whose celebrated forms of freedom are inextricable from catastrophic losses to erect a material memorial to herself and to her children militates against the necessary and ongoing destruction of memory within and beyond the archive on which future narratives of the Bangladeshi state rely. Throughout the film, Gurudashi refuses public and cinematic pressure to name herself *birangona*; she recognizes the emptiness of it as a category and its inability to do for her the work it promises to a national imagination. She undoes the gap between the personal, intimate life of trauma and the public life of politics with her insistence that her losses be memorialized, but does so in a different idiom than that which the state demands. The rumors of a fire in the archive and the call for a memorial in Kopolmoni operate within a shared but vexed economy of violence, its repair, and its repetition. It is, then, perhaps not surprising that when Gurudashi Mondal died, several years after the release of *Shadhinota*, she was—in the Hindu tradition and against her repeated requests—cremated. The ashes of her body, traces of her embeddedness in Kopolmoni as a reminder of the war, were spread in the river with no memorial.

5

Machine Made

On December 6, 1971, just ten days before Bangladesh would become independent from Pakistan following a nine-month war, U.S. Secretary of State Henry Kissinger gathered the National Security Council's Washington Special Action Group (WSAG) to discuss Indo-Pak hostilities. India had formally entered the war just three days earlier, responding both to the refugee crisis at its West Bengal border, as up to 10 million civilians fled from what was still East Pakistan, and to long-standing animosities with Pakistan. India's military capacities presaged a swift end to the war. Even while the WSAG considered how much and how publicly to continue to support the Pakistani army as it faced imminent defeat, concerns turned to the future of postwar Bangladesh and the aid it would require. Ambassador U. Alexis Johnson, in a phrase that would be attributed to Kissinger for decades to come, declared that despite its rich natural resources, Bangladesh would be "an international basket case."[1] Less well known is Kissinger's response: "But not necessarily our basket case."[2] Kissinger's marked disdain, as much for the "bleeding hearts" of the American public who might sympathize with the "dying Bengalis" as for those famine-stricken Bengalis, is of a piece with his abiding admiration of the Pakistani President Yahya Khan, his undisguised animosity toward Indian Prime Minister Indira Gandhi, and his general apathy toward the newly emerging Bangladeshi nation. Bangladesh, Kissinger was quick to avow, would not be a burden on a single country but the newest and perhaps neediest recipient of a multilateral aid infrastructure.

The sobriquet for the country has stuck, as referential shorthand for Bangladesh's dependence on foreign development assistance and as uncanny metaphor for neocolonial violence. Derived from the World War I description of a soldier who, having lost both arms and legs, had to be carried around in a basket, the term "basket case" is haunted by the detritus of battle. Stripped of independence in service of a nation, the basket case of war is the grotesque reminder of its cost. Now reliant on those for whose safety he ostensibly lost his independence, the basket case is the moral weight of war upon the body of his nation. The psychological evocation of the term, too, is a war relic: shell-shocked soldiers who returned from the front with limbs but not psyches intact. Their care became the purview of national gratitude even as they had to be shuttled from sight to preserve the possibility of a postwar future uncrippled by trauma. When American officials declared Bangladesh a "basket case," they recalled with it the long history of empire and its extractions implicated within the pathologization of this postcolonial state.

The fears of famine Johnson and the WSAG cited cannot be disaggregated from the catastrophic Bengal famines under the Raj in 1770, 1896, and 1943. Nor can concerns that rates of raw jute production in Bangladesh would be retarded by the lack of industrial infrastructure be disaggregated from the 1789 subsidies of the Dundee jute mills and the 1905 partition that demarcated urban industry in Calcutta from the lower Brahmaputra cultivation fields. Nor can either of those challenges be disaggregated from the quarter-century of Pakistani rule over East Bengal, which drew its administrative inspiration from the Raj's policies toward the eastern wing of the subcontinent. Like the limbless war veteran leaning upon the goodwill of the very state apparatus whose policies sent him to the front to begin with, Bangladesh as international basket case would require enormous external funding and support structures to repair two centuries of economic exploitation.[3]

Coded within the prescription of Bangladesh's dependence is also the repudiated possibility of its abundance, that it might have been breadbasket rather than basket case. Although the highly fertile floodplains of the Ganges-Brahmaputra had produced rice, jute, and tea for much of the eastern subcontinent, its outlined plan to be food self-sufficient by 1985 was deemed overly ambitious by many in the international aid community—a particularly cutting irony.[5] But the challenges facing the fledgling nation were more than just those of bare subsistence. Chief among the concerns of the World Bank (particularly its development wing, the International Bank for Reconstruction and Development [IBRD]) and other aid-giving agencies was the demographic situation in East Pakistan. As there had not been a census since 1961, their population figures were rough estimates based on an extraordinary projected 3 percent growth rate. Officials at IBRD warned of impending food scarcities and recommended that the first order of business be a regimented family planning program to decelerate the population boom.[6]

Though not for the reasons IBRD recommended, the new republic did set family planning as one of its earliest projects. As I argue in chapter 4, the contraceptive intervention into the bodies of women who had been raped during the war laid the groundwork for a revived ethnic nationalism—a nation without Pakistani blood—and primed the site for development aid. Bangladesh was prescient in its recognition that the reproductive possibilities of its female citizens would be inextricable from its economic growth. For the past half-century, the markers of its development progress have been dependent on measures of women's reproductive health: maternal mortality, infant mortality, and access to contraception. Women's bodies are in this way the justification for and the benchmark of foreign intervention and international aid. They are the litmus test of the developing state. In a moment when, following the horrific and preventable factory accidents between 2005 and 2015, Bangladeshi women's bodies are central to the international scrutiny of industrial labor, the familiar development language of *empowerment* and *agency* takes on a new guise. Female garment workers are figured in this global discourse as being exploited by a system that absorbs their labor and exhales only precarity. They, like the representative women of the international aid apparatus, aver the failures of a weak state to protect its citizen-subjects and warrant its condemnation to the waiting room of history. At the same time, whether in terms of the economic possibilities of the garment industry or the empowerment rhetoric of microcredit systems, women's public labor in Bangladesh is now seen through the neoliberal lens as the vehicle of self-determination—a very different kind of sovereignty than that with which this book began. From within this paradox, this chapter asks how else we might conceive of women's labor and their own relationship to it in Bangladesh; that is, other ways of understanding the material and symbolic conditions of a good life. *by non-Western standards!*

Fundamentally, the purported success of Bangladesh, growth of internationally recognized development markers, and move toward middle-income country status has come through liberalizing, globalizing policies that promote flexible labor. The World Bank notes that this has happened despite weak governance, a testament to the force of these global growth policies.[7] Bangladesh, it seems, succeeds in spite of itself. The question of what determines a life worth living is thus played out on an uneven global field. For this reason, this chapter traces how the people who are figured as the true engines of Bangladesh's growth—its female labor force—engage a relationship to work, to the nation, and to their objects of their labor.

Central to the international concern over the rights and well-being of Bangladeshi women is the pernicious, latent assumption that these women fundamentally misrecognize what is good for them or make choices against their own best interest. This global paternalism suggests a task of ideological rescue that uncannily (and purposefully) echoes the imperial projects of rescuing women from the clutches of a native culture. We hear the echo of Gayatri Spivak's famous phrase, "White men saving brown women from brown men."[8] But, let us disrupt that diagnosis. Like Pritilata Waddedar in chapter 1, who within and in response to patriarchal forces that sought to yoke women between victim and martyr, vividly and intentionally articulated the terms of her life and death, so too do these Bangladeshi women. This is no false consciousness. It is a powerful assertion of political will and self-determination that does not depend on the structures of the state or the international development system. The economic labor of women in Bangladesh is political labor. Unpacking the category of "empowerment" at the heart of national and international projects for women reveals forms of agency, desire, legibility, and possibility compressed within it, and illuminate how those affective forces operate in women's lives. In this chapter, I enjoin us to think otherwise about freedom, to imagine alongside Bangladeshi women what conditions of possibility look like unpinned from the normative expectations of a global economic order.

By tracing two forms of women's labor oriented around textiles, which are both culturally and economically central to the idea of Bangladesh (NGO-supported handicrafts and industrial garments), I show how the forms of micro-credit for which Bangladesh has garnered such acclaim have a longer history on the subcontinent tied to textiles and manufacture, and that the entrance of women into this space is inaugurated by an expansion of the sphere of the home to include forms of wage labor. The intimacy between these valorized projects of individual uplift—relying on but paradoxically at the expense of a collective—and the collectivized language around garment work proves the discourse of empowerment to be a red herring, distracting from how women's labor in Bangladesh clothes a global narrative of postcolonial neoliberalism and transnational capital. Ultimately, this discourse reproduces a familiar colonial commonplace in which Bengali women are objects of intervention, capture, and catalog by a paternalist structure of governance. This chapter also seeks to bridge the gap between the quantitative examinations of Bangladesh as a development state and the qualitative narratives of postcolonial resistance by showing the common thread of women's labor through them. This labor, economically undervalued and institutionally marginalized, offers a vision of political possibility that has abided on the subcontinent, and in East Bengal in particular, in a kind of rupturing proximity to our most familiar narratives yet refuses to be subsumed by them.

I. Women's Work

Women's Work, the monthly progress report sent out by the National Board of Bangladesh Women's Rehabilitation Programme (BWRP), opens its September 1972 issue with an account of a conversation between a visitor and one of the program's trainees in which the trainee shares how she plans to use her skills in the future: "I shall learn the work, and then go back to my home. Produce the items I have learnt. Conspire [trainee means negotiate] with a shop-keeper or tailor in the neighbourhood and arrange marketing of the products and earn a living."[9] The unnamed trainee articulates the primary goals of the state rehabilitation program: economic self-sufficiency, community reintegration, and market development. As I discuss in chapter 4, the BWRP was originally conceived as a five-year program, seeking to prepare women for a new national landscape while simultaneously priming an economic base for their entrance into formal sectors. Focused on artisanal craft—from weaving and embroidery to clay modeling and jute work—it engaged an aesthetic and cultural economy of valued and valorized labor. Reintegrating poor and displaced women into communities in which they could remain economically self-sufficient included the challenge of finding a market for the products of this project other than the BWRP's own handicraft outlet, Unmesh. The cooperative model that the trainee identified was central to this project, in which women's handicraft work could circulate within a more mainstream market of goods. Women working together, and with established sellers, could be incorporable in a way that a single woman could not.

In this way, through the form of the productive collective, women were positioned as the standard-bearer of the newly independent nation. Recognizing that they would be significant contributors to the economic development of the country, even before the UN Decade of Women, the BWRP and the Bangladesh Rehabilitation Assistance Committee (BRAC) focused extensive efforts on laying the groundwork for this new economic life of women. *Women's Work* suggests, "Willingness to work and earn is also a part of the mental process for which motivation to pursue and to adopt a changed way of life is a determining factor for the individual. Women's participation in economic activity can hardly be encouraged without helping them to attain desired literacy, ensuring needed enlightenment and orientation to the women in their bid for a planned and prosperous life."[10] Prophesying the development apparatus's discourse on women's empowerment, Bangladeshi nongovernmental organizations (NGOs) established themselves as intermediaries between state-based citizen services for women and private economic mechanisms. By supporting women's literacy and promoting a handicraft sector, NGOs built a shadow economy that remains one of the most significant global brands of Bangladesh.

BRAC, today the world's largest NGO with programs in twelve countries, began through the relatively local project of small-scale relief support for returning war refugees. As the central government struggled to provide for the millions of displaced Bangladeshis after the war, BRAC stepped in to offer civil services like medical centers, infrastructural repair, and home building. NGOs who participated in rehabilitation efforts following the war echoed the official BWRP sentiment that women's handicrafts were a particularly resonant and compelling material referent of repair and of economic possibility. In 1978, Ayesha Abed, wife of BRAC's founder Sir Fazle Abed, set up Aarong as BRAC's private handicraft retail chain; it continues to source much of its products from the women's collectives established in this period. While the BWRP announced its own planned obsolescence, as the project of state-sponsored rehabilitation was necessarily limited to produce the narrative of a successful, future-oriented nation, BRAC and other NGOs from this period were not so curtailed and benefited from their pledge to communities of continued support and development aid.

The name "Aarong," which comes from the Bangla for "market fair," explicitly references the cultural memory of the local *mela*, temporary fairs that were set up in villages to celebrate festivals, at which local artisans would sell their goods—terra cotta sculptures, woven cloth, wood carvings, and embroidery. These were a form of markedly indigenous commerce in which a common Bengali aesthetic imagination was espoused through handicraft. As a commercial venture in Dhaka, Aarong set out to remind an urban elite of that prior form of art and manufacture and to hone a new patriotic aesthetic. A revival of Bengali art and craft was central to a broad nationalist project in the postwar years, a reclamation of a particularly Bengali identity seen as having been suppressed under Pakistani rule. To shop at Aarong, which engaged in nominally fair-trade practices, was to announce yourself a steward of Bengali culture. Similarly, to support the work of women who were being trained through BWRP endeavors was to associate yourself with a project of removing the stigma of sexual violence through shared touch.

Though the range of BWRP training was extensive, the focus on handmade objects reveals tactility to be the central organizing principle of technologies of repair. Abiding traces of the women whose bodies, having been harmed, brought them to the BWRP adhered to the objects that would be touched, valued, and displayed. Social worker Maleka Khan notes that much of the initial handicraft work at the Rehabilitation Centre was the occupational therapy of intimate muscle memory. Rather than speak the words of what happened to them, women would take into their hands the objects of a prior life and be physiologically reminded of what preceded the war.[11] They would also instill in inanimate objects the memory trace of their touch, of their presence, ensuring that some small sign of their experience endured, even and especially in the face of personal and national traumatic aphasia. What could not be uttered aloud took on a new life as the appreciable remains of contact and manipulation. Women were encouraged to share family practices, those so instinctive they defied the limits of language, to produce memories of homes to which they might not return, in the resurgent form of embroidery patterns, recipes, and figural designs. Occupational therapy at the Rehabilitation Centre was, in this way, a somatic memory therapy as well. When handicrafts made by women at the Centre or, later, through BWRP initiatives, were sold at Unmesh or Aarong, they circulated across the new nation material remains of the violence of war and its afterlife. In particular, textile training—from the handloom to the sewing machine—knit together valorized objects of Bengali manufacture, material referents of a prior prosperity and aesthetics, with sanctified gendered rituals of care and contact. Those porous objects, suffused with particles of flesh and of recollection, drew together a new national body. Like the *khadi* that Gandhi in the 1930s hoped would weave together a common filial fabric, handicrafts made by these displaced women bound Bangladesh to the bodies it both valorized and hoped to disappear.

Artisanal handicraft projects of the BWRP go on to have a global life in the hands of international NGOs, which I will examine later in this chapter, but strangely they share a genealogy too with the phenomenon of microcredit that has led to enormous international celebration of Bangladesh. In 2006, Muhammad Yunus and the Grameen Bank were awarded the Nobel Peace Prize "for their efforts to create economic and social development from below."[12] The third Bengali to win a Nobel (Rabindranath Tagore and Amartya Sen, both of whom make cameo appearances in this chapter, won in 1913 for literature and 1998 for economics, respectively), Yunus started the Grameen Bank in 1976, two years after BRAC's first microcredit program targeted at rural agriculture producers, with personal loans to forty-two landless women. Operating against the economic commonsense notion that credit should be extended only if equivalent collateral is available to the individual, the Grameen model addresses the capital demands of the landless, rural poor. It has garnered international acclaim and celebration because it targets women as borrowers. The bank now records more than 8 million borrowers, 97 percent of whom are women.[13] Traditionally excluded from financial transactions, rural Bangladeshi women have had little access to capital other than property transactions and liquidating inherited gold. By lending to them, Grameen Bank upends the normative structure of credit systems and cultural expectations.

Grameen works on the premise that women's social embeddedness, their interdependence, is an assurance rather than a liability for a loan. Lending to "solidarity groups" instead of individuals, it produces a socially enforced debt system in which co-borrowers monitor and administer repayment. The laudatory image with which Grameen burrowed itself into the international imagination shows the phone plan in which one woman, using a microloan, purchases a mobile phone, the cost of which she raises through renting out minutes, thus bringing a technological good to a community in need and financially benefiting herself. However, it is in practice about individual and collective goods. Microcredit loans are directed toward small-scale venture investments that ostensibly earn their own repayment. But the 98 percent repayment rate that Grameen touts is made possible by an economy of pressure, shame, and occasional physical threats. Caught together in a web of debt, women who borrow through Grameen Bank are encouraged to monitor each other's investments to ensure collective repayment. Lamia Karim notes the prevalence of "house-breaking," the violent, sanctioned strategy of collection in which homes of delinquent borrowers are literally taken apart for scrap by their collective, many of whom are often kin.[14] In the chasm between the vaunted Nobel Peace Prize discourse of microcredit as an agent of dignity and the coercive mechanisms of shaming that make possible its financial success lies the transformation of structures of trust and affiliation between women.

As a global product, Grameen Bank traffics in the neoliberal fantasy of entrepreneurship, individualism, and "bootstrap capitalism in one of the poorest countries of the world, where shoeless women lift themselves up by the bootstraps" as a universal means to "empowerment."[15] It seeks to capitalize on the beguiling hope that agency can be monetized, that debt can give way to prosperity, and that women are the barometers of development. It thus repeats a familiar trope of Bengali women as metonyms of the nation, unruly signifiers of its conditions of possibility. What is more, as an emblem of Bangladesh, this model trades on the assumption that, so quantified, women's empowerment is universally recognizable in its production of the individual as agentive and political. Debt and intimate violence are central to this individuality and self-sufficiency, suggesting that communal and social interdependencies cannot coexist with this capitalist frame. The price of this form of empowerment, aimed at the poorest Bangladeshi women, is a new form of vulnerability in which homosocial affiliation is collected as surety against individual opportunity—a far cry from the relational ties that bound women like Pritilata Waddedar and Kalpana Dutt to each other in their revolutionary communities.

But even as the Grameen model pursues a project of gender individuation and debt as development, an alternative political imagination perseveres.

Grassroots organizations like Nijera Kori (We Do It Ourselves) turn to the techniques of feminist solidarity as a model for self-sufficiency. Without eschewing an emphasis on women, Nijera Kori begins with the question of political access for the rural poor as a collective. It espouses uplift as a people's movement, rather than the neoliberal projects of alleviating poverty and empowering individual women. In this way, it imagines the possibility of broad-scale change in Bangladesh, led by the rural poor who have in international discourse been the symptoms of underdevelopment rather than the engines of growth. Ultimately, its socialist project returns to the ideals of the early republic, while shedding the representative burden of Bangladesh as the litmus test of a global development program and its women as the symbols of freedom. It also, unfortunately, is in the scantest minority among grassroots organizations in Bangladesh with its now heterodoxic vision.

II. Dropped Stitches

The Grameen Bank model, hallowed as a vehicle of women's empowerment in the contemporary neoliberal world, takes the object of its intervention from an older corporate structure that identified women as its consumer and ideological base. In an essay published in *Young India* in November 1924, Mahadev Desai describes a conversation between Gandhi and a young G. Ramachandran who had come to visit from Santiniketan. Ramachandran, who was a devoted follower of Gandhi's *satyagraha* program, had begun an art education at Visva Bharati University in the middle of the public debate between Gandhi and Tagore around the machines of self-determination (examined in chapter 2). Ramachandran presses upon this concern to ask Gandhi about his objection to machinery, and Gandhi clarifies that his critique is not the machine as such but its supremacy over man. Echoing his debates with Tagore (and Tagore's own stance), Gandhi insists that the machine, in its limited application, should serve man rather than command him. He offers as an example of a machine in man's employ the Singer sewing machine:

> It is one of the few useful things ever invented and there is a romance about the device itself. Singer saw his wife laboring over the tedious process of sewing and seaming with her own hands and simply out his love for her he devised the sewing machine in order to save her from unnecessary labor. He, however, saved not only her labor but also the labor of everyone who could purchase a sewing machine.... The sewing machine had love at its back.[16]

The use-value of the machine is calculated by its unintended collective value. Intended to save the labor of one woman, as an intimate intervention, the sewing machine extends its benefit across a broader constituency. For Gandhi, this distributive property exports the memory of personal care, exonerating this particular machine from claims of alienation and automation. The romance of the Singer sewing machine, of which by 1924 there were more than one million in circulation in India, retains the mnemic promise of that transaction between husband and wife, the fantasy of millions of husbands so aggrieved by their wives' toil. This is a machine of and for the home, of the conjugal union, genteel work.

Ultimately, what drove the popularity of the Singer sewing machine was not this vision of reproductive domesticity but a shifting socioeconomic landscape that expanded the sphere of domestic labor for women. Indeed, the micro-credit model of gender uplift for which Bangladesh has been so lauded in the twenty-first century actually reverberates out of a financial system normalized on the subcontinent by the machine that has been the hallmark of women's work since the late nineteenth century. Singer's hire-to-buy installment plan helped to pioneer consumer credit culture in America, where it originated, and then across the world. In India, where the initial popularity of the name-brand machine faltered when cheaper counterfeit machines also bearing the Singer name and insignia entered the market, the installment credit system bridged the gap between cost and quality for a population for whom the machine would be a livelihood.

Middle-class families, for whom the machine was a proprietary eponym of class status, could often afford to buy the machines outright, so the economic benefits they might bring to the women of the household were kept private. Whether it was in saving the costs of sending clothing out to the tailor or bringing in money by selling manufactured clothing, financial gain for middle-class women that the machine represented was cloaked in the aura of gentility that it symbolized. David Arnold notes that "the sewing machine enabled women to exploit the practical advantages and prestige of machine use and earn money while remaining within the respectability of the home."[17] The sewing machine, for this social stratum, offered a narrow but alluring pathway into a labor market that did not imperil the rigid strictures of respectability. But India could not have been such a lucrative market for the corporation if it did not expand its consumer base to include women for whom visible forms of public labor were neither foreign nor forbidden. Despite the common image from the nineteenth century of the Indian woman as confined to the proprietary limits of the home that circulated through colonial and nationalist discourse alike, poor women have long been in the formal and informal labor forces as cooks, caretakers, cleaners, companions, servants, farmers, and rural manufacturers. The euphemization of the domestic space as that of tradition rather than politics is undone by the material labor of women at its antipodes.

The arrival of the sewing machine transformed one form of intimate labor into the possibility of wages, as Singer's installment plan enabled a male member of the household to gain access to the credit system for those who could not buy the machines outright or were not gifted them through a dowry. More often, still the machines entered circulation in these sectors secondhand or through a more informal network of shared purchase. In the latter model, which will be familiar to readers in its resemblance to the Grameen phone plan, a single machine would be purchased under the name of one buyer while the payments and significant interest were to be borne by several individuals who divided use of it. This was how, by 1907, the Royal Commission on Decentralization noted the presence of Singer sewing machines in what appeared to be every village in East Bengal.[18] The romantic marital machine took on a communal life on the subcontinent, where informal economic uplift rested on the shoulders of poor women who could monetize but not professionalize their labor—a fantasy also central to Gandhian *satyagraha*.

We might see the sewing machine as a crucial transitional technology in Bengal—the metal hinge between muslin handlooms and industrial garment factories.[19] Indeed, its popularity announced the textural slippage away from the fine but irregular weave of the handlooms by way of the rise of the Manchester mills toward a cotton cloth at once affordable and uniform. Sewing machines, as a domestic technology that drew women into the labor force, depended on the imperial redesignation of fabrics of value and their cultivation. Manchester mill cotton made way for the broadcloth, jersey, modal, and denim that Bengali women stitch on Singer machines today inside the factory space. This shift also allows for the entrance of women into the formal labor force; whereas weaving has traditionally been marked as men's work, with women contributing significantly to spinning and starching thread but not to loom-work, new imperial textiles invite the touch of women's hands.

Professional textile work in general was masculinized by its reliance on courtly patronage; the *darzi* (tailor) served as the bodily barrier between consumer and cloth. C. A. Bayly notes that *darzis*, unlike weavers, were seen as machinic even before the advent of the sewing machine.[20] Dhaka weavers, whose produce was limned by a natural transcendence reverberating in the names for their cloth, were artisans who transformed mere thread into gossamer. Working from patterns, *darzis* were seen as mindless replicators of an artistic design not their own. In addition to the rise of demand for Western clothing for private citizens and as civil uniform, *darzis* responded to the changing sartorial demands of a local population.[21] The image of *darzis* as cutters is not the image of feminized, personal labor evoked by Gandhi's valorization of *khadi* and its promise of purifying tactility that we saw in chapter 2. Darzis were low caste or Muslim; their touch would be prohibited in any context other than their textile manipulation. Although spinning and weaving in the *satyagrahan* model denuded the thread of contagion, replacing it with hallowed traces of indigenous labor, tailoring cut cloth into forms recognizable to an imperial imagination, carrying with it the threat of contact. These were men whose fingers skimmed the contours of the body to be clothed and who left on the cloth itself the accumulated particles of their own skin, spit, and sweat.

This form of labor, unromantic and professional, existed in the public. Sewing machines brought *darzis* out of the narrow bazaar stalls ill-suited to their size and into communal space.[22] Sewing machines, in the hands of *darzis*, not only took up visual space, changing the landscape of the public bazaar with their machinic form; they altered its soundscape as well. The distinctive whirring and clacking announced their technological presence and proved their use-value. In the hands of women, however, those machines retreated into private spaces, leaving as trace that familiar but muffled noise. The sewing machine remained in this way an intimate technology, not yet disrupting the normative flows of domestic life even as it prophesied the movement of women out of the space of the home and into the formal workforce. However, the new sewing machine's entrance into the middle-class home as a mark of respectable conjugal life was only a part of its machinic existence.

The latter-day life of the sewing machine in Bengal is one of reuse, of semi-commercialization, and of wage labor. When the Women's Rehabilitation Training Foundation offered training in mechanical stitching, it did so on used machines donated after the war.[23] Once found in the hallowed spaces of the home, these machines reappeared in the hands of women whose access to that domestic space had been imperiled. They were a part of the vocational training in several rehabilitation programs, each of which asked how the simple machine might open up new economic possibilities for women. Unlike the embroidery and sewing training that were figured as artisanal and reparative, the tactile practices of genteel life, sewing-machine training oriented itself to the public world of industrialization and the possibility that women might enter into the workforce. The efficiency and speed offered by the machine made it a gateway into the formal economy for women, not just those trained in the centers but more broadly—an evolution of the *darzi* into a new body in this new nation.

The photograph in figure 5.1, taken by American photographer Jill Sabella at the rehabilitation center in Dhaka in 1972, frames the integration of body and machine, imagining anew the acclaimed Margaret Bourke-White photograph of Gandhi at the *charkha* reproduced in chapter 2. Unlike that singular figure of

Figure 5.1 A sewing class at the rehabilitation center of the Women's Central Welfare Association in Dacca. Photo by Jill Sabella. Private Collection.

the iconic man, instantly recognizable, in glancing contact with the archetypal machine, this is an image crowded by bodies in contact with machine and each other. Though the sewing machine is central to the *mise-en-scène*, it nearly vanishes into the shared space between the three women on the ground. Cloth fed under its needles draws a continuous line back to the white sari of the woman whose hand blurs in movement at the flywheel. That unstitched white cotton cloth that drapes across one woman's body slips and binds hers to the women around her. Together they create a white space of touch that surrounds the machine's black metal form. The women in dark saris, both standing, are sutured together in their shared shadow. These women, unnamed and unrecognized by the camera, are a very different symbol of national futurity and purity than the emaciated man spinning his thread. Their bodies are subject to the purifying machine of the nation that will transform the violence done to them into war labor and make them into viable vessels for the work of reconstruction and restoration.

This image eerily reveals another emergent contingency. Captured by the light of a Japanese machine in the hands of an American woman, the stilled forms of these Bengali bodies converging with another American machine avail themselves to the gaze of a sympathetic consumer public. This photograph is part of the box of material that Sabella sent to me during my research for chapter 4, among photos she had originally planned to use in an article for *National Geographic* that never came to be.

In her research, Sabella collected interviews with women at the Centre and its administration, as well as official correspondence and documents from the BWRP. Included in them is a plea from Justice K. M. Subhan, the first chairman of the Women's Rehabilitation Board, to publicize the BWRP in her article: "Though the National Board has been catering on a mostly emergency basis to the needs of thousands of war-affected women in Bangladesh for their rehabilitation in the society, so far international assistance both in kind and cash received for this programme fell far short of our requirement, among many reasons, one is the lack of publicity, which if done effectively could have incited responses internationally."[24] Subhan hoped that the conjoined image of the women at work, objects of their manufacture close at hand, with an account of the commercial endeavors that funded the BWRP would elicit an international response. Aid in cash or in kind did finally arrive to support women's handicraft endeavors, but it did not come to the BWRP and it did not come in response to Sabella's article. Finding herself, upon her return to the United States, unable to narrativize—to give form and body—to the violence she witnessed and her time with the women at the Rehabilitation Centre, Sabella never wrote the article.[25] Like the stuttered speech of national memory that struggles to speak of war violence against women examined in chapter 4, Sabella's material recollections were relegated to the realm of the private. The global circulation of textile and handicraft by Bengali women, aimed at their uplift, happened not through *National Geographic* coverage but through the transnational structures of NGOs, which traffic in objects promising the touch of foreign bodies.

III. From the Throat

One common form of stitching that spans across but is insistently local to Bengal, and East Bengal in particular, is the *nakshi kantha* embroidered quilts that are archetypical of a feminized folk aesthetic. Made from scraps of discarded fabrics of the body—cotton *saris, lungis,* and *dhotis* pressed into one another and then sutured together—*kanthas* give new life to material worn soft by use and touch. Even the thread of *kantha* embroidery was traditionally pulled from old saris, making it a form of artistic labor available to women across socioeconomic differences, a shared practice of textile work that warmed the body with the reborn remnants of familiar cloth. Because *kanthas* consist of the most pedestrian and ubiquitous of materials, they are a democratic and commonplace art form that nonetheless demands rigorous training and detail. These familiar worn textiles attend the lives of Bengalis, from the blankets in which infants are swaddled at birth to family bedspreads to ceremonial puja mats to Koran covers. Textures of contact and care are woven into the *kantha* with elaborately stitched designs that illustrate a deeply local sense of home and place, condensing the memory of touch into an intimate fabric. For young women who sewed *kanthas* for their trousseaus, the *kantha* was not just proof of their marriageability but also a material trace of their families that could travel with them to their new lives and homes with their in-laws. In the materiality of the *kantha*, we find a particularly rich gathering of corporeal intimacy, aesthetic training, and affective possibility. Stella Kramrisch, an early proponent of *kanthas* as fine rather than folk art who taught for years at Visva Bharati at the invitation of Rabindranath Tagore, writes, "The *kanthas* of East Bengal are saturated with and express a numinous power, the *Shakti* of the region, working through its women and given form by innumerable disciplined stitches."[26]

Nakshi kanthas announce their location with motifs and designs particular to East Bengal, though a *kantha* tradition exists throughout the northern subcontinent. *Nakshi*, from the Persian *naqsh* نقش, indicates its figuralism, the embroidered design that binds together layers of fabric and renders them anew. *Kantha* কাঁথা has a less certain etymology: It has commonly been linked to the Bangla *khet* ক্ষেত, for "field"—*kheta* is the vernacular word for the simply stitched coverlet used by the rural poor—and to the Sanskrit *kanthA* কন্থা, for "rags," which are reconstituted into the form of the quilt.[27] Indeed, these are material kin of the *kantha*, but its symbolic force might best be understood through an unexplored linguistic and discursive affinity to the Sanskrit *kaNTha* কণ্ঠ (in Bangla, কণ্ঠ), "throat." The seat of utterance, the throat gives rise to *katha* কথা, to speech and to story. *Kanthas* are a vehicle of speech, the utterances of material labor and continual contact, the discourse of design for the women who exclusively make them. They are intensely personal art objects, the content and composition of which are entirely in women's hands. Unlike the artisanal fabric for which East Bengal was so hallowed, no courtly patronage shaped the political and aesthetic demands of *kanthas*. Women's work, despite its public life, operated in a personal economy of creative valuation and possibility. Indeed, the expansive potential of the *kantha* form is possible in part because of its domestic stricture. Within the home, through the routinization of stitch and touch, women attached their personal narratives and artistic visions to the fabric of familial life. From the throat, then, *kanthas* tell the stories of the women who make them and bear the traces of their labor and their investment.

The motifs of the embroidery attest to the genealogical character of the *kantha*, as common features of lotuses and geometric design are interwoven with highly local features passed down between women through kinship. In Bengal, where *kantha* tradition cuts across communal bounds, the motifs further reflect a syncretic aesthetic. Despite traditional Islamic aniconism, *kanthas* made by both Hindu and Muslim women depict animals, people, and scenes of rural life. In part this speaks to a Bengali aesthetic imagination that did not align with the theological rigors of the Wahhabi Sunni Islam that arrived much later in the region. Though much of the historical scholarship on *kanthas* has focused on those produced by Hindu artisans and their engagement with religious motifs, and it is true that some Muslim women produce largely nonfigural *kantha* designs, we also glimpse in the stitches of the *kantha* how the communal divisions of Bengal have not been cleaved entirely along cultural lines. There remain in the *kantha* tradition in Bangladesh today, even as it is most commonly manufactured by Muslim women, images and symbols that disrupt any religious categorization. Perhaps some modicum of imaginative synthetic possibility abides in the apparently private labors of women, refusing the public discipline of an increasingly Islamist national culture.

Kanthas often depict the most intimate aspects of life; the textural space opens up a vast terrain of possibility, unregulated by public demands or patriarchal oversight. As more women developed basic literacy in the nineteenth century, *kantha* designs began to include names, aphorisms, and verse. Following the 1905 partition and the rise of Bengali nationalism, patriotic phrases began to pop up on *kanthas* nominally far removed from the sphere of politics, demonstrating how the idiom of resistance had woven itself into the fabric of Bengali life. *Kanthas* are, in this way, spaces of articulation, imagination, and self-conception for women that are both deeply personal and relentlessly social. Their use is never limited to the women who produce them; thus, they bind together bodies and intentions through accumulated touch. In 1939, Kramrisch wrote, "It takes from six months to three generations to make a *Kantha*. No commercial incentive accelerates or vitiates the process of making a whole out of discarded, worthless bits. They are joined and reinforced by innumerable small stitches which give to the ground with its figures a new life and an ageless meaning."[28]

Today, however, in Bangladesh, *nakshi kanthas* have become consumer goods sold through the NGO handicraft sector and largely stripped of their functional origins as artifacts of familial care and contact. This new life of the *nakshi kantha* is synchronized with the life of the new Bangladeshi nation, as its revival as a valued art form was sponsored by the development NGO apparatus that BRAC established in 1972.[29] Though never the most prominent of local artifacts, *kanthas* nonetheless came into a wider field of sight, in part through Stella Kramrisch's patronage in the global art world. As a domestic practice, however, *kantha* work suffered from the movement of women into the formal labor force and the liberalization of import markets that brought in cheap blankets and coverings. BRAC's postwar commitment to handicraft revival as a mechanism of rural development drew the *kantha*, as a material signifier of an indigenous Bengali aesthetic, into a public marketplace into which it had never before crossed. Unlike the *jamdani* cotton fabric, which BRAC also targeted for commercial production, *kantha* manufacture was not a highly specialized skill and had a readily available labor force. Formerly familial practices of women could be resurrected with relatively low cost and training, drawing women into the workforce as makers of this markedly Bangladeshi object. What was once the deeply personal and insistently irreproducible technology of women's self-articulation, their *katha*, was transformed into a representative technology of a new national imagination.

What happens when this intimate practice is commercialized into a commodity? These *kantha* designs are shorn from the utility of their origins, now produced on a single layer of new cotton cloth. All trace of the used and worn and embodied is lifted from the threads of the *kantha*, its new artifice the romantic pastoral image of a Bengal frozen in time. Aarong, for example, markets a broad range of *kantha*-stitch products, from saris to tablecloths to wall hangings. The decorative hangings especially betray the transformation of the *kantha* practice into commodity, as they eschew the geometric and iconic structure of traditional *kanthas* in favor of highly figural scenes of Bangladeshi peasants, thatched huts, and teeming rivers. The neopastoral imagination figured in the *kantha* hangings stand in as the representation of "real" Bengal, a return in form and technology to a prior way of life. This vision is fundamentally unchanged from Rabindranath Tagore's depiction of it a century earlier in his writings and art as the archetypical image and condition of Purba-Banga, the ancestral and timeless font of national futurity. It is also a highly regulated and reproduced image, stripped clean of the particularity and personal intimacies of the *kantha* form.

If the *kantha*-stitch figural hanging circulates within an upwardly mobile and urban Bangladeshi population, bringing the rural and "authentic" Bengal to the increasingly globalized city of Dhaka, a more traditional and yet less emblematic incarnation of the art form travels overseas through the NGO market. Supported by the Mennonite Central Committee (MCC), several NGOs in Bangladesh focus on fair-trade *kantha* work as a vehicle for the general project of women's empowerment. For example, the collective Sacred Mark distributes *kantha*-stitch throws and bags through the MCC's global retail outpost, Ten Thousand Villages. The group—like all of those the MCC supports in Bangladesh—places a premium on the promise of uplift and opportunity, but with a distinctive focus on supporting women who have left sex work in Dhaka's red-light district. Evoking, without citing, the projects of handicraft therapy offered to women raped during the war in 1971, Sacred Mark endorses a markedly neoliberal and moralizing agenda. Its promotional material offers little insight into the subjectivities of its artisans outside of their sexual labor, but draws together the circulation of capital, labor, and the promissory notes of liberation central to their discourse. Using single-layer sari scraps to recall traditional *kantha* work, Sacred Mark's products stitch together not the memory of domestic life and its somatic traces but the purifying potential of tactility we encountered in Gandhi's *satyagrahan* imagination. It is perhaps, then, unsurprising that the other good the group manufactures is soap.

Ten Thousand Villages offers an account of Sacred Mark as

> a workshop of Bangladeshi women who have broken away from the sex trade and now earn their living making soap and handicrafts. The name 'Sacred Mark' was inspired by Bengali poet Rabindranath Tagore, the first non-European to win the Nobel Prize in Literature: 'O rub out, wipe out the writing of disgrace from my forehead. Today, O Friend, let me wear, O let me wear secretly on my forehead the sacred mark impressed by your own hand.'[30]

Sacred Mark cites Tagore to vouchsafe the local color of the project, its Bengaliness assured by the reference to the *ur*-Bengali—and the *ur*-Bengali patriarch, at that. The livelihood and the liberation of the women of the collective are thus warranteed through the figure of masculine national celebrity. This is a curious application of a verse from Tagore's 1915 collection *Gitali*, which is not invested in theological expiation but rather in the intimate touch between a personal god and her supplicant.

In the poem, the poet asks his friend, in the Sufi tradition of calling God by the familiar, who is still removed from him (*neebhrito* নিভৃত, the word by which Gurudashi Mondal in the previous chapter was described in her madness) to reach toward him and with her own hand wipe away the mark of *aupoman* অপমান, which may be as much insult as disgrace, on his brow and leave in its place the *tika* টিকা (the holy mark). It is a poem of longing for the touch of the divine upon the body of the poet, for the ability to wear vividly—not in secret—the sign of her contact, the proof of her presence. Tagore, in the Brahmo tradition, did not traffic in an Abrahamic idiom of sin and absolution. Recasting this verse to promote a project of purifying sexualized bodies through tactile labor, replacing the mark of sin with the mark of the saved, engages a moral economy that can quantify the cost of salvation. Each bar of soap produced by Sacred Mark is impressed with the thumbprint of the woman who made it, the mark of the saved now recast as the mark of the sacred. A strange afterlife of the colonial technology developed in Bengal more than a century earlier (as we saw in chapter 1) to identify and individuate criminals, fingerprinting in this incarnation is the proof of a reclaimed innocence and market presence. It is the mark, too, of the handmade and artisanal; it is the very promise of the identifiable, sovereign body. Sacred Mark's *kanthas* bear on their form the promise of purchasing corporeal intimacy with bodies whose labor has been moved away from the realm of the shameful to that of the valorized. Recalling the material history of *kanthas* as intimate sites of comfort and contact between women and their beloveds, this fair-trade model monetizes one set of labor practices while condemning both sex work and garment work as exploitative.

IV. From Oppression to Opportunity

The fair-trade model through which Bangladeshi handicrafts circulate in a global market, like the revival of *kantha* work, originates from programs of rehabilitation in the early republic. The Mennonite Central Committee first arrived in Bangladesh to offer aid after the 1970 cyclone that killed half a million people. They were already on the ground, so to speak, when NGOs began to engage in refugee relief during and following the war in 1971. The fair-trade supply chain they had established in the 1950s in Ukraine was well-suited to the Bangladeshi situation, in which the central government would cede a large portion of the distribution of basic services and fundamental governances to NGOs and international aid agencies. Setting up artisan collectives incorporated under the name Prokritee, with which they would then cultivate a long-term trade relationship, the MCC was one of a handful of influential groups in Bangladesh following the war that made handicrafts, particularly textiles, a valuable commodity and their production a relatively lucrative endeavor. Globally, their marketing espouses a now-familiar neoliberal credo to buy the change you wish to see in the world.

Ten Thousand Villages, the most prominent retail outlet for fair-trade handicrafts from Bangladesh today, includes with each purchase a short story about the artisan producer. Their products, they promise, are "Always handmade. Always fair trade."[31] The price of the product is supplemented by a qualitative account of what the sale of that product will mean to its always-female producer, from "providing classes on literacy, nutrition and legal rights" to "improving women's standard of living and helping them send their children to school" to encouraging self-reliance.[32] These are translatable, transnational aspirations to which a consumer in the Global North can relate: universal markers of women's empowerment. Indeed, the discourse of empowerment is central to the NGO sector's gender-directed programs. Fair trade's traffic in women's uplift suggests on the one hand that the markers of a good life are generalizable and mobile, and on the other hand that Bangladeshi women—and other women targeted through this paradigm—can be ideologically and economically primed for this good life. Moreover, its commercial profitability relies on the accompanying promise that consumers can fund this developmental project through the purchase of commodities.

Fair trade's focus on direct supply lines pragmatically produces the fantasy that physical distance between artisan and consumer can be bridged by the material promise of shared touch and the ideological promise of progress. Buying handmade products from female artisans in the Global South in this way conveys an intimacy between those who are willing and able to pay a premium and those whom they believe directly benefit from it. "Handmade" connotes contact, implies familiarity, bears the trace. That bodily trace of the artisan that attaches to the object is circulated through the fair-trade model, undiluted by multinational supply chains, and arrives in the hands of consumers to bind them to the development project. Transnational commerce is thereby personalized and sentimentalized, engaging an affective economy of sympathy and altruism. This contingent valuation of labor relies on the expectation that the made object is not the primary valued good but, rather, that it is what the process of production represents that produces a willingness to pay.[33] Consumers of the fair-trade model imagine themselves as purchasing a life for the artisan that they themselves might be willing to live.

Postcolonial feminist critics have already cogently examined the construction of the Third World woman as an object to be rescued by Western feminists, so I will not repeat that argument here; instead I want to point to the gendered neoliberal pivot of the fair-trade movement.[34] Purchasing power is political. Take, for example, Nicholas Kristoff's "Half the Sky Movement," a project which assembled Hollywood celebrities like Meg Ryan, Gabrielle Union, Diane Lane, and America Ferrera together with prominent public figures like Hillary Clinton, Desmond Tutu, Gloria Steinem, and Melinda Gates to "turn oppression into opportunity for women worldwide" through social-media games, books, and films. Fair-trade retail aims to confer moral capital on mundane acts and objects.[35] In the Facebook game of the same name, players—ostensibly around the world, but significantly from the Global North—can digitally embody women from the Global South, purport to experience their challenges, and, with just a click of a mouse, help them make good decisions. Appalling moral condescension of the game notwithstanding, it relies on an imperially upheld assurance that sympathetic identification with virtual "oppressed" women benefits not only the player but also the represented woman. This is because these projects of women's empowerment presuppose the uniformity of Third World women, the modes of their subjugation, and the vehicles of their liberation.

The thumbprint embossed on fair-trade soap, the mark of the identifiable unique individual, vouchsafes the particularity of the object of its intervention-ist project and simultaneously depersonalizes the producer into the generaliz-able category of "oppressed woman." This paradox enables the fantasy of global engagement through commerce and virtuality, markers of opportunity thus also reduced into economics and ideology.

Transnational projects like fair-trade retail and Half the Sky media barter in the common currency of gender discourse in Bangladesh more generally, that of *empowerment*. At its most basic, empowerment is the recognizable access to decision-making, a central conception of the liberal individual sovereign subject. Its discourse operates in a markedly different idiom than the self-articulated language of desire and will expressed by several of the women—historical and figural—in this book. Empowerment, unlike political desire or revolutionary investment, is an honorific bestowed within deeply unequal and impossibly distant power relations, between gender, race, coloniality, and class.

In practice, women's empowerment projects in Bangladesh cut across two major formations: economic and political empowerment for the individual and for collectives.[36] Undergirding this, and simultaneously international devel-opment policy, is the sense that empowerment has a moral dimension as well. Amartya Sen, one of three Bengali Nobel laureates, developed the capability approach, which is now the basis of the Human Development Index (HDI), uti-lized by the United Nations to measure quality of life in developing countries. Fundamentally, the capability approach offers one response to the abiding ques-tion of this book: What constitutes a good life? In particular, its investment in examining "adaptive preferences," which consider the interrelation between nominally objective measures of well-being and articulated subjective experi-ences, orients the capability approach to qualitative evaluations of welfare and development. Capabilities, Sen writes, "are notions of freedom, in the positive sense: what real opportunities you have regarding the life you may lead."[37] Capabilities are thus a mediation of the concern raised earlier about whether notions of well-being travel and translate. Apparently normative ideals like free-dom, development, and justice, when approached through the question of real conditions of possibility, are, to borrow Dipesh Chakrabarty's play on the term, provincialized.[38] Qualitative litmus tests of progress depend on a construction of development potential against the lived conditions of the so-called under-developed world, whereas the capability approach considers representational technologies through which these conditions are negotiated. As a hermeneu-tic, it does not dispense with the aspirational foundations of development eco-nomics, nor with the desire for improved circumstances and increased access to resources and opportunities—"more freedom to lead the kinds of lives we have reason to value"—but refuses a single normative measure of that development.[39] In practice, this has made for an interdisciplinary project in which economists, social scientists, and philosophers have collaborated to determine qualitative and quantitative measures of quality of life.

What universal freedom looks like, however, in practice and in discourse, is hardly a settled matter. Indeed, the kind of life we value change radically depending on who we are and what we conceive of as a thriving life. This is not to undermine the critical ways in which the capability approach has broadened the spectrum of analysis of development, but to posit a disciplinary intervention. Where economics necessarily seeks to measure inequality and to prescribe restorative policies, it cannot ask after the texture of life, the ways conceptions of future possibility are inextricable from their historical referents, of the lived experience of power, and of how people imagine otherwise. Neither, for that matter, can the particular orientation of philosophical discourse that is central to the capability approach.

Legal scholar and philosopher Martha Nussbaum who, along with Sen, Sudhir Anand, and James Foster, helped to develop the theory, focuses particularly on the concept of "human dignity" and gender and has identified specific capabilities as its determinant. Nussbaum uses as example anecdotal accounts from women affiliated with the Self-Employed Women's Association of India (SEWA), a trade union founded by Gandhian Ela Bhatt in 1972 as a branch of the Textile Labor Association, which was also one of the early adopters of microcredit loans on the subcontinent, to argue for what she calls "universal" values. They are better described as cosmopolitan ones. She writes, "Women in developing nations are important to the project in two ways: as people who suffer pervasively from acute capability failure, and also as people whose situation provides an interesting test of this and other approaches, showing us the problems they solve or fail to solve."[40] This "philosophical" account of quality of life suggests a primary set of desires toward which all women should express commitment and implies that as these women move away from their condition of "acute capability failure," they move toward what Nussbaum sees as full, universally recognizable human subjecthood. This nominally qualitative measure of well-being, which has adhered to the capabilities turn in development studies, fixes women of the Global South—and subcontinent in particular—as objects of policy decisions about and scholarly measures of a markedly narrow and fundamentally imperial conception of life and its possibilities.

Indeed, international discourse about Bangladeshi women has been caught in the groove of a record of empowerment. As a catchword and insignia of development, *empowerment* suggests the salutary, incremental increase of autonomy and self-determination. It is the movement from subjugated to agential, from dependence to independence. Ratifying familiar liberal ideals of sovereignty and individuality that so uneasily bore the weight of nationalist discourse in the late nineteenth and early twentieth centuries, this global fixation on empowerment yokes Third World women to precisely the normative measures of subjectivity against which their discursive lives have been built. In the end, it leaves little room for women themselves, the supposed beneficiaries of global good will, outside of congratulations or despair.

Throughout this book, I have endeavored to highlight moments at which other figurations of possibility emerge, ones in which politics and agency are not distilled into their most recognizable and liberal forms. It is thus exigent to ask, by way of conclusion, how the normative and prescriptive markers of well-being might be reconciled with a reading practice that refuses the notion that the terms of liberalism exhaust all political possibility. Holding to the insistence that women do not undermine their own needs and desires, let us consider the relationship between those personal articulations and their global life.

In adopting the capability approach as the foundation of the quantitative measure of the Human Development Index, the United Nations Development Programme (UNDP) recognized that, historically, development and aid have been adjudicated through the economic life of a nation, while directing their interventions toward the somatic and social lives of people. The HDI assesses quality of life in three categories: health, education, and income. Explicitly, it does not engage the most recognizable and marketable terms of development politics, like empowerment, inequality, and poverty. Rather, as a starting point for the measure of human choices—capabilities as positive freedoms—HDI quantifies the framework for basic conditions of well-being. By this measure, Sen announced in 2013, Bangladesh had far outstripped India because of gender-based state and international policies.[41] Empowering the Bangladeshi woman improved the condition of the nation as a whole. But let us attend more closely to what that development looks like.

Driving Bangladesh's rise through the HDI has been a nexus of policies and programs aimed at improving maternal health, increasing female literacy, and increasing participation in the labor force. Bangladesh's success story depends on women's labor—reproductive, educational, and material. In particular, as the garment industry and microcredit structures are individually credited with the exponential growth of both Bangladesh's wealth and women's economic possibility, the material work of women bears on its back the measure of Bangladesh's possibility. There is a disavowed but essential consanguinity between this ostensibly reparative and internationally celebrated labor of the fair-trade handicrafts industry, supported by microcredit structures, and the devalued, anonymous labor of female garment-industry workers—a shared traffic in vulnerable female bodies around the production of the material of national repair and development.

V. Generational Cloth

The fabric produced by contemporary garment labor, the object of international scrutiny after a series of recent catastrophic factory incidents, participates in the international prestige economy of its handwoven kin only in the most disavowed ways. Garment work's alleged distance from the touch of the human hand, its industrialized and mechanized anonymity, is precisely what quantifies its labor value so inexpensively as to ensure that Bangladeshi-made garments are profitable as a transnational commodity. The name bears the promise that machine, not human, manufactures the clothing and elides the strenuous physicality of the process. Disappearing the presence of the body, it suggests a kind of magical process by which garments do not have to be created because they preexist themselves. This is, of course, a very different kind of supernatural textile than the muslin made in the same city two centuries earlier. Where the mythos around that fabric dispelled the memory of human touch by evoking a naturalistic alchemy—woven thread perfected into woven air and water—the readymade garments of contemporary Dhaka void the human through the late global imperial form of commodity fetishism.

We have thus far charted the fabric genealogy between muslin, *khadi*, and *kantha* as aesthetic objects. Their kinship is manifested through the shared sensorial invocation of beauty, pleasure, tactility. But we do not speak of readymade garments in aesthetic terms. Their mass reproducibility and mundane circulation recall neither the work of the master artisan nor the communal singularity of the atelier. Ready-made garment work produces a strange relationship between woman and machine, one more reminiscent of Tagore's fear of the mindless spinning of useless thread than the romantic intimacy between Gandhi's feminized body and the *charkha*. There is no space in the tight weave of its knit fabric, it would seem, out of which to ask after the intentionality and desire prefigured by aesthetic critique. Indeed, aesthetics demands the consideration of desire in its technical, psychoanalytic sense as that which cathects to an object outside of the self. It is for this reason that the previous chapters have turned to textile as a site of political articulation. The contemporary life of ready-made garments, devoid of art and beauty, in turn appears to be one in which only the failure or lack of political agency can be demonstrated. Nevertheless, in insisting on the lineage between this cotton knit and those prior textiles, I want to restore to its commodity form the sensuous aura of the fetish through a contemporary kin, to think it a technology of self-articulation and preservation as much as the *Dhakai* muslin that the art agency Drik spent such time and money in 2013 trying to resurrect.

Kashmiri poet Agha Shahid Ali rewrites a snippet of Oscar Wilde's 1890 *The Picture of Dorian Gray* as an epigraph to his poem "Dacca Gauzes" (1987) about that muslin, ". . . for a whole year he sought to accumulate the most exquisite Dacca gauzes." Textile's promised impermanence hints at a melancholic dread of finitude, in which Dorian Gray is "almost saddened by the reflection of the ruin that Time brought on beautiful and wonderful things."[42] Against the commonsense temporality in which collected material objects outlive their mortal human owners and are passed on as an inheritance, Gray is the unchanging, atemporal remainder. He, unlike his collected muslins, gauzes, silks, and laces, will not decay and disappear. Thus, they become a "means of forgetfulness, modes by which he could escape, for a season, from the fear that seemed to him at times to be almost too great to be borne."[43]

In Ali's hands, those gauzes that veiled from Gray's sight the terror of his own decline are talismans against time of a different order:

> Those transparent Dacca gauzes
> known as woven air, running
> water, evening dew:
>   a dead art now, dead over
> a hundred years. "No one
> now knows," my grandmother says,
>   "what it was to wear
> or touch that cloth." She wore
> it once, an heirloom sari from
>   her mother's dowry, proved
> genuine when it was pulled, all
> six yards, through a ring.[44]

Despite the fact that the Dacca fabric no longer exists, its fleeting touch exists in the bodily memory of the poet's grandmother. What Dorian Gray hoards, while displacing from his own body the ravages of time, recalls to the grandmother the touch of fabric that lay on her body as it had her mother's—which then in turn comes to be repurposed in fragments by the women of her family. These are fabrics of use, meant to be held, washed, and, when worn, revived as intimate instruments of matrilineal care. The poet's grandmother does not mourn the historical violences by which that fabric has ceased to be produced, but mourns instead the loss of their touch. "Years later when it tore, / many hand-kerchiefs embroidered / with gold-thread paisleys / were distributed among / the nieces and daughters-in-law. / Those too now lost."[45] The length of a prized sari no longer available to be offered as inheritance, women now make do with its fragments. Those too, imbued with the touch of mothers and grandmothers woven as gold thread, are now just memory.

But weaving of this mode has far from vanished in Bengal; indeed, it con-tinues today in the celebrated production of *jamdani*. In essence, the method is nearly identical and calls upon the same practices of the body, its routinized movements, its tactile perceptibility, as the original muslin. In this way, muslin remains, or returns spectrally, within the form of contemporary *jamdani*. Many of those who today make *jamdani* fabric come from the hereditary weaver com-munity employed by the Mughal court to produce muslin, weaving saris now for a domestic bourgeoisie. In the same year that Drik dove into the history of muslin manufacture, the Bangladesh Small and Cottage Industries Corporation (BSCIC) filed an application with the World Intellectual Property Organisation (WIPO) for a Geographical Indication (GI) patent on *jamdani*. When registered with the WIPO, the patent affords propriety rights binding name to place; when approved, only fabric woven in Dhaka by the some four hundred recognized members of the weaver community can be sold domestically or internationally under the name *jamdani*. *Jamdani* comes to be fixed by its geolocality such that all *jamdani*s must be *Dhakai*.

In the face of growing competition by Indian weavers from West Bengal, where this manufacture is as historical and familiar as in the East, to Tamil Nadu, the mark of the local translates as market influence. To secure the pat-ent, which would ostensibly allow weavers to set prices commensurate with the singularity—and rarity—of its manufacture, BSCIC had both to establish a material genealogy linking *jamdani* to a historical cloth of a similar variety pro-duced in Dhaka (a wistful nod to spectral muslin) and to identify a determinate difference from cloth of a similar variety produced across the political border in West Bengal. Dhaka, in this application, stands in for contemporary Bangla-desh and its historical antecedent, East Bengal, sliced by international property law off of its former twin. The division of the region in 1905 and again in 1947 by colonial decree is reified through the competition of the global free market. For weavers struggling to compete with machine-made fabric made to look like *jamdani*, the patent represents a kind of reproductive futurity. Faced with the possibility of sending their children into garments work to secure a daily wage, *jamdani* weavers see the GI patent as the possibility that their children will remain in their heredity occupation. For many of the weavers who remain, the uncertainty of the market, the decline of relative prices with the influx of cheap cotton-polyester thread imported from Korea, and the unremunerated labor of producing a single sari are costs of an ancestral commitment they themselves will bear but balk at inflicting on their own children. Without market protections, *jamdani* weaving—once a hallowed courtly trade—appears radically devalued and strenuous in comparison to the hourly regularity of industrial wage labor. Garment work now stands to inherit the muscle memory of the hereditary work of weaving for which Dhaka was known—but in a curious inversion of its gendered image.

The figure of the male master weaver and his son to whom this proprietary knowledge would be passed has given way to the girl-child who will get a primary education and then enter into the formal, urban labor force. In many ways, the neoliberal promise of the garment industry as the vehicle of a particularly gendered development echoes the rehabilitative state policies of the early republic. The kinship between the artisanal textiles and industrial garments is rooted in a shared social vulnerability, a shared contingency between the bodies that manufactured them (that is, made them through the touch of the hand), between women whose labor and dispensability produce the fabric and fable of a neoliberal postcolonial possibility. This fabric, made through and for the human touch, politically constitutes a relationship not just between the bodies of *birangonas* and garment workers but, in retaining traces of the touch of those hands, between those porous lives and our own. This is a form of global contact that orients itself around the ethics of attachment made possible by intimate contact. In the tactile encounter between skin and fabric there resides the possibility of imagining otherwise what political commitment and shared life might look in the face of our own materiality.

VI. Made in Bangladesh

On April 24, 2013, an eight-story factory building in Savar, just outside the Dhaka city limits, collapsed, killing 1,129 people and injuring over 2,500 more. The majority of those killed were female garment workers, employed by the collection of mid-sized garment factories that rented space inside the building. International media were instantly flooded with images of pulverized concrete heaps teeming with volunteers, relatives, and gawkers; women frozen mid-keen, held by loved ones in their anguish; and the now iconic photograph by Taslima Akhter of two bodies—a man and a woman—clasped to one another under a flood of rubble and cloth scraps. Bangladesh, the predominant image of which had for so long been the malnourished child whom Sally Struthers promised late-night television viewers could be saved for just pennies a day, now came to be identified with the dead bodies of female garment workers, crushed under the products of their own labor.

The Rana Plaza factory collapse, the deadliest industrial accident in history, drew attention not only to the dangerous—"primitive" was the language of some media coverage—labor conditions, but also to what was produced in those factories. In 2012, more than a hundred workers were killed in a fire at the Tazreen Fashion factory. Clothing distributed to Benetton, Children's Place, MANGO, and Walmart brought the disasters close for the Western world. The cost of the cheap cotton knits pressed upon the bodies watching the aftermath of the disaster revealed itself as human life and bodily harm. But outrage at the factory conditions was yoked to a more difficult question: In the face of these catastrophes, how could people choose to work under such risky conditions?

Throughout this book, I have argued for a reconceptualization of what constitutes political labor. I want to suggest here that the issue of worker safety in fact depoliticizes the labor of Bangladeshi garment workers precisely by turning to the language of liberal choice. Consent to work in factories under unsafe conditions becomes a symptom of the failure to choose. Reanimating the issues of consent and political subjectivity from *sati* regulation that I examined in chapter 1, this global debate about workers' rights in Bangladesh produces these women as objects in need of saving, devoid of the critical self-conception that is the hallmark of the fantasy of the liberal subject. Paradoxically, in order to be humanized, Bangladeshi garment workers themselves must be manufactured as objects.

The ready-made garment industry constitutes more than 80 percent of Bangladesh's export economy and employs more than 3 million people, of which more than 85 percent are women. These numbers are startling in their magnitude and in their reflection of how women's labor has been absorbed into flows of global capital. The 1973 Multi Fibre Arrangement, which created preferential market access for textiles produced in the newly industrializing Global South, allowed Bangladesh to enter into a transnational circuit of manufacture. But women emerged as the primary workforce through a shift in what Naila Kabeer describes as "an intersection of the 'economics' of demand and the 'culture' of supply."[46] As the case of the Singer sewing machine illustrates, women in Bengal have long been generating income to support their families, but this, unlike men's employment, has largely been within informal sectors and in addition to full-time domestic labor. Of course, poor women have been far more mobile than middle-class women, as they have long participated in both the formal and informal workforces. In this way, both microfinance and garment work target a population that is primed for a public relationship to work and to money.[47]

However, several disparate factors coincided to radically transform women's economic force in Bangladesh after independence: first, the decline in family-based subsistence agriculture, which shifted poor rural women into a more formal economy; second, the decline in fertility rates, especially among rural populations; and third, liberalization policies targeted at export-oriented manufacture. Each of these also relates to the HDI measures. The relationship between fertility rates and the garment industry demonstrates the symbiosis between women's bodies, the global development apparatus, and a national narrative of progress. It is from this vantage point that we are able to see Bengali women's work as an articulation of political possibility expressed by the women themselves.

As the new Bangladeshi government was laying out its reconstruction plan following the war, international donor countries and agencies pressured the government to make population control a primary concern. For USAID and its affiliates, Bangladesh's population rate pointed to a host of problems, not the least of which were resource scarcity and food insecurity. Therefore, it established a comprehensive family-planning initiative, building on the auspices of the changes in contraceptive distribution policy implemented to deal with war rapes and unwanted pregnancies. The 1974 famine, which killed 1.5 million and is widely understood to have been precipitated by the United States' withholding of its pledged food aid until Bangladesh ceased jute exports to Cuba, was used as rationale for the exigent need to curtail population growth.[48] By 1975, when the International Centre for Diarrhoeal Disease Research, Bangladesh (ICDDR,B) set up the Matlab project to track demographic trends, there were already declines in fertility rates. From 1968, when estimated fertility rates were between 6 and 7.8 percent, to 1994, when they fell to 3.3 percent, there was a proportionate increase in contraceptive use of nearly 70 percent. This is coterminous with and depends on another critical indicator of women's empowerment, that of education. As more women gain access to primary and secondary education in the years following Bangladesh's independence, their access to reproductive choices increases as infant and maternal mortality decrease. Now able to give birth to fewer, healthier children, women's relationship to domestic labor shifts to allow them to enter more formal work sectors.

The increase in female literacy that drove lowered fertility rates in Bangladesh also primed a labor force that could operate industrial machinery. The very same industry that is now a synecdoche for failed development and women's exploitation came into being in Bangladesh through the effects of joint international, state, and NGO initiatives to increase women's access to decision-making and resources. Kabeer points out, within both Bangladeshi society and the literature on development, a virulent discourse of poor women as "the passive dupes of patriarchal culture."[49] Despite the broad ethos of empowerment as form and function of aid policy toward Bangladeshi women, their figuration as outside of the domain of liberal consent and agency remains potent and constitutive. Like Pritilata Waddedar, whose self-naming as revolutionary was muffled by accounts of her as dupe and victim, Bangladeshi women who enter into the workforce on the wing of gendered policies designed to increase decision-making can nonetheless never be empowered enough by this calculus. There is a Gordian knot of gender and development in Bangladesh: while projects of national uplift depend intimately on the symbolic and material labor of women, those women are subsequently produced as victims of that very progress.

Garment work, so vilified in the international press for its exploitative practices, is hardly a perfect industry in Bangladesh. But given that it draws millions of women into its workforce and has been the engine of substantial socioeconomic changes in Bangladesh over the past quarter-century, it behooves us to ask—without the assumption of patriarchal victimhood—why women choose to work in this way, under these conditions, and what worlds they braid together through their labor. Kabeer notes that women began to enter the garment industry in large numbers following the 1982 New Industrial Policy, which privatized export manufacturing for reasons that perhaps demonstrate most vividly the limits of the liberal paradigm according to which their well-being has been measured. Whether by necessity, with the loss of the primary wage-earner (traditionally, of course, male and engaged in either the formal labor force or subsistence agriculture), or to improve the lives and the prospects of their families, women often cite highly relational and contingent reasons for coming to garment work. Scholars of the industry have noted that its attendant social benefits have come from the fact that women put their income toward familial and community development, whereas men tend to prioritize their own needs.[50] Put another way, the very bonds of domestic obligation and care that seemingly kept women out of the workforce now uphold both industry and home.

Indeed, the garment sector became the major site of women's formal labor in Bangladesh because of its symbolic association with the home. Textile work and stitching, imbued with the benign and sympathetic aura of familial labor and recalling the bodies of mothers and grandmothers making useful and beautiful things in the home, could market itself as safe work for women even when industrialized. A *Lakshman rekha* of gender propriety—the impermeable circle of safety around which Lakshman enclosed Sita in the *Ramayana* to protect her and which has become a metaphor for the limits of feminine possibility—extends to include the factory space, which has historically been designated masculine. Recognizing a social anxiety about sending women into the workforce, the industry sought to sanitize its effect by promoting garment work as safe for young, newly educated women (their target demographic), economically profitable while socially innocuous. Summoning the memory of stitching as respectable labor, the industry promised to funnel women back into the home eventually. Though studies show that women who enter garment work largely stay in it even after they are married, the time of that labor is markedly circumscribed so as not to intervene in and disrupt national-domestic time. If the industry could promise that women could be both "empowered" financially and reincorporable into a traditional sphere, it could widen its labor base and draw from even more conservative social sectors.

Having been paradoxically produced as a site of safety despite its abiding industrial risks, garment work now engages women whose very presence in the public spaces of the city and among unmarried men would otherwise rend the social fabric. For example, at 6:00 a.m., when the streets of Dhaka flood with women streaming toward factories, it is common to see burqas and niqabs. Moreover, factories tout themselves as sites of paternalistic protection and oversight, taking on the mantle of the conservative state. Under this guise of this expanded familial space, the garment industry has in part been able to sidestep twenty-first-century industrial norms like unionization, standardized safety practices, and collective bargaining.[51] Figured as a "soft" industry in the objects of its manufacture and its targeted labor force, the ready-made garment sector in Bangladesh has made a global practice of financially benefiting from gendered cultural practices and economic relationships. While conditions in factories vary wildly, from the unregulated and treacherous makeshift sites erected by subcontractor companies to the flagship campuses of the few large corporations that work directly with multinational clients, prevailing industrial practices and a lack of state oversight ensure that the lived insecurity of many workers constitutes the shared insecurity of the entire industry, nearly 4 million workers.

As the body of the female garment worker becomes the new metonym for Bangladesh, supplanting in the international, if not the national, imagination the nineteenth-century figure of Mother Bengal, the objects of her labor are strenuously sanitized, despite the accompanying memory of factory catastrophes. The very term "ready-made garments" suggests that the labor of garment work is not manual, not tactile, not skilled; that cut knit pieces arrive from the manufacturer and are rotely stitched together by machine. The body at the machine, who in this vision neither touches cloth nor controls its form, is automated. She can usefully be feminized because this is a form of labor that requires no musculature, no heft; she can be illiterate because this is mechanical work, training fingers rather than minds; she can earn little because the labor value of her product is so low, her skills are so limited, her effort is so little.

This is the fantasy that feeds the global appetite for cheap garments from places like Bangladesh. Consumers deeply wish to believe the cost of their T-shirt to be less than its price. Although the horrific images from recent factory disasters interrupt this narrative, they do not challenge its prevailing images.

That "ready-made garments" is a misnomer should of course be clear. Those cotton shirts that bear the tag "Made in Bangladesh" bear the bodily traces of a highly physical and even exertional manufacture. Blood, dust, spit, and sweat from workers are embedded in the tight, regular knit weave. Though the process promises mechanization, much of the work is done by hand. From grading to marking to spreading to cutting to sewing to finishing, each step of the manufacture engages the body of the worker. Industrial machines purchased from Korea and China are often ill-suited to the physical spaces of the factories; when they break, replacement parts have to be supplemented by ad hoc measures—what in Hindi are called *jugaad* and have been studied by anthropologists and management specialists as improvisational practices to address problems that arise when an environment does not have the resources to maintain its technology.[52] As a result, what in the model of the industry is an almost entirely mechanized process, in reality is largely manual. Moreover, this is a form of manual labor that is in practice a world away from its purported feminized, genteel origins.

In this way, the garment industry, in Bangladesh and globally, explicitly benefits from the promise of an unskilled, automated, and disembodied labor practice such that the response to outcries after factory incidents can attend to structural insecurities without acknowledging their material reality. Because Bangladesh depends on garment exports and because such a large portion of its population depends either directly or indirectly on wages, a willful inertia colors these industry reforms. While factory work remains highly undercompensated and unregulated, it has gained a monopoly on employment and administration. By offering services such as on-site child care and health screenings, factories tend to the needs of a population that the state apparatus has ignored. They take up the work begun in 1971 by NGOs and foreign aid. Moreover, in the wake of the Rana Plaza collapse and the heightened scrutiny, more affluent companies have attempted to move beyond simply attending to worker safety and factory infrastructure. The Mohammadi Group, one of the largest factory groups, for example, has been among those attempting to respond to the needs and demands of its workforce, not just to international scrutiny.

Targeting two of the most prominent material signs of "empowerment," the Mohammadi Group is currently in the process of building the first ever low-cost, rent-to-buy housing for its workers and is participating in a scholarship program with the Asian Women's University (AWU) in Chittagong.[53] Many women who work in the factories move to the city from their villages and send back biweekly remittances to support nuclear and extended families. Children often live with them, splitting the form of the family across lines of rural and urban, wage-earning and subsistence, mobile and moribund. An obverse effect of the flow of women into the most lucrative labor force is the declining rates of employment among men in Bangladesh; male migrant labor to the Gulf States staunchly parallels the movement of female workers into Dhaka. Moreover, as more women become the primary family breadwinners, the gap between their consumer and property purchasing power becomes clear. Only an estimated 2 percent of women in Bangladesh own land, a phenomenon regulated by religion-based inheritance law.[54] Although Muslim women, under Islamic law, are entitled to half the amount of property as their brothers, Hindu and Buddhist women have no direct legal pathway to inherit property. The possibility that a formerly rural, poor population of women might have the opportunity to buy personal property in Dhaka stands to alter the socioeconomic cartography of Bangladesh. In the face of entirely valid critiques of garment work, let us also not ignore the irony that women (an admittedly tiny fraction) in the industry so undervalued are in a position to purchase homes, whereas women engaged in Grameen microcredit programs are positioned to break one another's homes to exact loan repayment. The unstable character of a global empowerment discourse falters . . .

Property ownership in a country whose abiding land distribution bears the trace of nearly four hundred years of colonial policy is not an abstract value. It offers a fundamentally new idiom through which women can express personal and political demands. Additionally, the scholarship initiative with AWU offers, for however small a selected group, the possibility of garment labor as a vehicle of mobility beyond the economic. Writing to the management in application, Afrozi Begum, who was forced to leave school in the sixth grade, now works in the factory as a "pulley-man" and sends a portion of her salary to fund her siblings' educations. She writes, "I hope to increase my own capabilities through hard work."[55] This is a common narrative (and indeed, oft-repeated phrasing) among the women who write to apply for the scholarship or for management positions: having been taken out of school because their families could not support them, they turn to garment work first to sustain those families and then to improve themselves. I do not here want to suggest that this evinces patriarchal oppression, but rather to pay attention to how these women see garment work as a dual vehicle in which their individual conditions of possibility are inextricable from their embeddedness in social structures of obligation, debt, and kinship.

For most of these women, the garment industry offers a matrix of quantifiable labor and return, in which demands for increased opportunity or safety are couched in dependence on the lives that the work makes possible for them. There is, of course, a commercial discourse around garment work that insists that it makes women more free. In the writings of the garment workers, the idiom of freedom is neither liberal sovereignty nor neoliberal purchasing power. If such a thing can be apprehended, freedom may be the space between the memory trace of their bodily labor and the ways its global circulation might bear them into a broader world.

The endeavors of the Mohammadi Group and other companies engaged in changing the perception of garment work are clearly not motivated by pure altruism. The capital of responsible management is enormous in the face of global scrutiny. Ready-made garment brands depend on maintaining their image as the site of economic possibility and empowerment for Third World women at minimal cost to their Western consumers. While by no means a cure for the extensive problems of worker safety, unfair wages, and unionization rights, they recognize that garment labor—like much of the material and symbolic labor of women—is not limited to the physicality of the work, but influences the very organization of life and intimacy. In this respect, attending to what may be the mundane and limited articulations of workers is particularly exigent when their bodies are the templates for imagining female agency and its failure.

In March 2014, less than a year after the Rana Plaza collapse, American Apparel released an ad campaign entitled "Made in Bangladesh." (Curiously, the ad has been removed from the company's website, which contains a searchable archive of their advertising.) Featuring a topless model whose breasts are emblazoned with the campaign phrase, the ad includes at the bottom copy that begins, "Meet Maks." Maks, it says, was born in Bangladesh but moved to Los Angeles as a child and now "doesn't feel the need to identify herself as American or Bangladeshi and is not content to fit herself into anyone else's conventional narrative."[56] This is revolutionary, we are to understand, because of the cultural expectations it claims to subvert by presenting the unclothed body of a Muslim woman, framed as being like the dead women whose images also come with that very tagline and yet not at all like them. Maks, the ad suggests, is free. Though she is "made in Bangladesh," bearing the mark of that site of female exploitation and unpaid labor, her freedom is constituted by her ability to expose her body and to earn a fair wage as a merchandiser. Indeed, as a merchandiser, she does not participate in the tactile practices of the women she repudiates. Her body—strong, unblemished, beautiful—is the commodity, exchanged for the broken bodies of the women crushed under the factory debris in Bangladesh. Using the image of a half-naked woman who is marketed as Bangladeshi yet represents the liberating power of American immigration to sell clothing that promises to be fair trade curiously doubles back to the other global life of Bangladeshi commodities.

Whereas those products, permeated by the somatic remains of the women whose hands formed them, radiate a communitarian possibility—that the fair-trade model benefits families and children and, in particular, empowers women as a group—American Apparel sells a national model of fair trade that saves one woman in particular. Though the campaign intends Maks to be the face and the breasts of freedom, she is reinscribed into the familiar form of the Bengali woman to be saved by the hand of Western paternalism. Although we are given to understand that Maks has already been saved, in the end she becomes a rep-etition (with difference) of those women against whose failed possibility her body is figured. To bear the title "Made in Bangladesh" is to bear the shared lineage of those bodies under rubble, but may also be to live with the laboring bodies who continue to suggest forms of being otherwise.

This book has traced the appearance over more than a century of women's desire as a potent, legible political force in East Bengal. In so doing, it has drawn together objects, bodies, and affects that often appear contingently but reveal the abiding traces of cathexis that cohere and create palimpsests in the objects of women's labor. For this reason, it ends with the articulations by women 110 years apart—from 1905, where this book began, and 2015, where it closes. Suturing these accounts to one another is a thread of speculative possibility on the transnational and transhistorical tactile, textual, and textural life of desire and attachment.

Begum Rokeya Sakhawat Hossain, a Bengali Muslim feminist activist, wrote the techno-utopian short story "Sultana's Dream" in 1905, the year of Bengal's first partition. Her vision of a world in which women, having come to power through scientific discovery and rational thought, have segregated men into *zenanas* (inner female apartments) for their own protection against their instincts for violence and conflict proffers a vision of political society in which virtue—a feminized condition—is the determinant of sovereignty. In Ladyland there is no danger and no potential strife, rendering the task of governance ancillary to the true task of womankind, the betterment of society through education and technological progress. In a sentiment that Tagore would echo twenty-five years later in "The Religion of Man," when he would write that "[p]rogress means that there is an ideal perfection which the individual seeks to reach by extending his limits in knowledge, power, love, enjoyment, thus approaching the universal," Hossain creates in Sultana's dreamscape a world in which women's access to universal education has resulted in material, spiri-tual, and social goods for the collective and individual both. [57] "We do not covet other people's land, we do not fight for a piece of diamond though it may be a thousand-fold brighter than the Koh-i-Noor, nor do we grudge a ruler his Pea-cock Throne. We dive deep into the ocean of knowledge and try to find out the precious gems, which nature has kept in store for us. We enjoy nature's gifts as much as we can."[58] True knowledge cultivates a form of personhood that is itself liberating, such that liberalism's political project of individual sovereignty is the means rather than the goal of political life. This liberation that Hossain suggests, though explicitly in terms of politics, is an almost perfect echo of the spiritual liberation that Ramakrishna described—the oceanic feeling that so confounded Freud (as we saw in chapter 3).

Hossain's extraordinarily prescient speculation about the possibilities of scientific knowledge in the hands of the worthier race—solar-powered machin-ery, electrical tillers, helicopters—emerges out of collective endeavor rather than individual ambition. The technology men condemned as a "sentimental nightmare" in its communal spirit facilitates a nation in which there is time for beauty and leisure even as state improvement continues apace. Sultana's Ladyland guide, Sister Sara, repairs the maligned feminine labor of embroi-dery, which, Sultana remarks, is all that women in her native Bengal have to do in the *zenana*. Sister Sara says, "But we do not trust our *zenana* members with embroidery as a man has not patience enough to pass thread through a needlehole even!"[59]

When Bimala, in *The Home and the World*, breaches the boundary between the *zenana* and the outer apartments at the call of the *swadeshi* movement, it cracks open in her a desire for destruction. She says, "As soon as the *swadeshi* storm reached my blood, I said to my husband: 'I must burn all my foreign clothes.'"[60] The feminine inner apartments in which women embroider instead of acting in service of the nation will, in Tagore's novel, ultimately be destroyed by the encroaching tide of a changing world. In Ladyland, the "covetous self-love" that becomes the idiom of Bimala's nationalist desire is transformed into an instru-ment of scientific endeavor.[61] Hossain's feminist utopia nurtures the hope that women's political life can be more than the eruption of desire that, in the face of the anesthetized sensibility of nationalism, appears destructive when it may indeed be productive. It may make possible another world.

More than a century after Hossain's short story was published, a garment worker named Rehana Yesmin would send the management of the Mohammadi Group an essay describing her path to the industry. Unlike her fellow workers, whose accounts largely follow the same structure and narrative arc, Rehana Yesmin comes from a middle-class family, has a college education, and is mar-ried to a man with a degree in computer engineering. She begins working at the factory not out of financial necessity, as is the almost unquestioned com-mon account, but out of psychic necessity. Four years after her marriage, she had given birth to a son who, despite Bangladesh's recent decline in infant mortality and her own access to medical care, died of a common cold at the age of nine months. Yesmin writes that after his death, she went nearly mad. "I paced inside the apartment all day, trapped. I couldn't breathe."[62] Getting a job at the factory as a "pulley-man," undeterred by the social breach this form of work represents to a woman of her class and education, Yesmin claims, gave her a reason to wish to live again. Yesmin's essay is striking not just for its account of incalculable grief but for how, in the face of the expected and justifiably over-determined vision of garment work as a site of death and foreclosed futurity, its tactile, manual regularity offers a bridge over the unrepaired trauma of her son's loss. The daily encounter between her body and the knits stretched taut in the pulley does not make up for his death but embeds on her form, as much as her body does into its weave, the promise of repetition and of remains. *Memories*, you may recall, was the word used in the nineteenth century to describe wrinkles in clothing.

This book began with the body of a young woman, dead outside of a colonial club on which she had just carried out an attack. Pritilata Waddedar, for whom we inquired into the legibility of female political desire in the postcolonial archive, demonstrated through her body and writing that, in the face of claims of its erasure, articulation never disappears. Signs are left to be read: the full feature of their expression cannot be mastered, but they are extant and insistent. That is the ethical gesture. Here, at the book's end, let us extend that gesture to Rehana Yesmin. From within the din of global diagnoses of her exploitation or her liberation, she speaks. Let us read her words and the aesthetic object of her making. That garment, like muslin, like *khadi*, like *kantha*, like text itself, is a site of self-articulation; a relational, intentional commitment manifested through labor and language. It is also the site of that commitment's preservation. Bearing the promise of psychoanalysis that nothing is ever lost, no object ever fully dislodged from the self, text, textile, and the fetish are the preservative technologies of our time. They bear on their surface the memory of touch, the possibility of history.

Epilogue

In April 2018, to mark the fifth anniversary of the Rana Plaza disaster, the *Bangladesh Garment Sromik Samhati* (Bangladesh Garment Workers Solidarity) organization mounted an exhibit in front of where the nine-story structure once perilously stood. Wild marsh grasses and water hyacinth had long since taken over the building footprint, testament to the pond on which the haphazard construction had taken place; the dogged fertility of East Bengal's alluvial soil for which it was so valued under the British empire covered up what remained of concrete and rebar wreckage. A dozen or so quilts were draped on bamboo stalks, next to hung shirts and *salwars*, in front of the memorial monument—a pair of hands rising out of the ground, fisting a hammer and sickle. These *kanthas* were stitched by family members of workers who died in Rana Plaza. Each *kantha* on display at the "*Smriti Katha O Kotha* (Memorial Quilts and Remembrances)" exhibit is a testament to the private grief of those whose loved ones became tokens of global outrage, abstracted evidence of corporate and state failure. Although they are displayed in memory of workers killed while manufacturing industrial cotton knit, these *kanthas*, like *kanthas* that have been made by Bengali women for generations, are made of saris worn soft with use, embroidered together with individualized icons of care. Unlike the tightly woven cloth which their loved ones measured, spread, cut, seamed, pressed, and finished, the structure of the saris from which the *kanthas* are made is loosened, permeated by the repeated contact with skin and water and dirt and sun. They are embedded with the bodily traces of intimate care and recalled loss.

"*Smriti Katha O Kotha*," while deeply local to the wreckage of Rana Plaza and the form of the East Bengali *nakshi kantha*, comes out of a global kinship of remembrance. In 2011, marking the centennial of the Triangle Shirtwaist Factory fire in New York, American artist and archivist Robin Berson began the Workers' Memorial Quilt project. Collaborating with a quilters guild and students at the Fashion Institute of Technology in New York, Berson constructed a quilt in the American folk tradition, consisting of individual squares patched together. The quilt blocks feature images of workers killed in the fire, with their names and ages culled from archival sources; printed labor songs and slogans; and quotes from notable Americans. The form of the "*Smriti Katha O Kotha*" *kanthas* clearly draws inspiration from the Triangle Shirtwaist memorial quilt: notably the inclusion of images of workers who died (a feature not endemic to *kanthas*) and indeed, are engaged in an internationalist commitment. But these textiles, first hung at the site of the loss they recall and then displayed for an urban public at the Drik gallery, are memory work of another order, of another materiality.

At the end of this book, I suggested we extend to Rehana Yesmin, who still works in perhaps the best existing and yet not even close to good enough conditions in a garment factory in Dhaka, a gesture I called *ethical*: to account for her articulation—textual and textilic—as the intentional concatenation of desire and labor, and, in so doing, to refuse the global humanitarian terms of her own objectification. When Marx wrote in 1844 of the production of worker as commodity—that the "realization of labor appears as *loss of realization* for the workers; objectification as *loss of the object and bondage to it*; appropriation as *estrangement*, as *alienation*"—he ironically has furnished terms taken up by twenty-first-century neoliberal rights-based critique.[1] There, these are not in service of the critique of the political economy of late capital that subtends labor and social relations, but of the postcolonial state as defender of individual agency. Feminist outcries against the exploitation of women in garment factories, women like and *not like* Rehana Yesmin, depend on the laborer derealized, on the object that she has become. Then, she can be saved—from the rapacious state, from stultified society, and from her own misrecognition of want and need. How convenient that the global project of women's empowerment borrows both from a psychological discourse of consciousness and an economic structure of accumulation and debt.

But Rehana Yesmin is not like the workers memorialized in the *kanthas* on display. Her education, class, and most importantly, aliveness make attending to the force and feature of her articulation a very different practice than that of the stitched-together mementos of grief. To "read" these *kanthas*, alongside and yet so far from the professional quilt in honor of the Triangle Shirtwaist factory on display in midtown Manhattan, is also to reconsider what global solidarity might materially look like. What is the ethical obligation enjoined that is not rescue or empathetic identification? The memorial function of the *kanthas* of "*Smriti Katha O Kotha*" recalls the somatic and social life of intimacy. Peter Stallybrass writes of the wrinkle as material memory: "Those wrinkles recorded the body that has inhabited the garment. They memorized the interaction, the mutual constitution, of person and thing."[2] These *kanthas* record the presence of that which remains, those who remain, as well as the inhabitation of those who are lost and loss itself. Killed by the very structure of their labor, the Rana Plaza workers for whom there are *kanthas* have come into a new use. Their deaths are a convenient, though perhaps necessary, proof of the failure of adequate safety, compensation, conditions of work and life for a local and global audience. Calls for reform and reparation accompany the conditional, "So that their deaths are not in vain." Their labor is made meaningful in the light of their deaths, in the absence of them as living actors. For their loved ones who labor at the making of *kanthas* in their memory, there is no affective, political, or financial renumeration for their loss. When they beseech the audience not to forget the names and faces of their loved ones, the *kantha*-stitchers do not cite death as that which gives them meaning. These *kanthas* are relics of personal loss. They recall life, not death. They memorialize the ongoing social relations in which these workers, named and pictured, continue to exist in everyday, mundane life: the daily, somatic, laboring existence that wore soft the saris from which the *kanthas* were stitched; the tactile, accumulative contact of bodies and cloth, adhering remains on top of remains.

Nasima Begum, whose daughter Aakhi was killed at Rana Plaza, says, "While I made this *kantha*, I remembered my daughter. With my pain, with my daughter's memory, with her essence, I thought of my child with every letter I stitched."[3] The touch of memory is here not a metaphor, not an abstraction. Nasima Begum insists on the corporeal traces of her own body and the memory of her daughter's body, on her, near her, imbued into the weave of cloth. Stella Kramrisch wrote in 1968, "The material of *kanthas* are rags and their threads. Joined afresh, these tatters are given a new wholeness. Their embroidered designs spring from this meaning. The *kantha* is a work that gives wholeness to things that were of no use any more, to fragments without any significance."[4] The *kanthas* of the exhibit can no more make whole the losses expressed within them than they can bring back to life those who were killed. Nevertheless, the work of their manufacture is the embodied, tactile articulation that insists on the significance and the necessity of those people who died. Their work may have been undervalued and their deaths may be reappropriated, but in the intimate touch of cloth to hand, their relational lives and desires abide.

The Worker's Memorial Quilt, sewn by artists and volunteers for whom the cause of labor rights and the practice of quilting gave meaning to the made-object, recalls those killed in the Triangle Shirtwaist fire from a great distance. One hundred years removed, without what Nasima Begum described as her daughter's essence imbuing her body as it labored over the *kantha*, the American quilt project is a recognizably political one. In reaching toward and insisting on kinship with the *kanthas* in Savar, the Worker's Memorial Quilt binds together the memory of labor conditions now repaired with the aspirational project of reform. Bangladesh in the future might hope to be that which the quilt recalls as no longer being, but the *kanthas* of the exhibit in front of Rana Plaza tell another story: not of a global political imagination but of an intimate, local one, though still oriented toward better factory conditions, higher wages, safer lives. In the form of the *kantha*, the memory trace of work is inextricable from cathexis, where what is recalled by the wrinkles in cloth is of the touch of bodies, at work and at rest.

Glossary

BABU: Name given to Bengalis who did clerical work for colonial authorities; later a satirical and stereotypical term for effeminate and overly bookish Bengalis

BANGA-BHANGA: The breaking of Bengal or first partition (1905)

BHADRALOK: Literally meaning "respectable class," the term for educated urban middle-class

BIDESHI: Foreign

BUDDHIJIBIS: Intellectuals (literally, those who live a life of the mind)

CHARKHA: Spinning wheel

DÉS/DESH: Country

DHOBI: Washer/launderman

JAMDANI: Flowered muslin

KHADI: Hand-woven cotton made famous by Gandhi

MUKTI BAHINI: Bengali guerilla and paramilitary forces during 1971 war (also called mukti juddha)

NAKSHI KANTHA: Embroidered quilt

RAZAKAR: Bengali who sympathized and collaborated with Pakistani forces during 1971 war

SAMĀJ: Society

SARI: Nine-yard length of cloth worn by Bengali women

SATI: Widow sacrifice, or an immolated widow

SATYAGRAHA: Holding onto truth, a form of nonviolent resistance (a Gandhian coinage and concept)

SHELAI: Stitching

SWADESHI: Movement for Indian self-sufficiency popularized after 1905; literally means "of a country of one's own)

SWARAJ: Self-rule

TAANT: Cotton; also, loom

ZAMINDAR: Landowner

ZAMINDARI: Territory administered by a zamindar as part of the tenancy system established by Permanent Settlement

ZENANA: Apartments in the home reserved for women

Notes

INTRODUCTION

1. The story, often recounted as a particularly visceral example of imperial violence, is likely not based in truth. For one thing, there are competing accounts, which I examine in chapter 1, in which weavers claimed to have cut off their own thumbs in protest of exorbitant taxes on the cloth. For another, the British East India Company did not exact its rule so visibly on the body of its subjects, relying instead on the far more onerous effects of taxation and export duties to stifle manufacture in the moments of the decline of its courtly patronage by the Mughals. Gandhi writes of the lost muslin that "[t]he East India Company came to buy, and remained to sell. It compelled us to cut off our thumbs. They stood over us and made us behave against our wills till thousands of us cut off our thumbs. This is no figment of my imagination but can be verified from the records of the East India Company." Mohandas K. Gandhi, *The Collected Works of Mahatma Gandhi*, vol. 30 (Ahmedabad: Navajivan Trust,1968), 123.
2. Clinton G. Gilroy, *The History of Silk, Cotton, Linen, Wool, and other Fibrous Substances* (London: Harper & Brothers, 1845).
3. Forbes J. Watson, *Textile Manufactures and the Costumes of the People of India* (London: Eyre & Spottiswoode, 1866), 65.
4. For more on the relationship between femininity, textile, and text, see Nancy K. Miller, "Arachnologies: The Woman, the Text, and the Critic," in *The Poetics of Gender*, ed. Nancy K. Miller (New York: Columbia University Press, 1986), 270–96; Liliane Weissberg, "Ariadne's Thread," *MLN* 125, no. 3 (2010): 661–81; Julia Bryan-Wilson, *Fray: Art and Textile Politics* (Chicago: University of Chicago Press, 2017); Caroline Rooney, "Deconstruction and Weaving," in *Deconstruction: A User's Guide*, ed. Nicholas Royle (London: Palgrave, 2000), 258–81.
5. Tim Ingold, "The Textility of Making," *Cambridge Journal of Economics* 34 (2010): 91–102.
6. Jacques Derrida, "A Silkworm of One's Own (Points of View Stitched on the Other Veil)," trans. Geoffrey Bennington, in *Derrida, Acts of Religion*, ed. Gil Anidjar (New York: Routledge, 2002), 313.

7. Karl Marx, *Capital: A Critique of Political Economy*, vol. 1., trans. Ben Fowkes (New York: Vintage, 1977), 163.

8. Madeline Bunting, "Amartya Sen: India's Dirty Fighter," *Guardian*, July 16, 2013, https://www.theguardian.com/world/2013/jul/16/amartya-sen-india-dirty-fighter.

9. See Sumathi Ramaswamy's excellent account of the co-constitution of a nationalist and cartographic imagination around the body of the woman: *Mother Goddesses and the Nation* (Durham, NC: Duke University Press, 2010).

10. Ranajit Guha, "On Some Aspects of the Historiography of Colonial India," in *Selected Subaltern Studies*, ed. Ranajit Guha and Gayatri Chakravorty Spivak (Oxford: Oxford University Press, 1988), 43 (emphasis in original).

11. Guha, "On Some Aspects," 40.

12. Erin Manning, *Politics of Touch: Sense, Movement, Sovereignty* (Minneapolis: University of Minnesota Press, 2006), 10.

13. Jacques Derrida, *Specters of Marx: The State of Debt, the Work of Mourning, and the New International* (London: Routledge, 1993), 6.

14. Many scholars of Freud, Peter Gay most prominently, have objected to Strachey's translation, arguing that it misrepresented Freud's term, which in German has a variety of connotations including that of troop occupation and electrical charge. Gay notes that even as Freud modified his own use of the term *Besetzung* over his life, it might be most easily translated as he did in a letter to Ernest Jones in 1908 as "interest (*Besetzung*)." Jean LaPlanche and Jean-Bertrand Pontalis, in contrast, do not object to the translation in *The Language of Psycho-Analysis*, tracing instead the various analogical contexts to which it is put to use in Freud's thinking. Peter Gay, *Freud: A Life of Our Time* (New York: Norton, 2006), 465; Jean LaPlanche and Jean-Bertrand Pontalis, "Cathexis," in *The Language of Psycho-Analysis*, trans. Donald Nicholson-Smith (New York: Norton, 1974), 62–65.

15. I am thinking here particularly of Arjun Appadurai on locality as "a phenomenological property of social life, a structure of a feeling that is produced by particular forms of intentional activity and that yields particular sorts of material effects." Arjun Appadurai, *Modernity at Large: Cultural Dimensions of Globalization* (Minneapolis: University of Minnesota Press, 1996), 182.

16. Derrida, *Specters of Marx*, 163.

17. Émile Durkheim, *The Elementary Forms of Religious Life* (Oxford: Oxford University Press, 2001).

18. Walter Benjamin, "Theses on the Philosophy of History," in *Illuminations: Essays and Reflections* (New York: Random House, 1968), 255.

19. Eve Kosofsky Sedgwick, "Paranoid Reading and Reparative Reading, or, You're So Paranoid, You Probably Think This Essay Is About You," in *Touching Feeling: Affect, Pedagogy, Performativity* (Durham, NC: Duke University Press, 2003), 149.

20. See Sukanya Banerjee, *Becoming Imperial Citizens: Indians in the Late Victorian Empire* (Durham, NC: Duke University Press, 2010); Andrew Sartori, *Liberalism in Empire: An Alternate History* (Berkeley: University of California Press, 2014); Gyan Prakash, "The Colonial Genealogy of Society: Community and Political Modernity in India," in *The Social in Question*, ed. Patrick Joyce (London: Routledge, 2002), 81–96.

21. Tanika Sarkar, "Nationalist Iconography: Image of Women in 19th Century Bengali Literature," *Economic and Political Weekly* 22, no. 47 (1987): 2011–15; see also Mrinalini Sinha's excellent examination of the co-construction of Bengali effeminacy and British masculinity in *Colonial Masculinity: The "Manly Englishman" and the "Effeminate Bengali" in the Late Nineteenth Century* (Manchester, UK: Manchester University Press, 1995).

22. Perhaps most famous is Arif Dirlik's critique of the Subaltern Studies' project as derivative of that of British Marxist historians and a form of elitist navel-gazing by which India—and Bengal in particular—comes to constitute the fantasy of a world much larger than it in fact is. Its claims to intellectual and political radicalism are, for Dirlik, thus undercut and overblown. Notable critiques in a similar vein have been posed by Aijaz Ahmad, Ramachandra Guha, and Rosalind O'Hanlon, among others. See Arif Dirlik, "The Postcolonial Aura: Third World Criticism in the Age of Global Capitalism," *Critical Inquiry* 20, no. 2 (1994): 328–56; Aijaz Ahmad, *In Theory: Classes, Nations, Literatures* (London: Verso, 1992); Ramachandra Guha, "Subaltern and Bhadralok Studies," *Economic and Political Weekly* 30, no. 33 (Aug. 19, 1995): 2056–58; Rosalind O'Hanlon and David Washbrook, "After Orientalism: Culture, Criticism, and Politics in the Third World," *Comparative Studies in Society and History* 34, no. 1 (January 1992): 141–67; Dorothy M. Figueira, *Otherwise Occupied: Pedagogies of Alterity and the Brahminization of Theory* (Albany: State University of New York Press, 2008).

23. The administrative rationale for the 1905 partition came significantly from the biopolitical technology of the 1871 census, the systemized organization of colonial subjects into populations marked by race, religion, caste, language, and occupation. The science of the census revealed, to *bhadralok* and administration alike, that the seeds of deep inequity, unequal development, and antagonistic possibility lay in the soil of Bengal. There, in the record of the Raj's quantification of subject life, begins to emerge the production of evidence to support the distinction between two lobes of an as-yet-singular linguicultural region. Crudely, the census "proved" that overall, Hindus (including Sikhs, though for Bengal this is a statistically insignificant population) constituted 62.18 percent of the population and Muslims 31.96 percent. That in and of itself was not out of line with the general trend across the Raj's purview, wherein Hindus made up 73 percent. Henry Waterfield, *Memorandum on the Census of British India 1871-72* (London: Eyre & Spottiswoode, 1875), 16.

24. David Ludden, "Spatial Inequity and National Territory: Remapping 1905 in Bengal and Assam," *Modern Asian Studies* 46, no. 3 (2011): 1–43.

25. David Scott, "The Aftermaths of Sovereignty: Postcolonial Criticism and the Claims of Political Modernity," *Social Text*, no. 48 (1996): 1–26.

26. Lauren Berlant and Lee Edelman, *Sex, or the Unbearable* (Durham, NC: Duke University Press, 2013): viii.

27. Dennis Dalton, in *Mahatma Gandhi: Nonviolent Power in Action* (New York: Columbia University Press, 2012), points out the similarities to Rousseau's and Hegel's theories of positive freedom, but also notes that this indigenous assertion of freedom was one in which the knowledge of the self led to unity within the social, not the liberal, conception of liberty.

28. Bipin Chandra Pal, *Writings and Speeches*, vol. 1 (Calcutta: Yugayatri Prakashak, 1954): 77–8.

29. Bruno Latour, "How to Talk About the Body? The Normative Dimension of Science Studies," *Body & Society* 10, nos. 2–3 (2004): 205–29, 210.

30. Indeed, this is a capacious conception of touch—phenomenological, psychological, metaphoric, and affective—which borrows in part from Laura Marks's argument that "[t]he phenomenological model of subjectivity posits a mutual permeability and mutual creation of self and other." Laura Marks, *The Skin of the Film* (Durham, NC: Duke University Press, 2000), 149.

31. This gloss, which has become paradigmatic of Spinoza's definition of *affect*, comes from Brian Massumi's description of "power" in his translator's note to Gilles Deleuze and Felix Guattari's *A Thousand Plateaus: Capitalism and Schizophrenia* (Minneapolis: University of Minnesota Press, 1987). Spinoza writes in *Ethics*, "By affect I understand affections of the body by which the

body's power of acting is increased or diminished, aided or restrained, and at the same time, the ideas of these affections." Benedictus de Spinoza, *Ethics*, ed. Edwin M. Curley (New York: Penguin Books, 1996), 70.

32. Ranjana Khanna, "Touching, Unbelonging, and the Absence of Affect," *Feminist Theory* 13, no. 2 (Aug. 2012): 215.

33. Partha Chatterjee, "The Nationalist Resolution of the Women's Question," in *Empire and Nation: Selected Essays* (New York: Columbia University Press, 2010), 116–35, 133.

34. See, among many others: B. R. Nanda, ed., *Indian Women: From Purdah to Modernity* (New Delhi: Vikas, 1962); Manmohan Kaur, *Women in India's Freedom Struggle* (New Delhi: Sterling, 1985); Geraldine Forbes, "In Search of the 'Pure Heathen,'" *Economic and Political Weekly* 21, no. 17 (April 26, 1986): WS2–WS8; Geraldine Forbes, "Goddesses or Rebels? The Women Revolutionaries of Bengal," in *Women, Politics and Literature in Bengal*, ed. Clinton Seely (East Lansing: Asian Studies Center, Michigan State University, 1981), 3–17; Geraldine Forbes, "The Politics of Respectability: Indian Women and the Indian National Congress," in *The Indian National Congress: Centenary Hindsights*, ed. D. A. Low (Delhi: Oxford University Press, 1988), 54–97; Meredith Borthwick, *The Changing Role of Women in Bengal 1849–1905* (Princeton, NJ: Princeton University Press, 1984); Radha Kumar, *The History of Doing: An Illustrated Account of Movements for Women's Rights and Feminism in India 1800–1990.* (New Delhi: Zubaan, 2003); Kumkum Sangari and Sudesh Vaid, eds., *Recasting Women: Essays in Indian Colonial History* (New Brunswick, NJ: Rutgers University Press, 1989); Tanika Sarkar, *Hindu Wife, Hindu Nation: Community, Religion, and Cultural Nationalism* (London: Permanent Black, 2003).

35. Gayatri Chakravorty Spivak, "Subaltern Studies: Deconstructing Historiography," in *Selected Subaltern Studies*, ed. Ranajit Guha and Gayatri Chakravorty Spivak (Oxford: Oxford University Press, 1988), 3–32.

36. Gayatri Chakravorty Spivak, *A Critique of Postcolonial Reason: Toward a History of the Vanishing Present* (Cambridge, MA: Harvard University Press, 1999).

37. Terry Eagleton, *After Theory* (London: Penguin, 2004).

38. On the postcritical turn, see Rita Felski, *The Limits of Critique* (Chicago: University of Chicago Press, 2015); Timothy Bewes, "Reading with the Grain: A New World in Literary Criticism," *Differences: A Journal of Feminist Cultural Studies* 21, no. 3 (2010): 1–33; Stephen Best and Sharon Marcus, "Surface Reading: An Introduction," *Representations* 108, no. 1 (2009): 1–21; Franco Moretti, *Distant Reading* (London: Verso, 2013); N. Katherine Hayles, "How We Read: Close, Hyper, Machine," *ADE Bulletin* 150 (2010): 62–79.

1. VIRGIN SUICIDES

1. The name "Indian Republican Army" was an explicit link to the Irish Republican Army, which significantly influenced revolutionary violence in Bengal. The relationship between Irish and Bengali revolutionary violence manifests in a variety of ways. Members of the Indian Republican Army were inspired by the writings of Dan Breen and Éamon de Valera and began each meeting with a reading of the Easter Uprising Manifesto. Their attack on the Chittagong Armory in April 1930 was intended as a homage to the Easter attacks in Ireland. Although the relationship between the Bengali IRA and the Sinn Fein has been examined in Silvestri

and Heehs, there has hitherto been no comprehensive study of the relationship between the two revolutionary movements that include other provocative points of contact, like the influence of Sister Nivedita, the Irish woman who so influenced Swami Vivekananda, and the construction of a revolutionary literary canon that spanned Bengal and Ireland to include works by Sarat Chandra Bose, Breen, Bankim Chandra Chatterjee, and de Valera. For more work on the intracolonial relations between India and Ireland, see S. B. Cook, *Imperial Affinities: Nineteenth-Century Analogies and Exchanges Between India and Ireland* (New Delhi: Sage, 1993); Peter Heehs, *The Bomb in Bengal: The Rise of Revolutionary Terrorism in India, 1900–1910* (New Delhi: Oxford University Press, 2004); Peter Heehs, "Foreign Influences on Bengali Revolutionary Terrorism, 1902–1908," *Modern Asian Studies* 28, no. 3 (1994): 533–56; Jeanette Herman, *Empire's Bodies: Images of Suffering in Nineteenth- and Twentieth-Century India and Ireland* (New York: Macmillan, 2004); Keith Jeffery, *An Irish Empire? Aspects of Ireland and the British Empire* (New York: Manchester University Press, 1996); Sean O'Ceallaigh, *India and Ireland* (New York: Friends of Freedom for India, 1924); Michael Silvestri, *Ireland and India: Nationalism, Empire, and Memory* (New York: Palgrave Macmillan, 2009).

2. Jugantar was itself an offshoot of the Anushilan Samiti (meaning, quite literally, Association for the Cultivation of Discipline), which emerged in Bengal in the late nineteenth century as a secret organization committed to liberating Bengal from colonial rule. Its anticolonial writings, published in the journal *Jugantar*, and its training of young men in hand-to-hand combat drew the attention of authorities and were explicitly cited as one of the rationales for the 1905 partition. It marked Bengal as a hotbed of anticolonial organization. Led by Pulin Behari Das, Auribindo, and Bipin Chandra Pal, the Anushilan Samiti gave rise to a set of loosely connected smaller organizations under its umbrella for whom violence was a central aspect of anticolonial agitation. In this chapter, I use these names interchangeably.

3. Please note that throughout this chapter, to follow the voices of these female revolutionaries and to take seriously the states in which the texts were written, I have avoided the intrusion of the *sic* and followed the spelling and wording of source texts without alteration or interruption.

4. Pritilata Waddedar, "An Appeal to Women," in *The Easter Rebellion in India: The Chittagong Uprising*, ed. Mallikarjuna Sharma (Calcutta: Marxist Study Forum, 1993), 122.

5. Achille Mbembe, "Necropolitics," *Public Culture* 15, no. 1 (2003): 13.

6. In this chapter, I use the word *revolutionary* in conjunction and interchangeably with *anticolonial* to retain something of its descriptive quality and to recognize the politics of self-naming at work in the writings of Waddedar and her comrades. The word *revolutionary* is itself a vexed term as a descriptor of both acts and actors but, unlike *terrorist* or *martyr*, does not engage a legalistic or heroic economy. Some—including Bhagat Singh, one of the most prominent members of the Hindustan Socialist Republican Association, with which Jugantar was affiliated—embraced the name *terrorist*. Singh writes, "We have been taken to task for our terroristic policy. Our answer is that terrorism is never the object of revolutionaries, nor do they believe that terrorism alone can bring independence. No doubt the revolutionaries think, and rightly, that it is only by resorting to terrorism alone that they can find a most effective means of retaliation. The British government exists, because the Britishers have been successful in terrorising the whole of India. How are we to meet this official terrorism? Only counterterrorism on the part of revolutionaries can checkmate effectively this bureaucratic bullying." Bhagat Singh, "Manifesto of the Hindustan Socialist Republican Association," in *Select Speeches & Writing* (New Delhi: National Book Trust, 2007), 137. Rather than shirk the extrajudicial mantle

of terrorism, Singh redoubles its accusation to suggest that revolutionary terrorism is in fact counterterrorism. It, unlike British official terrorism, works in service of the rule of law and of true freedom. Whereas Waddedar uses the word *revolutionary* in English in her writing, Bangla writing by other members of Jugantar employs the words বিদ্রোহ (*bidrohi*) and বিপ্লবী (*biplabi*). *Biplabi*, which means "revolutionary," appears mostly in formal writing by the group, while *bidrohi*, or "rebel," evokes a literary quality, likely following the prominence of Kazi Nazrul Islam's 1921 poem by the same name. Unlike the pastoral romanticism of Rabindranath Tagore's *swadeshi* verse, Nazrul Islam's poem, with the repetition of the phrase আমি বিদ্রোহী ("I am rebel") and each line beginning with "I," celebrates the individual at war. Surya Sen cites Nazrul throughout his journals, describing him as inspiration.

7. Home Ministry/Political Department, 1933 File Number 45/5/33, National Archives of India, New Delhi.

8. There is a wealth of historiographic work on women who participated in the anticolonial insurgency in the 1930s, though it has primarily been biographic in nature and is generally available only in Bangla. Niranjan Ghosh and Tirtha Mandal have both written brief accounts of the lives of Bengali revolutionaries, male and female, and Manini Chatterjee's recounting of the Chittagong Armory raid of 1930 is comprised in part of individual accounts of the planning, execution, and aftermath of the raid. See Niranjan Ghosh, *Role of Women in the Freedom Movement in Bengal, 1919-1947: Midnapore, Bankura, and Purulia District* (Midnapore: Tamralipta Prakashani, 1988); Tirtha Mandal, *The Women Revolutionaries of Bengal, 1905-1939* (New Delhi: Minerva, 1991); Manini Chatterjee, "1930: Turning Point in the Participation of Women in the Freedom Struggle," *Social Scientist* 29, no. 7/8 (2001): 39–47; *Do and Die: The Chittagong Uprising, 1930-34* (New Delhi: Penguin, 1999). For other examples, see Usha Bala and Anshu Sharma, *Indian Women Freedom Fighters, 1857-1947* (New Delhi: Manohar, 1986); Manmohan Kaur, *Women in India's Freedom Struggle* (New Delhi: Sterling, 1985); Amit Kumar Gupta, "Defying Death: Nationalist Revolutionism in India, 1897–1938," *Social Scientist* 25, no. 9/10 (1997): 3–27; P. K. Ray, *Down Memory Lane: Reminiscences of a Bengali Revolutionary* (New Delhi: Gian, 1990).

9. The appellation *agnikanya* is idiomatically multivalent. Commonly translated as "firebrand daughter," it also literally refers to the daughter of Lord Agni, god of fire and sacrifice. Interestingly, Lord Agni's consort, Swaha (the offering), is figured as the daughter of Daksha and sister to the goddess Sati. Called *agnikanya*, Waddedar is thus anointed as the product of divine sacrifice. The trope of women born of fire in the Vedic tradition commonly denotes the dual processes of purification and deification through *agnipariksha*, "the test of fire." The most visible example is that of Sita, the consort of Lord Ram, who is thrice asked to prove her purity by walking through fire. For a further examination of this trope, see Ananda Coomaraswamy, "Self-Sacrifice," *Harvard Journal of Asiatic Studies* 6, no. 3/4 (February 1942): 358–98.

10. Chittagong, one of the most important port cities in all of British India, is at once an obvious and strange site for this form of anticolonial resistance. Its strategic value is clear: to disrupt transportation and communication in the city would be to cost colonial commercial enterprises significant losses. However, Chittagong, on the far eastern side of the Bay of Bengal, had only recently and nominally been made a part of Bengal. Historically, linguistically, and culturally, it stood apart from much of the rest of the state—both East and West. Originally a part of the Arakan kingdom, it became a Portuguese holding in the sixteenth century before being taken over by the Mughals in the seventeenth. During British rule, prior to the 1905 partition, Chittagong was a part of British Burma. The partition consolidated western portions of Burma, southern Assam, and Mizoram into the territory of East Bengal. Only thereafter was

Chittagong significantly incorporated into the state of Bengal. The local Chatgaya dialect is only loosely and nominatively related to standard Bangla. Moreover, Chittagong's proximity to northeastern territories that are racially and culturally distinct from Bengal and the large indigenous population in the Chittagong Hill Tracts differentiated Chittagong from what we might call mainland East Bengal.

11. Pritilata Waddedar, "Assault on the European Club," in *The Easter Rebellion in India: The Chittagong Uprising*, ed. Mallikarjuna Sharma (Calcutta: Marxist Study Forum, 1993), 264.

12. Although this chapter focuses on Waddedar, it remains attuned to the force of the invocation of *sati* as a collective enunciation by other women who participated in revolutionary violence.

13. Gayatri Chakravorty Spivak, "Can the Subaltern Speak?," in *Colonial Discourse and Post-Colonial Theory: A Reader*, ed. Patrick Williams and Laura Chrisman (New York: Columbia University Press, 1994), 103–4.

14. Though I refer to Waddedar predominantly by her surname throughout, I follow Spivak in her use of Bhubaneswari's first name, for the sake of continuity.

15. Spivak, "Can the Subaltern Speak?," 104.

16. Ranajit Guha, "On Some Aspects of the Historiography of Colonial India," in *Selected Subaltern Studies*, ed. Ranajit Guha and Gayatri Chakravorty Spivak (Oxford: Oxford University Press, 1988), 40.

17. Rajeswari Sunder Rajan, "Death and the Subaltern," in *Can the Subaltern Speak? Reflections on the History of an Idea*, ed. Rosalind Morris (New York: Columbia University Press, 2010), 119.

18. Spivak, "Can the Subaltern Speak?," 104.

19. Sandhya Shetty and Elizabeth Jane Bellamy, "Postcolonialism's Archive Fever," *Diacritics* 30, no. 1 (March 1, 2000): 47.

20. Rosalind Morris, "Introduction," in *Can the Subaltern Speak? Reflections on the History of an Idea*, ed. Rosalind Morris (New York: Columbia University Press, 2010), 3–4.

21. The works of Lata Mani and Rajeswari Sunder Rajan are particularly useful here, as they represent two dominant and compelling poles of postcolonial scholarship on *sati*. Mani argues in *Contentious Traditions* that the debate around *sati* depended on an ideological fixing of the widow as an object of intervention and never as a subject in action. See Lata Mani, *Contentious Traditions: The Debate on Sati in Colonial India* (Berkeley: University of California Press, 1998). Rajan's project in *Real and Imagined Women* is a phenomenological inquiry into the question of pain, the widow as woman on fire; see *Real and Imagined Women: Gender, Culture, and Postcolonialism* (New York: Taylor and Francis, 2004). This chapter is deeply indebted to these feminist inquiries into the discursive production of subjectivity within the debate around *sati*. For more on *sati*, see also V. N. Datta, *Sati: A Historical, Social, and Philosophical Enquiry into the Hindu Rite of Widow Burning* (New Delhi: Manohar Publications, 1988); Jörg Fisch, "Dying for the Dead: Sati in Universal Context," *Journal of World History* 16, no. 3 (2005): 293–325; Jörg Fisch, "Sati and the Task of the Historian," *Journal of World History* 18, no. 3 (2007): 361–68; Sophie Gilmartin, "The Sati, the Bride, and the Widow: Sacrificial Woman in the Nineteenth Century," *Victorian Literature and Culture* 25, no. 1 (1997): 141–58; A. Laxshmi, "The Liminal Body: The Language of Pain and Symbolism around Sati," *Feminist Review* 74, no. 1 (2003): 81–97; Lata Mani, "Production of an Official Discourse on 'Sati' in Early Nineteenth Century Bengal," *Economic and Political Weekly* 21, no. 17 (1986): WS32–WS40; Ashis Nandy, "Nationalism, Genuine and Spurious: Mourning Two Early Post-Nationalist Strains," *Economic and Political Weekly* (2006): 3500–4; Ajit Kumar Ray, *Widows Are Not for Burning: Actions and Attitudes of the Christian Missionaries, the Native Hindus, and Lord William Bentinck* (Calcutta: ABC, 1985); Kumkum Sangari and Sudesh

Vaid, eds., *Recasting Women: Essays in Indian Colonial History* (New Brunswick, NJ: Rutgers University Press, 1989); and Arvind Sharma, ed., *Sati: Historical and Phenomenological Essays* (New Delhi: Motilal, 1988).

22. It is worth noting that *sati* is one of a handful of "native practices" having to do with the female body that aroused the attention of authorities and became a significant site of contestation between Hindu leaders and the Raj. The 1891 Age of Consent Act, which raised the age of sexual consent within marriage for girls from ten to twelve years old, incited enormous debate about the limits of imperial rule and its intrusion into the domestic sphere and onto the body of the Indian (Hindu) woman. For an excellent account of the ways a juridico-medical discourse was employed to justify the Act, see Ishita Pande, "Phulmoni's Body: The Autopsy, the Inquest and the Humanitarian Narrative on Child Rape in India," *South Asian History and Culture*, 4, no. 1 (2013): 9–30. There is additionally a wealth of scholarship on the debate more broadly. See Mrinalini Sinha, *Colonial Masculinity: The "Manly Englishman" and the "Effeminate Bengali" in the Late Nineteenth Century* (Manchester, UK: Manchester University Press, 1995); Tanika Sarkar, "Rhetoric Against Age of Consent: Resisting Colonial Reason and Death of Child Wife," *Economic and Political Weekly* (September 4, 1993): 1869–73.

23. Paul de Man, "The Rhetoric of Temporality," in *Blindness and Insight: Essays in the Rhetoric of Contemporary Criticism* (New York: Psychology, 1983), 227.

24. Bina Das, "Statement before the Special Tribunal of the Calcutta High Court," Appendix, *Bina Das: A Memoir*. Trans. Dhira Dhar. (New Delhi: Zubaan, 2010).

25. Purnima Bose, *Organizing Empire: Individualism, Collective Agency, and India* (Durham, NC: Duke University Press, 2003), 130–31.

26. Talal Asad, *On Suicide Bombing* (New York: Columbia University Press, 2007), 43.

27. Quoted in Ishanee Mukherjee, "Scaling the Barrier: Women, Revolution, and Abscondence in Late Colonial Bengal," *Indian Journal of Gender Studies* 6, no. 61 (1999): 69.

28. See *Oxford English Dictionary Online*, s.v. "Immolate," accessed June 12, 2016, http://www.oed.com/view/Entry/91950?rskey=8SQBTa&result=2.

29. Shiva's violence is only quelled when Lord Vishnu, with his *sudharshana chakra*, destroys Sati's body, slicing it into fifty-one pieces. The weight of her mortal frame quite literally lifted from his shoulders, Shiva ends his divine destruction and sets to the work of forgiveness and repair. Her body is the corporeal engine of his rage: Finally destroyed, it no longer holds sway over him. The fifty-one pieces of Sati's body, said to have been strewn across the world, are now sites of worship—Sati Peethas—and historically the sites of widow immolations.

30. Ania Loomba writes, "The *sati*'s 'power' lies in her will to die and comes into being only when she expresses that will." Ania Loomba, "Dead Women Tell No Tales: Issues of Female Subjectivity, Subaltern Agency, and Tradition in Colonial and Post-Colonial Writings on Widow Immolation in India," *History Workshop* 36 (Autumn 1993): 221.

31. Mani, *Contentious Traditions*, 31.

32. William Lord Bentinck, "Preamble to 1829 Bengal Regulation of *Sati*," in *The Bengal Code: Bengal Regulations, Local Acts of the Governor General in Council and the Regulations Made under 33 Victoria, Cap. 3, in Force in Bengal*, ed. Charles Herman Oertel and Frederic George Wigley (Calcutta: Superintendent of Government Print, Legislative Department, 1889), 267.

33. Herman, *Empire's Bodies*; Mani, *Contentious Traditions*.

34. In *The Nation and Its Fragments*, Partha Chatterjee identifies the ways nationalists sought to resolve "the women's question" in Bengal by identifying domestic space as an ideological battleground upon which to wage their anticolonial struggle. He writes that, to the

nationalist, "The world is the external, the domain of the material; the home represents one's inner spiritual self, one's true identity. The world is a treacherous terrain of the pursuit of material interests, where practical considerations reign supreme. It is typically the domain of the male. The home in its essence must remain unaffected by the profane activities of the material world—and woman is its representation." *The Nation and Its Fragments: Colonial and Postcolonial Histories* (Princeton, NJ: Princeton University Press, 1993), 120. In other words, the inner feminine domain harbors all that is untainted by the forces of colonization and is therefore a particularly efficacious space in which to converge an anticolonial discourse intended to be inaccessible and nominally incomprehensible to colonial forces. Chatterjee's argument that Bengali nationalism successfully redirected the question of women's rights and advancement onto a patriarchal discourse of protecting the "essence" of culture identifies the double move of isolating the domestic space and publicizing it as representative of all Bengal. Consecrating the domestic space in Bengali nationalist discourse removed it from the purview of colonial politics, converging on it a patriarchal form that reified traditional notions of domesticity.

35. The 1857 Mutiny, also called the Sepoy Mutiny, began as a soldier rebellion in Meerut and spread to other military and civilian uprisings. Spurred by that initial uprising by members of the Bengal Presidency Army, Bahadur Shah Zafar, the last Mughal Emperor of India, declared himself Emperor of All India and marshaled anticolonial forces. Most famously, perhaps, the uprising in Jhansi, led by Rani Laxshmi Bai, attempted to liberate the city of Gwalior. The Rani, to whom I will return later, was killed during the battle and has since become an icon of female militancy on the subcontinent. The rebellion, quashed by July 1858—mostly due to a lack of central organization and large geographic regions untouched by the violence—saw the end of the British East India Company's rule in India. The Government of India Act of 1858 dissolved the company and transferred its powers to the Crown. One result thereof was the solidification of a penal code in the 1858 Act.

36. Thomas Metcalf argues that representations of *sati* as a female practice of self-renunciation were, in fact, remarkably in line with the idealized woman of the dominant domestic ideology of Britain at the time. He writes, "For the British themselves, however, such female 'self-renunciation' was not meant to be that of the sati who followed her husband onto the pyre. From this act the British recoiled in horror. It was, nevertheless, as the ultimate 'self-sacrifice,' not so far removed from the 'self-abasement' or 'self-annihilation' that, especially for feminist critics, defined the core of the domestic ideology. In a Britain where gender roles were contested, the existence of a connection between Indian self-immolation and the ideals of domesticity could not be avowed. To the contrary, only a vigorous attack on sati could effectively deny such similarities by displacing them onto an India seen as barbaric and inhumane." Thomas Metcalf, *Ideologies of the Raj* (Cambridge: Cambridge University Press, 1994), 98.

37. Metcalf, *Ideologies*, 29.

38. The claim of liberal personhood under empire is of course a difficult one, as the model by which this relationship is forged comes through the liberal vision of individuals by whose consent a government rules. Ranajit Guha's seminal work on hegemony points to the ways in which the colonial state limited the liberal right of citizenship only to the British, while Indians remained subjects. Thus, they were co-opted into forms of liberal personhood while simultaneously denied full entry into its ranks. Ranajit Guha, *Dominance Without Hegemony: History and Power in Colonial India*. (Cambridge, MA: Harvard University Press, 1998).

39. "Statute 298: Voluntary Culpable Homicide by Consent," *Indian Penal Code.* (1858).

40. "Statute 298."

41. "Statute 298."

42. Prior to the consolidation of governance under the British Crown in 1858, a *cordon sanitaire* had been erected around matters of religious or familial practice. In his 1722 *Plan for the Administration of Justice*, Governor Warren Hastings decreed that "in all suits regarding inheritance, marriage, caste and other religious usages or institutions, the laws of the Koran with respect to the Mohamedans and those of the Shaster with respect to the Gentoos shall invariably be adhered to" (quoted in Jonathan Israel, *Democratic Enlightenment: Philosophy, Revolution, and Human Rights 1750-1790* [Oxford: Oxford University Press, 2011], 56). It is in deference to this earlier noninterventionist policy that the statute of voluntary culpable homicide by consent comes to be so periphrastically figured. More than forbidding a single practice, the statute does the synecdochic work of representing a new form of governmentality. *Sati* has to be the shibboleth, unuttered but illustrated.

43. Thomas Babington Macaulay, "Introductory Report upon the Indian Penal Code," in *Miscellanies* (New York: Houghton Mifflin, 1901), 423.

44. The illustration further intends to regularize across all regions of India the prohibition against *sati* first codified in the Bengal presidency by the 1829 regulation and in other presidencies thereafter. The purpose of the newly drafted penal code, after all, was to provide a common law across presidencies to consolidate the legislative and punitive force of the British government in India and to commission the force of law into a single administrative body.

45. Crimes that fall under the mitigated class of offenses do so, according to Macaulay, for two reasons. First, they are motivated by affects "generally far more respectable" than those that incite the crime of murder ("Introductory Report," 423). The moral economy evoked here suggests a normative baseline for what constitutes "respectable" in terms of motives. Indeed, the normative force of law depends intimately upon the shared deontic experience of affect and motivation: The logic of respectability in the law is universalizing and intended to be objective. Macaulay goes on to offer an illustration of that respectability of motive in the "high-born native of India who stabs the females of his family at their own entreaty in order to save them from the licentiousness of a band of marauders" ("Introductory Report," 423). He suggests that they would, anywhere but in "Christian societies," not be culpable and, even in those societies, not be regarded by the public as "assassins." The legalistic condition of respectability depends on a translatability of intent and value; the respectable, like consent, must be appreciable.

46. Jeannette Herman argues that, "in order for the practice to fall under the definition of legal *sati*, the widow's burning must be an expression of her own will. In British accounts of *sati*, however, there is often a slippage from consent to desire, so that regardless of spoken consent, witnesses either based findings of legality or illegality, or of 'good' or 'bad' *satis*, on their readings of the widow's desire, or else lamented the law's definition of consent in the face of ambiguous desire." Herman, *Empire's Bodies*, 323.

47. *Oxford English Dictionary Online*, s.v. "Consent," accessed September 25, 2018, http://www.oed.com/view/Entry/91950?rskey=8SQBTa&result=2.

48. Spivak, "Can the Subaltern Speak?," 93.

49. Gayatri Chakravorty Spivak, "History," in *A Critique of Postcolonial Reason: Toward a History of the Vanishing Present* (Cambridge, MA: Harvard University Press, 1999), 127.

50. Paul de Man, *Allegories of Reading: Figural Language in Rousseau, Nietzsche, Rilke, and Proust* (New Haven, CT: Yale University Press, 1979), 205.

51. Pritilata Waddedar, "Long Live Revolution," in *The Easter Rebellion in India: The Chittagong Uprising*, ed. Mallikarjuna Sharma (Calcutta: Marxist Study Forum, 1993), 266.

52. Kalpana Joshi Dutt, *Chittagong Armoury Raiders' Reminiscences* (Delhi: People's Press, 1979), 32.

53. Lindsey Harlan, *Religion and Rajput Women: The Ethic of Protection in Contemporary Narratives* (Berkeley: University of California Press, 1992), 192.

54. "Arrest of Woman in Male Attire," *Times of India*, June 23, 1932, *Proquest Historical Newspapers (1861-Current)*.

55. The British overseers of Calcutta University did not confer her degree upon her at the time, because she was wanted by authorities. She and Bina Das were both posthumously awarded their degrees by the university in 2012.

56. Intelligence Branch Files, CID, June 19, 1932, No. 115/1932, West Bengal State Archives, Calcutta.

57. Quoted in Chatterjee, *Do and Die*, 257 (italics in original).

58. Spivak, "Can the Subaltern Speak?," 104.

59. Her name meaning "invincible, unassailable," this warrior deity is commonly depicted in Bengal in the midst of battle against the demon Mahishasura and came to be central to the nationalist iconography that dovetailed Hindu revivalism in the late nineteenth century with anticolonialism.

60. The IRA and other revolutionary groups in Bengal distanced themselves from Gandhi in 1931 when he signed the Gandhi-Irwin Pact, calling off the civil disobedience movement in exchange for the removal of the salt tax and the release of all political prisoners not convicted of a violent crime.

61. In *Colonial Masculinity*, Mrinalini Sinha argues that that the notion of the Bengali *babu* was constructed as a perverted form of masculinity within a discourse of conquest and empire mobilized by British authorities. The construction of the effeminate Bengali in popular culture developed alongside the British cult of masculinity in the nineteenth century, as part of a project to reify and bolster the image of the virile British Empire. Sinha's analysis critically pinpoints the ways in which the very structure of empire necessitated the discursive project of identifying Bengal, and its residents, as at once dutiful and innocuous. Thomas Macaulay, in his 1840 biography of Lord Robert Clive, referred to Bengalis as "the race by whom this rich tract was peopled, enervated by a soft climate and accustomed to peaceful employments, bore the same relation to other Asiatics which the Asiatics generally bear to the bold and energetic children of Europe. The Castilians have a proverb, that in Valencia the earth is water and the men women; and the description is at least equally applicable to the vast plain of the Lower Ganges. . . . There never, perhaps, existed a people so thoroughly fitted by nature and by habit for a foreign yoke." *Macaulay's Essay on Lord Clive* (New York: Macmillan, 1840). Unlike the martial races of Northern India, who struggled against the vicissitudes of climate and conquest, colonial authorities saw the Bengalis as an effeminate race made weak by abundance and peace, not only in relation to the British but also to the other races and peoples in India.

The notion of the effete Bengali may have had its roots in a colonial discourse of appropriate masculinities, but it soon sprouted a domestic logic. Indeed, concerns over how to fortify a seemingly dwindling Bengali manliness were central to the discourse of the Bengal Renaissance in the nineteenth century. Swami Vivekananda, a monk in the Ramakrishna Order and a central figure in Hindu revivalism at the end of the century, preached a distinctly masculinized Hinduism tied to nationalist concerns. His philosophy marked a departure from the teachings of Ramakrishna, his *guru*, whose androgynous attachment to the

Mother Goddess was infamous. Vivekananda imagined a relationship between goddess and nation: "Say, brother: 'The soil of India is my highest heaven, the good of India is my good,' and repeat and pray day and night, 'O Thou Lord of Gauri, O Thou Mother of the Universe, vouchsafe manliness unto me! O Thou Mother of Strength, take away my weakness, take away my unmanliness, and make me a Man!'" Swami Vivekananda, "Modern India," in *The Complete Works of Swami Vivekananda*, vol. 4: Translation, Prose (Calcutta: Advaita Ashrama, 1962); accessed April 12, 2009, http://www.ramakrishnavivekananda.info/vivekananda/volume_4 /translation_prose/modern_india.htm). Vivekananda's prayer for manliness produced a vision of masculinity and strength acquired through action, a teleological narrative into which the discourse of revolutionary violence in Bengal in the 1930s actively posited itself.

62. Quoted in I. Mallikarjuna Sharma, *Easter Rebellion in India: The Chittagong Uprising*, (Hyderabad: Marxist Study Forum, 1993), 373. The pamphlet is undated but likely was printed between 1930 and 1933.

63. In "The Quest for Manhood," Subho Basu and Sikata Banerjee argue: "When such a revolutionary project of elite nationalism faced steep competition from Gandhian mass nationalism in the aftermath of World War I, Bengali elites searched for an alternative international revolution through vanguard political organizations. . . . The quest for masculine heroism did not die out. It instead assumed new forms by integrating itself with wider political currents of diverse forms of global revolutionary movements of the early twentieth century that provided alternative methods of articulation of such masculine anxiety within the matrix of modernizing movements." Subho Basu and Sikata Banerjee, "The Quest for Manhood: Masculine Hinduism and Nation in Bengal," *Comparative Studies of South Asia, Africa and the Middle East* 26, no. 3 (2006): 478.

64. Ananta Singh's surrender in 1932, after he had successfully eluded the authorities for two years, has been read in a variety of ways, ranging from an attempt to silence any jailed revolutionaries who might confess and turn evidence to a result of a power struggle within the ranks of the organization. His letter of surrender, however, provides an alternate explanation. He writes, "I could have committed suicide or could have fought in frontal battle to die. But I have a secret desire in me. I want to see and know the reaction of my fast and close friend during my death. This is why I preferred the process not of a quick death but a rather prolonged one in horror and at the same time to have time to read what position I actually occupied in your heart so long." Ananta Singh surrendered to elicit a response from an unrequited love. This declaration is closely bound to the mechanisms of affect in the revolutionary forces: His letter to his IRA comrade Ganesh Ghosh suggests that Ghosh is that "fast and close friend." Ananta Singh's surrender occasions an assessment of Ghosh's love for him, one to be measured in articulations of love and attachment. The political and the erotic are inextricable from one another here, and, I argue, more generally within these nationalist groups. Thus, we might understand Singh's fear of the inclusion of women in their collectivity as a disruption of the homoerotic structure of the group. Quoted in Chatterjee, *Do and Die*, 168. For an excellent account of the forms of homosociality and masculine community in these revolutionary groups, see Durba Ghosh, *Gentlemanly Terrorists: Political Violence and the Colonial State in India, 1919-1947*. (Cambridge: Cambridge University Press, 2017)

65. Dutt, *Chittagong Armoury Raiders*, 21.

66. de Man, "The Rhetoric of Temporality," 299.

67. Although Pritilata Waddedar's diary was destroyed by colonial authorities following the trial, the portions of it introduced at trial were, ironically, preserved in the court records and

subsequently reprinted in *Chittagong Uprising Golden Jubilee Souvenir*. (New Delhi: Chittagong Uprising National Golden Jubilee Committee and People's Publishing House, 1980); and I. Mallikarjuna Sharma, ed., *The Easter Rebellion in India: The Chittagong Uprising* (Hyderabad: Marxist Study Forum, 1993).

68. "High Court Judgment—Surya Sen Case. Special Bench: Pankridge, Ameer Ali and M. G. Ghose, J. J. Emperor v. Surjya Kumar Sen and Other-Accused-Appellents," in Mallikarjuna Sharma, *The Easter Rebellion in India*, 438–57.

69. "Girl, Believed to Be Mesmerised," *Times of India* (November 11, 1933), *Proquest Historical Newspapers 1861-Current*.

70. Quoted in Chatterjee, *Do and Die*, 257.

71. "Girl, Believed to Be Mesmerised."

72. In *Mesmerized: Powers of the Mind in Victorian Britain* (Chicago: University of Chicago Press, 1998), Alison Winter offers a useful account of colonial India as a laboratory for mesmerist experiments and of its prevalence as social referent in this period.

73. Durga, along with Sati, Uma, Gauri, and Parvati, is figured in a variety of texts and Vedic traditions as the consort of Shiva. The relationship between her and the others is a synchronic compression made possible by the logic of reincarnation and the range of goddess-worship traditions that came, during British rule, to be collated under "Hinduism" as a singular religion. Unlike the others, whose primarily discursive function is the representation of proper wifeliness, Durga is the blazing and fearsome mother goddess, compelled to Earth by Shiva to fight the demon who had thus far proven undefeatable. She is at once an incarnation of those other consorts and exalted above all others. She and the goddess Kali are figured as the most powerful manifestations of Shakti, a primordial, cosmic feminine energy.

74. Surya Sen, "Vijaya," in Mallikarjuna Sharma, *The Easter Rebellion in India*, 269.

75. "High Court Judgment—Surya Sen Case. Special Bench: Pankridge, Ameer Ali and M. G. Ghose, J. J. Emperor v. Surjya Kumar Sen and Other-Accused-Appellents," in Mallikarjuna Sharma, *The Easter Rebellion in India*, 438–57.

76. Sen, "Vijaya," 271.

77. Sen, "Vijaya," 272.

78. Judith Butler, *Precarious Life: The Powers of Mourning and Violence* (London: Verso, 2004), 34.

79. Though the prosecution offered several witnesses to support their case that Sen was involved in the terrorist activities in Chittagong, their primary argument emerged through the juxtaposition of Sen's "Vijaya" and the pamphlet "Long Live Revolution" found on Waddedar's body at the time of her death. The two texts, when read together by the prosecution, paint a causal relationship "of close association" in which shared intimacies equate projected guilt. This is not, of course, to claim that Sen was not complicit in the attacks; he indeed planned and helped to execute them. It is important to acknowledge, however, the ways in which the prosecution's argument does not ascribe to Sen the control over and investment in the Pahartali raid and others that he imagines in his essay. Sen, in other words, evinced a stronger investment in his own material causality—and the corresponding image of himself as a man of action—than did his prosecutors.

80. Bina Das, *Bina Das: A Memoir* (New Delhi: Zubaan, 2010), 24.

81. Karl Marx, "The Indian Revolt," *New York Daily Tribune* (September 4, 1857).

82. David Scott, "Colonial Governmentality," *Social Text* 43 (1995): 205 (emphasis in original).

83. Foucault describes the move to governmentality as "not in terms of the replacement of a society of sovereignty by a disciplinary society and the subsequent replacement of a disciplinary

society by a society of government; in reality one has a triangle, sovereignty-discipline-government, which has as its primary target the population and its essential mechanism the apparatuses of security." Michel Foucault, *The Foucault Effect: Studies in Governmentality* (Chicago: University of Chicago Press, 1991), 102. For Foucault, governmentality emerges alongside the state, whereas scholars of colonial governmentality argue that in the case of colonial India in particular, governmentality becomes a mechanism of a changing state apparatus. For more on colonial governmentality, see Peter Pels, "The Anthropology of Colonialism: Culture, History, and the Emergence of Western Governmentality," *Annual Review of Anthropology* 26 (1997): 163–83; Gyan Prakash, *Another Reason: Science and the Imagination of Modern India* (Princeton, NJ: Princeton University Press, 1999); Jean Comoroff and John Comoroff, *Of Revelation and Revolution: Christianity, Colonialism, and Consciousness in South Africa*, vol. 1 (Chicago: University of Chicago Press, 1991); Stephen Legg, *Spaces of Colonialism: Delhi's Urban Governmentalities* (Malden, MA: Blackwell, 2007); Mark Brown, *Penal Power and Colonial Rule* (New York: Routledge, 2014).

84. The 1872 Indian Evidence Act explicitly sought to offer a single, uniform system of judicial procedure to be applied to all of British India, concretizing and unifying previously disparate procedures from the Nizamat Adalat and religious legal systems. In "Bureaucratic Recruitment and Subordination in Colonial India," Arnold argues that the Indian Evidence Act, the Criminal Tribes Act, and the India Police Act of 1871 drew upon ethnological techniques to strengthen colonial rule over the populations identified to be least incorporable into a Victorian domestic and social sensibility. David Arnold, "Bureaucratic Recruitment and Subordination in Colonial India," in *Subaltern Studies No. 4: Writings of South Asian History and Society*, ed. Ranajit Guha (New Delhi: Oxford University Press, 1985), 1–53.

85. Statistics and demography are perhaps the other two most prominent such sciences of imperialism, as techniques of identification, taxonomy, and quantification. I describe in the introduction how the Raj turned to statistics as a vehicle of statecraft in its regulation and division of Bengal in 1905.

86. Intelligence Branch Files, CID, June 19, 1932, No. 115/1932, West Bengal State Archives, Calcutta.

87. Intelligence Branch Files, No. 115/1932.

88. Michel Foucault, *Society Must Be Defended: Lectures at the Collège de France, 1975–1976*, trans. David Macey (New York: Picador, 2003), 243.

89. Anand Yang, Anjali Arondekar, and others have argued that the CTA demonstrates an imperial fixation on collective criminality and deviance—a marker of population pathology—in lieu of individual culpability. Unlike the British Habitual Criminals Act of 1869, which allowed for the surveillance and detention of any individual who had been previously convicted of a crime, the CTA targeted "any tribe, gang or class of persons [who] is addicted to the systematic commission of non-bailable offenses." Act No. XXVII of 1871, "An Act for the Registration of Criminal Tribes and Eunuchs," in *The Bengal Code* (Calcutta: Office of the Superindent of Government Printing India, 1872). For more on the CTA, see Anand A. Yang, "Dangerous Castes and Tribes: The Criminal Tribes Act and the Magahiya Doms of Northeast India," in *Crime and Criminality in British India*, ed. Anand A. Yang (Tucson: University of Arizona Press, 1985), 108–27; Anjali Arondekar, *For the Record: On Sexuality and the Colonial Archive* (Durham, NC: Duke University Press, 2009); Meena Radhakrishna, *Dishonoured by History: Criminal Tribes and British Colonial Policy* (New Delhi: Orient Longman, 2001); Sanjay Nigam, "Disciplining and Policing the 'Criminals by Birth,' Part 1: The Making of a Colonial Stereotype—The Criminal Tribes and Castes of North India," *Indian Economic and Social History Review* 27 (1990): 131–64;

Anand Pandian, "Pastoral Power in the Postcolony: On the Biopolitics of the Criminal Animal in South India," *Cultural Anthropology* 23, no. 1 (2008): 85–117; Andrew J. Major, "State and Criminal Tribes in Colonial Punjab: Surveillance, Control and Reclamation of the 'Dangerous Classes,'" *Modern Asian Studies* 33, no. 3 (1999): 657–88; Rachel J. Tolen, "Colonizing and Transforming the Criminal Tribesman: The Salvation Army in British India," *American Ethnologist* 18, no. 1 (1991): 106–25; Jessica Hinchy, "Deviant Domesticities and Sexualised Childhoods: Prostitutes, Eunuchs and the Limits of the State Child 'Rescue' Mission in Colonial India," in *Divine Domesticities: Christian Paradoxes in Asia and the Pacific*, ed. Hyaeweol Choi and Margaret Jolly (Canberra, Australia: ANU Press, 2014), 247–80; Mark Brown, "Ethnology and Colonial Administration in Nineteenth-Century British India: The Question of Native Crime and Criminality," *British Journal for the History of Science* 36, no. 2 (2003): 201–19.

90. The Habitual Criminals Act, Thomas Metcalf points out, did not target any person other than who had already been convicted of a crime, whereas for Indian subjects, criminal behavior came to be typologized; the British were individual subjects under the law while Indians were collectives. Metcalf, *Ideologies of the Raj*, 124.

91. Indeed, the CTA was the culmination of a decades-long colonial enterprise to give material body to a formation that seemed to elude its disciplinary apparatus; it followed from a series of Thuggee and Dacoity Suppression Acts between 1836 and 1848 and the establishment of the Thuggee and Dacoity Department. There is a wealth of work on Thuggees and the colonial imagination, of which Roy's is particularly rich. See also Parama Roy, *Indian Traffic: Identities in Question in Colonial and Postcolonial India* (Berkeley: University of California Press, 1998); Kim Wagner, *Thuggee: Banditry and the British in Early Nineteenth-Century India* (London: Palgrave, 2007); Leon F. Fannin, "Thuggee and Professional Criminality," *Michigan Sociological Review* 3 (1989): 34–44; Radhika Singha, " 'Providential' Circumstances: The Thuggee Campaign of the 1830s and Legal Innovation," *Modern Asian Studies* 27, no. 1 (1993): 83–146.

92. The CTA offered a phylogenetic order to the Thuggees, identifying their patrilineal practice as one that could be codified and regulated. The aura of scientific rationality offered by ethnological accounts of behavior, embodiments, and habits highlighted what authorities took to be recognizable characteristics of a population that simultaneously captured the imperial imagination for its apparent mystery. Parama Roy argues that "the campaign for its exposure and extirpation was to form a significant constitutive component of the authoritarian and interventionary reform of the 1830s and 1840s, and to contribute to the still emerging project of 'discovering India.'" Parama Roy, "Discovering India, Imagining Thuggee," *Yale Journal of Criticism* 9, no. 1 (1996): 121–45, at 121.

93. Section 377 of the Indian Penal Code, which is currently being examined by the High Court following an appeal of the Naz Foundation ruling of 2011, was instituted in 1860 under Crimes of the Body as "Unnatural Offences": "Whoever voluntarily has carnal intercourse against the order of nature with any man, woman or animal, shall be punished with 1 [imprisonment for life], or with imprisonment of either description for a term which may extend to ten years, and shall also be liable to fine." For more on Section 377, see Arondekar, *For the Record*; Gayatri Reddy, *With Respect to Sex: Negotiating Hijra Identity in South India* (Chicago: University of Chicago Press, 2005); Gee Imaan Semmalar, "Unpacking Solidarities of the Oppressed: Notes on Trans Struggles in India," *Women's Studies Quarterly* 42, no. 3–4 (2014): 286–91; Rahul Rao, "Hijra," in *Key Concepts in Modern Indian Studies*, ed. Gita Dharampal-Frick, Monika Kirloskar-Steinbach, Rachel Dwyer, and Jahnavi Phalkey (New York: New York University Press, 2015), 99–101; Act No. XXVII of 1871, "An Act for the Registration of Criminal Tribes and Eunuchs."

94. By the terms of the CTA, *hijras* are somatically castrated and verifiably impotent; they bear on their bodies the garments and marks of a gender not biologically their own; their labor is at once performative and sexual; their threat is of visibility, contagion, and pleasure.

95. The stitched cloth that limned the contours of Waddedar's body in life and in death bound her to the trace of contact between the Muslim hand of the tailor who sewed together her garments to the modes of local identification that would have rendered her body recognizable and thus protected within the Muslim neighborhoods through which she passed. The garments on her body, logged in as evidence of her crime, are evidence too of an intent to make her body speak, of an articulation of refusal, of illegibility, of the gap between the surface and its interior filled by traces of contact and histories of touch.

96. "Orders by His Excellency, The Governor of Bengal: No. 2496P," *Calcutta Gazette*, March 16, 1933.

97. Interestingly, Charles Tegart, commissioner of the Calcutta Police at this time, was famous for his disguises. A red-headed Irishman who was more than six feet tall, he is said to have been able to infiltrate any community within India, though he never bothered to change his hair color.

98. The history of "habit" as a marker of both practice and bodily form goes back to the early modern period, when it came to indicate both costume (as in the habit of a nun) and morals. Traub argues, "If phenotype is a concept based on visible characteristics, then what developed in the early modern period was not a phenotype based on the privileging of skin color, but a strategy of marking differences and similarities through a visual mimesis of nation, religion, lineage, costume, as well as skin color—in a word, *habit*." See Valerie Traub, "Mapping the Global Body," in *Early Modern Visual Culture: Representation, Race, and Empire in Renaissance*, ed. Peter Eriksen and Clark Hulse (Philadelphia: University of Pennsylvania Press, 2000), 59.

99. Emma Tarlo argues, in *Clothing Matters: Dress and Identity in India* (Chicago: University of Chicago Press, 1996), that there is evidence of stitched clothing in India as early as the eleventh century, even though the Muslim conquest is seen as radically reconceiving forms of dress and religion.

100. In Bengal—particularly Muslim-majority East Bengal—the distinction was often marked by the conflation of stitched cloth with both Islam and British modernity. "Modern" Bengali Hindu men might don suits and pants, fashioned in the style of British authorities, in public and then change into draped *dhotis* and *lungis* at home. For young women, however, saris remained the common dress for both Hindus and Muslims. The *salwar-kameez* (long tunic and pajama pants) worn by Muslim women in Northern India did not come into fashion until after partition. Authorities feared that in a city so markedly cleaved by its religious distinctions, the evidence of which was visible upon the body of the population, wearing clothing associated with Muslims would let the members of Jugantar—all themselves of Hindu families—pass into a population that the Raj saw as apolitical or antagonistic to the anticolonial cause. Home Ministry/Political Department, 1933 File Number 45/5/33, National Archives of India, New Delhi.

101. Watson wrote, "About two hundred million of souls form the population of what we commonly speak of as India; and, scant though the garments of the vast majority may be, an order to clothe them all would try the resources of the greatest manufacturing nation on earth. It is clear, therefore, that India is in a position to become a magnificent customer." *Textile Manufactures and the Costumes of the People of India* (London: Eyre & Spottiswoode, 1866), 3.

102. Watson, *Textile Manufactures*, 6.

103. Watson, *Textile Manufactures*, 56.

104. Best and Marcus suggest that the opposition between surface and depth that so guides symptomatic modes of reading is misleading and produces a kind of romantic epistemophilia toward depth. Stephen Best and Marcus Sharon, "Surface Reading: An Introduction," *Representations* 108, no. 1 (2009): 1–21.

105. Anne Anlin Cheng, "Skins, Tattoos, and Susceptibility," *Representations* 108, no. 1 (2009): 98–119.

106. H. G. Cooke to Chief Secretary to the Government of Bengal, January 6, 1891; India Home Department, "Papers Relating to a Bill to Provide for the More Effectual Surveillance and Control of Habitual Offenders in India," in Selections from the Records of the Government of India, no. 300 (Calcutta, 1893). Quoted in Simon Cole, *Suspect Identities: A History of Fingerprinting and Criminal Identification* (Cambridge, MA: Harvard University Press, 2002), 69.

107. Galton's later work on the reliability of fingerprint identification drew its empirical authority from Hershel's data. Colonial bodies offer the template for the claim of fingerprinting's universalism. In 1892, Sir Edward Henry, inspector general of the Bengal Police, instituted the use of fingerprints for criminal identification to replace the prior imperfect anthropometric system, transforming the site of Herschel's experimentation into that of its practice.

108. For the British, who were so chagrined by the apparent disinterest of Bengalis in individuation and who so struggled to differentiate between them, the promise of visible and verifiable determination of identity was significant. Fingerprints bore the mark of liberal personhood. On the body of every Bengali (indeed, every Indian, every human) lay empirical proof that they must be individual subjects under the law; fingerprinting in this way became a metaphor for the possibility of governing individuals and not just types.

109. Several prominent members of the Chittagong branch of Jugantar, including Surya Sen, Nirmal Sen, Tarkeswar Dastidar, and Ananta Singh, had been jailed for suspicion of seditious activity under the 1925 Criminal Law Amendment (Supplementary) Act, and released in 1928 having served the maximum possible time. The CID files contain the identification photographs taken of them at Hijli Jail; these images are the most common, and perhaps only available, remaining photographs of them.

110. Roland Barthes, *Camera Lucida: Reflections on Photography*, trans. Richard Howard (New York: Farrar, Straus and Giroux, 1981), 13.

111. Barthes, *Camera Lucida*, 87.

112. In *Event, Memory, Metaphor: Chauri Chaura, 1922-1992* (Berkeley: University of California Press, 1995), Shahid Amin describes meeting relatives of those who took part in the 1922 riots and feeling like a colonial police officer, paralleling the experience of the police office, seeking to authenticate documents and proof by the encounter with the culprits, to his own of seeking to authentic archival documents with an encounter with their descendants. I am grateful to him for sharing his thoughts on the relationship between photography and the imperial gaze with me.

113. This description was reproduced as part of an exhibition at the Bangladesh Liberation War Museum in 2014.

114. Dutt writes in her memoir of Waddedar, "And now . . . the sudden, impossible news that she was dead! If only I were by her side, in action together, I would never have let her commit suicide. Later on, Masterda (Surjya Sen) told me that she had died in order to show our people that women too can fight and die for their country like their menfolk. But I was convinced that she could have done much more by coming back alive" (Dutt, *Chittagong Armoury Raiders'*

Reminiscences, 46). The pedagogical or inspirational value of Waddedar's death, in Dutt's intimate calculus, is unequal to the loss of her as a friend and comrade.

115. In 1943, Dutt married P. C. Joshi, then General Secretary of the Communist Party of India (CPI). It is likely that the continued surveillance of Dutt after Indian independence was because of Joshi's often contentious relationship to the Party until it split in 1964 into CPI Marxist and CPI wings. Dutt lived in relatively anonymity as a full-timer in a Delhi commune until her death in 1995. Her daughter-in-law Manini Chatterjee is the author of *Do and Die: The Chittagong Uprising 1930–1934*, on which the Gowariker film discussed in this chapter is based.

116. Intelligence Branch Files, CID, June 17, 1993, Item 18, No. 493/1931, West Bengal State Archives, Calcutta.

117. We might recall here Spivak's remark that her own encounter with the Rani of Sirmur, who occasioned her examination of *sati*, was made possible "because of the commercial/territorial interests of the East India Company." Gayatri Chakravorty Spivak, "The Rani of Sirmur: An Essay in Reading the Archives," *History and Theory* 24, no. 3 (1985): 247–72, 263.

118. Quoted in Chatterjee, *Do and Die*, 257.

119. Police Commissioner Charles Tegart described the initial confusion over Waddedar's body in his unpublished biography, which is available at the British Library in the Asia, Africa, Pacific Collections Private Papers.

120. Spivak, "Can the Subaltern Speak?," 104.

121. Spivak, "History," 273.

122. Spivak, "History," 273.

123. We might here think of Disney's 1989 animated feature *The Little Mermaid*, in which the mermaid Ariel gives up her voice in exchange for human legs. Her voice is figured as organ-like, extractable and transplantable. In the scene, Ariel sings the scales, the light of her voice glowing through her translucent skin; Ursula the witch, hypersexualized with phallic tentacles, wildly cackles, "Keep singing!" as she conjures phantom hands to reach into Ariel's throat to extract the glowing orb. The phantasmically solidified sound is then transplanted into the grotesquely vulvic shell around Ursula's neck. Ariel is made, if not to unspeak herself, to unsing herself: a melodic castration into humanness. The limbs she is offered in recompense are, we are to understand, an utterly inadequate prosthesis, bringing her within proximity of her object of desire, the hapless and administratively befuddled Prince Eric, but preventing her from being human enough. It is her speechlessness that allures him—for who does not want a silent supplicant as paramour?—but it is her voice, uncannily reembodied by Ursula in the guise of a human woman, with which he believes himself in love. There, even, it is her voice in song—only the melodic simulacrum of what she sacrificed. Ariel's voice is both the condition of her human possibility and its betrayal.

124. Spivak, "History," 308; "Can the Subaltern Speak?," 104.

125. Spivak, "History," 309.

126. I am following here, to a degree, Derrida's notion of hauntology from *Specters of Marx* (New York: Routledge, 1994) in taking seriously the spectral presence of that which history marks as its debris and erases.

127. Nicolas Abraham and Maria Torok, *The Shell and the Kernel: Renewals of Psychoanalysis*, trans. Nicholas T. Rand (Chicago: University of Chicago Press, 1994), 113.

128. Avery Gordon, *Ghostly Matters: Haunting and the Sociological Imagination* (Minneapolis: University of Minnesota Press, 1997), 8.

129. Spivak, "History," 208.

2. THE FETISH TOUCH

The epigraph that opens this chapter is from Maurice Merleau-Ponty, *Le Visible et L'invisible* (Paris: Gallimard, 1976), 328.

1. Quoted in Amartya Sen, *The Argumentative Indian: Writings on Indian History, Culture and Identity* (New York: Macmillan, 2006), 94.

2. Quoted in Reba Som, *Rabindranath Tagore: The Singer and His Song* (New York: Penguin, 2009), 123.

3. Michel Foucault, *The Order of Things: An Archeology of the Human Sciences* (New York: Pantheon, 1970), 9.

4. Rabindranath Tagore, *Nationalism* (London: Macmillan, 1917), 38.

5. Eve Kosofsky Sedgwick, "Paranoid Reading and Reparative Reading, or, You're So Paranoid, You Probably Think This Essay Is About You," in *Touching Feeling: Affect, Pedagogy, Performativity* (Durham, NC: Duke University Press, 2003), 146.

6. Karl Marx, "The Leading Article in No. 179 of the *Kölnische Zeitung*: Religion, Free Press, and Philosophy," in *The Writings of the Young Marx on Philosophy and Society*, ed. and trans. Loyd D. Easton and Kurt H. Guddat (New York: Hackett, 1975), 115.

7. Georg Wilhelm Friedrich Hegel, *Lectures on the Philosophy of History* (London: G. Bell and Sons, 1902), 96.

8. Hegel, *Lectures*, 96.

9. Sigmund Freud, "Fetishism" (1927), in *The Standard Edition of the Complete Psychological Works of Sigmund Freud*, vol. 21, ed. and trans. James Strachey (New York: Norton, 1953), 152.

10. *Oxford English Dictionary Online*, s.v. "Fetish," accessed April 14, 2009, http://www.oed.com/view/Entry/69611.

11. Pietz writes, "The fetish, then, not only originated from, but remains specific to, the problematic social value of material objects as revealed in situations formed by the encounter of radically heterogeneous social systems, and a history of the idea of the fetish may be guided by identifying those themes that persist throughout the various discourses and disciplines that have appropriated the term." William Pietz, "The Problem of the Fetish I," *RES: Anthropology and Aesthetics*, no. 9 (1985): 5–17, 7.

12. Pietz, "The Problem of the Fetish I," 12.

13. Pietz, "The Problem of the Fetish I," 12.

14. Tagore, *Nationalism*, 23.

15. Tagore, *Nationalism*, 23.

16. Quoted in Partha Chatterjee, *Lineages of Political Society: Studies in Postcolonial Democracy* (New York: Columbia University Press, 2011), 104.

17. We might here find echoes of Emersonian self-reliance. Indeed, Tagore deeply admired the writer, who himself deeply admired Vedic texts, and remarked during his travels to the United States in 1916: "I love your Emerson. In his work one finds much that is of India. In truth he made the teachings of our spiritual leaders and philosophers a part of his life." Quoted in Bailey Millard, "Rabindranath Tagore Discovers America," *The Bookman* 44 (1916): 247–48.

18. Tagore, *Nationalism*, 127.

19. The self-rule of *swadeshi* played out in Tagore's 1916 novel *The Home and the World*, which I examine in chapter 3, and in Bengal itself, as a kind of un-rule in which communities turned against each other in communal riots, rather than together against imperial rule.

20. The history of jute as cash crop and representative of the (failed) possibility of East Bengali development is perhaps the ghost of this chapter. It haunts questions of raw material and

valuation, as well as indicating the ways in which questions of Bangladesh's postindependence development were prophesied early in the colonial period. On labor in jute production, see Sugata Bose, *Peasant Labour and Colonial Capital: Rural Bengal Since 1770*, vol. 2 (Cambridge: Cambridge University Press, 1993); Dipesh Chakrabarty, *Rethinking Working-Class History: Bengal, 1890–1940* (Princeton, NJ: Princeton University Press, 2000); Samita Sen, *Women and Labour in Late Colonial India: The Bengal Jute Industry*, vol. 3 (Cambridge: Cambridge University Press, 1999). a more recent source is the dissertation of Tariq Omar Ali, *A Local History of Global Capital: Jute and Peasant Life in the Bengal Delta* (Princeton, NJ: Princeton University Press, 2018).

21. Rabindranath Tagore, "Amar Sonar Bangla," in *Encyclopedia of National Anthems*, ed. Xing Hang (Lanham, MD: Scarecrow Press, 2003), 450.

22. *Oxford English Dictionary Online*, s.v. "Thrill," accessed April 14, 2009, http://www.oed.com /view/Entry/201256.

23. Quoted in Joseph Parisi and Stephen Young, *Dear Editor: A History of Poetry in Letters: The First Fifty Years, 1912-1962* (New York: Norton, 2002), 46.

24. Rabindranath Tagore, "Amar Sonar Bangla," "Gitabidan: Swadesh" in *Rabindra-Rachanabali*, vol. 4. (Kolkata: Paschim Banga Sarkar, 1980), 189.

25. Tagore, "Amar Sonar Bangla," *Encyclopedia of National Anthems*, 450.

26. *Samsad Bengali-English Dictionary*, 3rd ed., s.v. "মলিন," accessed September 27, 2018, http://dsal .uchicago.edu/dictionaries/biswas-bengali.

27. Tagore, "Amar Sonar Bangla," *Rabindra Rachanabali*. Translation my own.

28. Jonathan Culler, "Apostrophe," in *The Pursuit of Signs: Semiotics, Literature, Deconstruction* (Ithaca: Cornell University Press, 1981), 139.

29. Barbara Johnson, "Apostrophe, Animation, and Abortion," *Diacritics* 16 (1986): 30.

30. Barbara Johnson, *Persons and Things* (Cambridge, MA: Harvard University Press, 2005), 10.

31. Rabindranath Tagore, "Jana Gana Mana," in *Encyclopedia of National Anthems*, ed. Xing Hang (Lanham, MD: Scarecrow Press, 2005), 450.

32. Ludden argues that the idea of an Indian national space, as opposed to the ancient figuration of Indian imperial, emerged in the late nineteenth century as a product of capital and its encounter with the imperial presence of the British Raj.

33. Rabindranath Tagore, "Jana Gana Mana," in "Gitabidan: Swadesh" *Rabindra-Rachanabali*, vol. 4. (Kolkata: Paschim Banga Sarkar, 1980) 194. Translation my own.

34. Monish R. Chatterjee, "Tagore and Jana Gana Mana," *Counter Currents*, August 31, 2003, accessed December 7, 2016, http://www.countercurrents.org/comm-chatterjee310803.htm. The report of the annual session of the Indian National Congress of December 1911 stated: "On the first day of 28th annual session of the Congress, proceedings started after singing Vande Mataram. On the second day the work began after singing a patriotic song by Babu Ravindranath Tagore. Messages from well wishers were then read and a resolution was passed expressing loyalty to King George V. Afterwards the song composed for welcoming King George V and Queen Mary was sung." This apparently led to the confusion around whether the song that Tagore sang was that which was composed for the emperor and his consort.

35. The painting, like much of Abanindranath Tagore's oeuvre, is considered an ideal example of the Bengal School of Art. Rabindranath Tagore, however, was deeply critical of what he saw as the regressive orientalist tropes of that style, its self-conscious eschewal of Western modernism. Tagore's own paintings, perhaps like his translated poems of the *Gitanjali*, played visibly with forms and media from Europe in particular. The Nation, Tagore suggests in his art practice, is an unsatisfactory principle for aesthetics.

36. Debashish Banerji, *The Alternate Nation of Abanindranath Tagore* (New Delhi: SAGE Publications India, 2010), xx.

37. Tagore, *Nationalism*, 122.

38. Rabindranath Tagore, *Greater India* (Madras: S. Ganesan, 1920), 70.

39. Rabindranath Tagore, *Selected Letters of Rabindranath Tagore*, ed. Krishna Dutt and Andrew Robinson (New York: Cambridge University Press, 1997), 72.

40. Tagore, *Nationalism*, 15.

41. Martha Nussbaum, for example, argues that Tagore's repudiation of nationalism is an explicit endorsement of and model for an ethical cosmopolitanism. She misreads his humanist ethics by ignoring his deeply felt local commitments and the philosophical ground for Tagore's notion of the world, which was not of citizenship or its abnegation but of a nondualist reality. Martha Nussbaum, "Patriotism and Cosmopolitanism," *Boston Review*, October 1, 1994. https:// bostonreview.net/martha-nussbaum-patriotism-and-cosmopolitanism.

42. Bruce Robbins, in "Uses of World Literature," in *The Routledge Companion to World Literature*, ed. Theo D'haen, David Damrosch, and Djelal Kadir (Abingdon, UK: Routledge, 2011), 383–92 (2011), avows this very distinction in order to make the case for world literature as a more democratic and useful category. Although I warrant that his argument that the temporal adherence of the postcolonial limits its scope, the turn away from the postcolonial has limited rather than expanded possibilities. Robbins, like Damrosch, Nussbaum, and others, aligns world literature with cosmopolitanism as an ethical project, in which a kind of critical national exile clears the ground for greater relationality. It seems to me that one of the great strengths of the project of postcolonial studies is to make visible the constitutive violences of romantic cosmopolitanism, its own imbrication in imperial knowledge production, and indeed the privileged condition of being able to self-estrange that is not distributed equally across the world.

43. Rabindranath Tagore, "Visva Sahitya," in *Rabindranath Tagore in the 21st Century*, ed. D. Banerji, trans. Rijula Das and Makarand Paranjape (New Delhi: Springer India, 2015): 286.

44. See David Damrosch, *What Is World Literature?* (Princeton, NJ: Princeton University Press, 2003); Barbara Herrnstein Smith, *Contingencies of Value: Alternative Perspectives for Critical Theory* (Cambridge, MA: Harvard University Press, 1988); Timothy Brennan, *At Home in the World: Cosmopolitanism Now* (Cambridge, MA: Harvard University Press, 1997); Bruce Robbins, *Feeling Global: Internationalism in Distress* (New York: NYU Press, 1999).

45. The word *gitanjali* comes from *git*, meaning "song," and *anjali*, meaning "offering."

46. Nobel Committee, "Rabindranath Tagore," *Nobelprize.org*, n.d., http://nobelprize.org/nobel _prizes/literature/laureates/1913/.

47. There was substantial controversy over Tagore's Nobel in terms of whether he was awarded the prize for the *Gitanjali* alone or, like the previous laureates, for a larger body of work. Critics claimed that he could not have been awarded it for other work because the committee would not have been able to read it in Bangla. However, one member of the five-person committee, Esaias Tegnér, could in fact read Bangla and appeared to have explored Tagore's other work. Michael Collins examines this at more length in "History and Postcolonial Thought: Rabindranath Tagore's Reception in London, 1912–1913," *International Journal of the Humanities* 4, no. 9 (2007): 71–83. In a note to William Rothenstein, dated June 1912, upon his arrival in London, accompanying the first translation of *Gitanjali*, Tagore wrote: "I send you some more of my poems rendered into English. They are far too simple to bear the strain of translation but I know you will understand them though their faded meanings" (Tagore, *Selected Letters*, 91–92). Days later,

he wrote to Kshiti Mohan Sen, after first meeting Yeats in June 1912, "I do not have much confidence in my own English—but he remarked that if someone were to say he could improve this piece of writing, that person did not understand literature" (Tagore, *Selected Letters*, 90).

48. Tagore, *Selected Letters*, 132.

49. Tagore, *Selected Letters*, 132.

50. Tagore, *Selected Letters*, 179.

51. Tagore, *Selected Letters*, 198.

52. Tagore, *Selected Letters*, 206.

53. Tagore, *Selected Letters*, 206.

54. "Letter to Editor," *Ananda Bazar Patrika* (August 19, 1929).

55. Tagore, *Selected Letters*, 179.

56. Tagore, *Selected Letters*, 179.

57. Tagore, *Selected Letters*, 29.

58. Bernard Cohn, *Colonialism and Its Forms of Knowledge* (Princeton, NJ: Princeton University Press: 1996).

59. Mohandas K. Gandhi (Mahatma), "The Uses of Khaddar," in *The Collected Works of Mahatma Gandhi*, vol. 17 (New Delhi: Publications Division, Ministry of Information and Broadcasting, Government of India, 1958), 251.

60. For an account of the symbolic and political relationship between *khadi* and Gandhian nationalism, see Lisa Trivedi, *Clothing Gandhi's Nation: Homespun and Modern India.* (Bloomington: Indiana University Press, 2007).

61. Rabindranath Tagore, "The Cult of the Charkha," in *The Mahatma and The Poet: Letters and Debates Between Tagore and Gandhi*, ed. Sabyashachi Bhattacharya (New Delhi: National Trust, 1997), 106.

62. Ajay Skaria, *Unconditional Equality: Gandhi's Religion of Resistance* (Minneapolis: University of Minnesota Press, 2016), 14.

63. Tagore, "Cult of the Charkha," 106.

64. "The Brahmo Trust Deed," *Thebrahmosamaj.net*, n.d., http://www.thebrahmosamaj.net/samajes /trustdeed.html.

65. Leaning heavily on rationalism, the Brahmos insisted that progress and enlightenment need not come from the imperial West but should rather be located within the Vedic tradition. Idolatry and ritual sacrifice were thus cast as artifacts of perversion rather than primitivism, Hinduism having strayed into the base and material despite what the Brahmos saw as its essential monotheistic, unitarian immanence.

66. Rabindranath Tagore, *Sadhana: The Realization of Life* (New York: Macmillan, 1914), 80.

67. Tagore, *Nationalism*, 92–93.

68. Freud, "Fetishism," 152.

69. Freud, "Fetishism," 152.

70. Sigmund Freud, "Mourning and Melancholia" (1917), in *The Standard Edition of the Complete Psychological Works of Sigmund Freud*, vol. 14, ed. and trans. James Strachey (New York: Norton, 1953), 178.

71. Rabindranath Tagore, "Letter to a Friend," in *The English Writings of Rabindranath Tagore, A Miscellany* (Calcutta: Sahitya Akademi, 1994), 245.

72. Tagore, "Cult of the Charkha," 112.

73. Shahid Amin, "Gandhi as Mahatma; Gorakhpur District, Eastern UP, 1921-2," in *Subaltern Studies III*, ed. Ranajit Guha (New Delhi: Oxford University Press, 1984).

74. Tagore, *Selected Letters*, 244.
75. Rebecca M. Brown, "Spinning Without Touching the Wheel: Anticolonialism, Indian National-ism, and the Deployment of Symbol," *Comparative Studies of South Asia, Africa and the Middle East* 29, no. 2 (2009): 230.
76. Ben Cosgrove, "Gandhi and His Spinning Wheel: The Story Behind a Famous Photo," *Time* (September 10, 2014), http://time.com/3639043/gandhi-and-his-spinning-wheel-the-story -behind-an-iconic-photo/.
77. Cosgrove, "Gandhi and His Spinning Wheel."
78. Mohandas K. Gandhi, *Young India* 40 (March 14, 1929), 143.
79. Pushpa Rani Mathur, *Costumes of the Rulers of Mewar* (Delhi: Abhinav Publications, 2004), 33.
80. William Bolts, *Considerations on Indian Affairs Particularly Respecting the Present State of Bengal and its Dependencies* (London: J. Almon, 1772), 194.
81. Tagore, "Cult of the Charkha," 104.
82. C. A. Bayly, "The Origins of Swadeshi," in *The Social Life of Things*, ed. Arjun Appadurai (Cambridge: Cambridge University Press, 1988), 291.
83. Bayly, "The Origins of Swadeshi," 294.
84. Peter Stallybrass, "Marx's Coat," in *Border Fetishisms: Material Objects in Unstable Spaces*, ed. Patricia Spyer (New York: Routledge, 1998), 184.
85. Stallybrass, "Marx's Coat," 186.
86. Michael Taussig, *The Nervous System* (New York: Routledge, 1992), 138–39.

3. OCEANIC FEELINGS

1. Girindrasekhar Bose and Sigmund Freud, *The Beginnings of Psychoanalysis in India: The Bose-Freud Correspondence* (Calcutta: Indian Psycho-analytical Society, 1964), 21.
2. Karl Marx and Friedrich Engels, *Capital; A Critique of Political Economy*, ed. Edward B. Aveling and Ernest Untermann, trans. Samuel Moore (Chicago: C. H. Kerr, 1906), 83.
3. See Richard C. Keller, *Colonial Madness: Psychiatry in French North Africa* (Chicago: University of Chicago Press, 2008); Warwick Anderson, Deborah Jenson, and Richard C. Keller, eds., *Unconscious Dominions: Psychoanalysis, Colonial Trauma, and Global Sovereignties* (Durham, NC: Duke University Press, 2011); Achille Mbembe, *On the Postcolony* (Berkeley: University of California Press, 2001); Ranjana Khanna, *Dark Continents: Psychoanalysis and Colonialism* (Durham, NC: Duke University Press, 2003); Sloane Mahone and Megan Vaughan, *Psychiatry and Empire* (London: Springer, 2007); Jock McCulloch, *Colonial Psychiatry and the African Mind* (Cambridge: Cambridge University Press, 1995); Mrinalini Greedharry, *Postcolonial Theory and Psychoanalysis: From Uneasy Engagements to Effective Critique* (London: Springer, 2008); Megan Vaughn, *Curing Their Ills: Colonial Power and African Illness* (London: John Wiley & Sons, 2013).
4. Rabindranath Tagore, "The Cult of the Charkha," in *The Mahatma and The Poet: Letters and Debates Between Tagore and Gandhi*, ed. Sabyashachi Bhattacharya (New Delhi: National Trust, 1997), 106.
5. Though Freud does not himself use the term *desire*, employing instead *wunsch*.
6. Jean Laplanche and Jean-Bertrand Pontalis, *The Language of Psycho-Analysis*, (London: Karnac Books, 1988): 483.

7. Dipesh Chakrabarty, "Postcoloniality and the Artifice of History: Who Speaks for 'Indian' Pasts?," *Representations* 37 (1992): 8.

8. Girindrasekhar Bose, "History of the Indian Psycho-Analytical Society," *International Journal of Psychoanalysis* 4 (January–April 1923): 250.

9. Christiane Hartnack, *Psychoanalysis in Colonial India* (Oxford: Oxford University Press, 2000); Ashis Nandy, "The Savage Freud: The First Non-Western Psychoanalyst and the Politics of Secret Selves in Colonial India," in *The Savage Freud and Other Essays on Possible and Retrievable Selves* (Princeton, NJ: Princeton University Press, 1995), 81–144.

10. Bose and Freud, *Beginnings of Psychoanalysis in India*, 7.

11. Girindrashekhar Bose, "The Genesis and Adjustment of the Oedipus Wish" (1928), in *Vishnu on Freud's Desk: A Reader in Psychoanalysis and Hinduism*, ed. T. G. Vaidyanathan and Jeffrey K. Kripal (Delhi: Oxford University Press, 1999), 26.

12. A. K. Ramanujan's "The Indian Oedipus" and Gananath Obeyesekere's *The Work of Culture* both offer comprehensive studies of instantiations of an "Indian Oedipus" in a variety of cultural forms, from early folklore and epic mythology onward. See Ramanujan, "The Indian Oedipus," in *Oedipus: A Folklore Casebook*, ed. Lowell Edmunds and Alan Dundes (Madison: University of Wisconsin Press, 1983), 234–64; Obeyesekere, *The Work of Culture* (Chicago: University of Chicago Press, 1990).

13. Bose, "Genesis and Adjustment," 34.

14. Ernest Jones, "Letter to Sigmund Freud, January 25, 1920," in Sigmund Freud, *The Complete Correspondence of Sigmund Freud and Ernest Jones 1908-1939*, ed. R. Andrew Paskauskas (Cambridge, MA: Harvard University Press), 364.

15. Sigmund Freud, "Letter to Ernest Jones, May 13, 1920," in Freud, *The Complete Correspondence*, 380.

16. C. D. Daly, "The Psychology of Revolutionary Tendencies," *International Journal of Psycho-Analysis* 11 (1930): 209 (emphasis added).

17. Bankimcandra Chatterji, *Anandamath, or The Sacred Brotherhood*, trans. Julius Lipner. (Oxford: Oxford University Press, 2005), 38.

18. Daly, "Psychology of Revolutionary Tendencies," 210.

19. Daly was likely referring to the 1857 Mutiny, the failure of which resulted in the establishment of formal colonial governance in India.

20. Daly, "Psychology of Revolutionary Tendencies," 210.

21. Freud, "Letter from Sigmund Freud to Ernest Jones, January 28, 1921," in Freud, *The Complete Correspondence*, 406.

22. Ernest Jones, *The Life and Work of Sigmund Freud, Volume Three: The Last Phase 1919-1939* (London: Hogarth Press, 1957), 204.

23. Freud, "Letter to Ernest Jones, April 12, 1921," in Freud, *The Complete Correspondence*, 418.

24. Bose and Freud, *Beginnings of Psychoanalysis in India*, 24.

25. Bose and Freud, *Beginnings of Psychoanalysis in India*, 27.

26. Ashis Nandy, *The Intimate Enemy: Loss and Recovery of Self Under Colonialism* (Oxford: Oxford University Press, 1989).

27. Sangeeta Ray has argued that Bankimcandra Chatterji's turn to allegorical figuration of the nationalist contest as one between the indigenous Hindu and imperial Muslim, rather than explicit critique of British rule, cohered region and religion into a single political formation. "His recovery of a glorious Hindu past consolidated as an exercise of *bahubol* (physical strength) against Muslim shows of strength imparted a 'purely Hindu' identity to the Indian

national character." Sangeeta Ray, *En-Gendering India: Woman and Nation in Colonial and Postcolonial Narratives* (Durham, NC: Duke University Press, 2000), 26.

28. Partha Chatterjee, *The Nation and Its Fragments: Colonial and Postcolonial Histories* (Princeton, NJ: Princeton University Press, 1993), 130–31 (emphasis added).

29. *Babu* is the term ascribed to those Bengalis who did clerical work for colonial authorities, though it was extrapolated out into a satirical and stereotypical term for effeminate, and overly bookish, Bengalis. Interestingly, *babu* is also a term of endearment for infants.

30. Mrinalini Sinha, *Colonial Masculinity: The "Manly Englishman" and the "Effeminate Bengali" in the Late Nineteenth Century* (Manchester, UK: Manchester University Press, 1995).

31. Thomas Babington Macaulay, *Macaulay's Essay on Lord Clive* (New York: Macmillan, 1840), 32.

32. Jasodhara Bagchi, "Representing Nationalism: Ideology of Motherhood in Colonial Bengal," *Economic and Political Weekly* 25, no. 42–43 (October 1990), WS65–WS71, WS65.

33. Swami Vivekananda, "Modern India," in *The Complete Works of Swami Vivekananda*, vol. 4 (Calcutta: Advaita Ashram, 1988), 480.

34. Tanika Sarkar argues that Bengali nationalism worshipped the feminine precisely because it could function in opposition to the masculine lion of empire; moreover, the construction of motherland referred back to the cult of Shakti worship in the region, which resulted in a blending "of the principles of abject victimhood and triumphant strength in the polysemic iconography deployed around the mother." Tanika Sarkar, *Hindu Wife, Hindu Nation: Community, Religion, and Cultural Nationalism* (London: Permanent Black, 2003), 253.

35. Sri Aurobindo's translation is included as an appendix in Chatterji, *Anandamath*, 298.

36. Quoted in Shukla Sanyal, *Revolutionary Pamphlets, Propaganda and Political Culture in Colonial Bengal* (Cambridge: Cambridge University Press, 2014), 159.

37. Sanyal, *Revolutionary Pamphlets*, 159.

38. Sigmund Freud, "Letter to Girindrasekhar Bose, March 9, 1929," in Bose and Freud, *Beginnings of Psychoanalysis in India*, 16.

39. Freud refers to the Oedipus complex as universal three times in *Three Essays on the Theory of Sexuality* and writes of Oedipus, in *The Interpretation of Dreams*, "His fate moves us only because it might have been our own, because the oracle laid upon us before our birth the very curse which rested upon him. It may be that we were all destined to direct our first sexual impulses toward our mothers, and our first impulses of hatred and violence toward our fathers; our dreams convince us that we were. King Oedipus, who slew his father Laius and wedded his mother Jocasta, is nothing more or less than a wish-fulfilment—the fulfilmentof the wish of our childhood." Sigmund Freud, *The Interpretation of Dreams* (London: Macmillan, 1913), 223.

40. Freud, *The Interpretation of Dreams*, 223.

41. Bose and Freud, *Beginnings of Psychoanalysis in India*, 15–16.

42. Hilda Doolittle (H.D.), *Tribute to Freud* (London: New Directions, 1956), 68.

43. Doolittle, *Tribute*, 68.

44. Doolittle, *Tribute*, 68.

45. Sigmund Freud, "Fetishism," in *The Standard Edition of the Complete Psychological Works of Sigmund Freud*, vol. 21, ed. and trans. James Strachey (New York: Norton, 1953), 154.

46. In the Rig-Veda, Vishnu is described as *"gopah sarvasya jagato rakshkah"* ("preserver of all the world)" which Sayana, the fourteenth-century scholar of the Vedas whose work was edited and published by Max Müller as the definitive commentary on the Rig-Veda, identifies as Vishnu's principle attribute. Edward Byles Cowells and William Frederick Webster, *Rig-Veda-Sanhitá: A Collection of Ancient Hindu Hymns* (London: W. H. Allen, 1866), 54.

47. In particular, Vaishnavism, which rose to enormous popularity in Bengal in the fifteenth and sixteenth centuries thanks in part to Chaitanya, focuses its worship on the singular aspect—here, Vishnu's incarnation as Krishna.

48. William Joseph Wilkins, *Hindu Mythology, Vedic and Puranic* (London: Thacker, Spink, 1882), 98.

49. Visnu is a commonly accepted variant spelling of Vishnu.

50. Alain Danielou, *The Myths and Gods of India* (London: Bear, 1991), 149.

51. Danielou, *Myths and Gods of India*, 152.

52. Sara Ahmed, noting the profusion of "Oriental" objects in Freud's study, writes, "The proximity of such objects are orientation devices, which bring the Orient home by providing a dwelling that secures the place of the body. . . . The arrival of such objects is a matter of their acquisition (we might speculate about the gifts, thefts, purchases, and payments). Of course, having arriving [*sic*] there, as objects that adorn the interior of Freud's room, the objects themselves are cut off from the history of past arrivals and of dwelling places that are not simply reachable through the objects being placed within reach. Having arrived, though, we still don't know what the objects will do, or what we will do with them." Sara Ahmed, *Queer Phenomenology: Orientations, Objects, Others* (Durham, NC: Duke University Press, 2006), 149.

53. Paul de Man, "Shelley Disfigured," in *The Rhetoric of Romanticism* (New York: Columbia University Press, 1984), 119. In "Blindness as Metaphor," Naomi Schor describes metaphor as "disfigurement," that which removes the body. See Schor, "Blindness as Metaphor," *Differences* 11, no. 2 (1999): 76–105.

54. This mode of nonmetaphorical reading takes its inspiration from what Elaine Freedgood has called a practice of "strong metonymic reading." Freedgood suggests that unlike its stable and structured cousin metaphor, metonymy works to destabilize meaning. "The contingency of metonymic relations may more properly rest, in many cases, on our ability and our willingness to recuperate historical necessity. Metonymy's apparently subversive ability to disrupt meaning, to be endlessly vagrant and open ended, may be attended by an equally subversive ability to recuperate historical links that are anything but random." Where metaphor is a relationship of similarity, condensation, and replacement, metonymy is one of contingency and displacement—and a fundamentally historicist technique. Barbara Johnson points out that metaphor and metonymy, "far from being a neutral opposition between equals [. . .] have always stood in hierarchical relation to each other. From Aristotle to George Lakoff, metaphor has always, in the Western tradition, had the privilege of revealing unexpected truth." In part this is because of the association of metaphor with necessity, and the contiguity of metonymy to chance that inspires a feminist reclamation of metonymy. Perhaps, though, this is equally due to the masculinist lineage of metaphor—strikingly, Lacan's figuration of body to phallus as metaphoric. Metonymy, in contrast, interrupts as much as it propels. Metaphor, as the privileged trope of both nationalism and psychoanalysis, enables by its structure their uneasy relationship to femininity and the place of women. For these reasons, I suggest we resist the imperial grasp of metaphor and displace, even briefly, its hierarchical place in rhetoric in favor of fugitive forms of materiality. Elaine Freedgood, *The Ideas in Things: Fugitive Meaning in the Victorian Novel* (Chicago: University of Chicago Press, 2006), 16; Barbara Johnson, "Metaphor, Metonymy, and Voice in *Their Eyes Were Watching God*," in *The Barbara Johnson Reader: The Surprise of Otherness*, ed. Melissa Feuerstein, Bill Johnson González, Lili Porten, and Keja Valens (Durham, NC: Duke University Press, 2014), 112.

55. The Vishnu has been the object of study for several scholars interested in the intersection between psychoanalysis and India. Christiane Hartnack, among others, has produced a

comprehensive study of the development of psychoanalytic thought in Bengal and the theories of Girindrasekhar Bose. See Hartnack, *Psychoanalysis in Colonial India*. Others, such as Ashis Nandy, Sudhir Kakar, and Salman Akhtar, have also written extensively about the rise of psychoanalysis in India and have themselves offered psychoanalytic readings—Kakar's being the most controversial—of prominent figures of subcontinental history. See Nandy, *The Savage Freud*; Sudhir Kakar, *Culture and Psyche: Selected Essays*, 2nd ed. (New York: Oxford University Press, 2008); Salman Akhtar, *Matters of Life and Death: Psychoanalytic Reflections* (London: Karnak, 2011); Rubén Gallo, *Freud's Mexico: Into the Wilds of Psychoanalysis* (Cambridge, MA: MIT Press, 2010). Additionally, though there are also many studies of Freud's art collection, to my knowledge, mine is the first examination of the Vishnu statuette's arrival in Vienna from its manufacture and purchase.

56. Suniti Kumar Chatterji, "Vienna—A Meeting with Freud," *Samiksa: The Journal of the Indian Psycho-analytical Society* 43, no. 3 (1993): 74–75.

57. This space, *ksheer sagar*, is also called the "ocean of milk," or the Milky Way. Depictions of the churning of the ocean of milk appear in the *Ramayana* and *Mahabharata* as well as the Vishnu Purana. This is not the same oceanic force as *satchitananda*, the absolute consciousness and bliss described in the Upanishads and central to Vedantic philosophy. This latter is more commonly called the ocean of bliss, the limitless unity with Brahman, and that to which Rolland and Ramakrishna refer in the accounts of the salt doll related later in this chapter.

58. Edward Alpers offers an exhaustive account of the trading relationships between India and East Africa in these valued commodities in *Ivory and Slaves in East Central Africa* (Berkeley: University of California, 1975).

59. *Statement of the Trade of British India with British Possessions and Foreign Countries for the Five Years* (London: Eyre & Spottiswoode, 1895), 53.

60. George Wyatt, *Indian Art at Delhi in 1903: Being the Official Catalogue of the Delhi Exhibit 1902-1903* (London: John Murray, 1904), 174.

61. Doolittle, *Tribute to Freud*, 68.

62. Freud goes on to describe what is in fact his favorite object of the collection, a Pallas Athena. He says of her to H.D., "She is perfect, only she has lost her spear" (quoted in Doolittle, *Tribute to Freud*, 178). Much can be, and has been, made of Freud's love of the figurine and its lack of phallic spear—her symbolic castration—but it is also worth noting the parallels between Athena, sprung from her father's head and Freud's own relationship to his daughter, who would come to curate the museum and afterlife of his work.

63. It should not escape our notice that the guarantor of his beloved collection, who would herself carry his favorite piece—the Athena—from Vienna to London, is the same woman to whom Freud would someday admit the limits of his understanding of the sexual and interior lives of women.

64. John Elsner and Roger Cardinal, eds., *The Cultures of Collecting* (London: Reaktion Books, 1994), 227.

65. Doolittle, *Tribute to Freud*.

66. Diana Fuss and Joel Sanders, "Berggasse 19: Inside Freud's Office," in *Stud: Architectures of Masculinity*, ed. Joel Sanders (Princeton, NJ: Princeton Architectural Press, 1996), 118.

67. Amber Jacobs, *On Matricide: Myth, Psychoanalysis, and the Law of the Mother* (New York: Columbia University Press, 2007), 68.

68. The Sigmund Freud Museum in Vienna offers this quote from *The Interpretation of Dreams* alongside the online image of the Horus. Janine Burke also connects this Horus to the account

of the dream in the text. Janine Burke, *The Sphinx on the Table: Sigmund Freud's Art Collection and the Development of Psychoanalysis* (London: Bloomsbury, 2009).

69. Sigmund Freud, *The Interpretation of Dreams*, in *The Standard Edition of the Complete Psychological Works of Sigmund Freud*, vol. 5, ed. and trans. James Strachey (New York: Norton, 1953), 583 (emphasis in original).

70. Freud, *The Interpretation of Dreams*, 583.

71. Burke, *The Sphinx on the Table*, 24.

72. Sigmund Freud, *Letters of Sigmund Freud*, ed. Ernst L. Freud, trans. Tania and James Stern (New York: Dover, 1960), 400.

73. Freud, *Letters of Sigmund Freud*, 400.

74. In *Antigone's Claim: Kinship Between Life and Death* (New York: Columbia University Press, 2000), 22, Judith Butler argues for the multivalences of Antigone's name: "Antigone is one for whom symbolic positions have become incoherent, confounding as she does brother and father, emerging as she does not as a mother but—as one etymology suggests—'in the place of the mother.' Her name is also construed as 'anti-generation (*gone* [generation]). She is, thus, already at a distance from that which she represents, and what she represents is far from clear." Antigone is both the surrogate and the failure of that sign. Indeed, Freud himself would refer to Anna as his "faithful Anna-Antigone" in letters to Arnold Zweig in 1935, declining an invitation to join Zweig on Mount Carmel, where he had just moved; and to Sandor Ferenczi as his "faithful Antigone-Anna" in 1928. See Ernst L. Freud, ed., *The Letters of Sigmund Freud and Arnold Zweig*, trans. Elaine Robson-Scott and William Robson-Scott (New York: Harcourt, 1970), 424, 382. In *Archive Fever*, Derrida reads Yerushalmi's invocation of this hyphenation as hope that Anna herself might speak in his name in front of the Psychoanalytic Congress instead of in her own name, even years after her father's death. This is, according to Derrida, both the sign of Yerushalmi's Oedipal fixation on Freud and its disavowal. See Jacques Derrida, *Archive Fever: A Freudian Impression*, trans. Eric Prenowitz (Chicago: University of Chicago Press, 1998).

75. That museological imagination would never come to pass: Freud's office in Vienna is now preserved as a museum with no objects other than Engleman's photographs, while in London, his *objets* and library stand in the site of his reluctant exile. But Aichhorn's insistence on the precision of the photographs, so that the order of things might be recreated perfectly in the years following the war, at once recognized the permanence of Freud's departure from that space and revealed that even that earlier analytic space—the one in which he lived before he went to London to die—was haunted. Fuss and Sanders, "Berggasse 19," 112.

76. Fuss and Sanders, "Berggasse 19," 119.

77. Paul Roazen, *Freud and His Followers* (Boston: Da Capo Press, 1992), 538.

78. Quoted in John Forrester, *Dispatches from the Freud Wars: Psychoanalysis and Its Passions* (Cambridge, MA: Harvard University Press, 1997), 111.

79. Bill Brown, "Thing Theory," *Critical Inquiry* 28, no. 1 (2001): 4.

80. Quoted in Roazen, *Freud and His Followers*, 540.

81. Quoted in Santanu Biswas, "Rabindranath Tagore and Freudian Thought," *International Journal of Psychoanalysis* 84, no. 3 (2003): 717.

82. Gyan Prakash writes of the work of museums in British India: "To know was to name, identify, and compare—this was the frame in which the questions of understanding India entered the discourse of colonial science. Museums were valuable because they provided an order of things by naming, classifying, and displaying Indian artifacts. In this respect, museological

practice differed from cabinets of curiosities: unlike those cabinets, museums organized objects to make them speak a language, reveal an order." Gyan Prakash, "Science 'Gone Native' in Colonial India," *Representations* 40 (1992): 155.

83. Rabindranath Tagore, *Selected Letters of Rabindranath Tagore*, ed. Krishna Dutt and Andrew Robinson (New York: Cambridge University Press, 1997), 170.

84. Quoted in Biswas, "Rabindranath Tagore and Freudian Thought," 720.

85. Quoted in Govinda Paramaswaran Pillai, *Representative Indians* (London: Routledge, 1897), 4.

86. Santanu Biswas, in "Rabindranath Tagore and Freudian Thought," offers an excellent account of the various intersections between Tagore and both members of the IPS and concepts of psychoanalysis more generally.

87. Tagore, *Selected Letters*, 408.

88. Sigmund Freud, *Civilization and Its Discontents*, ed. and trans. James Strachey (New York: Norton, 1962), 12.

89. Freud, *Civilization and Its Discontents*, 27.

90. December 5, 1927: "Mais j'aurais aimé à vous voir faire l'analyse du sentiment religieux spontané ou, plus exactement, de la sensation religieuse qui est tout différente Desdemona religions propement dites . . . le fait simple et direct de la sensation de l'éternel (qui peut très bien n'être pas éternel, mais simplement sans bornes perceptibles, et comme océanique)." Translation my own. Quoted in Jeffrey Masson, *The Oceanic Feeling: The Origins of Religious Sentiment in Ancient India* (Berlin: Springer, 2012), 34.

91. July 14, 1929. Ernst L. Freud, ed., *Letters of Sigmund Freud, 1873–1939*, trans. Tania Stern and James Stern (London: Hogarth Press, 1961), 388–92.

92. Freud, *Civilization and its Discontents*, 37. The original Grabbe reads, as Freud pointed out in a footnote, "*Ja, aus der Welt warden wir nicht fallen. Wir sing einmal darin.*" [Indeed, we shall not fall out of this world. We are in it once and for all.]

93. Freud, *Civilization and its Discontents*, 37.

94. Kaja Silverman, *Flesh of My Flesh* (Stanford, CA: Stanford University Press, 2009), 30.

95. Freud, *Letters of Sigmund Freud*, 392.

96. For an alternative or heterodox account arguing that the psychoanalytic subject is not the same as the post-Enlightenment one, see Mikkel Borch-Jacobsen, *The Emotional Tie: Psychoanalysis, Mimesis, Affect* (Stanford, CA: Stanford University Press, 1993).

97. Frantz Fanon, *The Wretched of the Earth*, trans. Richard Philcox (New York: Grove Press, 2004), 11.

98. Sigmund Freud, *Beyond the Pleasure Principle* (New York: Norton, 1975), 45.

99. Jeffrey Masson, in his extensive examination of psychoanalysis and Indian mysticism, argues that Rolland was likely referring to another moment from the life of Ramakrishna in which, faced with the fear he might never have a vision of the mother goddess, he goes to kill himself and then falls into a state of ecstasy: "Round me rolled an ocean of ineffable joy. And in the depths of my being I was conscious of the presence of the Divine Mother." See Masson, *The Oceanic Feeling*, 36.

100. Ramakrishna, and Mahendra Nath Gupta, *The Gospel of Sri Ramakrishna: Originally Recorded in Bengali by M., a Disciple of the Master*, trans. Swami Nikhilananda (New York: Ramakrishna-Vivekananda Center, 1952), 197.

101. A perhaps more apt account of Ramakrishna's sense of *jadi samadhi* is to be found in the Baul song that he was fond of singing, "*Dub Dub Dub Rupsagare, Amar Mon* (Dive, Dive, Dive into the Ocean of God's Beauty, My Heart)." That song is about the desire to dive into the depths of an

unknown ocean for the gem of holy love. This is in keeping with a Bhakti tradition in which utter immersion into the form of the Beloved is the ultimate telos. Ramakrishna and Gupta, *The Gospel of Sri Ramakrishna*, 178.

102. Ramakrishna and Gupta, *The Gospel of Sri Ramakrishna*, 603.

103. In "On the Seashore of Endless Worlds," Mark Epstein compares Freud's engagement with the oceanic feeling to D. W. Winnicott's citation of Tagore's poem "On the Seashore" as an epigraph in *Playing and Reality*. Epstein suggests that Winnicott's engagement with Tagore, unlike Freud's unease with the oceanic feeling, demonstrates the influence of Eastern, particularly Buddhist (though Tagore was not Buddhist), thought to Winnicott's argument that the experience of culture was a "transitional phenomenon." See Epstein, "On the Seashore of Endless Worlds," in *Freud and the Buddha: The Couch and the Cushion*, ed. Axel Hoffer (New York: Karnac Books, 2015), 108.

104. Rabindranath Tagore, "Ramakrishna Paramahamsa," in *The English Writings of Rabindranath Tagore: A Miscellany* (New Delhi: Sahitya Akademi, 1994), 955.

105. Tagore, *Sadhana: The Realization of Life* (New York: Macmillan, 1914), 163.

106. Doolittle, *Tribute*, 175.

107. Sigmund Freud, *The Diary of Sigmund Freud 1929–1939: A Record of the Final Decade*, trans. Michael Molnar (London: Hogarth Press, 1992), 115.

108. Freud, *The Diary of Sigmund Freud*, 80.

109. Partha Chatterjee, *The Nation and Its Fragments*, 120.

110. Sigmund Freud, *The Question of Lay Analysis: An Introduction to Psychoanalysis*, 1st American ed. (New York: Norton, 1950), 38.

111. Megan Vaughan provides a particularly incisive examination of the development of psychiatry and other medical discourses alongside colonialism in Africa in *Curing Their Ills: Colonial Power and African Illness* (Stanford, CA: Stanford University Press, 2013).

112. Mary Ann Doane argues that Freud's racialized description of female sexuality can, and ought to, be traced to the developmental narrative from which is born his claim that civilization develops at the expense of sexuality. Those less civilized peoples of the world who, according to Freud, are able to enjoy profligate sexual lives are akin to—indeed, starkly reminiscent of—the children who have sexual license which is later relinquished to the authority and repressive power of civilization. The less civilized peoples, who never so surrender their autonomous desires, thus constitute the limits of psychoanalytic knowledge, and Freud's designation of female sexuality as a dark continent renders it too marginal to psychoanalytic epistemology. Doane writes, "When Freud needs a trope for the unknowability of female sexuality, the dark continent is close at hand. Psychoanalysis can, for this point of view, be seen as a quite elaborate form of ethnography—as a writing of the ethnicity of the white Western psyche. Repression becomes the prerequisite for the construction of a white culture that stipulates that female sexuality act as the trace *within* of what has been excluded." Mary Ann Doane, *Femmes Fatales: Feminism, Film Theory, and Psychoanalysis* (New York: Routledge, 2013), 211 (emphasis added).

113. Rabindranath Tagore, *Nationalism* (London: Macmillan, 1917), 21.

114. Tagore, *Nationalism*, 57.

115. Tagore, *Nationalism*, 15.

116. Rabindranath Tagore, *The Home and the World*, ed. William Radice, trans. Surendranath Tagore (London: Penguin UK, 2005), 50.

117. Tagore, *The Home and the World*, 31–32.

118. Tagore, *The Home and the World*, 26.

119. Tagore, *The Home and the World*, 33.

120. Tagore, *The Home and the World*, 31.

121. Tagore, *The Home and the World*, 27.

122. Michel Serres, *The Five Senses: A Philosophy of Mingled Bodies* (New York: Continuum Books, 2008), 80.

123. Ann Rosalind Jones and Peter Stallybrass offer an excellent account of the mnemonic and commercial qualities of cloth as second skin in *Renaissance Clothing and the Materials of Memory* (Cambridge: Cambridge University Press, 2000).

124. The film adaptation's play on the bookended images of flames—as much those of the communal riots as augurs of Nikhil's pyre—evoke the purifying and transformative force of fire, an image that appears in chapter 2 regarding the discourse of *sati*, in which the wife/widow is said to make herself into a goddess on the pyre. Bimala, then, having "walked through the fire," makes herself a widow and goddess both.

125. Tagore, *The Home and the World*, 27.

126. Tagore, *The Home and the World*, 32.

127. Tagore, *The Home and the World*, 179.

128. Tagore, *The Home and the World*, 146.

129. Tagore, *The Home and the World*, 146.

130. Tagore, *The Home and the World*, 74.

131. Tagore, *The Home and the World*, 73.

132. Tagore, *The Home and the World*, 43.

133. Tagore, *The Home and the World*, 38.

134. Tagore, *The Home and the World*, 157.

135. Tagore, *The Home and the World*, 125.

136. Tagore, *The Home and the World*, 93.

137. Andrew Sartori, *Bengal in Global Concept History: Culturalism in the Age of Capital* (Chicago: University of Chicago Press, 2008), 149.

138. See Jeanne Openshaw, *Seeking the Bauls of Bengal* (Cambridge, MA: Cambridge University Press, 2002).

139. Lukács, in his essay on the novel, argues the opposite, suggesting that Sandip and Nikhil are foils for one another in the manner of Tagore and Gandhi to one another. However, in 1916 when the novel was written, Gandhi had not yet returned to India and was not the figure of resistant nationalist possibility he became by the 1920s, as discussed in chapter 2. Georg Lukács, "Tagore's Gandhi Novel. Review of Rabindranath Tagore: The Home and the World," in *Essays and Reviews*, trans. Peter Palmer (London: Merlin Press, 1983), 8–11.

140. Tagore, *The Home and the World*, 200.

141. In *Between Men*, Eve Kosofsky Sedgwick argues that that nineteenth-century British culture relied on homosocial bonds between men to maintain social order but that homosociality, presumed antithetical to homosexuality, in fact collapses into an economy of sexualized feeling. She writes, "The normative man uses a woman as a 'conduit of a relationship' in which the true *partner* is a man." Eve Kosofsky Sedgwick, *Between Men: English Literature and Male Homosocial Desire* (New York: Columbia University Press, 1985), 26.

142. Sedgwick, *Between Men*, 187.

143. In Bangla, there are three distinct signifiers of "home": *bhitte, bari,* and *basha*. The term *bhitte* is always linked to *mati*, "soil," and designates one's ancestral land. *Bari* refers to a home that

may be occupied for generations but is not on or connected to the ancestral home. *Bhitte mati* is defined by landedness, whereas *bari* is not. It is a home that may or may not be landed. *Bhitte mati* is literally "the soil of one's ancestors" and is the foundational site of a Bengali sense of home. *Basha*, then, connotes the house which one historically rented away from the ancestral home and the native soil. The word is extricated from land, from a connection to a soil, from a rootedness to place altogether. No matter how many generations a family might live in an urban area, there is a notion of home that recalls a genealogical and physical connection to the soil. Indeed, it is the soil that marks the familial history and connection to Bengal. To be dislocated from one's *bhitte mati* is a primal loss. In "Remembered Villages," Dipesh Chakrabarty writes that "the home that the Hindu refugee has lost is meant to be more than his home alone; it is the home of the Bengali nationality, the village in which in the 1880s nationalist writers had found the heart of Bengal." See Chakrabarty, "Remembered Villages: Representation of Hindu-Bengali Memories in the Aftermath of the Partition," *Economic and Political Weekly* 31, no. 32 (August 10, 1996): 2149. The irreversible move away from this *bhitte mati* in the text is also Tagore's mournful final disavowal of that early nationalist dream, lost to remembrance in its original connection to the rural and "real" Bengal.

144. Tagore, *The Home and the World*, 188.
145. Tagore, *The Home and the World*, 190.
146. Samir Dayal, "Repositioning India: Tagore's Passionate Politics of Love," *Positions: East Asia, Cultures, Critique* 15, no. 1 (2007): 187.

4. ARCHIVE ASYLUM

1. Spivak suggests in her essay that the goal of the humanities pedagogy, especially in the American academy, is to move beyond cultural relativism. She writes, "Its undoing is best produced by way of the training of reflexes that kick in at the time of urgency, of decision and policy. However unrealistic it may seem to you, I would not remain a teacher of the Humanities if I did not believe that at the New York end—standing metonymically for the dispensing end as such—the teacher can try to rearrange desires noncoercively—as I mentioned earlier—through an attempt to develop in the student a habit of literary reading, even just 'reading,' suspending oneself into the text of the other—for which the first condition and effect is a suspension of the conviction that I am necessarily better, I am necessarily indispensable, I am necessarily the one to right wrongs, I am necessarily the end product for which history happened, and that New York is necessarily the capital of the world. . . . Although literature cannot speak, this species of patient reading, miming an effort to make the text respond, as it were, is a training not only in poiesis, accessing the other so well that probable action can be prefigured, but teleo-poiesis, striving for a response from the distant other, without guarantees." Gayatri Chakravorty Spivak, "Righting Wrongs," *South Atlantic Quarterly* 103, no. 2–3 (March 20, 2004): 526, 532.

2. Act No. XIX of 1973, "The International Crimes (Tribunal) Act, 1973," Bangladesh Code. http:// bdlaws.minlaw.gov.bd/print_sections_all.php?id=435.

3. Jacques Derrida, *Archive Fever: A Freudian Impression*, trans. Eric Prenowitz (Chicago: University of Chicago Press, 1998), 12.

4. I thank Binayak Sen for this critical insight.

5. Michel Foucault, *The History of Sexuality: An Introduction* (New York: Knopf Doubleday, 2012), 17.

6. Nayanika Mookherjee argues that "the public secrecy of rape makes it indispensable to the operations of power and subservience because it enchants a community into silence and shame." See Mookherjee, *The Spectral Wound: Sexual Violence, Public Memories, and the Bangladesh War of 1971* (Durham, NC: Duke University Press, 2015), 69.

7. I would not have come to this term without Aarti Sethi's incisive work on the social emptiness and political mobilization of the figure of the farmer suicide. The term is hers and her work to theorize this category of the politically mobile and socially barren significantly shifts the politics of naming and state intervention. See: Aarti Sethi, *The Life of Debt in Rural India*. PhD Diss., Department of Anthropology, Columbia University, 2017.

8. Derrida, *Archive Fever*, 36.

9. Anjali Arondekar describes this as the "recast[ing of] the colonial archive as a site of endless promise, where new records emerge daily and where accepted wisdom is both entrenched and challenged." Anjali Arondekar, "Without a Trace: Sexuality and the Colonial Archive," *Journal of the History of Sexuality* 14, no. 1 (2005): 10.

10. Ranajit Guha, *Elementary Aspects of Peasant Insurgency in Colonial India* (Delhi: Oxford University Press, 1983).

11. This image appears in Mookherjee's *The Spectral Wound*.

12. For example, see William J. Drummond, "Ravages of War Hurt Bengali Women Most," *Los Angeles Times (1923-Current File)*, December 22, 1971; Shelley Steinberg and Marlene Fine, "Outcast Bengali Women" (letter to the editor), *New York Times*, February 9, 1972; Girilal Jain, "Pakistan's Military Elite: Influence of Racism and Bigotry," *Times of India (1861-Current)*, June 16, 1971; M. V. Kamath, "The Psychosis of Massacre: Bangladesh's Place in History," *Times of India (1861-Current)*, November 15, 1973; Amita Malik, "The Rape of Sara Bridge," *Times of India (1861-Current)*, December 24, 1971; Aubrey Menen, "The Rapes of Bangladesh: The Rapes," *New York Times*, July 23, 1972, http://www.cbgr1971.org/files/NYTimes/RapeBangladeshNYT .pdf; Lee Patterson, "Mass Rape in Bangladesh," *Times of India (1861-Current)*, October 1, 1972, http://search.proquest.com/docview/609777844?accountid=14496; "The Rape of Bangladesh," *Irish Times (1921-Current File)*, December 5, 1972; Jill Tweedie, "The Rape of Bangladesh," *Guardian (1959-2003)*, March 6, 1972; Robert Trumbull, "The Unwanted Children of a New Nation," *New York Times*, May 29, 1972, http://query.nytimes.com/mem/archive-free/pdf?res =9E04EFDF1F3EE63BBC4151DFB3668389669EDE.

13. See Susan Brownmiller, *Against Our Will: Men, Women and Rape* (New York: Fawcett Colum- bine, 1975); Mustafa Chowdhury, *Picking Up the Pieces: 1971 War Babies' Odyssey from Bangladesh to Canada* (New York: Xlibris, 2015); Bina D'Costa, *Nationbuilding, Gender and War Crimes in South Asia* (New York: Routledge, 2011); William J. Drummond, "Ravages of War Hurt Bengali Women Most," *Los Angeles Times (1923-Current File)*, December 22, 1971, part 1; Anthony Macarehas, *The Rape of Bangla Desh* (New Delhi: Vikas, 1971), http://search.proquest.com /docview/38246472/84381F2B111C4D12PQ/1; Menen, "The Rapes of Bangladesh."

14. Sharmila Bose, *Dead Reckoning: Memories of the 1971 Bangladesh War* (New York: Columbia Uni- versity Press, 2011).

15. Yasmin Saikia, *Women, War, and the Making of Bangladesh* (Durham, NC: Duke University Press Books, 2011).

16. *Bangabondhu*, the affectionate sobriquet for Sheikh Mujib, translates literally to "Friend of Bengal."

17. Kaberi Gayen, in "Women, War, and Cinema: Construction of Women in the Liberation War Films of Bangladesh," *French Journal for Media Research* 3, no. 2 (2015), http://frenchjournal formediaresearch.com/index.php?id=478, offers the date of December 22, 1971, without source citation. However, Nayanika Mookherjee clarifies this claim with a report published in the Bangla-language daily *Purbodesh* on December 23, 1971 (Mookherjee, *Spectral Wound*, 129). Bina D'Costa argues that Sheikh Mujib used the term regularly both in public and private. See "*Birangona*: Bearing Witness in War and 'Peace,'" in *Of the Nation Born: The Bangladesh Papers*, ed. Hameeda Hossain and Amena Mohsin (Chicago: University of Chicago Press, 2016), 76.

18. *Purbodesh*, quoted in Mookherjee, *Spectral Wound*, 36.

19. See Jasodhara Bagchi and Subhoranjan Dasgupta, eds., *The Trauma and the Triumph: Gender and Partition in Eastern India* (Kolkata: Stree, 2003); Suvir Kaul, ed., *The Partitions of Memory: The Afterlife of the Division of India* (Delhi: Permanent Black, 2001); Gargi Chakravartty, *Coming Out of Partition: Refugee Women of Bengal* (New Delhi: Bluejay, 2005); Jill Didur, *Unsettling Partition: Literature, Gender, Memory* (New Delhi: Pearson, 2007); Ritu Menon, ed., *No Women's Land: Women from Pakistan, India and Bangladesh Write on the Partition of India* (New Delhi: Women Unlimited, 2004); Ritu Menon and Kamala Bhasin, eds., *Borders and Boundaries: Women in India's Partition* (New Delhi: Kali for Women, 1998).

20. Pippa Virdee offers a rich account—one of the only accounts to my knowledge—of the representation of the Pakistani rehabilitation process in newspapers and official records. See Virdee, "Negotiating the Past: Journey through Muslim Women's Experience of Partition and Resettlement in Pakistan," *Cultural and Social History* 6, no. 4 (2009): 467–83.

21. Urvashi Butalia, *Other Side of Silence: Voices from the Partition of India* (Durham, NC: Duke University Press, 2000), 3.

22. Butalia, *Other Side of Silence*, 150.

23. From the private archive of Maleka Khan, accessed December 18, 2014, in Dhaka, Bangladesh. Translation my own.

24. Maleka Khan, personal interview by author, Dhaka, Bangladesh, December 18, 2014.

25. The word *Razakar* (রাজাকার), which in Bangla literally means "one in service of the king (Raja)" comes from the Urdu رضا کار, meaning "volunteer." It now entirely connotes "traitor" in Bangla, having become the shorthand for all those who were seen as opposing the Bangladeshi war for independence.

26. K. Subramanyam, "The Ghosts of 1971," *Indian Express* (March 5, 2009), http://archive.indian express.com/news/the-ghosts-of-1971/431017/.

27. David Ludden, "Forgotten Heroes," *Frontline* 20, no. 15 (2003), http://www.sas.upenn.edu /~dludden/LuddenFrontlineHeroes.htm.

28. D'Costa, "*Birangona*," 131.

29. U.S. Consulate (Dacca) Cable, *Killings at University* (March 30, 1971), Confidential, Source: Record Group 59, Subject Numeric File 1970–73, Pol and Def, Box 2530, http://nsarchive.gwu .edu/NSAEBB/NSAEBB79/.

30. On this figure, see Penelope Deutscher's *Foucault's Futures: A Critique of Reproductive Reason* (New York: Columbia University Press, 2017).

31. "Assistance and Aid to East Pakistan by UK for Prevention of Economic Disaster (Folder 1)." Government Papers, The National Archives, Kew (1970), 33, http://www.archivesdirect .amdigital.co.uk/Documents/Details/FCO_37_705.

32. Nilima Ibrahim, *Ami Birangona Bolchhi* (Dhaka: Jagriti Prokashoni, 1998), 18. Translation my own.

33. Khan, personal interview by author, December 18, 2014.
34. *Taant* saris are often called by their local appellation, Tangail saris, for the district of central Bangladesh that has been their historical producer since the Mughal era. They are in this way also distinguished from the *taant* woven in Dhaniakhali and Bishnupur in West Bengal. To consider these demarcations now, in light of the Radcliffe Line, however, would be to ignore how this artisanal weaving practice emerged from a particularly Bengali locale, responding to courtly demands and relying on the low-lying cotton-producing fields of the Brahmaputra. West and East is a far less productive distinction than that between cities within Bengal, each of which modified its process depending on local resources.
35. Anwar Huq, Mohammed Yunus, Syed Salahuddin Sohel, Abbas Bhuiya, Michael Emch, Stephen P. Luby, Estelle Russek-Cohen, G. Balakrish Nair, R. Bradley Sack, and Rita R. Colwell, "Simple Sari Cloth Filtration of Water Is Sustainable and Continues to Protect Villagers from Cholera in Matlab, Bangladesh," *mBio* 1, no. 1 (May 18, 2010): e00034-10. doi:10.1128/mBio.00034-10. I am grateful to Peter Betzer for drawing my attention to this phenomenon.
36. Rural women now largely supplement this sari filtration with water purification tablets, largely provided by international NGOs.
37. Naila Kabeer, "The Quest for National Identity: Women, Islam and the State in Bangladesh," *Feminist Review* 37 (1991): 40.
38. Indeed, as I discuss later, the state went so far as to ban Tagore's songs from the radio, effectively cementing his lyrics as the Bangla idiom of resistance against its rule. Kabeer, "Quest for National Identity," 41. See also Samia Huq, "Piety, Music, and Gender Transformation: Reconfiguring Women as Culture Bearing Markers of Modernity and Nationalism in Bangladesh," in *Islam, Culture and Women in Asia: Complex Terrains*, ed. Firdous Azim (London: Routledge, 2013), 59.
39. Akhtar Payami recounts Ayub Khan's arrival in Dhaka just prior to the outbreak of the war, during which time, according to Payami, he pointed to a crowd that had gathered outside the airport and said, "Pahle inko Musalman karo." [First, make them Muslims.] See Akhtar Payami, "Why Distort History?" *Dawn*, March 22, 2002, http://www.dawn.com/news/1062853; Kabeer, "Quest for National Identity," 39.
40. Louis Smith, ed., "Transcript of Telephone Conversation Between President Nixon and His Assistant for National Security Affairs, March 29, 1971," in *Foreign Relations of the United States, 1969–1976, Volume XI, South Asia Crisis, 1971* (Washington, DC: United States Department of State, 2005), 64.
41. This anecdote appears throughout the newspaper accounts on rape cited earlier, as well as in personal interviews with Maleka Khan.
42. In addition to scholarly records and news accounts, classified telegrams and correspondence to the U.S. National Security Council record the targeted violence on Hindus. See US Consulate (Dacca) Cable, *Selective Genocide* (March 28, 1971), Record Group 59, Subject Numeric File 1970–73, Pol and Def, Box 2530; US Consulate (Dacca) Cable, *Sitrep: Army Terror Campaign Continues in Dacca; Evidence Military Faces Some Difficulties Elsewhere* (March 31, 1971), Record Group 59, Subject Numeric File 1970–73, Pol and Def, Box 2530.
43. We might also think here of Draupadi in the *Mahabharata* who, having been wagered and lost by her husband Yudhishtira in a game of dice, is dragged out to the royal court. Despite her insistence that she could not have been wagered by Yudhishtira because he had already staked himself and lost, she is called a whore for having five husbands, and Dushasana begins to pull at her sari to disrobe her while holding her hair. But the sari will not end—its six yards of fabric that looped Draupadi's body are conjured by Krishna to extend limitlessly to

protect her modesty. Dushasana, finally exhausted, releases Draupadi's sari and hair both, and Draupadi vows not to tie her hair again until she can decorate its braid with his blood.

44. Sarah Lamb, *White Saris and Sweet Mangoes: Aging, Gender, and Body in North India* (Berkeley: University of California Press, 2000).

45. Meherjaan, one of the women whose account is included in Nilima Ibrahim's narrative *Ami Birangona Bolchhi (I Am Speaking as Birangona)*, recalls that the food she and other women received in the encampments was only rice and lentils. The army, according to the local woman who brought them food, could not be sure of religious dietary restrictions and so did not offer them meat. The irony of this attention to detail in the face of the repeated rapes and continued imprisonment scarcely requires comment.

46. Michelle Goldberg, *The Means of Reproduction: Sex, Power, and the Future of the World* (New York: Penguin, 2009).

47. Malcolm Potts, personal interview by author, Berkeley, California (May 25, 2016). This account repeats a quote from Potts in Lee Patterson's 1972 article, "Mass Rape in Bangladesh," *Times of India (1861–Current)*, http://search.proquest.com/docview/609777844?accountid=14496.

48. Potts, personal interview (May 25, 2016).

49. Khan, personal interview by author (December 18, 2014).

50. "Bangladesh Women's Emancipation Programme," unpublished document, Jill Sabella Private Collection, Dhaka, Bangladesh (February 1972).

51. Khan, personal interview (December 18, 2014).

52. Khan, personal interview.

53. Yasmine Kabir, dir., *Shadhinota (A Certain Liberation)* (Dhaka, Bangladesh: Magic Lantern Films, 2005). Translation my own.

54. Sigmund Freud, "The Origin and Development of Psychoanalysis," *American Journal of Psychology* 21 no. 2 (April 1910): 181–218.

55. Kabir, *Shadhinota (A Certain Liberation)*.

56. Kabir, *Shadhinota*.

57. Kabir, *Shadhinota*.

58. Mahasweta Devi, "The Breast-Giver," in *In Other Worlds: Essays in Cultural Politics*, 2nd ed., ed. Gayatri Chakravorty Spivak (New York: Routledge, 2006), 330.

59. This was confirmed by a visit to the temple and hospital in 2014.

60. Rabindranath Tagore, "Dui Bigha Jomi," *Chitra*, in *Rabindra-Rachanabali*, vol. 1 (Kolkata: Paschim Banga Sarkar, 1980), 597–59. Translation my own.

61. Dipesh Chakrabarty, "Remembered Villages: Representation of Hindu-Bengali Memories in the Aftermath of the Partition," *Economic and Political Weekly* 31, no. 32 (Aug. 10, 1996), 2144.

5. MACHINE MADE

1. "Texts of Secret Documents on Top-Level U.S. Discussions of Indian-Pakistani War," *New York Times (1923-Current File)*, January 6, 1972.

2. "Texts of Secret Documents."

3. A report on the economic landscape of East Bengal noted a USAID official's conservative estimate that at least $95 million was transferred ("disguised") from East to West Pakistan

through colonial money laundering. See U.S. National Security Council, *Conflict in East Pakistan; Attached to Cover Memorandum Dated June 21, 1971*

4. Indeed, West Bengal is considered the "rice bowl" of India.

5. Roger J. Robinson, *Bangladesh: Progress Through Partnership: Country Assistance Review* (Washington, DC: World Bank Publications, 1999).

6. "Assistance and Aid to East Pakistan by UK for Prevention of Economic Disaster," UK Foreign Office Files for India, Pakistan and Afghanistan, 1965–1971 (1970). FCO 37/705.

7. Naomi Hossain, "The Ugly Truth about Bangladesh's Successful Attack on Poverty," Institute of Development Studies (October 14, 2016), http://www.ids.ac.uk/opinion/the-ugly-truth-about-bangladesh-s-successful-attack-on-poverty.

8. Gayatri Chakravorty Spivak, "Can the Subaltern Speak?," in *Colonial Discourse and Post-Colonial Theory: A Reader*, ed. Patrick Williams and Laura Chrisman (New York: Columbia University Press, 1994), 93.

9. "Women's Work: A Monthly Progress Report," National Board of Bangladesh Women's Rehabilitation Programme, Dhaka, Bangladesh (September 1972).

10. "Women's Work."

11. Maleka Khan, personal interview by author (December 18, 2014).

12. Nobel Committee, "Nobel Peace Prize 2006," *Nobelprize.org*, n.d., https://www.nobelprize.org/prizes/peace/2006/summary/.

13. Lamia Karim, *Microfinance and Its Discontents: Women in Debt in Bangladesh* (Minneapolis: University of Minnesota Press, 2011).

14. Karim, *Microfinance and Its Discontents*, 110.

15. Karim, *Microfinance and Its Discontents*, xxii.

16. Mohandas K. Gandhi (Mahatma), *Young India* 6 (November 13, 1924), 378.

17. David Arnold, *Everyday Technology: Machines and the Making of India's Modernity* (Chicago: Chicago University Press, 2013), 81.

18. British Parliament House of Commons, *Parliamentary Papers, House of Commons and Command*, vol. 45 (London: H. M. Stationery Office, 1908), 23.

19. Nira Wickramasinghe's excellent account of the machines of life in Sri Lanka—including the Singer sewing machine, the gramophone, and the bicycle—demonstrates the connection between commodity life and social structure. Its history of the sewing machine was particularly generative for my thinking here and I thank Tariq Omar Ali for drawing my attention to it. Nira Wickramasinghe, *Metallic Modern: Everyday Machines in Colonial Sri Lanka* (New York: Berghahn Press, 2014).

20. Arnold, *Everyday Technology*, 37.

21. Arnold, *Everyday Technology*, 37.

22. See Edgar Thurston and K. Rangachari, *Castes and Tribes of Southern India* (Madras: Government Press, 1909); Anand A. Yang, *Bazaar India: Markets, Society, and the Colonial State in Bihar* (Berkeley: University of California Press, 1999).

23. Jill Sabella, personal interview with author (July 10, 2015).

24. K. M. Subhan, personal correspondence with Jill Sebella (September 13, 1972), Jill Sabella Private Collection.

25. Jill Sabella, personal interview.

26. Stella Kramrisch, "Unknown India: Ritual Art in Tribe and Village (1968)," in *Exploring India's Sacred Art: Selected Writings of Stella Kramrisch*, ed. Barbara Stoller Miller (Benaras: Motilal Banarsidass, 1994), 112.

27. Parveen Ahmed, "Aesthetics and Vocabulary of Nakshi Kantha," *The Indira Gandhi National Centre for the Arts News Letter* 2, no. 1–4 (1999); Niaz Zaman, *The Art of Kantha Embroidery* (Dhaka, India: The University Press, 1995).

28. Stella Kramrisch, "Kantha," in *Kantha: The Embroidered Quilts of Bengal from the Jill and Sheldon Bonovitz Collection and the Stella Kramrisch Collection of the Philadelphia Museum of Art*, ed. Darielle Mason (Philadelphia: Philadelphia Museum of Art, 2009), 169.

29. See Martha Alter Chen, "Kantha and Jamdani: Revival in Bangladesh," *India International Centre Quarterly* 11, no. 4 (1984): 45–62.

30. Ishrat Jahan Deepa, "Artesan Profile: Sacred Mark Enterprise, Bangladesh," *The Artesan Gateway* (July 25, 2016), http://theartesangateway.org/2016/07/25/artesan-profile-sacred -mark-enterprise-bangladesh.

31. Ten Thousand Villages, "Ten Thousand Villages, n.d.," http://www.tenthousandvillages.com/.

32. Ten Thousand Villages, "Dhaka Handicrafts," n.d., http://www.tenthousandvillages.com /bangladesh/dhaka-handicrafts.

33. Adam Smith, in his 1759 *The Theory of Moral Sentiments* (ed. Ryan Patrick Hanley (New York: Penguin, 2009)), argued that men are motivated primarily by sympathy, the ability and willingness to identify ourselves as another, and that this, not pure self-interest, makes economic ambition possible. See Emma Rothschild's excellent account of the interconnection between philosophy, politics, and economic imagination in *Economic Sentiments: Adam Smith, Condorcet, and the Enlightenment* (Cambridge, MA: Harvard University Press, 2013). In the field of economics, specifically work on contingent valuation and price of sympathy, see Paul Milgrom, "Is Sympathy an Economic Value? Philosophy, Economics, and the Contingent Valuation Method," in *Contingent Valuation: A Critical Assessment*, ed. Jerry A. Hausman (Amsterdam: Elsevier Science, 1993), 417–41.

34. Chandra Talpade Mohanty's "Under Western Eyes: Feminist Scholarship and Colonial Discourses," *Feminist Review* 30 (1988): 61–88, is of course the definitive essay on this.

35. Half the Sky: Turning Oppression into Opportunity for Women Worldwide, "Celebrities/Activists," *Half the Sky*, n.d., accessed December 9, 2016, http://www.halftheskymovement.org/videos /celebrities.

36. Sohela Nazneen, Maheen Sultan, and Naomi Hossain, "National Discourses on Women's Empowerment in Bangladesh: Enabling or Constraining Women's Choices?" *Development* 53, no. 2 (2010): 239–46.

37. Amartya Sen, "The Standard of Living: Lecture II, Lives and Capabilities," in *The Standard of Living*, ed. Geoffrey Hawthorne (Cambridge: Cambridge University Press, 1988), 36.

38. Dipesh Chakrabarty, *Provincializing Europe: Postcolonial Thought and Historical Difference* (Princeton, NJ: Princeton University Press, 2001).

39. Amartya Sen, *Development as Freedom* (New York: Knopf Doubleday, 2011), 14.

40. Martha Nussbaum, "Women's Capabilities and Social Justice," *Journal of Human Development* 1, no. 2 (July 1, 2000): 223.

41. Quoted in Staff Reporter, "Bangladesh Ahead of India in Gender Equality: Amartya Sen," *The Hindu*, January 5, 2013, http://www.thehindu.com/news/national/bangladesh-ahead-of-india -in-gender-equality-amartya-sen/article4277151.ece.

42. Oscar Wilde, *The Picture of Dorian Gray and Other Writings* (New York: Simon & Schuster, 2014), 148.

43. Wilde, *The Picture of Dorian Gray*, 150.

44. Agha Shahid Ali, "Dacca Gauzes," in *The Veiled Suite: The Collected Poems* (New York: Norton, 2009), 42.

45. Ali, "Dacca Gauzes."

46. Naila Kabeer, *The Power to Choose: Bangladeshi Garment Workers in London and Dhaka* (London: Verso, 2002), 5.

47. Karim, *Microfinance and Its Discontents.*

48. For analyses of the famine, its causes and effects, see Amartya Sen, *Poverty and Famines: An Essay on Entitlement and Deprivation* (Oxford: Oxford University Press, 1982); Rehman Sobhan, "Politics of Food and Famine in Bangladesh," *Economic & Political Weekly* 14, no. 48 (1979): 1973–80; Abdur Razzaque, Nurul Alam, Lokky Wai, and Andrew Foster, "Sustained Effects of the 1974–5 Famine on Infant and Child Mortality in a Rural Area of Bangladesh," *Population Studies* 44, no. 1 (1990): 145–54.

49. Kabeer, *Power to Choose*, 40.

50. Chen, "Kantha and Jamdani"; Katy Gardner, *Global Migrants, Local Lives: Travel and Transformation in Rural Bangladesh* (Oxford: Clarendon Press, 1995); Kabeer, *Power to Choose.*

51. Activists like Kalpona Akter have been pushing international regulatory bodies and the state to establish and enforce industrial safety measures and allow unionization.

52. See Amit S. Rai, "The Affect of Jugaad: Frugal Innovation and Postcolonial Practice in India's Mobile Phone Ecology," *Environment and Planning D: Society and Space* 33, no. 6 (December 1, 2015): 985–1002; Navi Radiou, Jaideep Prabhu, and Simone Ahuja, *Jugaad Innovation* (Delhi: Random House India, 2012); Ananya Roy, "The Agonism of Utopia: Dialectics at a Standstill," *Traditional Dwellings and Settlements Review* 23, no. 1 (2011): 15–24; Kavita Phillip, Lilly Irani, and Paul Dourish, "Postcolonial Computing: A Tactical Survey," *Science, Technology, & Human Values* 37, no. 1 (2012): 3–29; Peter Capelli, Harbir Singh, Jitendra Singh, and Michael Useem, "The India Way: Lessons for the U.S.," *Academy of Management Perspectives* 24, no. 2 (2010): 6–24.

53. Rubana Huq, Mohammadi Group Managing Director, personal interview by author, Dhaka, Bangladesh, December 2, 2015.

54. Gardner, *Global Migrants, Local Lives.*

55. Afrozi Begum, "Untitled" (unpublished personal essay, 2015). Translation my own.

56. Official images of the advertisement have been scrubbed from the Internet, but copies of the campaign are archived with several online magazine essays on it: "Meet Maks, American Apparel's New Bengali Muslim Model," *Dazed*, March 10, 2014, http://www.dazeddigital .com/artsandculture/article/19188/1/maks-bengali-muslim-made-in-bangladesh-topless -american-apparel-ad.

57. Rabindranath Tagore, "Religion of Man," in *The English Writings of Rabindranath Tagore: A Miscellany* (New Delhi: Sahitya Akademi, 1994), 91.

58. Roushan Jahan Rokeya, *Sultana's Dream and Selections from The Secluded Ones*, ed. Hanna Papanek (New York: Feminist Press at City University of New York, 1988), 17.

59. Rokeya, *Sultana's Dream*, 10.

60. Rabindranath Tagore, *The Home and the World*, ed. William Radice, trans. Surendranath Tagore (London: Penguin, 2005), 27.

61. Tagore, *The Home and the World*, 43.

62. Rehana Yesmin, "Untitled" (unpublished personal essay, 2015). Translation my own.

EPILOGUE

1. Karl Marx, "The Economic and Philosophical Manuscripts of 1844," in *Karl Marx: A Reader*, ed. Jon Elster (Cambridge: Cambridge University Press, 1989), 35–47.

2. Peter Stallybrass, "Marx's Coat," in *Border Fetishisms: Material Objects in Unstable Spaces*, ed. Patricia Spyer (New York: Routledge, 1998), 196.

3. Taslima Akhter, "স্মৃতি কাঁথা ও কথা / Memorial quilt on 24th April," filmed [April 2018]. YouTube video, 1:06. Posted [April 2018]. https://www.youtube.com/watch?v=foUw3YAhTEw

4. Stella Kramrisch, "Kantha," in *Kantha: The Embroidered Quilts of Bengal from the Jill and Sheldon Bonovitz Collection and the Stella Kramrisch Collection of the Philadelphia Museum of Art*, ed. Darielle Mason (Philadelphia: Philadelphia Museum of Art, 2009), 108.

Bibliography

Archival Sources

British Library

"Alipore Bomb Case." India Office Records and Private Papers. IOR/L/PJ/3171/12.

"An article, entitled 'Bomb and Pistol in a Bengal District' (1930–32) and a speech dated 1936 by Sir Robert Reid on terrorism in Bengal, 1930–35 (typescript)." India Office Records and Private Papers. 1930–1936. Mss Eur E278/2.

"Bengal and Calcutta: Papers Relating to the Chittagong Armoury Raids, Calcutta." India Office Records and Private Papers. 1930. Mss Eur F161/38.

"Bengal Ordinances; Indian Conciliation Group; terrorism in Bengal." India Office Records and Private Papers. 6 Nov 1931–31 Dec 1931. IOR/L/PO/6/75.

"Bengal terrorism: attempted murder of Mr C.G. Grassby IPS, and murder of Babu K Prasad Sen, special magistrate, Dacca; conviction of assailant." India Office Records and Private Papers. 1 Jul 1932–20 Feb 1933. IOR/L/PJ/7/390.

"Charles Tegart of the Indian Police." N.d. MS. British Library, Asia, Africa, Pacific Collections. Private Papers. Mss Eur C235 1881–1946.

"Chittagong Armoury Raid 1930: action against absconders" India Office Records and Private Papers. IOR/L/PJ/7/331.

"Chittagong Armoury Raid: newspaper articles including brief account of its leader Suriya Sen Dated as: 1961; 1976." India Office Records and Private Papers. Mss Eur F341/172.

"File 938(B)/29 –Terrorism in India: printed Bengal govt reports." India Office Records and Private Papers. April- June 1934. IOR/L/PJ/12/399.

"Forbes Collection: publications and papers relating to Indian women and womens studies collected by Prof Geraldine Hancock Forbes (b 1943) on which her 'Women in modern India' (Cambridge 1996) was based." India Office Records and Private Papers. Mss Eur F341.

"Indian Police Collection: topographical files." India Office Records and Private Papers. Mss Eur F161/26-137.

"Joshi, Kalpana (nee Dutt)." India Office Records and Private Papers. Mss Eur F341/144.

"Letters by John Younie in Khulna, Calcutta, Chittagong including a description of the Chittagong Armoury Raid, and aboard SS Naldera and SS Rawalpindi, to his sister Annie and his wife Dorothy." India Office Records and Private Papers. Mss Eur D939/18.

"Measures to suppress terrorism in Bengal. Promulgation of Bengal Emergency Powers Ordinances 1931 and 1932 and action under." India Office Records and Private Papers. 2 Oct 1931-26 Jul 1933. IOR/L/PJ/7/242.

"Papers concerning revenue, terrorism, and the political situation in Bengal, and martial law in Ireland. Dated as: May 1932, nd." India Office Records and Private Papers. May 1932. Mss Eur F207/12.

"Pronouncement of Chittagong Armoury Raid prisoners." India Office Records and Private Papers. IOR/L/PJ/7/5155.

"Re-enactment of Bengal Criminal Law Amendment Act (1930)." IOR/L/PO/6/18.

"Revolutionary Activities in India." IOR/L/PJ/12/393.

"Sir Stanley Jackson, Governor of Bengal: Attempted Assassination and Conviction of Assailant." IOR/L/PJ/1436/32.

"Terrorism in India." India Office Records and Private Papers. IOR/L/PJ/1000/33.

"Terrorism in Bengal, Measures to Suppress." IOR/L/PJ/754/1933.

National Archives of England

UK Foreign Office Files for India, Pakistan and Afghanistan, 1965–1971. (1970). FCO 37/705.

National Archives of India

"Bengal Revolutionary Leaflets and History Sheets." Home Ministry/Political Department 379/3/.

"Reports on the operations against terrorists and absconders in the district of Chittagong." Home Ministry/Political Department, 45/5/33.

"Reports on the Operation of the Bengal Emergency Ordinance in the District of Chittagong." Home Ministry/Political Department, 13/32.

"Report on the raid by military on a house in Chittagong Distrct: the subsequent arrest of Tarakeswar Dastidar, Kalpana Dutt, and others." Home Ministry/Political Department, 45/16/3.

"Revolutionary Propoganda in Bengal." Home Ministry/Political Department, 249/1925.

West Bengal State Archives

"Assassination of CGB Stevens." Intelligence Branch Files, CID, 850/31.

"Kalpana Dutta." Intelligence Branch Files, CID, June 17, 1933, Item 18, No. 493/1931.

"Outbreak by Revolutionaries in Chittagong." Intelligence Branch Files, CID, 176k/1930.

"Priti Waddedar." Intelligence Branch Files, CID, June 19, 1932, No. 115/1932.

"Proscription of Leaflet Titled 'Indian Republican Army.'" Intelligence Branch Files, CID, 178/30.

"Revolutionaries of Bengal." Intelligence Branch Files, CID, 164/1925, 495/25/.

"Revolutionary Press Propaganda in Bengal." Home Ministry/Political Department, 612/26.

"Terrorist Outrages in Chittagong." Intelligence Branch Files, CID, 1930–1933, Nil/31.

National Archives of the United States

"Situation in East Pakistan." US Consulate (Dacca) Cables, Record Group 59, Subject Numeric File 1970–73, Pol and Def, Box 2530.

Other Sources

"মলিন." *Samsad Bengali-English Dictionary*, 3rd ed. http://dsal.uchicago.edu/dictionaries/biswas
-bengali.

Abraham, Nicolas, and Maria Torok. *The Shell and the Kernel: Renewals of Psychoanalysis*. Trans. Nicholas T. Rand. Chicago: University of Chicago Press, 1994.

Act No. XIX of 1973. "The International Crimes (Tribunal) Act, 1973." *Bangladesh Code*. http://bdlaws
.minlaw.gov.bd/print_sections_all.php?id=435.

Act No. XXVII of 1871. "An Act for the Registration of Criminal Tribes and Eunuchs." *The Bengal Code*. Calcutta: Office of the Superintendent of Government Printing India, 1872.

Ahmad, Aijaz. *In Theory: Classes, Nations, Literatures*. London: Verso, 1992.

Ahmed, Parveen. "Aesthetics and Vocabulary of Nakshi Kantha." *The Indira Gandhi National Centre for the Arts News Letter* 2, no. 1–4 (1999). http://ignca.nic.in/nl_01310.htm

Ahmed, Sara. *Queer Phenomenology: Orientations, Objects, Others*. Durham, NC: Duke University Press, 2006.

Akhtar, Salman. *Matters of Life and Death: Psychoanalytic Reflections*. London: Karnac, 2011.

Ali, Agha Shahid. "Dacca Gauzes." In *The Veiled Suite: The Collected Poems*, 42. New York: Norton, 2009.

Ali, Tariq Omar. *A Local History of Global Capital: Jute and Peasant Life in the Bengal Delta*. Princeton, NJ: Princeton University Press, 2018.

Alpers, Edward. *Ivory and Slaves in East Central Africa*. Berkeley: University of California, 1975.

Alter, Joseph S. "Celibacy, Sexuality, and the Transformation of Gender into Nationalism in North India." *Journal of Asian Studies* 53, no. 1 (February 1994): 45–66.

Amin, Shahid. *Event, Memory, Metaphor: Chauri Chaura, 1922–1992*. Berkeley: University of California Press, 1995.

——. "Gandhi as Mahatma; Gorakhpur District, Eastern UP, 1921–2." In *Subaltern Studies III*, ed. Ranajit Guha, 288–342. New Delhi: Oxford University Press, 1984.

Anderson, Warwick, Deborah Jenson, and Richard C. Keller, eds. *Unconscious Dominions: Psychoanalysis, Colonial Trauma, and Global Sovereignties*. Durham, NC: Duke University Press Books, 2011.

Appadurai, Arjun. *Modernity at Large: Cultural Dimensions of Globalization*. Minneapolis: University of Minnesota Press, 1996.

Arnold, David. "Bureaucratic Recruitment and Subordination in Colonial India." In *Subaltern Studies No. 4: Writings of South Asian History and Society*, ed. Ranajit Guha, 1–53. New Delhi: Oxford University Press, 1985.

——. *Everyday Technology: Machines and the Making of India's Modernity*. Chicago: Chicago University Press, 2013.

Arondekar, Anjali. *For the Record: On Sexuality and the Colonial Archive*. Durham, NC: Duke University Press, 2009.

——. "Without a Trace: Sexuality and the Colonial Archive." *Journal of the History of Sexuality* 14, no. 1 (2005): 10–27.

"Arrest of Woman in Male Attire." *Times of India*, June 23, 1932; *Proquest Historical Newspapers (1861–Current)*.

Asad, Talal. *On Suicide Bombing*. New York: Columbia University Press, 2007.

Bagchi, Jasodhara. "Representing Nationalism: Ideology of Motherhood in Colonial Bengal." *Economic and Political Weekly* 25, no. 42–43 (October 1990), WS65–WS71.

Bagchi, Jasodhara, and Subhoranjan Dasgupta, eds. *The Trauma and the Triumph: Gender and Partition in Eastern India*. Kolkata: Stree, 2003.

Bala, Usha, and Anshu Sharma. *Indian Women Freedom Fighters, 1857–1947*. New Delhi: Manohar, 1986.

Banerjee, Sukanya. *Becoming Imperial Citizens: Indians in the Late Victorian Empire*. Durham, NC: Duke University Press, 2010.

Banerji, Debashish. *The Alternate Nation of Abanindranath Tagore*. New Delhi: SAGE India, 2010.

"Bangladesh Ahead of India in Gender Equality: Amartya Sen." *The Hindu*, January 5, 2013. http://www.thehindu.com/news/national/bangladesh-ahead-of-india-in-gender-equality-amartya-sen/article4277151.ece.

Barthes, Roland. *Camera Lucida: Reflections on Photography*. Trans. Richard Howard. New York: Farrar, Straus and Giroux, 1981.

Basu, Subho, and Sikata Banerjee. "The Quest for Manhood: Masculine Hinduism and Nation in Bengal." *Comparative Studies of South Asia, Africa and the Middle East* 26, no. 3 (2006): 476–490.

Bayly, C. A. "The Origins of Swadeshi." In *The Social Life of Things*, ed. Arjun Appadurai, 285–321. Cambridge: Cambridge University Press, 1988.

Benjamin, Walter. "Theses on the Philosophy of History." In *Illuminations: Essays and Reflections*, 253–264. New York: Random House, 1968.

Bentinck, William Lord. "Preamble to 1829 Bengal Regulation of Sati." In *The Bengal Code: Bengal Regulations, Local Acts of the Governor General in Council and the Regulations Made under 33 Victoria, Cap. 3, in Force in Bengal*, ed. Charles Herman Oertel and Frederic George Wigley, 267–69. Calcutta: Superintendent of Government Print, Legislative Department, 1889.

Berlant, Lauren and Lee Edelman. *Sex, or the Unbearable*. Durham, NC: Duke University Press, 2013.

Best, Stephen, and Sharon Marcus. "Surface Reading: An Introduction." *Representations* 108, no. 1 (2009): 1–21.

Bewell, Alan. *Romanticism and Colonial Disease*. Baltimore, MD: Johns Hopkins University Press, 2003.

Bewes, Timothy. "Reading with the Grain: A New World in Literary Criticism." *Differences: A Journal of Feminist Cultural Studies* 21, no. 3 (2010): 1–33.

Biplabi: A Journal of the 1942 Open Rebellion. Kolkata: K. P. Bagchi, 2002.

Biswas, Santanu. "Rabindranath Tagore and Freudian Thought." *International Journal of Psychoanalysis* 84, no. 3 (2003): 717–32.

Bolts, William. *Considerations on Indian Affairs Particularly Respecting the Present State of Bengal and its Dependencies*. London: J. Almon, 1772.

Borch-Jacobsen, Mikkel. *The Emotional Tie: Psychoanalysis, Mimesis, Affect*. Stanford, CA: Stanford University Press, 1993.

Borradori, Giovanna, and Jacques Derrida. *Philosophy in a Time of Terror*. Chicago: University of Chicago Press, 2004.

Borthwick, Meredith. *The Changing Role of Women in Bengal 1849–1905*. Princeton, NJ: Princeton University Press, 1984.

Bose, Girindrasekhar. "The Genesis and Adjustment of the Oedipus Wish" (1928). In *Vishnu on Freud's Desk: A Reader in Psychoanalysis and Hinduism*, ed. T. G. Vaidyanathan and Jeffrey K. Kripal. Delhi: Oxford University Press, 1999.

——. "History of the Indian Psycho-Analytical Society." *International Journal of Psychoanalysis* 4 (January–April 1923): 249–52.

Bose, Girindrasekhar, and Sigmund Freud. *The Beginnings of Psychoanalysis in India: The Bose-Freud Correspondence.* Calcutta: Indian Psycho-analytical Society, 1964.

Bose, Purnima. *Organizing Empire: Individualism, Collective Agency, and India.* Durham, NC: Duke University Press, 2003.

Bose, Sharmila. *Dead Reckoning: Memories of the 1971 Bangladesh War.* New York: Columbia University Press, 2011.

Bose, Sugata. *Peasant Labour and Colonial Capital: Rural Bengal Since 1770,* vol. 2. Cambridge: Cambridge University Press, 1993.

Bourke-White, Margaret. "Mohandas K. Gandhi," January 1, 1946. Los Angeles: The LIFE Picture Collection.

"The Brahmo Trust Deed." *Thebrahmosamaj.net,* n.d. http://www.thebrahmosamaj.net/samajes/trustdeed.html.

Brennan, Timothy. *At Home in the World: Cosmopolitanism Now.* Cambridge, MA: Harvard University Press, 1997.

British Parliament House of Commons. *Parliamentary Papers, House of Commons and Command* (vol. 45). London: H. M. Stationery Office, 1908.

Brown, Bill. "Thing Theory." *Critical Inquiry* 28, no. 1 (2001): 1–22.

Brown, Mark. "Ethnology and Colonial Administration in Nineteenth-Century British India: The Question of Native Crime and Criminality." *British Journal for the History of Science* 36, no. 2 (2003): 201–19.

——. *Penal Power and Colonial Rule.* New York: Routledge, 2014.

Brown, Rebecca M. "Spinning Without Touching the Wheel: Anticolonialism, Indian Nationalism, and the Deployment of Symbol." *Comparative Studies of South Asia, Africa and the Middle East* 29, no. 2 (2009): 230–45.

Brownmiller, Susan. *Against Our Will: Men, Women and Rape.* New York: Fawcett Columbine, 1975.

Bryan-Wilson, Julia. *Fray: Art and Textile Politics.* Chicago: University of Chicago Press, 2017.

Bunting, Madeline. "Amartya Sen: India's Dirty Fighter." *Guardian,* July 16, 2013. https://www.theguardian.com/world/2013/jul/16/amartya-sen-india-dirty-fighter

Burke, Janine. *The Sphinx on the Table: Sigmund Freud's Art Collection and the Development of Psychoanalysis.* London: Bloomsbury, 2009.

Burton, Antoinette M. *Dwelling in the Archive: Women Writing House, Home, and History in Late Colonial India.* Oxford: Oxford University Press, 2003.

Butalia, Urvashi. *Other Side of Silence: Voices from the Partition of India.* Durham, NC: Duke University Press, 2000.

Butler, Judith. *Antigone's Claim: Kinship Between Life and Death.* New York: Columbia University Press, 2000.

——. *Precarious Life: The Powers of Mourning and Violence.* London: Verso, 2004.

Capelli, Peter, Harbir Singh, Jitendra Singh, and Michael Useem. "The India Way: Lessons for the U.S." *Academy of Management Perspectives* 24, no. 2 (2010): 6–24.

Chakrabarty, Dipesh. "Postcoloniality and the Artifice of History: Who Speaks for 'Indian' Pasts?" *Representations* 37 (1992): 1–26.

——. *Provincializing Europe: Postcolonial Thought and Historical Difference.* Princeton, NJ: Princeton University Press, 2001.

——. "Remembered Villages: Representation of Hindu-Bengali Memories in the Aftermath of the Partition." *Economic and Political Weekly* 31, no. 32 (August 10, 1996): 2143–2145, 2147–2151.

——. *Rethinking Working-Class History: Bengal, 1890–1940*. Princeton, NJ: Princeton University Press, 2000.

Chakravartty, Gargi. *Coming Out of Partition: Refugee Women of Bengal*. New Delhi: Bluejay, 2005.

Chatterjee, Manini. *Do and Die: The Chittagong Uprising, 1930–34*. New Delhi: Penguin, 1999.

——. "1930: Turning Point in the Participation of Women in the Freedom Struggle." *Social Scientist* 29, no. 7/8 (2001): 39–47.

Chatterjee, Monish R.. "Tagore and Jana Gana Mana." *Counter Currents*, August 31, 2003, http://www .countercurrents.org/comm-chatterjee310803.htm.

Chatterjee, Partha. *Lineages of Political Society: Studies in Postcolonial Democracy*. New York: Columbia University Press, 2011.

——. "The Nationalist Resolution of the Women's Question." In *Empire and Nation: Selected Essays*, 116–35. New York: Columbia University Press, 2010.

——. *The Nation and Its Fragments: Colonial and Postcolonial Histories*. Princeton, NJ: Princeton University Press, 1993.

Chatterjee, Sarat Chandra. *Pather Dabi = the Right of Way*. New Delhi: Rupa, 1993.

Chatterji, Bankimcandra. *Anandamath, or The Sacred Brotherhood*. Trans. Julius Lipner. Oxford: Oxford University Press, 2005.

Chatterji, Suniti Kumar. "Vienna—A Meeting with Freud." *Samiksa: The Journal of the Indian Psycho-analytical Society* 43, no. 3 (1993): 74–75.

Chen, Martha Alter. "Kantha and Jamdani: Revival in Bangladesh." *India International Centre Quarterly* 11, no. 4 (1984): 45–62.

Cheng, Anne Anlin. "Skins, Tattoos, and Susceptibility." *Representations* 108, no. 1 (2009): 98–119.

Chittagong Uprising Golden Jubilee: 18 April 1980–18 April 1981. Calcutta: Chittagong Uprising Golden Jubilee Committee, 1981.

Chittagong Uprising Golden Jubilee Committee. *Bibliography of Freedom Movement in India, 1757 to 1947*. Calcutta: Chittagong Uprising Golden Jubilee Committee, 1982.

Chowdhury, Indira. *The Frail Hero and Virile History: Gender and the Politics of Culture in Colonial Bengal*. Delhi: Oxford University Press, 1998.

Chowdhury, Mustafa. *Picking Up the Pieces: 1971 War Babies' Odyssey from Bangladesh to Canada*. New York: Xlibris, 2015.

Clements, Ron, and John Musker, dirs. *The Little Mermaid*. Walt Disney Home Video, 1989.

Cohn, Bernard. *Colonialism and Its Forms of Knowledge*. Princeton, NJ: Princeton University Press, 1996.

Cole, Simon. *Suspect Identities: A History of Fingerprinting and Criminal Identification*. Cambridge, MA: Harvard University Press, 2002.

Collins, Michael. "History and Postcolonial Thought: Rabindranath Tagore's Reception in London, 1912–1913." *International Journal of the Humanities* 4, no. 9 (2007): 71–83.

Comoroff, Jean, and John Comoroff. *Of Revelation and Revolution: Christianity, Colonialism, and Consciousness in South Africa*, vol. 1. Chicago: University of Chicago Press, 1991.

Cook, S. B. *Imperial Affinities: Nineteenth-Century Analogies and Exchanges Between India and Ireland*. New Delhi: Sage, 1993.

"Consent." *Oxford English Dictionary Online*, http://www.oed.com/view/Entry/91950?rskey=8SQBTa &result=2.

Coomaraswamy, Ananda. "Self-Sacrifice." *Harvard Journal of Asiatic Studies* 6, no. 3/4 (February 1942): 358–98.

Cosgrove, Ben. "Gandhi and His Spinning Wheel: The Story Behind a Famous Photo." *Time*, (September 10, 2014), http://time.com/3639043/gandhi-and-his-spinning-wheel-the-story -behind-an-iconic-photo/.

Cowells, Edward Byles, and William Frederick Webster, trans. *Rig-Veda-Sanhitá: A Collection of Ancient Hindu Hymns*. London: W. H. Allen, 1866.

Culler, Jonathan. "Apostrophe." In *The Pursuit of Signs: Semiotics, Literature, Deconstruction*, 135–54. Ithaca, NY: Cornell University Press, 1981.

Dalton, Dennis. *Mahatma Gandhi: Nonviolent Power in Action*. New York: Columbia University Press, 2012.

Daly, C. D. "The Psychology of Revolutionary Tendencies." *International Journal of Psycho-Analysis* 11 (1930): 193–210.

Daly, F. C. *First Rebels: Strictly Confidential Note on the Growth of the Revolutionary Movement in Bengal*. Calcutta: Riddhi-India, 1981.

Damrosch, David. *What Is World Literature?* Princeton, NJ: Princeton University Press, 2003.

Danielou, Alain. *The Myths and Gods of India*. London: Bear, 1991.

Das, Bina. *Bina Das: A Memoir*. New Delhi: Zuban, 2010.

——. "Statement Before the Special Tribunal of the Calcutta High Court." *Bina Das: A Memoir*. New Delhi: Zuban, 2010.

——. *Shrinkal Jhankal*. Calcutta: Jayashi Prakashan, 1956.

Datta, V. N. *Sati: A Historical, Social, and Philosophical Enquiry into the Hindu Rite of Widow Burning*. Riverdale, MD: Riverdale, 1988.

Dayal, Samir. "Repositioning India: Tagore's Passionate Politics of Love." *Positions: East Asia, Cultures, Critique* 15, no. 1 (2007): 165–208.

D'Costa, Bina. "*Birangona*: Bearing Witness in War and 'Peace.' " In *Of the Nation Born: The Bangladesh Papers*, ed. Hameeda Hossain and Amena Mohsin. Chicago: University of Chicago Press, 2016.

——. *Nationbuilding, Gender and War Crimes in South Asia*. New York: Routledge, 2011.

Deepa, Israt Jahan. "Artesan Profile: Sacred Mark Enterprise, Bangladesh." *The Artesan Gateway*, July 25, 2016, http://theartesangateway.org/2016/07/25/artesan-profile-sacred-mark-enterprise-bangladesh.

Deleuze, Gilles, and Félix Guattari. *A Thousand Plateaus: Capitalism and Schizophrenia*. Minneapolis: University of Minnesota Press, 1987.

de Man, Paul. *Allegories of Reading: Figural Language in Rousseau, Nietzsche, Rilke, and Proust*. New Haven, CT: Yale University Press, 1979.

——. *Blindness and Insight: Essays in the Rhetoric of Contemporary Criticism*. New York: Psychology, 1983.

——. *The Rhetoric of Romanticism*. New York: Columbia University Press, 1984.

Derrida, Jacques. *Archive Fever: A Freudian Impression*. Trans. Eric Prenowitz. Chicago: University of Chicago Press, 1998.

——. "Deconstruction and the Other: A Conversation with Jacques Derrida." In *Dialogues with Contemporary Continental Thinkers: The Phenomenological Heritage: Paul Ricoeur, Emmanuel Levinas, Herbert Marcuse, Stanislas Breton, Jacques Derrida*, ed. Richard Kearney, 139–56. Manchester, UK: Manchester University Press, 1984.

——. "A Silkworm of One's Own (Points of View Stitched on the Other Veil)." Trans. Geoffrey Bennington. In *Acts of Religion*, ed. Gil Anidjar. New York: Routledge, 2002.

——. *Specters of Marx: The State of Debt, the Work of Mourning, and the New International*. London: Routledge, 1993.

Deutscher, Penelope. *Foucault's Futures: A Critique of Reproductive Reason*. New York: Columbia University Press, 2017.

de Valera, Eamon. *India and Ireland*. New York: Friends of Freedom for India, 1920.

Devi, Mahasweta. "The Breast-Giver." In *In Other Worlds: Essays in Cultural Politics*, 2nd ed., ed. Gayatri Chakravorty Spivak, 305–31. New York: Routledge, 2006.

Didur, Jill. *Unsettling Partition: Literature, Gender, Memory.* New Delhi: Pearson, 2007.

Dirlik, Arif. "The Postcolonial Aura: Third World Criticism in the Age of Global Capitalism." *Critical Inquiry* 20, no. 2 (1994): 328–56.

Doane, Mary Ann. *Femmes Fatales: Feminism, Film Theory, and Psychoanalysis.* New York: Routledge, 2013.

Doolittle, Hilda (H.D.). *Tribute to Freud.* London: New Directions, 1956.

Drummond, William. "Ravages of War Hurt Bengali Women Most." *Los Angeles Times (1923-Current File).* December 22, 1971, part 1.

Durkheim, Émile. *The Elementary Forms of Religious Life.* Oxford: Oxford University Press, 2001.

Dutt, Kalpana Joshi. *Chittagong Armoury Raiders' Reminiscences.* Delhi: People's Press, 1979.

Eagleton, Terry. *After Theory.* London: Penguin, 2004.

Elsner, John, and Roger Cardinal, eds. *The Cultures of Collecting.* London: Reaktion Books, 1994.

Epstein, Mark. "On the Seashore of Endless Worlds." In *Freud and the Buddha: The Couch and the Cushion,* ed. Axel Hoffer. New York: Karnac Books, 2015.

Fannin, Leon F. "Thuggee and Professional Criminality." *Michigan Sociological Review* 3 (1989): 34–44.

Fanon, Frantz. *The Wretched of the Earth.* Trans. Richard Philcox. New York: Grove Press, 2004.

Felski, Rita. *The Limits of Critique.* Chicago: University of Chicago Press, 2015.

"Fetish." *Oxford English Dictionary Online,* http://www.oed.com/view/Entry/69611.

Figueira, Dorothy M. *Otherwise Occupied: Pedagogies of Alterity and the Brahminization of Theory.* Albany: State University of New York Press, 2008.

Fisch, Jörg. "Dying for the Dead: Sati in Universal Context." *Journal of World History* 16, no. 3 (2005): 293–325.

——. "Sati and the Task of the Historian," *Journal of World History* 18, no. 3 (2007): 361–68.

Forbes, Geraldine. "Goddesses or Rebels? The Women Revolutionaries of Bengal." In *Women, Politics and Literature in Bengal,* ed. Clinton Seely, 3–17. East Lansing: Asian Studies Center, Michigan State University, 1981.

——. "In Search of the Pure Heathen." *Economic and Political Weekly (EPW)* 21, no. 17 (April 26, 1986): WS2–WS8.

——. "The Politics of Respectability: Indian Women and the Indian National Congress." In *The Indian National Congress: Centenary Hindsights,* ed. D. A. Low, 54–97. Delhi: Oxford University Press, 1988.

Forrester, John. *Dispatches from the Freud Wars: Psychoanalysis and Its Passions.* Cambridge, MA: Harvard University Press, 1997.

Foucault, Michel. *The Foucault Effect: Studies in Governmentality.* Chicago: University of Chicago Press, 1991.

——. *The History of Sexuality: An Introduction.* New York: Knopf Doubleday, 2012.

——. *The Order of Things: An Archeology of the Human Sciences.* New York: Pantheon, 1970.

——. *Society Must Be Defended: Lectures at the Collège de France, 1975-1976.* Trans. David Macey. New York: Picador, 2003.

Freedgood, Elaine. *The Ideas in Things: Fugitive Meaning in the Victorian Novel.* Chicago: University of Chicago Press, 2006.

Freedom Struggle and Anushilan Samiti. Calcutta: Anushilan Samiti, 1979.

Freud, Ernst L., ed. *Letters of Sigmund Freud, 1873-1939.* Trans. Tania Stern and James Stern. London: Hogarth Press, 1961.

Freud, Ernst L., ed. *The Letters of Sigmund Freud and Arnold Zweig*. Trans. Elaine Robson-Scott and William Robson-Scott. New York: Harcourt, 1970.

Freud, Sigmund. *Beyond the Pleasure Principle*. New York: Norton, 1975.

——. *Civilization and Its Discontents*. Ed. and trans. James Strachey. New York: Norton, 1962.

——. *The Complete Correspondence of Sigmund Freud and Ernest Jones 1908–1939*. Ed. R. Andrew Paskauskas. Cambridge, MA: Harvard University Press.

——. *The Diary of Sigmund Freud 1929–1939: A Record of the Final Decade*. Trans. Michael Molnar. London: Hogarth Press, 1992.

——. "Fetishism" (1927). In *The Standard Edition of the Complete Psychological Works of Sigmund Freud*, vol. 21, ed. and trans. James Strachey, 152. New York: Norton, 1953.

——. *The Interpretation of Dreams*. In *The Standard Edition of the Complete Psychological Works of Sigmund Freud*, vol. 5, ed. and trans. James Strachey. New York: Norton, 1953.

——. *Letters of Sigmund Freud*. Ed. Ernst L. Freud. Trans. Tania and James Stern. New York: Dover, 1960.

——. "Mourning and Melancholia" (1917). In *The Standard Edition of the Complete Psychological Works of Sigmund Freud*, vol. 14, ed. and trans. James Strachey, 237–58. New York: Norton, 1953.

——. "The Origin and Development of Psychoanalysis." *American Journal of Psychology* 21, no. 2 (April 1910): 181–218.

——. *The Question of Lay Analysis: An Introduction to Psychoanalysis*, 1st American ed. New York: Norton, 1950.

——. *Three Essays on the Theory of Sexuality*. Ed. and trans. James Strachey. New York: Basic Books, 1962.

Fuss, Diana, and Joel Sanders. "Berggasse 19: Inside Freud's Office." In *Stud: Architectures of Masculinity*, ed. Joel Sanders, 112–39. Princeton, NJ: Princeton Architectural Press, 1996.

Gallo, Rubén. *Freud's Mexico: Into the Wilds of Psychoanalysis*. Cambridge, MA: MIT Press, 2010.

Gandhi, Mohandas K. *The Collected Works of Mahatma Gandhi*. New Delhi: Publications Division, Ministry of Information and Broadcasting, Government of India, 1958.

——. *The Collected Works of Mahatma Gandhi*, vol. 30. Ahmedabad: Navajivan Trust, 1968.

——. *Young India* 6 (November 13, 1924): 378.

——. *Young India* 40 (March 14, 1929): 143.

Gardner, Katy. *Global Migrants, Local Lives: Travel and Transformation in Rural Bangladesh*. Oxford: Clarendon Press, 1995.

Gay, Peter. *Freud: A Life of Our Time*. New York: Norton, 2006.

Gayen, Kaberi. "Women, War, and Cinema: Construction of Women in the Liberation War Films of Bangladesh." *French Journal for Media Research* 3, no. 2 (2015). http://frenchjournalformediaresearch.com/index.php?id=478.

Ghosh, Durba. *Gentlemanly Terrorists: Political Violence and the Colonial State in India, 1919–1947*. Cambridge: Cambridge University Press, 2017.

Ghosh, Niranjan. *Role of Women in the Freedom Movement in Bengal, 1919–1947: Midnapore, Bankura, and Purulia District*. Midnapore: Tamralipta Prakashani, 1988.

Ghosh, Satyavrata. *Decades of Daring Deeds*. Delhi: B.R. Publishing, 1991.

Ghosh, Satyavrata, and Marxist Study Forum. *Remembering Our Revolutionaries*. Hyderabad: Marxist Study Forum, 1994.

Gilmartin, Sophie. "The Sati, the Bride, and the Widow: Sacrificial Woman in the Nineteenth Century." *Victorian Literature and Culture* 25, no. 1 (1997): 141–58.

"Girl, Believed to Be Mesmerised." *Times of India* (November 11, 1933). *Proquest Historical Newspapers 1861–Current*.

Gokhale, B. G. "Swami Vivekananda and Indian Nationalism." *Journal of Bible and Religion* 32, no. 1 (January 1964): 35–42.

Goldberg, Michelle. *The Means of Reproduction: Sex, Power, and the Future of the World.* New York: Penguin, 2009.

Gordon, Avery. *Ghostly Matters: Haunting and the Sociological Imagination.* Minneapolis: University of Minnesota Press, 1997.

Gordon, Leonard A. *Bengal: The Nationalist Movement, 1876–1940.* New York: Columbia University Press, 1974.

Greedharry, Mrinalini. *Postcolonial Theory and Psychoanalysis: From Uneasy Engagements to Effective Critique.* London: Springer, 2008.

Grewal, Inderpal. *Home and Harem: Nation, Gender, Empire, and the Cultures of Travel.* Durham, NC: Duke University Press, 1996.

Guha, Ramachandra. "Subaltern and Bhadralok Studies." *Economic and Political Weekly* 30, no. 33 (August 19, 1995): 2056–58.

Guha, Ranajit. *Elementary Aspects of Peasant Insurgency in Colonial India.* Delhi: Oxford University Press, 1983.

——. "On Some Aspects of the Historiography of Colonial India." In *Selected Subaltern Studies,* ed. Ranajit Guha and Gayatri Chakravorty Spivak, 37–45. Oxford: Oxford University Press, 1988.

——. *Dominance Without Hegemony: History and Power in Colonial India.* Cambridge, MA: Harvard University Press, 1998.

Gupta, Amit Kumar. "Defying Death: Nationalist Revolutionism in India, 1897–1938." *Social Scientist* 25, no. 9/10 (1997): 3–27.

Habermas, Jurgen. *Philosophy in a Time of Terror: Dialogues with Jurgen Habermas and Jacques Derrida.* Chicago: University of Chicago Press.

Half the Sky. "Turning Oppression into Opportunity for Women Worldwide; Celebrities/Activists." *Half the Sky,* n.d. http://www.halftheskymovement.org/videos/celebrities.

Haq, Jalalul. *Nation and Nation-Worship in India.* New Delhi: Genuine Publications, 1992.

Harlan, Lindsey. *Religion and Rajput Women: The Ethic of Protection in Contemporary Narratives.* Berkeley: University of California Press, 1992.

Hartnack, Christiane. *Psychoanalysis in Colonial India.* Oxford: Oxford University Press, 2000.

Hayles, N. Katherine. "How We Read: Close, Hyper, Machine." *ADE Bulletin* 150 (2010): 62–79. https://doi.org/10.1632/ade.150.62.

Heehs, Peter. *The Bomb in Bengal: The Rise of Revolutionary Terrorism in India, 1900–1910.* New Delhi: Oxford University Press, 2004.

——. "Foreign Influences on Bengali Revolutionary Terrorism, 1902–1908." *Modern Asian Studies* 28, no. 3 (1994): 533–56.

Hegel, Georg Wilhelm Friedrich. *Lectures on the Philosophy of World History—Introduction: Reason in History.* Trans. H. B. Nisbet. Cambridge: Cambridge University Press, 1975.

Herman, Jeanette. *Empire's Bodies: Images of Suffering in Nineteenth- and Twentieth-Century India and Ireland.* New York: Macmillan, 2004.

——. "Men and Women of Feeling: Conventions of Sensibility and Sentimentality in the Sati Debate and in Mainwaring's *The Suttee.*" *Comparative Literature Studies* 42, no. 2 (2005): 223–63.

"High Court Judgment—Surya Sen Case. Special Bench: Pankridge, Ameer Ali and M. G. Ghose, J. J. Emperor v. Surjya Kumar Sen and Other-Accused-Appellents." In I. M. Sharma, *The Easter Rebellion in India: The Chittagong Uprising,* 438–57. Calcutta: Marxist Study Forum, 1963.

Hills, Carol, and Daniel C. Silverman. "Nationalism and Feminism in Late Colonial India: The Rani of Jhansi Regiment, 1943–1945." *Modern Asian Studies* 27, no. 4 (October 1993): 741–60.

Hinchy, Jessica. "Deviant Domesticities and Sexualised Childhoods: Prostitutes, Eunuchs and the Limits of the State Child 'Rescue' Mission in Colonial India." In *Divine Domesticities: Christian Paradoxes in Asia and the Pacific*, ed. Hyaeweol Choi and Margaret Jolly, 247–80. Canberra, Australia: ANU Press, 2014.

Hossain, Anwar. *Muslim Women's Struggle for Freedom in Colonial Bengal (1873–1940)*. Kolkata: Progressive Publishers, 2003.

Hossain, Naomi. "The Ugly Truth about Bangladesh's Successful Attack on Poverty." *Institute of Development Studies*, October 14, 2016. http://www.ids.ac.uk/opinion/the-ugly-truth-about -bangladesh-s-successful-attack-on-poverty.

Huq, Anwar, Mohammed Yunus, Syed Salahuddin Sohel, Abbas Bhuiya, Michael Emch, Stephen P. Luby, Estelle Russek-Cohen, G. Balakrish Nair, R. Bradley Sack, and Rita R. Colwell. "Simple Sari Cloth Filtration of Water Is Sustainable and Continues to Protect Villagers from Cholera in Matlab, Bangladesh." *mBio* 1, no. 1 (May 18, 2010): e00034-10. doi:10.1128/mBio.00034-10.

Huq, Samia. "Piety, Music, and Gender Transformation: Reconfiguring Women as Culture Bearing Markers of Modernity and Nationalism in Bangladesh." In *Islam, Culture and Women in Asia: Complex Terrains*, ed. Firdous Azim, 225–39. London: Routledge, 2013.

Ibrahim, Nilima. *Ami Birangona Bolchhi*. Dhaka: Jagriti Prokashoni, 1998.

"Immolate." *Oxford English Dictionary Online*. http://www.oed.com/view/Entry/91950?rskey=8SQBTa &result=2.

Ingold, Tim. "The Textility of Making." *Cambridge Journal of Economics* 34 (2010), 91–102.

Israel, Jonathan. *Democratic Enlightenment: Philosophy, Revolution, and Human Rights, 1750–1790*. Oxford: Oxford University Press, 2011.

Jacobs, Amber. *On Matricide: Myth, Psychoanalysis, and the Law of the Mother*. New York: Columbia University Press, 2007.

Jain, Girilal. "Pakistan's Military Elite: Influence of Racism and Bigotry." *Times of India (1861-Current)*, June 16, 1971.

Jeffery, Keith. *An Irish Empire? Aspects of Ireland and the British Empire*. New York: Manchester University Press, 1996.

Johnson, Barbara. "Apostrophe, Animation, and Abortion." *Diacritics* 16 (1986): 28–47.

——. "Metaphor, Metonymy, and Voice in *Their Eyes Were Watching God*." In *The Barbara Johnson Reader: The Surprise of Otherness*, ed. Melissa Feuerstein, Bill Johnson González, Lili Porten, and Keja Valens, 108–125. Durham, NC: Duke University Press, 2014.

——. *Persons and Things*. Cambridge, MA: Harvard University Press, 2005.

Jones, Ann Rosalind, and Peter Stallybrass. *Renaissance Clothing and the Materials of Memory*. Cambridge: Cambridge University Press, 2000.

Jones, Ernest. *The Life and Work of Sigmund Freud, Volume Three: The Last Phase 1919-1939*. London: Hogarth Press, 1957.

Kabeer, Naila. *The Power to Choose: Bangladeshi Garment Workers in London and Dhaka*. London: Verso, 2002.

——. "The Quest for National Identity: Women, Islam and the State in Bangladesh." *Feminist Review* 37 (1991): 38–58.

Kabir, Yasmine, dir. *Shadhinota (A Certain Liberation)*. Dhaka, Bangladesh: Magic Lantern Films, 2005.

Kakar, Sudhir. *Culture and Psyche: Selected Essays*. 2nd ed. New York: Oxford University Press, 2008.

Kamath, M. V. "The Psychosis of Massacre: Bangladesh's Place in History." *Times of India (1861-Current)*, November 15, 1973.

Karim, Lamia. *Microfinance and Its Discontents: Women in Debt in Bangladesh*. Minneapolis: University of Minnesota Press, 2011.

Kaul, Suvir, ed. *The Partitions of Memory: The Afterlife of the Division of India.* New Delhi: Permanent Black, 2001.

Kaur, Manmohan. *Women in India's Freedom Struggle.* New Delhi: Sterling, 1985.

Keller, Richard C. *Colonial Madness: Psychiatry in French North Africa.* Chicago: University of Chicago Press, 2008.

Khanna, Ranjana. "Touching, Unbelonging, and the Absence of Affect." *Feminist Theory*, 13, no. 2 (August 2012): 213–32.

——. *Dark Continents: Psychoanalysis and Colonialism.* Durham, NC: Duke University Press, 2003.

Kramrisch, Stella. "Kantha." In *Kantha: The Embroidered Quilts of Bengal from the Jill and Sheldon Bonovitz Collection and the Stella Kramrisch Collection of the Philadelphia Museum of Art*, ed. Darielle Mason, 169–84. Philadelphia: Philadelphia Museum of Art, 2009.

——. "Unknown India: Ritual Art in Tribe and Village" (1968). In *Exploring India's Sacred Art: Selected Writings of Stella Kramrisch*, ed. Barbara Stoller Miller, 85–120. Benaras: Motilal Banarsidass, 1994.

Kumar, Radha. *The History of Doing: An Illustrated Account of Movements for Women's Rights and Feminism in India 1800–1990.* New Delhi: Zubaan, 2003.

Lamb, Sarah. *White Saris and Sweet Mangoes: Aging, Gender, and Body in North India.* Berkeley: University of California Press, 2000.

Lane, Christopher. *The Ruling Passion: British Colonial Allegory and the Paradox of Homosexual Desire.* Durham, NC: Duke University Press, 1995.

Laplanche, Jean, and Jean-Bertrand Pontalis. *The Language of Psycho-Analysis.* Trans. Donald Nicholson-Smith. New York: Norton, 1974.

Latour, Bruno. "How to Talk About the Body? The Normative Dimension of Science Studies." *Body & Society* 10, no. 2–3 (2004): 205–29.

Laushey, David M. *Bengal Terrorism & the Marxist Left: Aspects of Regional Nationalism in India, 1905–1942.* Calcutta: Firma K. L. Mukhopadhyay, 1975.

Laxshmi, A. "The Liminal Body: The Language of Pain and Symbolism around Sati." *Feminist Review* 74, no. 1 (2003): 81–97.

Legg, Stephen. *Spaces of Colonialism: Delhi's Urban Governmentalities.* Malden, MA: Blackwell, 2007.

"Letter to Editor." *Ananda Bazar Patrika* (August 19, 1929).

Loomba, Ania. "Dead Women Tell No Tales: Issues of Female Subjectivity, Subaltern Agency, and Tradition in Colonial and Post-Colonial Writings on Widow Immolation in India." *History Workshop* 36 (Autumn 1993): 209–27.

Ludden, David. "Forgotten Heroes." *Frontline* 20, no. 15 (2003). http://www.sas.upenn.edu/~dludden/LuddenFrontlineHeroes.htm.

——. "Spatial Inequity and National Territory: Remapping 1905 in Bengal and Assam." *Modern Asian Studies* 46, no. 3 (2011): 1–43.

Lukács, Georg. "Tagore's Gandhi Novel. Review of Rabindranath Tagore: The Home and the World." In *Essays and Reviews*, trans. Peter Palmer, 8–11. London: Merlin Press, 1983.

Macarehas, Anthony. *The Rape of Bangla Desh.* New Delhi: Vikas, 1971.

Macaulay, Thomas Babington. "Introductory Report upon the Indian Penal Code." In *Miscellanies*, 415–29. New York: Houghton Mifflin, 1901.

——. *Macaulay's Essay on Lord Clive.* New York: Macmillan, 1840.

——. "Minute on Indian Education." In *Speeches by Lord Macaulay: With His Minute on Indian Education*, ed. G. M. Young, 356–57. Oxford: Oxford University Press, 1979.

Mahone, Sloane, and Megan Vaughan. *Psychiatry and Empire*. London: Springer, 2007.

Major, Andrew J. "State and Criminal Tribes in Colonial Punjab: Surveillance, Control and Reclamation of the 'Dangerous Classes,'" *Modern Asian Studies* 33, no. 3 (1999): 657–88.

Majumdar, R. C. *The Revolutionary Movement in Bengal and the Role of Surya Sen* (Surya Sen lecture). Calcutta: University of Calcutta, 1978.

Malik, Amita. "The Rape of Sara Bridge." *Times of India (1861–Current)*, December 24, 1971.

Mandal, Tirtha. *The Women Revolutionaries of Bengal, 1905–1939*. New Delhi: Minerva, 1991.

Mani, Lata. *Contentious Traditions: The Debate on Sati in Colonial India*. Berkeley: University of California Press, 1998.

——. "Production of an Official Discourse on 'Sati' in Early Nineteenth Century Bengal." *Economic and Political Weekly* 21, no. 17 (1986): WS32–WS40.

Manning, Erin. *Politics of Touch: Sense, Movement, Sovereignty*. Minneapolis: University of Minnesota Press, 2006.

Marks, Laura. *The Skin of the Film*. Durham, NC: Duke University Press, 2000.

Marx, Karl. *Capital: A Critique of Political Economy*, vol. 1. Trans. Ben Fowkes. New York: Vintage, 1977.

——. "The Economic and Philosophical Manuscripts of 1844." In *Karl Marx: A Reader*, ed. Jon Elster, 35–47 (Cambridge: Cambridge University Press, 1989).

——. "The Indian Revolt." *New York Daily Tribune* (September 4, 1857).

——. "The Leading Article in No. 179 of the *Kölnische Zeitung*: Religion, Free Press, and Philosophy." In *The Writings of the Young Marx on Philosophy and Society*, ed. and trans. Loyd D. Easton and Kurt H. Guddat, 115. New York: Hackett, 1975.

Masson, Jeffrey. *The Oceanic Feeling: The Origins of Religious Sentiment in Ancient India*. Berlin: Springer, 2012.

Massumi, Brian. "Translator's Note." In *A Thousand Plateaus: Capitalism and Schizophrenia*, ix–xv. Minneapolis: University of Minnesota Press, 1987.

Mathur, Pushpa Rani. *Costumes of the Rulers of Mewar*. Delhi: Abhinav Publications, 2004.

Mayo, Katherine. *Mother India*. Ann Arbor: University of Michigan Press, 2000.

Mbembe, Achille. "Necropolitics." *Public Culture* 15, no. 1 (2003): 11–40.

——. *On the Postcolony*. Berkeley: University of California Press, 2001.

McClintock, Anne. *Imperial Leather: Race, Gender, and Sexuality in the Colonial Conquest*. New York: Routledge, 1995.

McCulloch, Jock. *Colonial Psychiatry and the African Mind*. Cambridge: Cambridge University Press, 1995.

McDaniel, June. *Offering Flowers, Feeding Skulls*. New York: Oxford University Press, 2004.

"Meet Maks, American Apparel's New Bengali Muslim Model." *Dazed*, March 10, 2014. http://www.dazeddigital.com/artsandculture/article/19188/1/maks-bengali-muslim-made-in-bangladesh-topless-american-apparel-ad.

Menen, Aubry. "The Rapes of Bangladesh: The Rapes." *New York Times*, July 23, 1972. http://www.cbgr1971.org/files/NYTimes/RapeBangladeshNYT.pdf.

Menon, Ritu, ed. *No Women's Land: Women from Pakistan, India and Bangladesh Write on the Partition of India*. New Delhi: Women Unlimited, 2004.

Menon, Ritu, and Kamala Bhasin, eds. *Borders and Boundaries: Women in India's Partition*. New Delhi: Kali for Women, 1998.

Merleau-Ponty, Maurice. *Le Visible et L'invisible*. Paris: Gallimard, 1976.

Metcalf, Thomas. *Ideologies of the Raj*. Cambridge: Cambridge University Press, 1994.

Milgrom, Paul. "Is Sympathy an Economic Value? Philosophy, Economics, and the Contingent Valuation Method." In *Contingent Valuation: A Critical Assessment*, ed. Jerry A. Hausman, 417–41. Amsterdam: Elsevier Science, 1993.

Millard, Bailey. "Rabindranath Tagore Discovers America." *The Bookman* 44 (1916): 247–48.

Miller, Nancy K. "Arachnologies: The Woman, the Text, and the Critic." In *The Poetics of Gender*, ed. Nancy K. Miller, 270–96. New York: Columbia University Press, 1986.

Moaddel, Mansoor. *Islamic Modernism, Nationalism, and Fundamentalism: Episode and Discourse*. Chicago: University of Chicago Press, 2005.

Mohanty, Chandra Talpade. "Under Western Eyes: Feminist Scholarship and Colonial Discourses." *Feminist Review* 30 (1988): 61–88.

Mookherjee, Nayanika. *The Spectral Wound: Sexual Violence, Public Memories, and the Bangladesh War of 1971*. Durham, NC: Duke University Press, 2015.

Moretti, Franco. *Distant Reading*. London: Verso, 2013.

Morris, Rosalind. "Introduction." In *Can the Subaltern Speak? Reflections on the History of an Idea*, ed. Rosalind Morris, 1–18. New York: Columbia University Press, 2010.

Mukherjee, Haridas. *India's Fight for Freedom: Or, The Swadeshi Movement (1905-1906)*. Calcutta: K. L. Mukhopadhyay, 1958.

Mukherjee, Ishanee. "Scaling the Barrier: Women, Revolution, and Abscondence in Late Colonial Bengal." *Indian Journal of Gender Studies* 6, no. 61 (1999): 61–78.

Nanda, B. R., ed. *Indian Women: From Purdah to Modernity*. New Delhi: Vikas, 1962.

Nandy, Ashis. *The Intimate Enemy: Loss and Recovery of Self Under Colonialism*. Oxford: Oxford University Press, 1989.

——. "Nationalism, Genuine and Spurious: Mourning Two Early Post-nationalist Strains." *Economic and Political Weekly* (2006): 3500–3504.

——. *The Savage Freud and Other Essays on Possible and Retrievable Selves*. Princeton, NJ: Princeton University Press, 1995.

Nazneen, Sohela, Maheen Sultan, and Naomi Hossain. "National Discourses on Women's Empowerment in Bangladesh: Enabling or Constraining Women's Choices?" *Development* 53, no. 2 (2010): 239–46.

Nigam, Sanjay. "Disciplining and Policing the 'Criminals by Birth,' Part 1: The Making of a Colonial Stereotype—The Criminal Tribes and Castes of North India." *Indian Economic and Social History Review* 27 (1990): 131–64.

Nobel Committee. "Nobel Peace Prize 2006." *Nobelprize.org*, n.d. https://www.nobelprize.org/prizes/peace/2006/summary/.

——. "Rabindranath Tagore." *Nobelprize.org*, n.d. http://nobelprize.org/nobel_prizes/literature/laureates/1913/.

Nussbaum, Martha. "Patriotism and Cosmopolitanism." *Boston Review*, October 1, 1994. https://bostonreview.net/martha-nussbaum-patriotism-and-cosmopolitanism.

——. "Women's Capabilities and Social Justice." *Journal of Human Development* 1, no. 2 (July 1, 2000): 219–47.

Obeyesekere, Gananath. *The Work of Culture*. Chicago: University of Chicago Press, 1990.

O'Ceallaigh, Sean. *India and Ireland*. New York: Friends of Freedom for India, 1924.

O'Hanlon, Rosalind, and David Washbrook. "After Orientalism: Culture, Criticism, and Politics in the Third World." *Comparative Studies in Society and History* 34, no. 1 (January 1992), 141–67.

Openshaw, Jeanne. *Seeking the Bauls of Bengal*. Cambridge: Cambridge University Press, 2002.

"Orders by His Excellency, The Governor of Bengal: No. 2496P." *Calcutta Gazette*, March 16, 1933.

Pal, Bipin Chandra. *Writings and Speeches*. Vol. 1. Calcutta: Yugayatri Prakashak, 1954.

Pande, Ishita. "Phulmoni's Body: The Autopsy, the Inquest and the Humanitarian Narrative on Child Rape in India." *South Asian History and Culture* 4, no. 1 (2013): 9–30.

Pandian, Anand. "Pastoral Power in the Postcolony: On the Biopolitics of the Criminal Animal in South India." *Cultural Anthropology* 23, no. 1 (2008): 85–117.

Parisi, Joseph, and Stephen Young. *Dear Editor: A History of Poetry in Letters: The First Fifty Years, 1912–1962*. New York: Norton, 2002.

Parker, Andrew, ed. *Nationalisms & Sexualities*. New York: Routledge, 1992.

Patterson, Lee. "Mass Rape in Bangladesh." *Times of India (1861–Current)*, October 1, 1972. http://search.proquest.com/docview/609777844?accountid=14496.

Payami, Akhtar. "Why Distort History?" *Dawn*, March 22, 2002. http://www.dawn.com/news/1062853.

Pels, Peter. "The Anthropology of Colonialism: Culture, History, and the Emergence of Western Governmentality." *Annual Review of Anthropology* 26 (1997): 163–83.

Phillip, Kavita, Lilly Irani, and Paul Dourish. "Postcolonial Computing: A Tactical Survey." *Science, Technology, & Human Values* 37, no. 1 (2012): 3–29.

Pietz, William. "The Problem of the Fetish I." *RES: Anthropology and Aesthetics*, no. 9 (1985): 5–17.

Pillai, Govinda Paramaswaran. *Representative Indians*. London: Routledge, 1897.

Prakash, Gyan. *Another Reason: Science and the Imagination of Modern India*. Princeton, NJ: Princeton University Press, 1999.

——. "The Colonial Genealogy of Society: Community and Political Modernity in India." In *The Social in Question*, ed. Patrick Joyce, 81–96. London: Routledge, 2002.

——. "Science 'Gone Native' in Colonial India." *Representations* 40 (1992): 153–78.

Radhakrishna, Meena. *Dishonoured by History: Criminal Tribes and British Colonial Policy*. New Delhi: Orient Longman, 2001.

Radiou, Navi, Jaideep Prabhu, and Simone Ahuja. *Jugaad Innovation*. Delhi: Random House India, 2012.

Rai, Amit S. "The Affect of Jugaad: Frugal Innovation and Postcolonial Practice in India's Mobile Phone Ecology." *Environment and Planning D: Society and Space* 33, no. 6 (December 1, 2015): 985–1002.

Rajan, Rajeswari Sunder. "Death and the Subaltern." In *Can the Subaltern Speak? Reflections on the History of an Idea*, ed. Rosalind Morris, 117–38. New York: Columbia University Press, 2010.

——. *Real and Imagined Women: Gender, Culture, and Postcolonialism*. New York: Taylor and Francis, 2004.

Ramakrishna, and Mahendra Nath Gupta. *The Gospel of Sri Ramakrishna: Originally Recorded in Bengali by M., a Disciple of the Master*. Trans. Swami Nikhilananda. New York: Ramakrishna-Vivekananda Center, 1952.

Ramanujan, A. K. "The Indian Oedipus." In *Oedipus: A Folklore Casebook*, ed. Lowell Edmunds and Alan Dundes, 234–64. Madison: University of Wisconsin Press, 1983.

Ramaswamy, Sumathi. *Mother Goddesses and the Nation*. Durham, NC: Duke University Press, 2010.

Rao, Rahul. "Hijra." In *Key Concepts in Modern Indian Studies*, ed. Gita Dharampal-Frick, Monika Kirloskar-Steinbach, Rachel Dwyer, and Jahnavi Phalkey, 99–101. New York: New York University Press, 2015.

"The Rape of Bangladesh." *Irish Times (1921–Current File)*, December 5, 1972.

Ray, Ajit Kumar. *Widows Are Not for Burning: Actions and Attitudes of the Christian Missionaries, the Native Hindus, and Lord William Bentinck*. Calcutta: ABC, 1985.

Ray, Asok Kumar. *Party of Firebrand Revolutionaries: The Dacca Anushilan Samiti, 1906–1918*. Calcutta: Minerva Associates, 1999.

Ray, Bharati. "Women of Bengal: Transformation in Ideas and Ideals, 1900–1947." *Social Scientist* 19, no. 5/6 (June 1991): 3–23.

Ray, Dalia. *The Bengal Revolutionaries and Freedom Movement.* New Delhi: Cosmo Publications, 1990.

Ray, Nisith Ranjan, and Chittagong Uprising Golden Jubilee Committee. *Challenge, a Saga of India's Struggle for Freedom.* New Delhi: People's Publishing House, 1984.

Ray, P. K. *Down Memory Lane: Reminiscences of a Bengali Revolutionary.* New Delhi: Gian, 1990.

Ray, Sangeeta. *En-Gendering India: Woman and Nation in Colonial and Postcolonial Narratives.* Durham, NC: Duke University Press, 2000.

Razzaque, Abdur, Nurul Alam, Lokky Wai, and Andrew Foster. "Sustained Effects of the 1974–5 Famine on Infant and Child Mortality in a Rural Area of Bangladesh." *Population Studies* 44, no. 1 (1990): 145–54.

Reddy, Gayatri. *With Respect to Sex: Negotiating Hijra Identity in South India.* Chicago: University of Chicago Press, 2005.

Roazen, Paul. *Freud and His Followers.* Boston: Da Capo Press, 1992.

Robbins, Bruce. *Feeling Global: Internationalism in Distress.* New York: NYU Press, 1999.

——. "Uses of World Literature." In *The Routledge Companion to World Literature*, ed. Theo D'haen, David Damrosch, and Djelal Kadir, 383–92. Abingdon, UK: Routledge, 2011.

Robinson, Roger J. *Bangladesh: Progress Through Partnership: Country Assistance Review.* Washington, DC: World Bank Publications, 1999.

Rokeya, Roushan Jahan. *Sultana's Dream and Selections from The Secluded Ones.* Ed. Hanna Papanek. New York: Feminist Press, 1988.

Rooney, Caroline. "Deconstruction and Weaving." In *Deconstruction: A User's Guide*, ed. Nicholas Royle, 258–81. London: Palgrave, 2000.

Rothschild, Emma. *Economic Sentiments: Adam Smith, Condorcet, and the Enlightenment.* Cambridge, MA: Harvard University Press, 2013.

Roy, Ananya. "The Agonism of Utopia: Dialectics at a Standstill." *Traditional Dwellings and Settlements Review* 23, no. 1 (2011): 15–24.

Roy, Parama. "Discovering India, Imagining Thuggee." *Yale Journal of Criticism* 9, no. 1 (1996): 121–45.

——. *Indian Traffic: Identities in Question in Colonial and Postcolonial India.* Berkeley: University of California Press, 1998.

Saikia, Yasmin. *Women, War, and the Making of Bangladesh.* Durham, NC: Duke University Press Books, 2011.

Sangari, Kumkum, and Sudesh Vaid, eds. *Recasting Women: Essays in Indian Colonial History.* New Brunswick, NJ: Rutgers University Press, 1989.

——. "Sati in Modern India: A Report." *Economic and Political Weekly* 16, no. 31 (1988): 1284–88.

Sanyal, Shukla. *Revolutionary Pamphlets, Propaganda and Political Culture in Colonial Bengal.* Cambridge: Cambridge University Press, 2014.

Sarkar, Tanika. *Hindu Wife, Hindu Nation: Community, Religion, and Cultural Nationalism.* London: Permanent Black, 2003.

——. "Nationalist Iconography: Image of Women in 19th Century Bengali Literature." *Economic and Political Weekly* 22, no. 47 (1987): 2011–15.

——. *Rebels, Wives, Saints: Designing Selves and Nations in Colonial Times.* Ranikhet: Permanent Black, 2009.

——. "Rhetoric Against Age of Consent: Resisting Colonial Reason and Death of Child Wife." *Economic and Political Weekly* (September 4, 1993): 1869–73.

Sartori, Andrew. *Bengal in Global Concept History: Culturalism in the Age of Capital.* Chicago: University of Chicago Press, 2008.

——. *Liberalism in Empire: An Alternate History*. Berkeley: University of California Press, 2014.

Schor, Naomi. "Blindness as Metaphor." *Differences* 11, no. 2 (1999): 76–105.

Scott, David. "The Aftermaths of Sovereignty: Postcolonial Criticism and the Claims of Political Modernity." *Social Text* 48 (1996): 1–26.

——. "Colonial Governmentality." *Social Text* 43 (1995): 191–220.

Sedgwick, Eve Kosofsky. *Between Men: English Literature and Male Homosocial Desire*. New York: Columbia University Press, 1985.

——. *Touching Feeling: Affect, Pedagogy, Performativity*. Durham, NC: Duke University Press, 2003.

Semmalar, Gee Imaan. "Unpacking Solidarities of the Oppressed: Notes on Trans Struggles in India." *Women's Studies Quarterly* 42, no. 3–4 (2014): 286–91.

Sen, Amartya. *The Argumentative Indian: Writings on Indian History, Culture and Identity*. New York: Macmillan, 2006.

——. *Development as Freedom*. New York: Knopf Doubleday, 2011.

——. *Poverty and Famines: An Essay on Entitlement and Deprivation*. Oxford: Oxford University Press, 1982.

——. "The Standard of Living: Lecture II, Lives and Capabilities." In *The Standard of Living*, ed. Geoffrey Hawthorne, 20–38. Cambridge: Cambridge University Press, 1988.

Sen, Samita. *Women and Labour in Late Colonial India: The Bengal Jute Industry*. Vol. 3. Cambridge: Cambridge University Press, 1999.

Sen, Surya. "Vijaya." In *Easter Rebellion in India: The Chittagong Uprising*, ed. I. Mallikarjuna Sharma, 268–73. Hyderabad: Marxist Study Forum, 1993.

Serres, Michel. *The Five Senses: A Philosophy of Mingled Bodies*. New York: Continuum Books, 2008.

Sethi, Aarti. *The Life of Debt in Rural India*. Doctoral Dissertation. Department of Anthropology, Columbia University, 2017.

Sethi, Manisha. "Avenging Angels and Nurturing Mothers: Women in Hindu Nationalism." *Economic and Political Weekly* 37, no. 16 (April 20, 2002): 1545–52.

Sharma, Arvind, ed. *Sati: Historical and Phenomenological Essays*. New Delhi: Motilal, 1988.

Sharma, I. Mallikarjuna, ed. *The Easter Rebellion in India: The Chittagong Uprising*. Calcutta: Marxist Study Forum, 1963.

Shetty, Sandhya, and Elizabeth Jane Bellamy. "Postcolonialism's Archive Fever." *Diacritics* 30, no. 1 (March 1, 2000): 25–48.

Silverman, Kaja. *Flesh of My Flesh*. Stanford, CA: Stanford University Press, 2009.

Silvestri, Michael. *Ireland and India: Nationalism, Empire, and Memory*. New York: Palgrave Macmillan, 2009.

——. " 'The Sinn Fein of India': Irish Nationalism and the Policing of Revolutionary Terrorism in Bengal." *Journal of British Studies* 39, no. 4 (2000): 454–86.

Singh, Bhagat. "Manifesto of the Hindustan Socialist Republican Association." In *Select Speeches & Writing*, 137. New Delhi: National Book Trust, 2007.

Singha, Radhika. " 'Providential' Circumstances: The Thuggee Campaign of the 1830s and Legal Innovation." *Modern Asian Studies* 27, no. 1 (1993): 83–146.

Sinha, Mrinalini. *Colonial Masculinity: The "Manly Englishman" and the "Effeminate Bengali" in the Late Nineteenth Century*. Manchester, UK: Manchester University Press, 1995.

——. *Specters of Mother India: The Global Restructuring of an Empire*. Durham, NC: Duke University Press, 2006.

Skaria, Ajay. *Unconditional Equality: Gandhi's Religion of Resistance*. Minneapolis: University of Minnesota Press, 2016.

Smith, Adam. *The Theory of Moral Sentiments*. Ed. Ryan Patrick Hanley. New York: Penguin, 2009.

Smith, Barbara Herrnstein. *Contingencies of Value: Alternative Perspectives for Critical Theory.* Cambridge, MA: Harvard University Press, 1988.

Smith, Louis, ed. *Foreign Relations of the United States, 1969–1976, Volume XI, South Asia Crisis, 1971.* Washington, DC: United States Department of State, 2005.

Sobhan, Rehman. "Politics of Food and Famine in Bangladesh." *Economic and Political Weekly* 14, no. 48 (1979): 1973–80.

Som, Reba. *Rabindranath Tagore: The Singer and His Song.* New York: Penguin, 2009.

Sontag, Susan. *Regarding the Pain of Others.* New York: Farrar, Straus and Giroux, 2003.

Spinoza, Benedictus de. *Ethics.* Ed. Edwin M. Curley. New York: Penguin Books, 1996.

Spivak, Gayatri Chakravorty. "Can the Subaltern Speak?" In *Colonial Discourse and Post-Colonial Theory: A Reader,* ed. Patrick Williams and Laura Chrisman, 66–111. New York: Columbia University Press, 1994.

——. *A Critique of Postcolonial Reason: Toward a History of the Vanishing Present.* Cambridge, MA: Harvard University Press, 1999.

——. "The Rani of Sirmur: An Essay in Reading the Archives." *History and Theory* 24, no. 3 (1985): 247–72.

——. "Righting Wrongs." *South Atlantic Quarterly* 103, no. 2–3 (March 20, 2004): 523–81.

——. "Subaltern Studies: Deconstructing Historiography." In *Selected Subaltern Studies,* ed. Ranajit Guha and Gayatri Chakravorty Spivak, 3–32. Oxford: Oxford University Press, 1988.

Stallybrass, Peter. "Marx's Coat." In *Border Fetishisms: Material Objects in Unstable Spaces,* ed. Patricia Spyer, 183–207. New York: Routledge, 1998.

Statement of the Trade of British India with British Possessions and Foreign Countries for the Five Years. London: Eyre & Spottiswoode, 1895.

"Statute 298. Voluntary Culpable Homicide by Consent." *Indian Penal Code.* 1858.

Steinberg, Shelley, and Marlene Fine. "Outcast Bengali Women" (letter to the editor). *New York Times,* February 9, 1972.

Subramanyam, K. "The Ghosts of 1971." *Indian Express,* March 5, 2009. http://archive.indianexpress.com/news/the-ghosts-of-1971/431017/.

Tagore, Rabindranath. "Amar Sonar Bangla." In *Encyclopedia of National Anthems,* ed. Xing Hang, 450. Lanham, MD: Scarecrow Press, 2003.

——. "Amar Sonar Bangla," "Gitabidan: Swadesh" in *Rabindra-Rachanabali,* vol. 4, 189. Kolkata: Paschim Banga Sarkar, 1980.

——. "The Cult of the Charkha." In *The Mahatma and The Poet: Letters and Debates Between Tagore and Gandhi,* ed. Sabyashachi Bhattacharya, 103–15. New Delhi: National Trust, 1997.

——. "Dui Bigha Jomi." *Chitra,* in *Rabindra-Rachanabali,* vol. 1, 597–559. Kolkata: Paschim Banga Sarkar, 1980.

——. *Greater India.* Madras: S. Ganesan, 1920.

——. *The Home and the World.* Ed. William Radice. Trans. Surendranath Tagore. London: Penguin UK, 2005.

——. "Jana Gana Mana." In *Encyclopedia of National Anthems,* ed. Xing Hang, 450. Lanham, MD: Scarecrow Press, 2005.

——. "Jana Gana Mana." *Rabindra Rachanabali.* "Gitabidan: Swadesh" in *Rabindra-Rachanabali,* vol. 4, 194. Kolkata: Paschim Banga Sarkar, 1980.

——. "Letter to a Friend." In *The English Writings of Rabindranath Tagore, A Miscellany,* 245. Calcutta: Sahitya Akademi, 1994.

——. *Nationalism.* London: Macmillan, 1917.

——. "Ramakrishna Paramahamsa." In *The English Writings of Rabindranath Tagore: A Miscellany*, 955. New Delhi: Sahitya Akademi, 1994.

——. "Religion of Man." In *The English Writings of Rabindranath Tagore: A Miscellany*, 91. New Delhi: Sahitya Akademi, 1994.

——. *Sadhana: The Realization of Life*. New York: Macmillan, 1914.

——. *Selected Letters of Rabindranath Tagore*. Ed. Krishna Dutt and Andrew Robinson. New York: Cambridge University Press, 1997.

——. "Visva Sahitya." In *Rabindranath Tagore in the 21st Century*, ed. D. Banerji, trans. Rijula Das and Makarand Paranjape, 286. New Delhi: Springer India, 2015.

Tarlo, Emma. *Clothing Matters: Dress and Identity in India*. Chicago: University of Chicago Press, 1996.

Taussig, Michael. *The Nervous System*. New York: Routledge, 1992.

Ten Thousand Villages. "Dhaka Handicrafts." n.d. http://www.tenthousandvillages.com/bangladesh /dhaka-handicrafts.

Ten Thousand Villages. "Ten Thousand Villages." n.d. http://www.tenthousandvillages.com/.

"Thrill." *Oxford English Dictionary Online*. http://www.oed.com/view/Entry/201256.

Thurston, Edgar, and K. Rangachari. *Castes and Tribes of Southern India*. Madras: Government Press, 1909.

Tolen, Rachel J. "Colonizing and Transforming the Criminal Tribesman: The Salvation Army in British India." *American Ethnologist* 18, no. 1 (1991): 106–25.

Traub, Valerie. "Mapping the Global Body." In *Early Modern Visual Culture: Representation, Race, and Empire in Renaissance*, ed. Peter Eriksen and Clark Hulse, 44–97. Philadelphia: University of Pennsylvania Press, 2000.

Trivedi, Lisa. *Clothing Gandhi's Nation: Homespun and Modern India*. Bloomington: Indiana University Press, 2007.

Trumbull, Robert. "The Unwanted Children of a New Nation." *New York Times*, May 29, 1972. http://query .nytimes.com/mem/archive-free/pdf?res=9E04EFDF1F3EE63BBC4151DFB3668389669EDE.

Tweedie, Jill. "The Rape of Bangladesh." *Guardian (1959-2003)*, March 6, 1972.

U.S. National Security Council. *Conflict in East Pakistan; Attached to Cover Memorandum Dated June 21, 1971.*

Vaughn, Megan. *Curing Their Ills: Colonial Power and African Illness*. Stanford, CA: Stanford University Press, 1991.

Virdee, Pippa. "Negotiating the Past: Journey through Muslim Women's Experience of Partition and Resettlement in Pakistan." *Cultural and Social History* 6, no. 4 (2009): 467–83.

Viswanathan, Gauri. *Masks of Conquest: Literary Study and British Rule in India*. New York: Columbia University Press, 1989.

Vivekananda, Swami. "Modern India." In *The Complete Works of Swami Vivekananda*, vol. 4, 438–80. Calcutta: Advaita Ashram, 1988.

Waddedar, Pritilata. "An Appeal to Women." In *The Easter Rebellion in India: The Chittagong Uprising*, ed. I. Mallikarjuna Sharma, 122. Calcutta: Marxist Study Forum, 1993.

——. "Assault on the European Club." In *The Easter Rebellion in India: The Chittagong Uprising*, ed. I. Mallikarjuna Sharma, 264. Calcutta: Marxist Study Forum, 1993.

——. "Long Live Revolution." In *The Easter Rebellion in India: The Chittagong Uprising*, ed. I. Mallikarjuna Sharma, 266. Calcutta: Marxist Study Forum, 1993.

Wagner, Kim. *Thuggee: Banditry and the British in Early Nineteenth-Century India*. London: Palgrave, 2007.

Waterfield, Henry. *Memorandum on the Census of British India 1871-72*. London: Eyre & Spottiswoode, 1875.

Watson, J. Forbes. *Textile Manufactures and the Costumes of the People of India*. London: Eyre & Spottis-woode, 1866.

Weissberg, Liliane. "Ariadne's Thread." *MLN* 125, no. 3 (2010): 661–81. https://doi.org/10.1353/mln.0.0267.

Wickramasinghe, Nira. *Metallic Modern: Everyday Machines in Colonial Sri Lanka*. New York: Berghahn Press, 2014.

Wilde, Oscar. *The Picture of Dorian Gray and Other Writings*. New York: Simon & Schuster, 2014.

Wilkins, William Joseph. *Hindu Mythology, Vedic and Puranic*. London: Thacker, Spink, 1882.

Winter, Alison. *Mesmerized: Powers of the Mind in Victorian Britain*. Chicago: University of Chicago Press, 1998.

"Women's Work: A Monthly Progress Report." National Board of Bangladesh Women's Rehabilita-tion Programme. Dhaka, Bangladesh, September 1972.

Wyatt, George. *Indian Art at Delhi in 1903: Being the Official Catalogue of the Delhi Exhibit, 1902–1903*. London: John Murray, 1904.

Yang, Anand A. *Bazaar India: Markets, Society, and the Colonial State in Bihar*. Berkeley: University of California Press, 1999.

——. "Dangerous Castes and Tribes: The Criminal Tribes Act and the Magahiya Doms of Northeast India." In *Crime and Criminality in British India*, ed. Anand A. Yang, 108–27. Tucson: University of Arizona Press, 1985.

Zaman, Niaz. *The Art of Kantha Embroidery*. Dhaka: The University Press, 1995.

Index

GENDER AND CULTURE

A Series of Columbia University Press

Nancy K. Miller and Victoria Rosner, *Series Editors*
Carolyn G. Heilbrun (1926–2003) and Nancy K. Miller, *Founding Editors*

In Dora's Case: Freud, Hysteria, Feminism, Edited by Charles Bernheimer and Claire Kahane

Breaking the Chain: Women, Theory, and French Realist Fiction, Naomi Schor

Between Men: English Literature and Male Homosocial Desire, Eve Kosofsky Sedgwick

Romantic Imprisonment: Women and Other Glorified Outcasts, Nina Auerbach

The Poetics of Gender, Edited by Nancy K. Miller

Reading Woman: Essays in Feminist Criticism, Mary Jacobus

Honey-Mad Women: Emancipatory Strategies in Women's Writing, Patricia Yaeger

Subject to Change: Reading Feminist Writing, Nancy K. Miller

Thinking Through the Body, Jane Gallop

Gender and the Politics of History, Joan Wallach Scott

The Dialogic and Difference: "An/Other Woman" in Virginia Woolf and Christa Wolf, Anne Herrmann

Plotting Women: Gender and Representation in Mexico, Jean Franco

Inspiriting Influences: Tradition, Revision, and Afro-American Women's Novels, Michael Awkward

Hamlet's Mother and Other Women, Carolyn G. Heilbrun

Rape and Representation, Edited by Lynn A. Higgins and Brenda R. Silver

Shifting Scenes: Interviews on Women, Writing, and Politics in Post-68 France, Edited by Alice A. Jardine and Anne M. Menke

Tender Geographies: Women and the Origins of the Novel in France, Joan DeJean

Unbecoming Women: British Women Writers and the Novel of Development, Susan Fraiman

The Apparitional Lesbian: Female Homosexuality and Modern Culture, Terry Castle

George Sand and Idealism, Naomi Schor

Becoming a Heroine: Reading About Women in Novels, Rachel M. Brownstein

Nomadic Subjects: Embodiment and Sexual Difference in Contemporary Feminist Theory, Rosi Braidotti

Engaging with Irigaray: Feminist Philosophy and Modern European Thought, Edited by Carolyn Burke, Naomi Schor, and Margaret Whitford

Second Skins: The Body Narratives of Transsexuality, Jay Prosser

A Certain Age: Reflecting on Menopause, Edited by Joanna Goldsworthy

Mothers in Law: Feminist Theory and the Legal Regulation of Motherhood, Edited by Martha Albertson Fineman and Isabelle Karpin

GENDER AND CULTURE READERS